CENSUS OF INDIA 1891

Census of India 1871-1951, 9 Sets In 384 Bindings (9788121258876) Rs. 700000

Census of India 1891, 28 Vols. In 49 Bindings (978-81-212-7129-5) Rs. 125000

1. General Report (9788121269834) Rs. 1450
2. General Tables For British Provinces And Feudatory States (9788121269810) Rs. 2710 (Vol. I)
3. General Tables For British Provinces And Feudatory States (9788121269797) Rs. 950 (Vol. II)
4. Assam - Report (9788121269773) Rs. 2390 (Vol. I, V.1)
5. Assam - Tables (9788121269759) Rs. 2210 (Vol. II, V.2)
6. Assam - Provincial Tables (9788121269735) Rs. 1310 (Vol. II, V.3)
7. The Lower Provinces of Bengal and their Feudatories - The Report (9788121269711) Rs. 1660 (Vol. III)
8. The Lower Provinces of Bengal and their feudatories - The Administrative Tables (9788121269698) Rs. 4200 (Vol. IV)
9. The Lower Provinces of Bengal and their feudatories - The Caste Tables (9788121269674) Rs. 2600 (Vol. V, Pt. 1)
10. Lower Provinces of Bengal - The Provincial Tables (9788121269650) Rs. 1980 (Vol. V, Pt. 2)
11. Berar or the Hyderabad Assigned Districts (9788121269636) Rs. 3360 (Vol. VI)
12. Bombay and Its Feudatories - Report (9788121269612) Rs. 4010 (Vol. VII, Pt. 1)
13. Bombay And Its Feudatories - Imperial Tables (9788121269599) Rs. 790 (Vol. VIII, Pt. 2)
14. Imperial Series - Burma Report (9788121269575) Rs. 2320 (Vol. IX-V.1)
15. Imperial Tables - Burma Report (9788121269551) Rs. 3360 (Vol. X-V.2)
16. Provincial Tables Burma Report (9788121269537) Rs. 3510 (Vol. X-V.3)
17. Provincial Tables Burma Report (9788121269513) Rs. 3630 (Vol. X-V.4)
18. The Central Provinces And Feudatories - The Report (9788121269490) Rs. 2290 (Vol. XI, Pt. 1)
19. The Central Provinces And Feudatories - Imperial tables and supplementary returns (9788121268936) Rs. 2010 (Vol. XII)
20. Madras The Report On The Census (9788121269476) Rs. 2870 (Vol. XIII)
21. Madras - Tables I to XVII-C, British Territory (9788121269452) Rs. 3490 (Vol. XIV)
22. Madras - Tables A TO E, British Territory. Tables for feudatory States and A Caste Index (9788121269438) Rs. 2820 (Vol. XV)
23. The North Western Provinces and Outh - Report and Provincial Tables (9788121268912) Rs. 3100 (Vol. XVI, Pt. 1)
24. The North - Western Provinces and Oudh- Imperial Tables (9788121269414) Rs. 2000 (Vol. XVII, Pt. 2)
25. The North - Western Provinces and Oudh- Imperial Caste Tables (9788121269391) Rs. 3020 (Vol. XVIII, Pt. 3)
26. Punjab and Its Feudatories - The Report on the Census (9788121269377) Rs. 2710 (Vol. XIX, Pt. 1)
27. Punjab and Its Feudatories - Imperial Tables and Supplementary Returns for the British Territory (9788121269353) Rs. 1370 (Vol. XX, Pt. 2)
28. Punjab and Its Feudatories - Imperial Tables and Supplementary Returns for the Native States, Together With A Caste Index (9788121269339) Rs. 4910 (Vol. XXI, Pt. 3)
29. Report on The Census of The Districts of Ajmere-Merwara (9788121269056) Rs. 720 (Vol. XXII)
30. His Highness The Nizam's Dominions - Report (9788121269315) Rs. 2240 (Vol. XXIII, Pt. 1)
31. His Highness The Nizam's Dominions - Report (9788121269292) Rs. 2410 (Vol. XXIII, Pt. 2)
32. His Highness The Nizam's Dominions - Imperial And Supplementry Tables and Caste Index (9788121269278) Rs. 3390 (Vol. XXIII, Pt. 3)
33. Baroda - Report (9788121269254) Rs. 3810 (Vol. XXIV, Pt. 1)
34. Baroda - Tables (9788121269230) Rs. 2620 (Vol. XXIV, Pt. 2)
35. Mysore - Report (9788121269216) Rs. 2590 (Vol. XXV, Pt. 1)
36. Mysore - Imperial Tables (9788121269193) Rs. 1600 (Vol. XXV, Pt. 2)
37. Mysore - Tables (9788121269179) Rs. 5320 (Vol. XXV, Pt. 3)
38. Mysore - Supplementary Tables (9788121269155) Rs. 3590 (Vol. XXV, Pt. 4)
39. Mysore- Supplement to the Mysore census report of 1891 being a list of villages in the Mysore province and : comparing the population as per Censuses of 1891, 1881 & 1871 (9788121279024) Rs. 5350 (Vol. XXV, Pt. 5)
40. Rajputana - The Report, Imperial Tables And Supplementary Returns (9788121269131) Rs. 2330 (Vol. XXVI, Pt. 1)
41. Rajputna - The Provincial Tables and Remarks (9788121269117) Rs. 550 (Vol. XXVI, Pt. 2)
42. Central India (9788121269094) Rs. 2000 (Vol. XXVII)
43. Kashmir State - The Report on the census and Imperial and supplementary Tables (9788121269070) Rs. 2290 (Vol. XXVIII)
44. The Census of Calcutta (9788121269032) Rs. 890
45. Report on the census of Cochin (9788121269018) Rs. 790 (Pt. 1)
46. Report on the census of Cochin - The Final Census Tables with Appendices (9788121268998) Rs. 910 (Pt. 2)
47. Report on the Census of Coorg (9788121268974) Rs. 730
48. Report on the census of Travancore -Report (9788121274029) Rs. 4220 (Vol. I)
49. Report on the census of Travancore -Appendix (9788121268950) Rs. 5300 (Vol. II)

Owing to the antiquity and rarity of this book, certain pages are regrettably absent, and readability is compromised due to the blurring of the original text. If you possess any insights regarding the availability of these missing sections, kindly inform us. Your assistance is crucial in ensuring the completion of this significant work for the benefit of future generations.

CENSUS OF INDIA, 1891

BOOK-13: VOL. VIII

Bombay and Its Feudatories

PART II.—IMPERIAL TABLES

W. W. DREW

GYAN

Published by

GYAN

Gyan Publishing House
5, Ansari Road
Daryaganj, New Delhi-110002
Phone: 011-47034999, 9811692060
E-mail: books@gyanbooks.com

Distribution Network
gyanbooks.com
India, USA, Canada, UK, Australia

ISBN: 978-81-212-7129-5 (Set) 28 Vols. In 49 Bindings
978-81-212-6959-9 (PB) Book-13, Vol. VII, Pt. II

First Published, 1892

2nd Impression 2024

Printed at: Gyan Press, Delhi.

CENSUS OF INDIA 1891

Census of India, 1891.

VOLUME VIII.

BOMBAY

AND

ITS FEUDATORIES.

PART II.—IMPERIAL TABLES.

BY

W. W. DREW,

OF THE INDIAN CIVIL SERVICE,

PROVINCIAL SUPERINTENDENT OF CENSUS OPERATIONS.

Bombay:

PRINTED AT THE GOVERNMENT CENTRAL PRESS.

1892.

FEUDATORIES.

TABLE I.

AREA, HOUSES AND POPULATION.

CONTENTS

IMPERIAL TABLES

BRITISH TERRITORY.

TABLE I.

Area, Houses and Population.

State.	Area in Square Miles.	Number of Towns.	Number of Villages.	Occupied Houses. Total.	Occupied Houses. Towns.	Occupied Houses. Villages.	Population. Total. Total.	Population. Total. Towns.	Population. Total. Villages.	Population. Males. Total.	Population. Males. Towns.	Population. Males. Villages.	Population. Females. Total.	Population. Females. Towns.	Population. Females. Villages.
Cutch	6,500	8	928	*122,476*	25,072	97,404	*558,415*	109,191	449,224	*278,441*	54,023	224,418	*279,974*	55,168	224,806
Pálanpur	7,775	2	1,175	*138,917*	9,143	129,774	*645,526*	35,267	610,259	*335,587*	18,052	317,535	*309,939*	17,215	292,724
Mahi Kántha...	9,300	6	1,861	*132,760*	9,023	123,737	*581,568*	33,496	548,072	*296,646*	16,243	280,303	*284,922*	17,153	267,769
Káthiáwár	20,559	48	4,151	*575,816*	118,804	457,012	*2,752,404*	554,846	2,197,558	*1,416,633*	282,840	1,133,793	*1,335,771*	272,006	1,063,765
Rewa Kántha	4,980	3	3,153	*148,957*	7,831	141,126	*733,506*	30,607	702,899	*376,146*	14,381	361,765	*357,360*	16,226	341,134
Cambay	350	2	86	*22,888*	10,104	12,784	*89,722*	37,347	52,375	*46,231*	18,589	27,642	*43,491*	18,758	24,733
Surat Agency	1,051	2	378	*33,275*	1,728	31,547	*181,208*	7,778	173,430	*92,457*	3,781	88,676	*88,751*	3,997	84,754
Total, Gujarát Group ...	50,515	71	11,732	*1,175,089*	181,705	993,384	*5,542,349*	808,532	4,733,817	*2,842,141*	408,009	2,434,132	*2,700,208*	400,523	2,299,685
Jawhár	534	1	106	*8,887*	533	8,354	*52,831*	2,991	49,840	*27,825*	1,528	26,297	*25,006*	1,463	23,543
Janjira	324	2	227	*16,491*	2,398	14,093	*81,780*	12,985	68,795	*39,629*	6,240	33,389	*42,151*	6,745	35,406
Sáwantwádi	926	1	226	*32,476*	1,382	31,094	*192,948*	9,269	183,679	*93,520*	4,465	89,055	*99,428*	4,804	94,624
Total, Konkan Group ...	1,784	4	559	*57,854*	4,313	53,541	*327,559*	25,245	302,314	*160,974*	12,233	148,741	*166,585*	13,012	153,573
The Dángs	660	...	343	*6,224*	...	6,224	*32,920*	......	32,920	*17,237*	...	17,237	*15,683*	...	15,683
Surgana	360	...	57	*2,246*	...	2,246	*12,398*	......	12,398	*6,545*	...	6,545	*5,853*	...	5,853
Bhor	1,491	1	472	*24,001*	790	23,211	*155,669*	5,250	150,419	*78,602*	2,651	75,951	*77,067*	2,599	74,468
Akalkot	498	1	105	*11,002*	1,018	9,984	*75,774*	6,551	69,223	*38,615*	3,319	35,296	*37,159*	3,232	33,927
Sátára Agency	844	1	142	*20,009*	1,838	18,171	*131,529*	10,564	120,965	*66,269*	5,154	61,115	*65,260*	5,410	59,850
Total, Deccan Group ...	3,853	3	1,119	*63,482*	3,646	59,836	*408,290*	22,365	385,925	*207,268*	11,124	196,144	*201,022*	11,241	189,781
Jat	979	1	118	*10,359*	721	9,638	*79,786*	5,264	74,522	*40,576*	2,669	37,907	*39,210*	2,595	36,615
Kolhápur	2,816	10	1,055	*151,748*	17,195	134,553	*913,131*	98,978	814,153	*467,572*	50,263	417,309	*445,559*	48,715	396,844
Southern Marátha Jághírs ...	2,919	30	578	*108,080*	34,385	73,695	*639,270*	202,055	437,215	*320,531*	101,260	219,271	*318,739*	100,795	217,944
Sawanúr	70	1	23	*2,901*	1,458	1,443	*16,976*	8,743	8,233	*8,330*	4,137	4,193	*8,646*	4,606	4,040
Total, Karnátak Group ...	6,784	42	1,774	*273,088*	53,759	219,329	*1,649,163*	315,040	1,334,123	*837,009*	158,329	678,680	*812,154*	156,711	655,443
Khairpur	6,109	1	148	*26,619*	1,257	25,362	*131,937*	6,240	125,697	*72,733*	3,170	69,563	*59,204*	3,070	56,134
Total, Feudatory States ...	**69,045**	**121**	**15,332**	**1,593,132**	**244,680**	**1,351,452**	**8,059,298**	**1,177,422**	**6,881,876**	**4,120,125**	**592,865**	**3,527,260**	**3,939,173**	**584,557**	**3,354,616**

TABLE II.

VARIATION IN THE ENUMERATED POPULATION SINCE LAST CENSUS.

FEUDATORIES.

BRITISH TERRITORY.

TABLE II.

Variation in the Enumerated Population since last Census.

State.	Total.			Males.			Females.		
	1891.	1881.	Variation.	1891.	1881.	Variation.	1891.	1881.	Variation.
Cutch	558,415	*512,084*	+ 46,331	278,441	*260,251*	+ 18,190	279,974	*251,833*	+ 28,141
Pálanpur	645,526	*576,478*	+ 69,048	335,587	*301,550*	+ 34,037	309,939	*274,928*	+ 35,011
Mahi Kántha	581,568	*517,485*	+ 64,083	296,646	*266,566*	+ 30,080	284,922	*250,919*	+ 34,003
Káthiáwár	2,752,404	*2,343,899*	+ 408,505	1,416,633	*1,218,803*	+ 197,830	1,335,771	*1,125,096*	+ 210,675
Rewa Kántha	733,506	*549,892*	+ 183,614	376,146	*283,445*	+ 92,701	357,360	*266,447*	+ 90,913
Cambay	89,722	*86,074*	+ 3,648	46,231	*44,018*	+ 2,213	43,491	*42,056*	+ 1,435
Surat Agency	181,208	*151,132*	+ 30,076	92,457	*77,633*	+ 14,824	88,751	*73,499*	+ 15,252
Total, Gujarát Group ...	5,542,349	*4,737,044*	805,305	2,842,141	*2,452,266*	389,875	2,700,208	*2,284,778*	+ 415,430
Jawhár	52,831	*48,556*	+ 4,275	27,825	*25,174*	+ 2,651	25,006	*23,382*	+ 1,624
Janjira	81,780	*76,361*	+ 5,419	39,629	*37,782*	+ 1,847	42,151	*38,579*	+ 3,572
Sáwantwádi	192,948	*174,433*	+ 18,515	93,520	*86,061*	+ 7,459	99,428	*88,372*	+ 11,056
Total, Konkan Group ...	327,559	*299,350*	28,209	160,974	*149,017*	11,957	166,585	*150,333*	+ 16,252
The Dángs	32,920	*31,280*	+ 1,640	17,237	*16,451*	+ 786	15,683	*14,829*	+ 854
Surgana	12,398	*14,205*	− 1,807	6,545	*7,334*	− 789	5,853	*6,871*	− 1,018
Bhor...	155,669	*145,876*	+ 9,793	78,602	*74,263*	+ 4,339	77,067	*71,613*	+ 5,454
Akalkot	75,774	*58,040*	+ 17,734	38,615	*29,470*	+ 9,145	37,159	*28,570*	+ 8,589
Sátára Agency	131,529	*117,318*	+ 14,211	66,269	*58,964*	+ 7,305	65,260	*58,354*	+ 6,906
Total, Deccan Group ...	408,290	*366,719*	41,571	207,268	*186,482*	20,786	201,022	*180,237*	+ 20,785
Jat	79,786	*55,493*	+ 24,293	40,576	*27,800*	+ 12,776	39,210	*27,693*	+ 11,517
Kolhápur	913,131	*800,189*	+ 112,942	467,572	*410,647*	+ 56,925	445,559	*389,542*	+ 56,017
Southern Marátha Jághirs ...	639,270	*523,753*	+ 115,517	320,531	*260,136*	+ 60,395	318,739	*263,617*	+ 55,122
Sawanúr	16,976	*14,763*	+ 2,213	8,330	*7,347*	+ 983	8,646	*7,416*	+ 1,230
Total, Karnátak Group ...	1,649,163	*1,394,198*	254,965	837,009	*705,930*	131,079	812,154	*688,268*	+ 123,886
Khairpur	131,937	*129,153*	+ 2,784	72,733	*70,746*	+ 1,987	59,204	*58,407*	+ 797
Total, Feudatory States ...	**8,059,298**	**6,926,464**	**+ 1,132,834**	**4,120,125**	**3,564,441**	**+ 555,684**	**3,939,178**	**3,362,023**	**+ 577,150**

TABLE III.

TOWNS AND VILLAGES CLASSIFIED BY POPULATION.

TABLE III.

Towns and Villages classified by Population,

State.	Total Number of Towns and Villages.	Total Population.	1 – 199.		200 – 499.		500 – 999.		1,000 – 1,999.		2,000 – 2,999.		3,000 – 4,999.		5,000 – 9,999.		10,000 – 14,999.		15,000 – 19,999.		20,000 – 49,999.		50,000 and over.	
			No.	Population.	No.	Population.	No.	Population.	No.	Population.	No	Population.	No.	Population.	No.	Population.	No.	Population.	No.	Population.	No.	Population.	No.	Population.
Cutch	936	558,415	416	35,903	225	74,360	161	115,438	92	122,938	19	41,846	17	64,782	2	12,206	2	24,886	...	...	2	63,576	...	...
Pálanpur	1,177	645,526	265	30,830	484	104,215	310	208,999	90	123,328	18	44,309	7	26,742	...	...	2	26,211	...	...	1	21,092	...	...
Mahi Kántha	1,867	581,568	1,101	100,183	479	152,274	172	121,478	89	120,094	16	38,544	6	20,478	4	28,622	...	...	...	...	...	...	...	...
Káthiáwár	4,199	2,752,404	948	116,735	1,647	545,788	1,078	734,591	378	502,398	78	177,023	34	125,913	29	193,500	5	60,595	7	115,168	4	122,140	1	57,653
Rewa Kántha	3,156	733,506	2,047	198,102	819	247,057	215	145,380	59	78,498	6	13,832	7	25,030	1	9,687	2	20,920	...	...	...	...	...	...
Cambay	88	89,722	21	2,729	23	7,014	32	24,384	6	7,422	3	7,540	1	3,288	1	5,957	...	...	...	...	1	31,390	...	...
Surat Agency	380	181,208	100	12,502	161	55,733	88	61,400	26	35,247	2	4,413	3	11,918	...	...	...	...	...	...	...	...	...	...
Total, Gujarát Group ...	*11,803*	*5,542,349*	*4,898*	*496,784*	*3,838*	*1,246,441*	*2,051*	*1,411,665*	*740*	*984,925*	*137*	*330,907*	*75*	*278,144*	*37*	*249,872*	*11*	*132,592*	*7*	*115,168*	*8*	*238,198*	*1*	*57,653*
Jawhár	107	62,831	31	3,868	39	12,928	26	18,419	9	11,879	1	2,991	1	3,246	...	...	...	...	...	...	...	...	...	...
Janjira	229	81,780	111	10,540	77	23,295	28	19,274	10	13,491	1	2,195	...	...	2	12,985	...	...	...	...	...	...	...	...
Sáwantwádi	227	192,948	38	3,404	61	21,547	69	49,479	38	53,081	15	36,016	5	20,152	1	9,269	...	...	...	...	...	...	...	...
Total, Konkan Group ...	*563*	*337,559*	*180*	*17,812*	*177*	*57,770*	*123*	*87,172*	*57*	*77,951*	*17*	*41,202*	*6*	*23,398*	*3*	*22,254*	...	...	...	...	...	...	...	...
The Dángs	343	32,920	315	25,365	28	7,555	...	...	...	...	...	...	...	...	...	...	...	...	...	...	...	...	...	...
Surgana	57	12,398	34	3,810	19	5,738	4	2,850	...	...	...	...	...	...	...	...	...	...	...	...	...	...	...	...
Bhor	473	155,669	203	24,403	182	59,005	75	49,426	10	12,708	2	4,877	...	...	1	5,250	...	...	...	...	...	...	...	...
Akalkot	106	75,774	27	2,777	35	12,137	25	18,738	11	16,970	4	9,889	3	10,205	1	6,551	...	...	...	...	...	...	...	...
Sátára Agency	143	131,529	7	804	50	17,004	43	30,370	31	40,366	7	15,781	3	11,244	1	5,446	1	10,564	...	...	...	...	...	...
Total, Deccan Group ...	*1,122*	*408,290*	*586*	*57,159*	*314*	*101,439*	*147*	*101,382*	*52*	*69,053*	*13*	*29,997*	*6*	*21,449*	*3*	*17,247*	*1*	*10,564*	...	...	...	...	...	...
Jat	119	79,788	19	2,400	45	15,842	34	24,722	15	18,801	4	9,651	1	3,106	1	5,264	...	...	...	...	...	...	...	...
Kolhápur	1,065	913,131	146	17,872	356	125,556	346	251,317	148	209,000	43	122,425	18	71,272	5	32,424	1	11,200	...	...	2	72,056	...	...
Southern Marátha Jaghirs	608	639,270	93	11,509	175	69,090	165	117,051	110	149,764	31	75,777	19	73,214	9	62,600	5	64,205	...	...	1	26,060	...	...
Sáwanúr	24	16,976	7	658	9	2,895	7	4,080	...	...	...	...	...	...	1	8,743	...	...	...	...	...	...	...	...
Total, Karnátak Group ...	*1,816*	*1,649,165*	*265*	*32,439*	*585*	*203,383*	*552*	*397,770*	*273*	*377,574*	*78*	*207,853*	*38*	*147,592*	*16*	*109,031*	*6*	*75,405*	...	...	*3*	*98,116*	...	...
Khairpur	149	131,937	18	2,546	46	16,335	49	35,493	22	31,162		16,836	5	18,254	2	11,201	...	...	...	...	...	...	...	...
Total, Feudatory States ...	15,453	8,059,298	5,947	608,740	4,960	1,625,418	3,922	2,033,482	1,144	1,540,665	253	628,795	130	458,837	61	409,685	18	213,561	7	115,168	11	338,314	1	57,653

TABLE IV.

TOWNS BY POPULATION.

TABLE IV.

Serial Number.	Town.	State or Agency.	Municipality, Suburbs or Cantonment.	Total Population. 1891.	Total Population. 1881.	Total Population. Difference.	Males. 1891.	Males. 1881.	Males. Difference.	Females. 1891.	Females. 1881.	Females. Difference.
1	Bháwnagar	Gohelwád, Káthiáwár ...	Municipality.	57,653	47,792	+9,861	31,116	25,626	+5,490	26,537	22,166	+4,371
2	Nawánagar	Hálár, Káthiáwár	Do. ...	48,530	39,668	+8,862	24,460	20,057	+4,403	24,070	19,611	+4,459
3	Kolhápur	Kolhápur	Do. ...	45,815	38,599	+7,216	23,393	19,335	+4,058	22,422	19,264	+3,158
4	Mándvi	Cutch	Do. ...	38,155	35,980	+2,175	18,407	17,285	+1,122	19,748	18,695	+1,053
5	Junágad	Sorath, Káthiáwár	......	31,640	24,679	+6,961	16,710	13,605	+3,105	14,930	11,074	+3,856
6	Cambay	Cambay	Municipality.	31,390	36,007	—4,617	15,273	17,580	—2,307	16,117	18,427	—2,310
7	Miraj	S. M. Jaghirs	Do. ...	26,060	20,616	+5,444	13,105	9,902	+3,203	12,955	10,714	+2,241
8	Bhúj	Cutch	Do. ...	25,421	22,308	+3,113	13,423	11,547	+1,876	11,998	10,761	+1,237
9	Rájkot City	Hálár, Káthiáwár	Do. ...	21,564	15,139	+6,425	11,300	7,725	+3,575	10,264	7,414	+2,850
10	Pálanpur	Pálanpur	......	21,092	17,547	+3,545	11,160	8,852	+2,308	9,932	8,695	+1,237
11	Dhoráji	Hálár, Káthiáwár	Municipality.	20,406	16,121	+4,285	9,547	7,785	+1,762	10,859	8,336	+2,523
12	Porbandar	Sorath, do.	......	18,805	14,570	+4,235	9,410	7,120	+2,290	9,395	7,450	+1,945
13	Wadhwán	Jháláwád, do.	Municipality.	17,440	16,949	+491	8,591	8,824	—233	8,849	8,125	+724
14	Morvi	Hálár, do.	Do. ...	16,325	15,345	+980	8,338	7,738	+600	7,987	7,607	+380
15	Mhowa	Gohelwád, do.	Do. ...	16,707	13,704	+3,003	9,230	7,523	+1,707	7,477	6,181	+1,296
16	Gondal	Hálár, Káthiáwár	Do. ...	15,343	13,524	+1,819	7,827	6,978	+849	7,516	6,546	+970
17	Verával	Sorath, do.	......	15,339	12,111	+3,228	7,726	5,744	+1,982	7,613	6,367	+1,246
18	Dhrángadra	Jháláwád, Káthiáwár ...	Municipality.	15,209	12,304	+2,905	7,721	6,283	+1,438	7,488	6,021	+1,467
19	Sángli	S. M. Jaghirs	Do. ...	14,798	13,272	+1,526	7,557	6,755	+802	7,241	6,517	+724
20	Anjár	Cutch	Do. ...	14,433	12,584	+1,849	6,966	6,066	+900	7,467	6,518	+949
21	Rádhanpur	Pálanpur	......	14,175	14,722	—547	6,892	7,500	—608	7,283	7,222	+61
22	Jaithpur	Sorath, Káthiáwár	......	13,646	11,813	+1,833	6,740	6,114	+626	6,906	5,699	+1,207
23	Limbdi	Jháláwád do.	Municipality.	13,497	12,873	+624	6,753	6,569	+184	6,744	6,304	+440
24	Mángrol	Sorath, do.	......	13,005	12,123	+882	6,201	5,666	+535	6,804	6,457	+347
25	Jamkhandi	S. M. Jaghirs	Municipality.	12,504	10,409	+2,095	6,318	5,159	+1,159	6,186	5,250	+936
26	Mangalwedha ...	Do.	Do. ...	12,270	9,156	+3,114	6,081	4,428	+1,653	6,189	4,728	+1,461
27	Sháhápur	Do.	Do. ...	11,961	10,732	+1,229	6,006	5,415	+591	5,955	5,317	+638
28	Lakshmeshwar ...	Do.	Do. ...	11,842	10,274	+1,568	5,821	5,011	+810	6,021	5,263	+758
29	Ichalkaranji ...	Do.	Do. ...	11,200	9,107	+2,093	5,740	4,538	+1,202	5,460	4,569	+891
30	Nándod	Rewa Kántha	Do. ...	10,819	10,777	+42	5,322	5,625	—303	5,497	5,152	+345
31	Phaltan	Phaltan	Do. ...	10,564	10,842	—278	5,154	5,438	—284	5,410	5,404	+6
32	Pálitána	Gohelwád, Káthiáwár ...	Do. ...	10,442	7,659	+2,783	5,467	3,958	+1,509	4,975	3,701	+1,274
33	Mandra	Cutch	Do. ...	10,433	8,900	+1,533	5,002	4,189	+813	5,431	4,711	+720
34	Lunáwáda	Rewa Kántha	Do. ...	10,101	9,059	+1,042	4,566	4,150	+416	5,535	4,909	+626
35	Sihor	Gohelwád, Káthiáwár ...	Do. ...	10,005	9,528	+477	4,963	4,804	+159	5,042	4,724	+318
36	Wádásinor	Rewa Kántha	Do. ...	9,687	9,718	—31	4,493	4,695	—202	5,194	5,023	+171
37	Khambhália	Hálár, Káthiáwár	Do. ...	9,591	8,576	+1,015	4,706	4,083	+623	4,885	4,493	+392
38	Katiana	Sorath, do.	......	9,480	8,177	+1,303	4,268	4,001	+267	5,212	4,176	+1,036
39	Bagasra	Do.	......	9,410	7,876	+1,534	4,958	4,195	+763	4,452	3,681	+771
40	Sáwantwádi	Sáwantwádi	Municipality.	9,269	8,584	+685	4,465	4,398	+67	4,804	4,186	+618
41	Kurundwád and Wádi	S. M. Jaghirs	Do. ...	9,136	7,671	+1,465	4,620	3,804	+816	4,516	3,867	+649
42	Sáwanúr	Sáwanúr	Do. ...	8,743	7,640	+1,103	4,137	3,669	+468	4,606	3,971	+635
43	Shirol	Kolhápur	Do. ...	8,705	6,944	+1,761	4,357	3,479	+878	4,348	3,465	+883
44	Rámdurg	S. M. Jaghirs	Do. ...	8,645	6,810	+1,835	4,333	3,289	+1,044	4,312	3,521	+791
45	Bántwa	Sorath, Káthiáwár	......	8,641	7,589	+1,052	3,744	3,437	+307	4,897	4,152	+745
46	Mánsa	Mahi Kántha	......	8,452	7,898	+554	4,166	3,898	+268	4,286	4,000	+286
47	Pattan	Sorath, Káthiáwár	......	7,853	6,644	+1,209	3,893	3,273	+620	3,960	3,371	+589
48	Upleta	Hálár, do.	Municipality.	7,785	6,240	+1,495	3,657	3,137	+520	4,078	3,103	+975
49	Botád	Gohelwád, do.	Do. ...	7,710	7,755	—36	3,996	4,068	—72	3,723	3,687	+36
50	Rájkot Civil Station...	Hálár, do.	Do. ...	7,683	6,013	+1,670	4,783	3,729	+1,054	2,900	2,284	+616
51	Wanthali	Sorath, do.	......	7,537	6,529	+1,008	3,728	3,295	+433	3,809	3,234	+575
52	Jodhia	Hálár, do.	Municipality.	7,404	6,842	+562	3,504	3,377	+127	3,900	3,465	+435
53	Una	Sorath, do.	......	7,309	5,980	+1,329	3,650	3,136	+514	3,659	2,844	+815
54	Wadhwán C. Station.	Jháláwád, do.	Municipality.	7,164	3,231	+3,933	4,268	2,066	+2,202	2,896	1,165	+1,731
55	Pethapur	Mahi Kántha	......	7,159	7,081	+78	3,526	3,567	—41	3,633	3,514	+119
56	Shriwardhan... ...	Jánjira	Municipality.	7,102	7,702	—600	3,304	3,838	—534	3,798	3,864	—66
57	Wánkáner	Jháláwád, Káthiáwár ...	Do. ...	7,100	5,533	+1,567	3,621	2,842	+779	3,479	2,691	+788
58	Idar	Mahi Kántha	......	7,086	6,223	+863	3,592	2,985	+607	3,494	3,238	+256
59	Nalia	Cutch	Municipality.	7,078	5,542	+1,536	3,430	2,720	+710	3,648	2,822	+826
60	Terdál	S. M. Jaghirs	Do. ...	7,043	5,764	+1,279	3,430	2,583	+847	3,613	3,181	+432
61	Kágal	Kolhápur	Do. ...	6,928	6,371	+557	3,490	3,143	+347	3,438	3,228	+210

TABLE IV—*continued.*

Serial Number.	Town.	State or Agency.	Municipality, Suburbs or Cantonment.	Total Population. 1891.	Total Population. 1881.	Total Population. Difference.	Males. 1891.	Males. 1881.	Males. Difference.	Females. 1891.	Females. 1881.	Females. Difference.
62	Mudhol	S. M. Jaghirs...	Municipality.	6,805	6,060	+745	3,364	2,971	+393	3,441	3,089	+352
63	Akalkot	Akalkot	......	6,551	5,836	+715	3,319	2,962	+357	3,232	2,874	+358
64	Kundla	Gohelwád, Káthiáwár ...	Municipality.	6,490	6,135	+355	3,409	3,244	+165	3,081	2,891	+190
65	Halwad	Jháláwád, do. ...	Do. ...	6,453	5,967	+486	3,077	2,865	+212	3,376	3,102	+274
66	Mahálingpur ...	S. M. Jaghirs	Do. ...	6,273	5,206	+1,067	3,106	2,531	+575	3,167	2,675	+492
67	Khairpur	Khairpur	Do. ...	6,240	6,005	+235	3,170	3,228	—58	3,070	2,777	+293
68	Kundgolpur	S. M. Jaghirs	Do. ...	6,146	6,720	—574	3,105	3,350	—245	3,041	3,370	—329
69	Tárápur	Cambay	Do. ...	5,957	5,590	+367	3,316	3,047	+269	2,641	2,543	+98
70	Murád	Janjira	Do. ...	5,883	5,251	+632	2,936	2,769	+167	2,947	2,482	+465
71	Bhâyáwadar... ...	Hálár, Káthiáwár ...	Do. ...	5,850	5,197	+653	2,935	2,691	+244	2,915	2,506	+409
72	Gad Hinglaj	Kolhápur	Do.	5,836	5,002	+834	3,054	2,529	+525	2,782	2,473	+309
73	Wadali	Mahi Kántha	......	5,825	5,477	+348	2,574	2,524	+50	3,251	2,953	+298
74	Dhrol	Hálár, Káthiáwár ...	Municipality.	5,721	4,613	+1,108	2,847	2,284	+563	2,874	2,329	+545
75	Rabkavi	S. M. Jaghirs	Do. ...	5,698	5,028	+670	2,800	2,417	+383	2,898	2,611	+287
76	Sáyla	Jháláwád, Káthiáwár ...	Do. ...	5,650	6,488	—838	2,697	3,357	—660	2,953	3,131	—178
77	Sávar Sáwápadar ...	Gohelwád, do.	......	5,574	4,565	+1,009	2,823	2,278	+545	2,751	2,287	+464
78	Wadgaon	Kolhápur	Municipality.	5,554	4,890	+664	2,726	2,355	+371	2,828	2,535	+293
79	Gadhada	Gohelwád, Káthiáwár ...	Do. ...	5,523	5,822	—299	2,864	3,015	—151	2,659	2,807	—148
80	Bilkha...	Sorath, do.	......	5,502	3,002	+2,500	3,023	1,652	+1,371	2,479	1,350	+1,129
81	Mulá	Jháláwád, do.	Municipality.	5,467	6,357	—890	2,668	3,457	—789	2,799	2,900	—101
82	Chuda...	Do. do. ...	Do. ...	5,326	5,061	+265	2,649	2,531	+118	2,677	2,530	+147
83	Maindargi	S. M. Jaghirs	Do. ...	5,311	4,064	+1,247	2,653	2,031	+622	2,658	2,033	+625
84	Umrala	Gohelwád, Káthiáwár	Do. ...	5,309	3,429	+1,880	2,935	1,795	+1,140	2,374	1,634	+740
85	Valà	Do. do.	Do. ...	5,298	4,956	+342	2,773	2,558	+215	2,525	2,398	+127
86	Jat	Jat	......	5,264	3,789	+1,475	2,669	1,830	+839	2,595	1,959	+636
87	Malgaon	S. M. Jaghirs	Municipality.	5,258	4,071	+1,187	2,665	2,021	+644	2,593	2,050	+543
88	Bhor	Bhor	Do. ...	5,250	4,572	+678	2,651	2,312	+339	2,599	2,260	+339
89	Láthi	Gohelwád, Káthiáwár ...	......	5,236	4,384	+852	2,695	2,180	+515	2,541	2,204	+337
90	Jáfarábád	Sorath do. ...	......	5,312	4,783	+429	2,419	2,258	+161	2,793	2,525	+268
91	Mandurda	Do. do. ...	......	5,164	5,406	—242	2,645	2,820	—175	2,519	2,586	—67
92	Jakháu	Cutch	Municipality.	5,128	5,040	+88	2,454	2,498	—44	2,674	2,542	+132
93	Katkol	Kolhápur	Do. ...	4,963	4,292	+671	2,403	2,083	+320	2,560	2,209	+351
94	Sureban Manihal and Shiwápeth.	S. M. Jaghirs	Do. ...	4,780	3,897	+883	2,354	1,970	+384	2,426	1,927	+499
95	Dharampur	Surat Agency...	......	4,775	4,806	—31	2,280	2,442	—162	2,495	2,364	+131
96	Bhochan	Cutch	......	4,530	3,722	+808	2,279	1,854	+425	2,251	1,868	+383
97	Banhatti	S. M. Jaghirs	Municipality.	4,506	3,582	+924	2,272	1,790	+482	2,234	1,792	+442
98	Lakhtar	Jháláwád, Káthiáwár ...	Do. ...	4,467	4,145	+322	2,267	2,110	+157	2,200	2,035	+165
99	Jasdan	Gohelwád, do. ...	......	4,402	3,873	+529	2,227	2,050	+177	2,175	1,823	+352
100	Shirahatti	S. M. Jaghirs	Municipality.	4,298	3,594	+704	2,157	1,715	+442	2,141	1,879	+262
101	Kawati Periana ...	Do.	Do. ...	4,235	3,710	+525	2,197	1,871	+326	2,038	1,839	+199
102	Ajra	Kolhápur	......	4,136	3,547	+589	2,085	1,711	+374	2,051	1,836	+215
103	Sawashi	S. M. Jaghirs	Municipality.	4,115	3,959	+156	2,047	1,952	+95	2,068	2,007	+61
104	Rápur...	Cutch	......	4,013	4,601	—588	2,062	2,429	—367	1,951	2,172	—221
105	Shegali	S. M. Jaghirs	Municipality.	3,964	3,429	+535	2,038	1,750	+288	1,926	1,679	+247
106	Gudageri	Do.	Do. ...	3,758	3,127	+631	1,911	1,553	+358	1,847	1,574	+273
107	Kawati	Do.	Do. ...	3,592	3,675	—83	1,766	1,838	—72	1,826	1,837	—11
108	Hunur	Do.	Do. ...	3,481	2,861	+620	1,763	1,461	+302	1,718	1,400	+318
109	Hatkalanguda ...	Kolhápur	Do. ...	3,198	2,415	+783	1,721	1,234	+487	1,477	1,181	+296
110	Ahmednagar ...	Mahi Kántha	......	3,135	3,289	—154	1,395	1,480	—85	1,740	1,809	—69
111	Budgaon	S. M. Jaghirs...	Municipality.	3,057	2,401	+656	1,553	1,209	+344	1,504	1,192	+312
112	Wánsda	Surat Agency	......	3,003	2,446	+557	1,501	1,274	+227	1,502	1,172	+330
113	Jawhár	Jawhár	......	2,991	2,277	+714	1,528	1,191	+337	1,463	1,086	+377
114	Kamdoli	S. M. Jaghirs...	Municipality.	2,878	2,618	+260	1,423	1,313	+110	1,455	1,305	+150
115	Dudhani	Do.	Do. ...	2,831	2,562	+269	1,499	1,286	+213	1,332	1,276	+56
116	Malkápur	Kolhápur	Do. ...	2,643	2,597	+46	1,294	1,314	—20	1,349	1,283	+66
117	Lokapur	S. M. Jaghirs...	Do. ...	2,508	2,321	+187	1,202	1,154	+48	1,306	1,167	+139
118	Sawalgi	Do.	Do. ...	2,430	1,755	+675	1,198	885	+313	1,232	870	+362
119	Sarsai	Hálár, Káthiáwár	Do. ...	2,020	1,744	+276	1,011	929	+82	1,009	815	+194
120	Yeliwal	S. M. Jaghirs	Do. ...	1,872	1,570	+302	916	764	+152	956	806	+150
121	Sadra	Mahi Kántha...	Do. ...	1,839	2,893	—1,054	1,090	1,557	—467	749	1,336	—587

TABLE V.

TOWNS ARRANGED TERRITORIALLY WITH POPULATION BY RELIGIONS.

The following are the details of Religions shown under "Others":—

	Buddhist.		Sikh.	
	M.	F.	M.	F.
Cutch	1	...	71	12

Deesa.

	Total Population.			Hindu.		Mussalman.		Christian.		Jain.		Pa'rsi.		Jew.	
	Total.	Males.	Females.	Males.	Females.	Males.	Females.	Males.	Females.	Males.	Females.	Males.	Females.	Males.	Females.
City	3,865	1,982	1,883	1,145	1,032	449	404	...	...	388	447	...	...	...	...
Civil Station... ...	8,452	4,360	4,092	2,936	2,640	1,163	1,225	15	15	104	105	75	97	7	10
Cantonment... ...	3,584	2,661	923	1,690	555	511	252	444	104	4	6	3	2	9	4
Total ...	15,901	9,003	6,898	5,771	4,227	2,123	1,881	459	119	556	558	78	99	16	14

Towns territorially by Religions.

State or Agency.	Town.	Total Population.			Hindu.			Mussalman.		
		Total.	Males.	Females.	Total.	Males.	Females.	Total.	Males.	Females.
Cutch	Mándvi	38,155	18,407	*19,748*	19,129	9,264	*9,865*	15,499	7,392	*8,107*
	Bhúj	25,421	13,423	*11,998*	14,350	7,713	*6,637*	9,357	4,788	*4,569*
	Anjár	14,433	6,966	*7,467*	9,726	4,752	*4,974*	3,699	1,762	*1,937*
	Mundra	10,433	5,002	*5,431*	3,887	1,818	*2,069*	5,262	2,636	*2,626*
	Nalia	7,078	3,430	*3,648*	3,218	1,605	*1,613*	2,639	1,226	*1,413*
	Jakháu	5,128	2,454	*2,674*	1,915	947	*968*	2,562	1,211	*1,351*
	Bhochan	4,530	2,279	*2,251*	2,967	1,511	*1,456*	409	205	*204*
	Rápur	4,013	2,062	*1,951*	2,978	1,525	*1,453*	580	306	*274*
	Total, Cutch ...	109,191	54,023	*55,168*	58,170	29,135	*29,035*	40,007	19,526	*20,481*
Pálanpur ...	Pálanpur	21,092	11,160	*9,932*	10,123	5,498	*4,625*	7,993	4,181	*3,812*
	Rádhanpur	14,175	6,892	*7,283*	6,723	3,342	*3,381*	4,660	2,235	*2,425*
	Total, Pálanpur ...	35,267	18,052	*17,215*	16,846	8,840	*8,006*	12,653	6,416	*6,237*
Mahi Kántha...	Mánsa	8,452	4,166	*4,286*	7,527	3,718	*3,809*	249	139	*110*
	Pethapur	7,159	3,526	*3,633*	5,685	2,881	*2,804*	431	178	*253*
	Idar	7,086	3,592	*3,494*	5,023	2,564	*2,459*	1,196	611	*585*
	Wadáli	5,825	2,574	*3,251*	4,880	2,131	*2,749*	307	149	*158*
	Ahmednagar	3,135	1,395	*1,740*	1,390	718	*672*	1,564	595	*969*
	Sadra	1,839	1,090	*749*	1,375	820	*555*	411	239	*172*
	Total, Mahi Kántha ...	33,496	16,343	*17,153*	25,880	12,832	*13,048*	4,158	1,911	*2,247*
Káthiáwár ...	Bháwnagar	57,653	31,116	*26,537*	42,021	22,846	*19,175*	10,267	5,454	*4,813*
	Nawánagar	48,530	24,460	*24,070*	28,600	14,503	*14,097*	16,049	7,981	*8,068*
	Junágad	31,640	16,710	*14,930*	15,331	8,356	*6,975*	15,240	7,817	*7,423*
	Rájkot City	21,564	11,300	*10,264*	15,375	8,071	*7,304*	3,877	2,027	*1,850*
	Dhoráji	20,406	9,547	*10,859*	8,616	4,470	*4,146*	10,560	4,460	*6,100*
	Porbandar	18,805	9,410	*9,395*	13,272	6,714	*6,558*	4,369	2,153	*2,216*
	Wadhwán	17,440	8,591	*8,849*	11,554	5,746	*5,808*	1,974	947	*1,027*
	Mhowa	16,707	9,230	*7,477*	11,565	6,542	*5,023*	3,935	2,043	*1,892*
	Morvi	16,325	8,338	*7,987*	10,735	5,634	*5,101*	3,586	1,606	*1,900*
	Gondal	15,343	7,827	*7,516*	9,428	4,877	*4,551*	3,847	1,880	*1,967*
	Veráwal	15,339	7,726	*7,613*	6,949	3,492	*3,457*	7,245	3,685	*3,560*
	Dhrángadra	15,209	7,721	*7,488*	11,136	5,641	*5,495*	1,879	985	*894*
	Jaithpur	13,646	6,740	*6,906*	7,268	3,732	*3,536*	5,135	2,363	*2,772*
	Limbdi	13,497	6,753	*6,744*	8,631	4,327	*4,304*	1,427	718	*709*
	Mángrol	13,005	6,201	*6,804*	5,433	2,599	*2,834*	6,425	3,133	*3,292*
	Pálitána	10,442	5,467	*4,975*	6,586	3,519	*3,067*	1,878	971	*907*
	Sihor	10,005	4,963	*5,042*	7,678	3,815	*3,863*	1,413	707	*706*
	Khambhália	9,591	4,706	*4,885*	7,740	3,826	*3,914*	1,698	799	*899*
	Katiána	9,480	4,268	*5,212*	2,518	1,238	*1,280*	6,879	2,991	*3,888*
	Bagasra	9,410	4,958	*4,452*	7,107	3,764	*3,343*	1,650	867	*783*
	Bántwa	8,641	3,744	*4,897*	1,944	967	*977*	6,650	2,757	*3,893*
	Pattan	7,853	3,893	*3,960*	3,457	1,685	*1,772*	4,084	2,070	*2,014*
	Upleta	7,735	3,657	*4,078*	4,160	2,131	*2,029*	3,380	1,421	*1,959*
	Botád	7,719	3,996	*3,723*	4,967	2,567	*2,400*	1,204	609	*595*
	Rájkot Civil Station .	7,683	4,783	*2,900*	5,297	3,353	*1,944*	1,941	1,181	*760*
	Wanthali...	7,537	3,728	*3,809*	3,227	1,675	*1,552*	4,009	1,923	*2,086*
	Jodhia	7,404	3,504	*3,900*	4,671	2,295	*2,376*	2,290	995	*1,295*
	Una	7,309	3,650	*3,659*	3,381	1,718	*1,663*	3,861	1,902	*1,959*
	Wadhwán City	7,164	4,268	*2,896*	4,356	2,651	*1,705*	1,043	616	*427*
	Wánkáner	7,100	3,621	*3,479*	3,697	1,897	*1,800*	2,388	1,182	*1,206*
	Kundla	6,490	3,409	*3,081*	4,689	2,486	*2,203*	934	474	*460*
	Halwad	6,453	3,077	*3,376*	5,124	2,495	*2,629*	1,114	467	*647*
	Bhâyáwadar	5,850	2,935	*2,915*	5,015	2,526	*2,489*	763	367	*396*
	Dhrol	5,721	2,847	*2,874*	3,926	2,012	*1,914*	1,352	616	*736*
	Sáyla	5,650	2,697	*2,953*	4,044	1,930	*2,114*	488	235	*253*
	Sávar Sáwápadar ...	5,574	2,823	*2,751*	4,452	2,262	*2,190*	1,041	516	*525*
	Gadhada	5,523	2,864	*2,659*	3,883	2,034	*1,849*	1,138	581	*557*
	Bilkha	5,502	3,023	*2,479*	4,142	2,268	*1,874*	1,125	630	*495*
	Mula	5,467	2,668	*2,799*	4,471	2,182	*2,289*	274	145	*129*
	Chuda	5,326	2,649	*2,677*	3,901	1,923	*1,978*	720	388	*332*
	Umrala	5,309	2,935	*2,374*	3,826	2,169	*1,657*	700	372	*328*
	Vala	5,298	2,773	*2,525*	4,382	2,262	*2,120*	412	232	*180*
	Láthi	5,236	2,695	*2,541*	3,912	2,026	*1,886*	933	456	*477*
	Jáfarábád	5,212	2,419	*2,793*	3,482	1,644	*1,838*	1,718	769	*949*
	Mandurda	5,164	2,645	*2,519*	3,837	1,947	*1,890*	890	489	*401*
	Lakhtar	4,467	2,267	*2,200*	3,541	1,803	*1,738*	482	245	*237*
	Jasdan	4,402	2,227	*2,175*	3,452	1,776	*1,676*	941	446	*495*
	Sarsái	2,020	1,011	*1,009*	1,655	835	*820*	246	114	*132*
	Total, Káthiáwár ...	554,846	282,840	*272,006*	348,434	181,231	*167,203*	155,374	75,785	*79,589*
Rewa Kántha .	Nándod	10,819	5,322	*5,497*	9,234	4,570	*4,664*	1,523	712	*811*
	Lunáwáda...	10,101	4,566	*5,535*	7,372	3,358	*4,014*	2,433	1,082	*1,351*
	Wadásinor	9,687	4,493	*5,194*	6,426	3,071	*3,355*	3,183	1,388	*1,795*
	Total, Rewa Kántha ...	30,607	14,381	*16,226*	23,032	10,999	*12,033*	7,139	3,182	*3,957*

Table V.

Towns territorially by Religions.

V.

Christian.			Jain.			Pársi.			Jew.			Animistic.			Others.		
Total.	Males.	Females.	Total.	Males.	Females.	Total.	Males.	Females.	Total.	Males.	Females.	Total.	Males.	Females.	Total.	Males.	Females.
54	46	8	3,437	1,684	1,753	30	16	14	...	...	...	...	...	...	6	5	1
116	91	25	1,224	611	613	73	40	33	47	26	21	186	94	92	68	60	8
...	...	...	997	445	552	2	1	1	...	...	...	...	...	...	9	6	3
...	...	...	1,280	547	733	4	1	3	...	...	...	...	...	...	...	...	...
...	...	...	1,220	598	622	1	1	...	...	...	...	...	...	...	...	...	...
...	...	...	651	296	355	...	...	...	...	...	...	...	...	...	...	...	...
...	...	...	1,154	563	591	...	...	...	...	...	...	...	...	...	...	...	...
...	...	...	430	218	212	...	...	...	...	...	...	24	12	12	1	1	...
170	137	33	10,393	4,962	5,431	110	59	51	47	26	21	210	106	104	84	72	12
12	10	2	2,935	1,454	1,481	25	15	10	4	2	2	...	...	...	...	...	...
...	...	...	2,792	1,315	1,477	...	...	...	...	...	...	...	...	...	...	...	...
12	10	2	5,727	2,769	2,958	25	15	10	4	2	2	...	...	...	...	...	...
5	3	2	671	306	365	...	...	...	...	...	...	...	...	...	...	...	...
...	...	...	1,043	467	576	...	...	...	...	...	...	...	...	...	...	...	...
13	13	...	853	403	450	1	1	...	...	...	...	...	...	...	...	...	...
...	...	...	638	294	344	...	...	...	...	...	...	...	...	...	...	...	...
2	2	...	179	80	99	...	...	...	...	...	...	...	...	...	...	...	...
11	5	6	42	26	16	...	...	...	...	...	...	...	...	...	...	...	...
31	23	8	3,426	1,576	1,850	1	1	...	...	...	...	...	...	...	...	...	...
308	180	128	4,761	2,461	2,300	296	175	121	...	...	...	...	...	...	...	...	...
47	40	7	3,781	1,908	1,873	41	20	21	12	8	4	...	...	...	...	...	...
30	27	3	1,017	499	518	13	7	6	9	4	5	...	...	...	...	...	...
9	3	6	2,297	1,195	1,102	5	3	2	1	1	...	...	...	...	...	...	...
1	1	...	1,213	602	611	16	14	2	...	...	...	...	...	...	...	...	...
17	13	4	1,090	500	590	57	30	27	...	...	...	...	...	...	...	...	...
31	18	13	3,873	1,875	1,998	8	5	3	...	...	...	...	...	...	...	...	...
15	12	3	1,183	627	556	9	6	3	...	...	...	...	...	...	...	...	...
33	26	7	2,024	1,057	967	21	12	9	6	3	3	...	...	...	...	...	...
37	31	6	2,022	1,033	989	9	6	3	...	...	...	...	...	...	...	...	...
15	13	2	1,124	531	593	6	5	1	...	...	...	...	...	...	...	...	...
4	4	...	2,184	1,087	1,097	6	4	2	...	...	...	...	...	...	...	...	...
...	...	...	1,242	644	598	1	1	...	...	...	...	...	...	...	...	...	...
3	3	...	3,427	1,698	1,729	9	7	2	...	...	...	...	...	...	...	...	...
4	1	3	1,140	467	673	3	1	2	...	...	...	...	...	...	...	...	...
20	20	...	1,957	956	1,001	1	1	...	...	...	...	...	...	...	...	...	...
1	1	...	913	440	473	...	...	...	...	...	...	...	...	...	...	...	...
...	...	...	153	81	72	...	...	...	...	...	...	...	...	...	...	...	...
...	...	...	83	39	44	...	...	...	...	...	...	...	...	...	...	...	...
8	5	3	629	314	315	9	6	3	7	2	5	...	...	...	...	...	...
...	...	...	47	20	27	...	...	...	...	...	...	...	...	...	...	...	...
...	...	...	312	138	174	...	...	...	...	...	...	...	...	...	...	...	...
...	...	...	186	99	87	9	6	3	...	...	...	...	...	...	...	...	...
7	5	2	1,541	815	726	...	...	...	...	...	...	...	...	...	...	...	...
115	74	41	94	63	31	204	98	106	28	13	15	4	1	3	...	...	...
...	...	...	301	130	171	...	...	...	...	...	...	...	...	...	...	...	...
2	2	...	441	212	229	...	...	...	...	...	...	...	...	...	...	...	...
...	...	...	58	25	33	9	5	4	...	...	...	...	...	...	...	...	...
21	15	6	1,672	942	730	48	29	19	24	15	9	...	...	...	...	...	...
5	4	1	1,005	534	471	5	4	1	...	...	...	...	...	...	...	...	...
...	...	...	867	449	418	...	...	...	...	...	...	...	...	...	...	...	...
...	...	...	215	115	100	...	...	...	...	...	...	...	...	...	...	...	...
1	1	...	69	39	30	...	...	...	2	2	...	...	...	...	...	...	...
1	1	...	442	218	224	...	...	...	...	...	...	...	...	...	...	...	...
...	...	...	1,118	532	586	...	...	...	...	...	...	...	...	...	...	...	...
5	3	2	76	42	34	...	...	...	...	...	...	...	...	...	...	...	...
...	...	...	502	249	253	...	...	...	...	...	...	...	...	...	...	...	...
1	1	...	233	123	110	1	1	...	...	...	...	...	...	...	...	...	...
...	...	...	722	341	381	...	...	...	...	...	...	...	...	...	...	...	...
...	...	...	704	337	367	1	1	...	...	...	...	...	...	...	...	...	...
...	...	...	782	393	389	1	1	...	...	...	...	...	...	...	...	...	...
2	2	...	499	275	224	3	2	1	...	...	...	...	...	...	...	...	...
...	...	...	387	211	176	4	2	2	...	...	...	...	...	...	...	...	...
...	...	...	7	3	4	5	3	2	...	...	...	...	...	...	...	...	...
...	...	...	437	209	228	...	...	...	...	...	...	...	...	...	...	...	...
...	...	...	439	215	224	5	4	1	...	...	...	...	...	...	...	...	...
...	...	...	9	5	4	...	...	...	...	...	...	...	...	...	...	...	...
...	...	...	119	62	57	...	...	...	...	...	...	...	...	...	...	...	...
763	506	257	49,397	24,910	24,587	805	459	346	89	48	41	4	1	3	...	...	...
10	5	5	13	8	5	35	24	11	4	3	1	...	...	...	...	...	...
...	...	...	298	126	170	...	...	...	...	...	...	...	...	...	...	...	...
...	...	...	75	33	42	...	...	...	2	1	1	1	...	1	...	...	...
10	5	5	384	167	217	35	24	11	6	4		1	...	1	...	...	...

Towns territorially by Religions.

TABLE

State or Agency.	Town.	Total Population. Total.	Males.	Females.	Hindu. Total.	Males.	Females.	Musalmán. Total.	Males.	Females.
Cambay ...	Cambay	31,390	15,273	16,117	20,952	10,360	10,592	7,466	3,504	3,962
	Tárápur	5,957	3,316	2,641	5,510	3,082	2,428	357	186	171
	Total, Cambay ...	37,347	18,589	18,758	26,462	13,442	13,020	7,823	3,690	4,133
Surat Agency .	Dharampur	4,775	2,280	2,495	3,718	1,763	1,955	1,036	500	536
	Wánsda	3,003	1,501	1,502	2,412	1,201	1,211	523	262	261
	Total, Surat Agency ...	7,778	3,781	3,997	6,130	2,964	3,166	1,559	762	797
Jawhár ...	Jawhár	2,991	1,528	1,463	2,758	1,399	1,359	226	124	102
Janjira ...	Shriwardhan	7,102	3,304	3,798	5,107	2,422	2,685	1,924	840	1,084
	Murud	5,883	2,936	2,947	5,227	2,595	2,632	574	285	289
	Total, Janjira ...	12,985	6,240	6,745	10,334	5,017	5,317	2,498	1,125	1,373
Sáwantwádi ...	Sáwantwádi	9,269	4,465	4,804	7,035	3,415	3,620	1,389	662	727
Bhor	Bhor	5,250	2,651	2,590	4,406	2,199	2,207	808	425	381
Akalkot ...	Akalkot	6,551	3,319	3,232	4,465	2,256	2,209	1,969	996	973
Sátára Agency.	Phaltán	10,564	5,154	5,410	9,200	4,492	4,708	753	361	392
Jat	Jat	5,264	2,669	2,595	4,643	2,358	2,284	539	270	269
Kolhápur ...	Kolhápur	45,815	23,393	22,422	40,070	20,492	19,578	4,193	2,089	2,104
	Ichalkaranji	11,200	5,740	5,460	9,096	4,642	4,454	1,060	559	501
	Shirol	8,705	4,357	4,348	7,902	3,949	3,953	393	206	187
	Kágal	6,928	3,490	3,438	5,897	2,965	2,932	659	330	329
	Gad Hinglaj	5,836	3,054	2,782	5,437	2,839	2,598	346	183	163
	Wádgaon	5,554	2,726	2,828	4,944	2,411	2,533	277	138	139
	Katkol	4,963	2,403	2,560	4,713	2,269	2,444	213	110	103
	A'jra	4,136	2,085	2,051	3,266	1,658	1,608	798	387	411
	Hátkalangda	3,198	1,721	1,477	2,571	1,398	1,173	344	183	161
	Malkápur	2,643	1,294	1,349	2,437	1,175	1,262	162	87	75
	Total, Kolhápur ...	98,978	50,263	48,715	86,333	43,798	42,535	8,445	4,272	4,173
Southern Marátha Jaghírs.	Miraj	26,060	13,105	12,955	20,046	10,160	9,886	5,244	2,531	2,713
	Sángli	14,798	7,557	7,241	11,755	6,009	5,746	2,057	1,043	1,014
	Jamkhandi	12,504	6,318	6,186	10,006	5,114	4,892	2,465	1,189	1,276
	Mangalwedha	12,270	6,081	6,189	11,096	5,496	5,600	1,092	546	546
	Sháhápur	11,961	6,006	5,955	10,331	5,186	5,145	1,078	547	531
	Lakshmeshwar	11,842	5,821	6,021	9,528	4,721	4,807	2,191	1,038	1,153
	Kurundwád and Wádi	9,136	4,620	4,516	6,593	3,314	3,279	1,293	648	645
	Rámdurg	8,645	4,333	4,312	7,580	3,826	3,754	1,023	484	539
	Terdál	7,043	3,430	3,613	4,598	2,278	2,320	906	460	446
	Mudhol	6,805	3,364	3,441	5,545	2,747	2,798	1,205	588	617
	Mahálingpur	6,273	3,106	3,167	5,738	2,830	2,908	525	271	254
	Kundgolpur	6,146	3,105	3,041	5,051	2,537	2,514	1,076	554	522
	Rabkavi	5,698	2,800	2,898	5,140	2,510	2,630	511	255	256
	Maindargi...	5,311	2,653	2,658	3,904	1,958	1,946	1,329	654	675
	Malgaon	5,258	2,665	2,593	4,162	2,097	2,065	294	161	133
	Sureban, Manihal and Shiwápeth	4,780	2,354	2,426	4,531	2,235	2,296	245	117	128
	Banhatti	4,506	2,272	2,234	4,081	2,059	2,022	406	202	204
	Shirhatti	4,298	2,157	2,141	3,374	1,700	1,674	921	454	467
	Kawati Periana	4,235	2,197	2,038	3,409	1,751	1,658	400	218	182
	Sawashi	4,115	2,047	2,068	3,447	1,702	1,745	656	337	319
	Shegali	3,964	2,038	1,926	3,650	1,865	1,785	303	166	137
	Gudageri	3,758	1,911	1,847	3,142	1,603	1,539	409	210	199
	Kawati	3,592	1,766	1,826	2,561	1,247	1,314	303	136	167
	Hunur	3,481	1,763	1,718	3,305	1,665	1,640	92	47	45
	Budgaon	3,057	1,553	1,504	2,835	1,424	1,401	209	111	98
	Kamdoli	2,878	1,423	1,455	2,147	1,043	1,104	718	370	348
	Dudhani	2,831	1,499	1,332	2,368	1,227	1,141	408	244	164
	Lokapur	2,508	1,202	1,306	2,161	1,027	1,134	344	172	172
	Satwalgi	2,430	1,198	1,232	2,179	1,071	1,108	110	56	54
	Yeliwal	1,872	916	956	1,682	822	860	190	94	96
	Total, Southern Marátha Jaghírs ...	202,055	101,260	100,795	165,946	83,234	82,711	28,003	13,903	14,100
Sáwanúr ...	Sáwanúr	8,743	4,137	4,606	4,893	2,326	2,567	3,848	1,809	2,039
Khairpúr ...	Khairpur	6,240	3,170	3,070	2,850	1,358	1,492	3,378	1,805	1,573

Table V.

Towns territorially by Religions.

V—*continued.*

Christian.			Jain.			Pa'rsi.			Jew.			Animistic.			Others.		
Total.	Males.	Females.	Total.	Males.	Females.	Total.	Males.	Females.	Total.	Males.	Females.	Total.	Males.	Females.	Total.	Males.	Females.
12	10	2	2,825	1,333	1,492	135	66	69	...	...	...	...	...	...	...	...	...
2	1	1	86	45	41	2	2	...	...	...	...	...	...	...	...	...	...
14	11	3	2,911	1,378	1,533	137	68	69	...	...	...	...	...	...	...	...	...
1	1	...	4	2	2	16	14	2	...	...	...	...	...	...	...	...	...
...	...	...	30	19	11	38	19	19	...	...	...	...	...	...	...	...	...
1	1	...	34	21	13	54	33	21	...	...	...	...	...	...	...	...	...
5	3	2	1	1	...	1	1	...	...	...	...	...	...	...	...	...	...
...	...	...	16	16	...	...	...	...	55	26	29	...	...	...	...	...	...
7	5	2	26	26	...	...	...	...	49	25	24	...	...	...	...	...	...
7	5	2	42	42	...	...	...	...	104	51	53	...	...	...	...	...	...
806	370	436	39	18	21	...	...	...	...	...	...	...	...	...	...	...	...
4	3	1	34	24	10	...	...	...	...	...	...	...	...	...	...	...	...
...	...	...	117	67	50	...	...	...	...	...	...	...	...	...	...	...	...
...	...	...	607	299	308	...	...	...	4	2	2	...	...	...	...	...	...
7	4	3	76	37	39	...	...	...	...	...	...	...	...	...	...	...	...
260	138	122	1,279	668	611	13	6	7	...	...	...	...	...	...	...	...	...
...	...	...	1,044	539	505	...	...	...	...	...	...	...	...	...	...	...	...
...	...	...	410	202	208	...	...	...	...	...	...	...	...	...	...	...	...
2	2	...	370	193	177	...	...	...	...	...	...	...	...	...	...	...	...
1	1	...	52	31	21	...	...	...	...	...	...	...	...	...	...	...	...
6	4	2	327	173	154	...	...	...	...	...	...	...	...	...	...	...	...
2	2	...	35	22	13	...	...	...	...	...	...	...	...	...	...	...	...
47	26	21	25	14	11	...	...	...	...	...	...	...	...	...	...	...	...
2	2	...	279	136	143	2	2	...	...	...	...	...	...	...	...	...	...
...	...	...	44	32	12	...	...	...	...	...	...	...	...	...	...	...	...
320	175	146	3,865	2,010	1,855	15	8	7	...	...	...	...	...	...	...	...	...
56	39	17	703	369	334	5	4	1	6	2	4	...	...	...	...	...	...
59	45	14	927	460	467	...	...	...	...	...	...	...	...	...	...	...	...
...	...	...	33	15	18	...	...	...	...	...	...	...	...	...	...	...	...
...	...	...	82	39	43	...	...	...	...	...	...	...	...	...	...	...	...
96	44	52	456	229	227	...	...	...	...	...	...	...	...	...	...	...	...
...	...	...	123	62	61	...	...	...	...	...	...	...	...	...	...	...	...
...	...	...	1,250	658	592	...	...	...	...	...	...	...	...	...	...	...	...
...	...	...	42	23	19	...	...	...	...	...	...	...	...	...	...	...	...
...	...	...	1,539	692	847	...	...	...	...	...	...	...	...	...	...	...	...
2	1	1	49	25	24	4	3	1	...	...	...	...	...	...	...	...	...
...	...	...	10	5	5	...	...	...	...	...	...	...	...	...	...	...	...
...	...	...	19	14	5	...	...	...	...	...	...	...	...	...	...	...	...
...	...	...	47	35	12	...	...	...	...	...	...	...	...	...	...	...	...
...	...	...	78	41	37	...	...	...	...	...	...	...	...	...	...	...	...
...	...	...	802	407	395	...	...	...	...	...	...	...	...	...	...	...	...
...	...	...	4	2	2	...	...	...	...	...	...	...	...	...	...	...	...
...	...	...	19	11	8	...	...	...	...	...	...	...	...	...	...	...	...
...	...	...	3	3	...	...	...	...	...	...	...	...	...	...	...	...	...
...	...	...	426	228	198	...	...	...	...	...	...	...	...	...	...	...	...
...	...	...	12	8	4	...	...	...	...	...	...	...	...	...	...	...	...
...	...	...	11	7	4	...	...	...	...	...	...	...	...	...	...	...	...
...	...	...	207	98	109	...	...	...	...	...	...	...	...	...	...	...	...
...	...	...	728	383	345	...	...	...	...	...	...	...	...	...	...	...	...
...	...	...	84	51	33	...	...	...	...	...	...	...	...	...	...	...	...
...	...	...	13	8	5	...	...	...	...	...	...	...	...	...	...	...	...
...	...	...	13	10	3	...	...	...	...	...	...	...	...	...	...	...	...
...	...	...	52	27	25	3	1	2	...	...	...	...	...	...	...	...	...
...	...	...	3	3	...	...	...	...	...	...	...	...	...	...	...	...	...
...	...	...	141	71	70	...	...	...	...	...	...	...	...	...	...	...	...
...	...	...	...	...	...	...	...	...	...	...	...	...	...	...	...	...	...
213	129	84	7,876	3,984	3,892	12	8	4	6	2	4	...	...	...	...	...	...
...	...	...	2	2	...	...	...	...	...	...	...	...	...	...	...	...	...
...	...	...	...	...	...	...	...	...	...	...	...	12	7	5	...	...	...

TABLE VI.

RELIGIONS.

In Mahi Kántha, Religion was not returned for Total 19,236, Males 10,579, Females 8,657.

Table VI.

Religions.

TABLE

Reli

State.	Total Population. Total.	Total Population. Males.	Total Population. Females.	Hindu. Total.	Hindu. Males.	Hindu. Females.	Mussalman. Total.	Mussalman. Males.	Mussalman. Females.	Christian. Total.	Christian. Males.	Christian. Females.
Cutch	558,415	278,441	279,974	351,620	176,765	174,855	133,492	66,552	66,940	173	140	33
Pálanpur	645,526	335,587	309,939	557,870	290,059	267,811	57,486	29,949	27,537	608	480	128
Mahi Kántha	581,568	296,646	284,922	525,897	267,730	258,167	22,570	11,610	10,960	35	29	6
Káthiáwár	2,752,404	1,416,633	1,335,771	2,279,423	1,175,886	1,103,537	358,061	181,196	176,865	898	593	305
Rewa Kántha	733,506	376,146	357,360	641,811	329,675	312,136	25,103	13,102	12,001	36	26	10
Cambay	89,722	46,231	43,491	73,590	38,351	35,239	12,712	6,218	6,494	21	16	5
Surat Agency	181,208	92,457	88,751	175,298	89,426	85,872	5,159	2,606	2,553	1	1	...
Total, Gujarát Group...	5,542,349	2,842,141	2,700,208	4,605,509	2,367,892	2,237,617	614,583	311,233	303,350	1,772	1,285	487
Jawhár	52,831	27,825	25,006	52,232	27,492	24,740	421	235	186	7	5	2
Janjira	81,780	39,629	42,151	66,803	32,898	33,905	14,136	6,284	7,852	12	10	2
Sáwantwádi...	192,948	93,520	99,428	183,749	89,115	94,634	4,455	2,120	2,335	4,597	2,209	2,388
Total, Konkan Group...	327,559	160,974	166,585	302,784	149,505	153,279	19,012	8,639	10,373	4,616	2,224	2,392
The Dángs	32,920	17,237	15,683	21,343	11,268	10,075	151	83	68	3	3	...
Surgana	12,398	6,545	5,853	12,118	6,397	5,721	131	68	63	...	...	...
Bhor	155,669	78,602	77,067	152,716	77,021	75,695	1,992	1,074	918	9	8	1
Akalkot	75,774	38,615	37,159	65,034	33,092	31,942	10,230	5,253	4,977	2	2	...
Sátára Agency	131,529	66,269	65,260	125,554	63,216	62,338	4,674	2,378	2,296	1	1	...
Total, Deccan Group..	408,290	207,268	201,022	376,765	190,991	185,771	17,178	8,856	8,322	15	14	1
Jat......	79,786	40,576	39,210	74,690	37,919	36,771	4,764	2,488	2,276	16	8	8
Kolhápur	913,131	467,572	445,559	822,526	419,783	402,743	38,272	20,127	18,145	1,413	700	713
Southern Marátha Jághirs.	639,270	320,531	318,739	558,469	279,858	278,611	52,197	26,280	25,917	403	233	170
Sávanúr	16,976	8,330	8,646	12,108	5,978	6,130	4,853	2,344	2,509	...	...	...
Total, Karnátak Group...	1,649,163	837,009	812,154	1,467,793	743,538	724,255	100,086	51,239	48,847	1,832	941	891
Khairpur	131,937	72,733	59,204	28,214	14,644	13,570	103,033	57,697	45,336	4	3	1
Total, Feudatory States.	**8,059,293**	**4,120,125**	**3,939,173**	**6,781,065**	**3,466,573**	**3,314,492**	**853,892**	**437,664**	**416,228**	**6,239**	**4,467**	**3,772**

VI.

gions.

Table VI.

Religions.

Buddhist.			Jain.			Sikh.			Pa'rsi.			Jew.			Animistic.		
Total.	Males.	Females.	Total.	Males.	Females.	Total.	Males.	Females.	Total.	Males.	Females.	Total.	Males.	Females.	Total.	Males.	Females.
1	1	...	71.988	34,355	37,633	94	81	13	118	64	54	47	26	21	882	457	425
...	...	...	29.149	14,896	14,253	...	...	...	205	96	109	34	18	16	174	89	85
...	...	...	13.818	6,690	7,128	...	...	...	8	5	3	4	3	1	...	...	...
...	...	...	113.005	58,379	54,626	...	...	...	908	524	384	105	54	51	4	1	3
..	...	...	1.308	721	587	...	...	...	386	228	158	6	4	2	64,856	32,390	32,466
...	...	...	3.262	1,578	1,684	...	...	...	137	68	69	...	...	...	...	...	...
...	...	...	126	69	57	...	...	...	618	352	266	6	3	3	...	...	...
1	1	...	232,656	116,688	115,968	94	81	13	2,380	1,337	1,043	202	108	94	65,916	32,937	32,979
...	...	...	4	4	...	...	...	...	46	31	15	...	...	...	121	58	63
...	...	...	71	62	9	...	...	...	...	...	...	599	282	317	159	93	66
...	...	...	147	76	71	...	...	...	...	...	...	...	...	...	...	...	...
...	...	...	223	142	80	...	...	...	46	31	15	599	282	317	280	151	129
...	...	...	1	1	...	...	...	...	20	14	6	...	...	...	11,402	5,868	5,534
...	...	...	...	...	...	...	...	...	28	19	9	...	...	...	121	61	60
..	...	...	680	356	324	...	...	...	1	1	...	271	142	129	...	...	...
...	...	...	508	268	240	...	...	...	...	...	...	...	...	...	..	...	..
...	...	...	1.296	672	624	...	...	...	...	...	...	4	2	2	...	...	
...	...	...	2,485	1,297	1,188	...	...	...	49	34	15	275	144	131	11 533	5,920	[illegible]
...	...	...	316	161	155	...	..	...	...	...	...	...	...	...	..	...	...
...	...	...	50.896	26,950	23,946	...	...	...	24	12	12	...	...	...	...	...	...
...	...	...	28.183	14,150	14,033	...	...	...	12	8	4	6	2	4	..	...	...
...	...	...	15	8	7	...	...	...	...	...	...	...	...	...	...	...	..
...	...	...	79,410	41,269	38,141	...	...	..	36	20	16	6	2	4	...	...	...
...	...	...	...	...	...	...	...	...	...	...	...	...	...	...	686	389	297
1	1	...	314.773	159,396	155,377	94	81	13	2,511	1.422	1.089	1,082	536	546	78,405	39,406	38.999

TABLE VII.

AGES BY RELIGIONS.

PART	A.—Total Population.	PART	F.—Jain.
,,	B.—Hindu.	,,	G.—Sikh.
,,	C.—Mussalman.	,,	H.—Pársi.
,,	D.—Christian.	,,	I.—Jew.
,,	E.—Buddhist.	,,	J.—Animistic.

The 19,236 persons—10,579 males, 8,657 females—in Feudatories, for whom religion and age were not returned, are excluded.

Ages by Religions.

TABLE

Part (A).—

State.	Total Population. Total.	Males.	Females.	Under 1 year. Males.	Females.	1 year. Males.	Females.	2 years. Males.	Females.	3 years. Males.	Females.	4 years. Males.	Females.	Total, 0—4. Males.	Females.	5—9. Males.	Females.
Cutch	553,415	278,441	279,974	9,310	9,057	4,332	4,691	7,885	8,447	8,824	9,168	8,469	8,746	38,820	40,093	40,583	[illegible]
Pálanpur	645,526	335,587	309,939	10,370	10,702	5,551	6,701	9,071	10,176	10,744	11,900	11,209	11,269	46,945	49,748	53,195	[illegible]
Mahi Kántha	562,332	286,067	276,265	8,397	8,892	4,390	4,614	8,028	9,163	8,669	9,783	9,667	10,253	39,151	42,605	46,684	[illegible]
Káthiáwár	2,752,404	1,416,633	1,335,771	42,351	43,230	25,355	27,087	41,649	43,971	43,925	47,157	41,114	41,269	194,194	202,694	200,775	[illegible]
Rewa Kántha	733,506	376,146	357,360	13,550	14,208	5,941	6,413	10,746	11,837	13,154	14,655	12,800	13,112	56,191	60,219	60,404	[illegible]
Cambay	89,722	46,231	43,491	1,109	1,171	754	801	1,155	1,149	1,216	1,180	1,212	1,222	5,515	5,613	5,945	[illegible]
Surat Agency	181,208	92,457	83,751	2,846	3,050	1,422	1,621	2,652	2,936	3,459	3,781	3,320	3,364	13,690	14,752	14,862	[illegible]
Total, Gujarát Group	5,523,113	2,831,562	2,691,551	87,893	90,304	47,745	50,828	81,086	87,679	90,000	97,689	87,791	89,234	394,515	415,734	422,398	[illegible]
Jawhár	52,831	27,825	25,006	681	705	501	520	906	987	916	1,079	1,101	1,165	4,105	4,456	4,384	[illegible]
Janjira	81,780	39,629	42,151	1,432	1,503	991	1,130	1,246	1,564	1,467	1,599	1,412	1,489	6,548	7,284	6,478	[illegible]
Sáwantwádi	192,948	93,520	99,428	2,636	2,931	1,409	1,406	2,926	3,281	3,016	3,375	2,865	3,026	12,843	14,019	12,688	[illegible]
Total, Konkan Group	327,559	160,974	166,585	4,749	5,138	2,892	3,056	5,078	5,833	5,399	6,053	5,378	5,680	23,496	25,759	23,550	[illegible]
The Dángs	32,920	17,237	15,683	459	465	123	172	412	659	624	719	693	774	2,311	2,789	3,052	[illegible]
Surgana	12,398	6,545	5,853	144	168	59	79	222	222	250	279	312	304	987	1,052	1,129	[illegible]
Bhor	155,669	78,602	77,067	2,483	2,490	1,375	1,509	2,700	2,981	2,842	2,950	2,716	2,787	12,116	13,717	11,918	[illegible]
Akalkot	75,774	38,615	37,159	1,212	1,237	1,120	1,148	1,403	1,647	1,192	1,267	1,383	1,391	6,310	6,590	5,086	[illegible]
Sátára Agency	131,529	66,269	65,260	2,292	2,366	1,192	1,219	2,267	2,566	2,167	2,362	2,103	2,134	10,091	10,647	9,055	[illegible]
Total, Deccan Group	408,290	207,268	201,022	6,590	6,726	3,869	4,127	7,004	7,975	7,076	7,577	7,206	7,390	31,804	33,795	30,235	[illegible]
Jat	79,786	40,576	39,210	1,615	1,707	821	854	1,597	1,680	1,436	1,504	1,561	1,618	7,030	7,363	5,949	[illegible]
Kolhápur	913,131	467,572	445,559	14,294	14,614	9,049	9,713	14,880	15,621	14,194	15,248	15,137	14,837	67,554	70,027	63,508	[illegible]
Southern Marátha Jaghirs	639,270	320,531	318,739	10,897	11,091	6,692	6,958	11,127	11,503	10,459	10,660	11,064	10,878	50,239	51,090	43,677	[illegible]
Sávanúr	16,976	8,330	8,640	303	300	144	143	259	365	279	283	306	281	1,291	1,371	1,176	[illegible]
Total, Karnátak Group	1,649,163	837,009	812,154	27,109	27,712	16,712	17,668	27,863	29,169	26,368	27,688	28,068	27,614	126,120	129,851	114,310	[illegible]
Khairpur	131,937	72,733	59,204	1,496	1,217	1,528	1,414	2,444	2,296	2,024	2,283	2,917	2,300	11,009	9,520	11,060	[illegible]
Total, Feudatory States	8,040,062	4,109,546	3,930,516	127,887	131,037	72,746	77,093	133,475	132,950	131,466	141,295	131,420	132,224	586,944	614,659	601,553	[illegible]

Part (B).—

State.	Total Population. Total.	Males.	Females.	Under 1 year. Males.	Females.	1 year. Males.	Females.	2 years. Males.	Females.	3 years. Males.	Females.	4 years. Males.	Females.	Total, 0—4. Males.	Females.	5—9. Males.	Females.
Cutch	351,620	176,765	174,855	5,762	5,524	2,690	2,795	4,794	5,187	5,565	5,666	5,283	5,403	24,108	24,575	25,200	[illegible]
Pálanpur	557,870	290,059	267,811	9,008	9,222	4,869	4,972	8,040	8,986	9,651	10,690	9,922	9,974	41,490	43,844	47,381	[illegible]
Mahi Kántha	525,897	267,730	258,167	7,889	8,384	4,118	4,283	7,598	8,647	8,222	9,317	9,172	9,735	38,999	40,246	44,163	[illegible]
Káthiáwár	2,279,423	1,175,886	1,103,537	34,883	35,539	20,955	22,281	34,550	36,657	36,615	39,449	33,988	34,076	160,991	168,002	166,747	[illegible]
Rewa Kántha	641,811	329,675	312,136	11,641	12,187	5,230	5,657	9,167	10,105	11,521	12,819	11,161	11,498	48,720	52,180	52,956	[illegible]
Cambay	73,590	38,351	35,239	974	939	662	675	964	971	1,041	1,081	1,013	1,019	4,644	4,685	4,991	[illegible]
Surat Agency	175,298	89,420	85,878	2,759	2,964	1,362	1,508	2,588	2,854	3,379	3,698	3,240	3,280	13,328	14,364	14,496	[illegible]
Total, Gujarát Group	4,605,809	2,367,892	2,257,617	72,916	74,639	39,885	42,151	67,698	73,407	75,994	82,720	73,779	74,985	330,270	347,902	355,934	[illegible]
Jawhár	53,232	27,492	24,740	676	606	496	613	893	978	907	1,069	1,094	1,158	4,066	4,408	4,348	[illegible]
Janjira	66,803	32,898	33,905	1,178	1,266	812	957	1,011	1,381	1,219	1,340	1,172	1,228	5,392	6,106	5,328	[illegible]
Sáwantwádi	183,749	89,115	94,634	2,496	2,761	1,314	1,322	2,780	3,103	2,855	3,202	2,718	2,870	12,163	13,264	11,988	[illegible]
Total, Konkan Group	302,764	149,505	153,279	4,350	4,783	2,622	2,792	4,684	5,402	4,981	6,011	4,984	5,250	21,621	23,778	21,664	[illegible]
The Dángs	21,343	11,268	10,075	308	298	89	107	289	418	406	426	430	483	1,522	1,785	1,950	[illegible]
Surgana	12,118	6,397	5,721	142	167	59	75	217	217	249	271	308	295	975	1,02?	1,103	1,0??
Bhor	152,716	77,021	75,695	2,425	2,441	1,353	1,488	2,653	2,987	2,797	2,911	2,672	2,744	11,900	12,511	11,744	[illegible]
Akalkot	65,034	33,092	31,942	1,023	1,082	972	904	1,217	1,337	1,053	1,101	1,298	1,190	5,470	5,704	4,834	4,135
Sátára Agency	125,554	63,216	62,338	2,204	2,254	1,136	1,157	2,166	2,464	2,076	2,279	2,070	2,047	9,652	10,201	8,642	7,971
Total, Deccan Group	376,765	190,994	185,771	6,101	6,248	3,609	3,831	6,542	7,357	6,681	6,988	6,686	6,758	29,619	31,166	27,773	[illegible]
Jat	74,690	37,919	36,771	1,515	1,611	777	803	1,495	1,571	1,357	1,405	1,462	1,520	6,596	6,908	6,689	6,516
Kolhápur	822,526	419,783	402,743	12,988	13,292	8,182	8,783	13,507	14,248	12,958	13,975	13,689	13,481	61,324	63,776	57,468	[illegible]
Southern Marátha Jaghirs	558,469	279,858	278,611	9,543	9,718	5,822	6,168	9,840	10,110	9,141	9,380	9,678	9,500	44,024	44,825	38,039	35,516
Sávanúr	12,108	5,978	6,130	204	206	99	68	186	250	191	196	213	208	893	958	822	[illegible]
Total, Karnátak Group	1,467,793	743,538	724,255	24,250	24,827	14,880	15,793	25,029	26,188	23,647	24,951	25,032	24,709	112,837	116,467	101,917	[illegible]
Khairpur	28,214	14,644	13,570	429	341	388	397	623	630	617	575	624	627	2,681	2,570	2,558	1,977
Total, Feudatory States	6,781,065	3,466,573	3,314,492	108,016	116,772	61,384	61,953	104,573	112,981	111,820	130,845	111,105	112,329	496,928	521,883	500,846	[illegible]

Table VII.

Ages by Religions.

VII.

Total Population.

10—14. Males.	10—14. Females.	15—19. Males.	15—19. Females.	20—24. Males.	20—24. Females.	25—29. Males.	25—29. Females.	30—34. Males.	30—34. Females.
33,103	27,466	22,611	20,559	23,274	26,060	21,877	23,676	28,864	24,271
39,919	32,037	28,776	31,348	29,740	27,791	30,219	27,619	30,927	26,369
38,651	29,016	27,794	21,333	25,626	25,128	25,785	25,051	24,141	22,941
147,469	118,119	120,644	99,649	142,095	142,837	136,375	127,876	129,865	117,847
41,410	32,205	32,609	26,784	32,669	28,638	35,452	33,094	31,017	30,839
4,865	3,694	4,210	3,654	4,774	4,649	4,458	3,098	4,090	3,695
10,991	9,040	7,072	6,461	7,103	7,560	7,734	7,738	7,209	7,089
313,428	251,677	243,615	200,283	265,081	260,661	261,900	249,061	252,003	233,111
2,969	2,274	2,099	1,953	1,967	1,944	2,677	2,064	2,297	2,177
4,199	3,692	2,802	3,227	2,248	3,211	3,253	4,066	3,260	3,620
10,430	8,694	8,395	7,508	6,319	8,346	8,163	9,646	7,267	9,143
17,598	14,660	13,296	12,690	10,534	13,501	14,013	15,776	12,824	14,840
2,219	1,602	1,358	1,115	1,191	1,336	1,632	1,648	1,452	1,367
821	636	508	458	408	404	656	544	528	498
8,934	7,349	5,541	5,097	5,170	6,513	7,332	7,376	6,539	6,606
3,114	2,519	2,628	2,436	2,922	3,434	4,020	3,752	3,518	3,719
6,982	5,431	4,721	4,653	4,433	5,651	6,159	6,043	5,439	6,815
22,070	17,437	14,756	14,359	14,124	17,397	19,799	19,363	17,476	18,005
3,168	2,532	2,018	2,408	2,979	3,449	3,881	3,784	3,660	3,831
50,454	40,581	34,194	29,456	33,371	36,117	42,400	41,871	40,325	40,071
30,520	24,987	23,447	21,620	23,442	27,776	28,948	29,771	27,436	29,802
900	741	593	571	687	856	743	705	665	723
85,068	68,771	60,852	54,061	60,479	68,208	76,032	76,151	72,086	74,487
6,044	3,579	4,833	4,004	5,560	5,955	6,135	6,031	6,601	6,062
444,178	356,124	337,383	285,336	355,784	371,712	377,879	366,351	360,990	346,505

35—39. Males.	35—39. Females.	40—44. Males.	40—44. Females.	45—49. Males.	45—49. Females.	50—54. Males.	50—54. Females.	55—59. Males.	55—59. Females.	60 and over. Males.	60 and over. Females.
15,046	13,837	17,050	19,272	7,911	6,750	13,516	14,522	5,289	4,237	16,547	18,680
15,866	14,436	20,342	19,613	8,193	7,780	14,398	14,788	4,009	3,915	13,058	15,677
15,554	15,135	17,165	18,364	7,503	7,752	10,799	13,112	2,690	2,974	6,624	10,174
84,999	72,227	88,469	86,707	41,227	34,177	59,046	58,497	16,615	14,427	54,820	68,680
25,150	21,647	22,061	21,851	12,775	11,837	12,651	13,737	4,323	4,369	8,734	12,566
2,941	3,711	3,150	3,415	1,534	1,575	2,231	2,381	680	654	1,809	2,291
7,201	5,886	4,803	4,646	4,234	3,337	2,790	2,883	1,659	1,567	3,100	3,837
160,757	145,779	173,049	173,867	83,377	73,208	116,422	119,910	35,295	33,043	104,692	131,955
2,620	1,506	1,404	1,181	1,827	895	781	783	622	420	774	1,085
2,713	2,265	2,371	2,488	1,653	1,304	1,567	1,831	830	772	1,707	2,334
6,642	5,236	5,840	6,949	4,024	3,322	4,621	4,998	2,140	1,748	5,219	7,884
10,784	9,057	9,714	10,619	7,004	5,519	6,969	7,612	3,492	2,940	7,700	11,303
1,419	878	766	692	621	421	498	457	180	115	438	431
458	359	395	308	261	154	200	160	54	59	140	113
4,713	4,191	4,934	4,938	3,009	2,291	3,557	3,364	1,300	1,018	3,456	4,243
2,362	1,905	2,920	2,624	1,618	1,079	1,735	1,721	710	428	1,072	2,081
3,884	3,501	4,592	4,649	2,714	2,154	3,372	3,087	1,164	1,000	3,793	4,263
12,836	10,834	13,607	13,202	8,223	6,099	9,302	8,785	3,498	2,648	9,408	11,136
2,510	2,027	2,976	2,609	1,482	1,109	1,910	1,655	688	500	1,719	2,272
29,693	24,466	32,518	30,317	19,378	14,763	21,935	21,161	8,555	6,906	23,617	30,049
19,933	17,697	23,422	21,935	12,014	10,012	14,988	15,685	5,504	4,905	16,355	21,504
494	461	552	524	282	222	400	468	152	164	395	595
52,630	44,651	59,468	55,385	33,756	26,106	39,233	38,949	14,899	12,475	42,086	54,429
3,917	3,195	5,216	4,499	2,556	2,100	4,053	2,581	1,121	774	4,592	3,137
216,954	213,516	261,054	257,571	134,916	113,032	175,039	173,237	58,305	50,887	168,558	211,949

Hindu.

10—14. Males.	10—14. Females.	15—19. Males.	15—19. Females.	20—24. Males.	20—24. Females.	25—29. Males.	25—29. Females.	30—34. Males.	30—34. Females.
20,847	16,996	14,865	12,951	15,273	16,454	14,230	14,836	15,544	15,283
34,842	27,798	24,841	18,768	25,352	23,890	25,997	24,037	26,890	22,665
34,400	27,041	26,117	19,967	23,730	23,338	24,021	23,393	22,569	21,591
121,009	96,486	101,309	82,479	119,164	118,604	114,748	106,753	109,114	97,619
36,738	28,510	28,898	23,434	28,453	28,085	30,790	28,716	27,915	26,871
4,100	3,000	3,690	2,975	3,995	3,678	3,714	3,257	3,340	2,982
10,653	8,756	6,668	6,263	6,798	7,259	7,472	7,501	6,955	6,804
262,589	208,587	206,488	160,830	222,763	221,888	220,972	208,493	212,323	193,675
2,942	2,860	2,073	1,934	1,037	1,923	2,544	2,043	2,254	2,151
3,406	2,914	2,316	2,595	1,931	2,609	2,809	3,201	2,812	2,892
9,918	8,231	8,032	7,166	6,051	7,964	7,850	9,175	6,938	8,717
16,266	13,595	12,420	11,696	9,019	12,495	13,203	14,419	12,004	13,670
1,539	1,036	928	686	700	833	1,034	1,036	979	866
800	680	497	460	403	460	639	634	514	480
8,764	7,219	5,422	5,575	5,040	6,384	7,177	7,240	6,394	6,515
2,650	2,141	2,241	2,116	2,494	2,965	3,495	3,240	2,987	3,190
6,528	5,173	4,487	4,418	4,229	5,416	5,884	5,776	5,188	5,568
20,290	16,179	13,575	13,246	12,926	16,048	18,229	17,826	16,062	16,609
2,949	2,394	2,449	2,267	2,778	3,224	3,029	3,538	3,385	3,593
45,045	36,495	30,717	26,668	29,822	32,763	38,135	37,989	36,184	36,206
26,386	21,657	20,505	19,010	20,528	24,383	25,377	26,079	24,022	26,168
638	532	427	413	501	594	554	495	473	525
75,018	61,068	54,098	48,348	53,629	60,964	67,695	68,102	64,074	66,492
1,327	995	1,098	974	1,081	1,313	1,163	1,2[illegible]	1,093	1,113
375,290	300,164	287,679	241,093	300,318	312,103	321,262	310,079	305,559	291,558

35—39. Males.	35—39. Females.	40—44. Males.	40—44. Females.	45—49. Males.	45—49. Females.	50—54. Males.	50—54. Females.	55—59. Males.	55—59. Females.	60 and over. Males.	60 and over. Females.
9,670	8,729	10,803	12,269	4,817	4,136	8,511	9,279	3,264	2,635	9,038	11,437
13,179	12,060	17,166	16,560	6,615	6,379	12,126	12,550	3,210	3,147	10,961	13,266
14,381	14,084	16,024	16,970	6,841	7,129	10,030	12,183	2,422	2,711	6,043	9,375
70,496	59,561	72,836	71,149	33,667	28,611	49,410	48,087	13,253	11,756	44,242	55,973
21,857	18,884	19,469	19,178	11,134	10,210	11,156	12,101	3,785	3,881	7,804	11,260
2,417	2,201	2,554	2,742	1,258	1,248	1,813	1,911	637	510	1,398	1,723
6,960	5,715	4,628	4,453	4,067	3,218	2,670	2,756	1,608	1,520	2,930	3,688
139,860	121,232	143,480	143,320	68,209	60,330	94,716	98,877	28,079	26,100	83,316	106,718
2,505	1,492	1,471	1,163	1,301	885	770	769	519	426	762	1,081
2,300	1,773	2,022	1,927	1,375	1,011	1,261	1,473	665	607	1,276	1,864
5,290	5,056	5,592	6,623	3,856	3,186	4,414	4,777	2,018	1,671	4,964	7,559
10,110	8,321	9,085	9,713	6,531	5,082	6,445	7,019	3,232	2,703	7,002	10,505
909	560	504	470	416	294	823	507	122	96	282	278
443	347	381	303	252	173	195	159	50	57	136	110
4,617	4,114	4,834	4,839	2,944	2,246	3,464	3,278	1,359	909	3,362	4,165
2,020	1,645	2,493	2,250	1,372	926	1,491	1,487	600	403	1,445	1,740
3,710	3,337	4,378	4,466	2,598	2,061	3,210	2,941	1,104	955	3,606	4,075
11,699	9,993	12,590	12,328	7,582	5,669	8,683	8,172	3,235	2,600	8,831	10,363
2,367	1,885	2,770	2,461	1,368	1,035	1,778	1,558	645	459	1,606	2,164
26,584	23,076	29,057	27,255	17,353	13,202	19,576	19,085	7,623	6,185	20,943	26,937
17,440	15,519	20,392	19,129	11,106	8,815	13,094	13,649	4,860	4,258	14,086	18,603
308	351	410	356	203	175	287	341	119	130	283	337
46,700	39,831	52,629	49,201	30,030	23,227	34,737	34,611	13,247	11,030	36,918	48,[illegible]
692	664	808	902	479	463	720	624	249	172	705	579
208,070	180,031	218,592	215,464	112,924	94,771	145,301	149,303	48,042	42,565	136,772	176,264

TABLE

Part (C).—

State.	Total Population. Total.	Males.	Females.	Under 1 year. Males.	Females.	1 year. Males.	Females.	2 years. Males.	Females.	3 years. Males.	Females.	4 years. Males.	Females.	Total, 0—4. Males.	Females.	5—9. Males.	Females.
Cutch	133,492	66,552	66,940	2,214	2,184	1,092	1,210	2,024	2,146	2,217	2,378	2,201	2,287	9,748	10,199	10,324	10,078
Pâlanpur	57,486	29,949	27,537	889	872	439	495	678	890	761	812	895	910	3,662	3,979	4,068	3,891
Mahi Kántha	21,670	11,610	10,060	304	352	154	168	287	361	323	324	318	353	1,386	1,558	1,712	1,536
Káthiáwár	358,081	181,196	176,885	5,661	5,874	3,406	3,754	5,459	5,750	5,629	5,973	5,602	5,659	25,757	27,010	26,384	25,237
Rewa Kántha	25,103	13,102	12,001	417	425	192	193	330	337	276	344	323	350	1,538	1,649	1,570	1,433
Cambay	12,712	6,218	6,494	144	172	69	101	161	132	140	161	167	144	681	710	749	681
Surat Agency	5,159	2,606	2,553	71	76	52	48	61	75	71	74	66	79	321	352	335	308
Total, Gujarát Group	614,583	311,233	303,350	9,700	10,045	5,404	5,969	9,000	9,691	9,417	10,066	9,573	9,812	43,093	45,483	45,142	45,965
Jawhár	421	235	186	3	8	3	4	8	6	6	4	4	7	24	29	22	32
Janjira	14,136	6,284	7,852	239	223	166	159	223	230	235	238	227	251	1,090	1,100	1,088	1,071
Sáwantwádi	4,455	2,120	2,335	57	74	49	48	64	83	70	91	73	78	313	368	330	319
Total, Konkan Group	19,012	8,639	10,373	299	304	218	205	294	319	311	333	304	336	1,426	1,497	1,440	1,423
The Dángs	151	83	68	..	..	..	..	2	1	3	1	2	1	7	3	10	19
Surgana	131	68	63	2	..	..	1	2	2	..	1	2	4	6	8	10	7
Bhor	1,992	1,074	918	46	34	13	28	29	33	34	27	38	33	160	145	130	116
Akalkot	10,230	5,253	4,977	181	144	142	151	178	204	136	160	169	195	806	854	721	669
Sátára Agency	4,674	2,378	2,296	68	94	49	58	80	85	75	73	74	76	346	379	343	315
Total, Deccan Group	17,178	8,856	8,322	297	272	204	222	291	325	248	261	285	309	1,325	1,389	1,214	1,126
Jat	4,764	2,488	2,276	95	92	46	48	99	103	75	96	107	94	422	433	330	318
Kolhápur	38,272	20,127	18,145	569	618	410	441	647	607	566	566	681	632	2,873	2,864	2,777	2,673
Southern Marátha Jaghirs	52,197	26,280	25,917	910	923	584	613	866	965	874	853	926	932	4,160	4,286	3,792	3,679
Sáwanúr	4,853	2,344	2,509	99	93	45	45	73	115	87	86	93	72	397	411	353	380
Total, Karnátak Group	100,086	51,239	48,847	1,673	1,726	1,085	1,147	1,685	1,790	1,602	1,601	1,807	1,730	7,852	7,994	7,252	6,773
Khairpur	103,033	57,697	45,336	1,059	838	1,134	1,010	1,805	1,652	1,994	1,706	2,273	1,669	8,265	6,905	8,433	5,855
Total, Feudatory States	853,892	437,664	416,228	13,038	13,215	8,045	8,553	13,075	13,677	13,573	13,967	14,241	13,858	61,961	63,268	63,481	57,613

Part (D).—

State.	Total.	Males.	Females.	Under 1 year. Males.	Females.	1 year. Males.	Females.	2 years. Males.	Females.	3 years. Males.	Females.	4 years. Males.	Females.	Total, 0—4. Males.	Females.	5—9. Males.	Females.
Cutch	173	140	33	1	2	2	..	3	..	..	2	4	..	10	4	3	3
Pálanpur	604	480	118	6	8	4	2	2	7	2	6	4	5	18	28	14	21
Mahi Kántha	35	29	6	..	..	..	..	1	1	..	..	3	..	4	1	..	2
Káthiáwár	898	593	305	10	13	6	9	17	8	5	12	11	11	49	53	31	33
Rewa Kántha	38	28	10	1	1	..	..	1	..	..	1	..	..	2	2	1	1
Cambay	21	16	5	..	..	..	..	..	..	1	..	..	..	1	..	..	..
Surat Agency	1	1	..	..	..	..	..	..	..	..	..	..	..	..	..	..	..
Total, Gujarát Group	1,772	1,285	487	18	24	12	11	24	16	8	21	22	16	84	88	49	60
Jawhár	7	5	2	..	..	..	..	..	..	..	1	..	..	..	1	..	..
Janjira	12	10	2	..	..	..	..	..	..	1	..	..	..	1	..	2	1
Sáwantwádi	4,597	2,209	2,388	80	92	87	40	78	93	88	81	72	70	355	376	366	317
Total, Konkan Group	4,616	2,224	2,392	80	92	87	40	78	93	89	81	72	70	356	377	368	318
The Dángs	3	3	..	..	..	..	..	..	..	..	..	..	..	..	..	..	..
Surgana	..	..	..	..	..	..	..	..	..	..	..	..	..	..	..	..	..
Bhor	9	8	1	..	..	..	..	..	..	..	..	..	..	..	..	..	..
Akalkot	2	2	..	..	..	..	..	..	..	..	..	..	..	..	..	..	..
Sátára Agency	1	1	..	..	..	..	..	..	..	..	..	..	..	..	..	..	..
Total, Deccan Group	15	14	1	..	..	..	..	..	..	..	..	..	..	..	..	..	..
Jat	16	8	8	..	..	1	..	..	1	..	..	..	1	1	2	..	2
Kolhápur	1,413	700	713	26	24	21	17	31	36	17	27	29	26	124	130	117	87
Southern Marátha Jaghirs	403	233	170	5	3	5	3	3	7	6	6	8	2	27	21	36	29
Sáwanúr	..	..	..	..	..	..	..	..	..	..	..	..	..	..	..	..	..
Total, Karnátak Group	1,832	941	891	31	27	27	20	34	44	23	33	37	30	152	163	153	118
Khairpur	4	3	1	..	..	..	..	..	..	..	..	..	..	..	..	..	..
Total, Feudatory States	6,239	4,467	1,772	139	143	76	71	136	153	130	136	131	115	692	618	570	496

Part (E).—

State.	Total.	Males.	Females.	Under 1 year. Males.	Females.	1 year. Males.	Females.	2 years. Males.	Females.	3 years. Males.	Females.	4 years. Males.	Females.	Total, 0—4. Males.	Females.	5—9. Males.	Females.
Cutch	1	1	..	..	..	..	..	..	..	..	..	..	..	..	..	..	..

Table VII.

Ages by Religions.

VII.

Mussalman.

10 — 14.		15 — 19.		20 — 24.		25 — 29.		30 — 34.		35 — 39.		40 — 44.		45 — 49.		50 — 54.		55 — 59.		60 and over.	
Males.	Females.	Males.	Females.	Males.	Females.	Males.	Females.	Males.	Females.	Males.	Females.	Males.	Females.	Males.	Females.	Males.	Females.	Males.	Females.	Males.	Females.
7,536	6,555	5,229	4,751	5,451	6,214	5,205	5,535	5,675	5,959	3,461	3,086	4,081	4,642	1,788	1,460	3,072	3,834	1,065	856	3,917	4,467
3,387	2,766	2,676	2,077	2,805	2,587	2,716	2,375	2,727	2,459	1,646	1,496	2,137	1,969	874	781	1,568	1,444	401	378	1,382	1,536
1,419	1,225	1,051	835	1,114	1,030	1,159	1,038	1,038	967	783	584	735	887	355	330	457	526	130	108	821	386
19,564	15,975	13,752	12,828	16,818	18,713	16,172	16,315	16,046	15,714	10,786	9,624	11,970	11,785	5,298	4,347	8,115	7,898	2,369	1,876	8,165	9,703
1,393	1,098	1,149	966	1,307	1,279	1,345	1,160	1,174	1,047	952	706	919	795	481	411	599	605	225	190	450	613
612	541	606	533	613	783	606	599	605	575	401	378	489	532	202	240	820	365	99	99	335	444
301	251	184	175	265	299	229	211	224	193	196	159	144	168	137	101	96	115	88	43	136	179
34,212	29,411	24,447	22,165	28,373	30,905	27,432	27,233	27,489	26,913	18,175	15,987	20,475	20,558	9,135	7,670	14,227	14,187	4,327	3,550	14,706	17,325
23	20	22	18	25	13	24	16	32	18	19	12	16	10	15	6	6	7	2	3	5	2
746	744	443	614	278	564	408	825	419	692	370	568	330	547	260	279	290	347	154	155	409	445
264	228	180	163	130	189	156	225	144	192	112	104	110	149	75	68	112	119	55	35	139	176
1,033	992	645	795	433	766	588	1,066	595	903	501	684	456	706	350	353	408	473	211	193	553	623
10	6	9	4	8	5	9	9	6	3	8	5	1	4	9	..	1	4	2	..	3	6
6	10	3	3	4	..	10	4	5	10	10	7	5	5	2	1	3	4	3	2	1	2
118	85	72	72	78	87	93	87	90	67	60	61	74	58	47	31	69	39	17	12	66	58
433	350	370	301	401	439	505	498	508	513	332	241	407	355	228	146	230	224	101	49	211	338
264	202	186	171	143	188	221	210	199	198	136	147	153	141	88	60	118	111	43	28	138	146
831	653	640	551	634	719	838	808	808	791	546	461	640	563	374	238	421	382	166	91	419	550
206	122	151	131	188	214	234	230	254	224	132	135	194	134	107	66	124	107	40	36	106	101
2,138	1,561	1,407	1,156	1,442	1,469	1,754	1,732	1,753	1,661	1,239	953	1,465	1,294	794	578	977	875	317	259	1,091	1,270
3,558	1,939	1,851	1,692	1,906	2,281	2,324	2,389	2,278	2,433	1,566	1,361	1,961	1,747	943	730	1,148	1,303	395	383	1,368	1,794
361	209	166	158	185	271	188	208	191	198	126	109	141	168	79	47	112	117	33	34	112	199
4,192	3,831	3,575	3,137	3,721	4,235	4,500	4,559	4,476	4,516	3,063	2,558	3,761	3,343	1,923	1,421	2,361	2,402	785	712	2,677	3,364
4,682	2,569	3,704	3,008	4,455	4,607	4,963	4,765	5,406	4,921	3,237	2,525	4,389	3,577	2,069	1,627	3,319	2,347	863	593	3,852	2,537
44,051	37,456	33,011	29,656	37,616	41,232	38,331	38,431	38,834	38,043	25,533	22,115	29,721	28,747	13,851	11,309	20,738	19,791	6,352	5,139	22,207	24,399
Christian.																					
2	1	6	4	16	7	18	6	30	3	36	2	11	3	6	..	1	..	1	..	..	1
6	11	11	8	148	8	178	19	42	14	22	8	22	6	9	..	5	2	3	1	2	2
..	..	3	..	12	..	2	2	1	..	2	..	1	1	2	..	2	..	..	..	..	..
19	19	43	27	90	35	90	57	87	22	54	13	48	18	34	9	22	12	12	2	14	6
..	1	..	1	3	1	3	1	8	3	3	..	4	..	1	..	1	..	..	..	..	..
..	..	2	1	4	2	2	..	2	..	2	1	1	1	..	..	1	..	1	..	..	..
..	..	..	..	..	..	..	..	1	..	..	..	..	..	..	..	..	..	..	..	..	..
27	32	65	41	273	53	293	84	171	42	119	24	87	29	52	9	32	14	17	3	16	8
..	..	..	..	..	1	2	..	..	..	1	..	..	..	1	..	..	..	..	..	1	..
3	..	..	..	1	..	..	..	1	..	..	1	1	..	1	..	..	..	..	..	..	..
240	231	172	174	133	184	170	240	179	228	129	122	144	171	88	65	90	98	35	40	108	142
243	231	172	174	134	185	172	240	180	228	130	123	145	171	90	65	90	98	35	40	109	142
..	..	..	..	..	..	8	..	..	..	..	..	..	..	..	..	..	..	..	..	..	..
..	..	..	..	..	..	..	..	..	..	..	..	..	..	..	..	..	..	..	..	..	..
..	..	..	1	1	..	2	..	3	..	..	..	1	..	..	..	1	..	..	..	..	..
..	..	..	..	1	..	..	..	..	..	..	..	1	..	..	..	..	..	..	..	..	..
..	..	..	..	1	..	..	..	..	..	..	..	..	..	..	..	..	..	..	..	..	..
..	..	..	1	3	..	5	..	3	..	..	..	2	..	..	..	1	..	..	..	..	..
..	..	..	..	2	1	1	2	1	1	2	..	..	..	..	..	..	..	..	..	1	..
61	66	52	53	69	77	64	73	54	57	38	28	28	39	21	17	31	34	9	9	32	43
31	26	25	15	13	6	17	19	18	14	12	12	21	9	9	5	13	7	5	3	6	4
..	..	..	..	..	..	..	..	..	..	..	..	..	..	..	..	..	..	..	..	..	..
92	92	77	68	84	84	82	94	73	72	52	40	49	48	30	22	44	41	14	12	39	47
..	..	..	..	..	..	1	..	1	1	..	..	1	..	..	..	..	..	..	..	..	..
[illegible]	355	314	284	494	322	553	418	428	343	301	187	284	248	172	96	167	153	66	55	164	197
Buddhist.																					
..	..	..	..	..	..	1	..	..	..	..	..	..	..	..	..	..	..	..	..	..	..

TABLE

Part (F).—

State.	Total Population. Total.	Males.	Females.	Under 1 year. Males.	Females.	1 year. Males.	Females.	2 years. Males.	Females.	3 years. Males.	Females.	4 years. Males.	Females.	Total, 0—4. Males.	Females.	5—9. Males.	Females.
Cutch	71,988	34,355	37,633	1,318	1,335	527	679	1,052	1,090	1,028	1,086	957	1,037	4,882	5,227	4,924	5,118
Pálanpur	29,149	14,896	14,253	459	505	237	229	346	378	319	381	382	379	1,743	1,872	1,712	1,738
Mahi Kántha	13,818	6,690	7,128	203	215	118	123	142	154	124	141	173	155	760	788	807	809
Káthiáwár	113,005	58,379	54,626	1,682	1,789	974	1,034	1,518	1,546	1,066	1,687	1,501	1,505	7,336	7,560	7,533	7,425
Rewa Kántha	1,308	721	587	16	20	7	5	13	13	13	10	18	13	67	61	68	55
Cambay	3,262	1,578	1,684	50	59	33	25	27	44	42	36	30	36	182	200	196	154
Surat Agency	126	69	57	7	1	1	...	3	...	8	...	1	...	15	1	4	15
Total, Gujarát Group	232,656	116,688	115,968	3,735	3,924	1,897	2,095	3,096	3,225	3,195	3,341	3,062	3,125	14,985	15,709	15,244	15,373
Jawhár	4	4	...	...	...	...	...	...	...	...	...	...	...	...	...	...	...
Janjira	71	62	9	...	...	...	1	...	...	...	...	1	...	1	1	1	1
Sáwantwádi	147	76	71	3	4	...	3	4	2	3	1	2	2	12	11	4	5
Total, Konkan Group	222	142	80	3	4	...	3	4	2	3	1	3	2	13	12	5	6
The Dángs	1	1	...	...	...	...	...	...	...	...	...	...	...	...	...	...	...
Surgana	...	...	...	...	...	...	...	...	...	...	...	...	...	...	...	...	...
Bhor	680	356	324	8	10	2	2	12	16	5	9	2	9	29	46	24	29
Akalkot	508	268	240	9	11	6	3	8	6	3	6	8	6	34	32	31	31
Sátára Agency	1,296	672	624	20	18	7	10	21	17	16	11	19	11	83	67	70	80
Total, Deccan Group	2,485	1,297	1,188	37	39	15	15	41	39	24	26	29	26	146	145	125	140
Jat	316	161	155	5	4	3	3	3	5	4	5	2	3	17	20	30	20
Kolhápur	50,896	26,950	23,946	711	680	436	472	695	789	653	676	738	697	3,233	3,314	3,144	3,023
Southern Marátha Jaghirs	28,183	14,150	14,033	439	447	280	234	418	412	438	421	451	443	2,026	1,957	1,811	1,824
Sáwanúr	15	8	7	...	1	...	...	...	...	1	...	...	1	1	2	1	1
Total, Karnátak Group	79,410	41,269	38,141	1,155	1,132	719	709	1,116	1,146	1,096	1,102	1,191	1,144	5,277	5,235	4,986	4,888
Khairpur	...	...	...	...	...	...	...	...	...	...	...	...	...	...	...	...	...
Total, Feudatory States	314,773	159,396	155,377	4,930	5,099	2,631	2,822	4,257	4,411	4,318	4,470	4,285	4,297	20,421	21,099	20,360	20,407

Part (G).—

State.	Total.	Males.	Females.	Under 1 year. Males.	Females.	1 year. Males.	Females.	2 years. Males.	Females.	3 years. Males.	Females.	4 years. Males.	Females.	Total, 0—4. Males.	Females.	5—9. Males.	Females.
Cutch	94	81	13	...	1	...	1	...	...	...	...	1	...	1	2	2	2

Part (H).—

State.	Total.	Males.	Females.	Under 1 year. Males.	Females.	1 year. Males.	Females.	2 years. Males.	Females.	3 years. Males.	Females.	4 years. Males.	Females.	Total, 0—4. Males.	Females.	5—9. Males.	Females.
Cutch	118	64	54	2	...	2	...	2	3	2	2	3	4	11	9	4	19
Pálanpur	205	96	109	3	2	1	2	4	1	3	5	2	...	13	10	10	18
Mahi Kántha	8	5	3	...	1	...	...	...	...	...	1	1	...	1	2	1	...
Káthiáwár	908	524	384	11	12	12	8	9	9	9	13	12	17	53	59	70	54
Rewa Kántha	386	228	158	6	4	4	3	8	7	9	8	4	5	28	27	17	61
Cambay	137	68	69	1	1	...	...	8	2	1	2	2	3	7	8	9	9
Surat Agency	618	352	266	9	8	7	5	5	7	6	9	13	5	40	34	27	45
Total, Gujarát Group	2,380	1,337	1,043	34	28	26	18	26	29	30	40	37	34	153	149	138	161
Jawhár	46	31	15	1	...	...	...	1	1	2	...	...	1	4	2	2	4
Janjira	...	...	...	...	...	...	...	...	...	...	...	...	...	...	...	...	...
Sáwantwádi	...	...	...	...	...	...	...	...	...	...	...	...	...	...	...	...	...
Total, Konkan Group	46	31	15	1	...	...	...	1	1	2	...	...	1	4	2	2	4
The Dángs	20	14	6	...	...	...	...	...	1	...	1	...	...	...	2	...	1
Surgana	28	19	9	...	...	...	...	...	...	...	...	...	...	...	...	...	2
Bhor	1	1	...	...	...	...	...	...	...	...	...	...	...	...	...	...	...
Akalkot	...	...	...	...	...	...	...	...	...	...	...	...	...	...	...	...	...
Sátára Agency	...	...	...	...	...	...	...	...	...	...	...	...	...	...	...	...	...
Total, Deccan Group	49	34	15	...	...	...	...	...	1	...	1	...	...	...	2	...	3
Jat	...	...	...	...	...	...	...	...	...	...	...	...	...	...	...	...	...
Kolhápur	24	12	12	...	...	...	...	...	1	...	1	...	1	...	3	2	1
Southern Marátha Jaghirs	12	8	4	...	...	1	...	...	...	...	...	1	...	2	...	...	1
Sáwanúr	...	...	...	...	...	...	...	...	...	...	...	...	...	...	...	...	...
Total, Karnátak Group	36	20	16	...	...	1	...	...	1	...	1	1	1	2	3	2	2
Khairpur	...	...	...	...	...	...	...	...	...	...	...	...	...	...	...	...	...
Total, Feudatory States	2,511	1,422	1,089	35	28	27	18	27	33	32	43	38	36	159	156	143	171

Table VII.

Ages by Religions.

VII.

Jain.

10—14.		15—19.		20—24.		25—29.		30—34.		35—39.		40—44.		45—49.		50—54.		55—59.		60 And over.	
Males.	Females.	Males.	Females.	Males.	Females.	Males.	Females.	Males.	Females.	Males.	Females.	Males.	Females.	Males.	Females.	Males.	Females.	Males.	Females.	Males.	Females.
3,854	3,872	2,453	2,798	2,457	3,337	2,335	3,250	2,546	2,987	1,944	2,003	2,120	2,437	1,288	1,137	1,915	1,980	947	743	2,070	2,750
1,659	1,434	1,333	1,078	1,414	1,284	1,308	1,169	1,240	1,217	1,010	860	1,004	1,067	686	612	691	776	387	284	709	864
832	750	623	531	670	752	601	618	542	583	437	467	405	566	305	293	310	403	138	155	260	413
6,845	5,743	5,498	4,276	5,953	5,442	5,313	4,707	4,555	4,460	3,610	3,106	3,583	3,794	2,295	1,791	2,470	2,480	990	789	2,380	2,954
72	38	67	55	70	61	71	67	72	68	43	39	68	50	41	17	37	39	18	15	27	47
143	143	135	119	160	181	132	136	134	134	118	131	113	137	73	84	81	102	42	45	60	118
5	7	6	3	8	1	5	4	5	11	8	6	4	1	3	2	6	3	...	...	...	3
13,410	11,987	10,115	8,860	10,732	11,058	9,785	9,941	9,094	9,450	7,170	6,613	7,297	8,048	4,691	3,936	5,519	5,792	2,531	2,031	6,115	7,177
...	...	...	...	1	...	...	...	2	...	1	...	...	...	...	...	...	...	...	...	...	...
8	2	17	1	14	1	9	...	4	...	4	1	...	...	...	...	2	...	1	1	1	1
8	4	11	5	5	9	7	5	6	6	2	4	3	6	3	3	5	4	2	2	8	7
16	6	28	6	20	10	16	5	12	6	7	5	3	6	3	3	7	4	3	3	9	8
...	...	...	...	1	...	...	...	...	...	...	...	...	...	...	...	...	...	...	...	...	...
...	...	...	...	...	...	...	...	...	...	...	...	...	...	...	...	...	...	...	...	...	...
37	27	34	34	39	32	44	35	39	19	28	12	20	24	17	11	18	20	12	7	16	19
31	28	17	19	26	30	20	14	23	16	10	19	19	19	18	7	14	10	9	6	16	9
70	56	47	64	60	47	54	56	52	59	38	27	61	42	27	33	44	35	17	17	40	41
138	111	98	117	126	100	118	105	114	94	76	58	100	85	62	51	76	65	38	30	80	69
13	16	18	10	11	10	17	14	10	14	9	7	12	14	7	8	8	10	3	5	6	7
3,118	2,457	2,017	1,588	2,039	1,808	2,505	2,077	2,334	2,148	1,880	1,404	1,966	1,728	1,210	966	1,348	1,159	606	455	1,551	1,803
1,518	1,305	1,066	909	905	1,105	1,229	1,283	1,117	1,246	915	804	1,046	1,050	556	462	783	726	243	259	895	1,103
1	...	...	...	1	1	1	1	1	...	...	1	1	...	...	...	1	...	...	...	...	1
4,650	3,778	3,101	2,507	3,045	2,924	3,752	3,375	3,462	3,406	2,804	2,218	3,025	2,792	1,773	1,436	2,090	1,895	852	719	2,462	2,920
...	...	...	...	...	...	...	...	...	...	...	...	...	...	...	...	...	...	...	...	...	...
18,214	15,883	13,343	11,490	13,923	14,101	13,671	13,423	12,683	13,958	10,057	8,893	10,435	10,925	6,529	5,426	7,693	7,756	3,421	2,788	8,656	10,173

Sikh.

10—14 M.	10—14 F.	15—19 M.	15—19 F.	20—24 M.	20—24 F.	25—29 M.	25—29 F.	30—34 M.	30—34 F.	35—39 M.	35—39 F.	40—44 M.	40—44 F.	45—49 M.	45—49 F.	50—54 M.	50—54 F.	55—59 M.	55—59 F.	60 and over M.	60 and over F.
3	1	2	1	27	1	19	2	6	3	6	...	5	...	4	...	5	1	...	...	1	1

Pársi.

10—14 M.	10—14 F.	15—19 M.	15—19 F.	20—24 M.	20—24 F.	25—29 M.	25—29 F.	30—34 M.	30—34 F.	35—39 M.	35—39 F.	40—44 M.	40—44 F.	45—49 M.	45—49 F.	50—54 M.	50—54 F.	55—59 M.	55—59 F.	60 and over M.	60 and over F.
12	5	8	3	3	4	3	6	4	6	4	...	4	1	1	3	2	1	5	1	3	4
13	26	6	8	6	11	10	9	9	7	6	9	6	8	6	3	5	2	4	3	2	5
...	...	...	...	...	1	2	...	...	...	1	...	...	...	...	...	...	...	...	...	...	...
43	48	40	34	68	41	60	35	40	29	47	23	30	29	30	16	17	10	9	4	18	11
19	18	19	11	24	13	23	18	25	13	21	16	19	9	14	2	7	4	3	2	9	6
10	10	7	6	2	5	4	6	9	4	3	6	2	3	1	3	6	3	1	...	7	[illegible]
31	26	14	12	33	21	28	23	24	21	37	8	26	25	27	16	18	9	13	4	34	17
128	117	94	83	136	96	120	96	120	79	119	62	87	62	79	43	55	29	35	14	73	53
3	1	1	...	3	...	3	2	5	1	1	1	4	3	2	1	1	...	1	...	1	...
...	...	...	...	...	...	...	...	...	...	...	...	...	...	...	...	...	...	...	...	...	...
...	...	...	...	...	...	...	...	...	...	...	...	...	...	...	...	...	...	...	...	...	...
3	1	1	...	3	...	3	2	5	1	1	1	4	3	2	1	1	...	1	...	1	...
1	...	1	1	2	...	3	...	2	2	1	...	2	...	1	...	1	...	...	...	...	...
1	...	...	1	...	1	4	1	3	2	1	1	2	...	7	...	...	...	1	...	...	1
...	...	...	...	...	...	...	...	1	...	...	...	...	...	...	...	...	...	...	...	...	...
...	...	...	...	...	...	...	...	...	...	...	...	...	...	...	...	...	...	...	...	...	...
...	...	...	...	...	...	...	...	...	...	...	...	...	...	...	...	...	...	...	...	...	...
2	...	1	2	2	1	7	1	6	4	2	1	4	...	8	...	1	...	1	...	...	1
...	...	...	...	...	...	...	...	...	...	...	...	...	...	...	...	...	...	...	...	...	...
2	2	1	1	...	...	2	...	...	1	2	3	2	1	...	...	1	...	...	...	...	...
2	...	...	...	...	1	1	1	1	1	...	...	1	...	...	...	...	...	1	...	...	...
...	...	...	...	...	...	...	...	...	...	...	...	...	...	...	...	...	...	...	...	...	...
4	2	1	1	...	1	3	1	1	2	2	3	3	1	...	...	1	...	1	...	...	...
...	...	...	...	...	...	...	...	...	...	...	...	...	...	...	...	...	...	...	...	...	...
137	120	97	85	141	98	133	100	133	86	134	67	98	66	89	44	58	29	38	14	74	53

Table VII.

Ages by Religions.

TABLE

Part (I).—

State.	Total Population. Total.	Total Population. Males.	Total Population. Females.	Under 1 year. Males.	Under 1 year. Females.	1 year. Males.	1 year. Females.	2 years. Males.	2 years. Females.	3 years. Males.	3 years. Females.	4 years. Males.	4 years. Females.	Total, 0 — 4. Males.	Total, 0 — 4. Females.	5 — 9. Males.	5 — 9. Females.
tch	47	26	21	2	...	...	...	1	...	3	1	1	...	7	1	3	7
lanpur	34	18	16	2	...	...	...	...	2	1	...	...	...	3	2	...	1
ahi Kántha	4	3	1	1	...	...	...	...	...	...	...	...	...	1	...	1	...
thiáwár	105	54	51	4	3	2	1	1	2	1	3	...	1	8	10	10	9
wa Kántha	6	4	2	...	...	...	...	1	...	...	...	...	...	1	...	...	...
mbay	...	...	...	...	...	...	...	...	...	...	...	...	...	...	...	...	...
rat Agency	6	3	3	...	1	...	...	...	...	...	...	...	...	...	1	...	...
Total, Gujarát Group ...	203	108	94	9	4	2	1	3	4	5	4	1	1	20	14	14	17
whár	599	282	317	11	13	7	11	12	8	7	19	9	11	46	63	49	48
njira	...	...	...	...	...	...	...	...	...	...	...	...	...	...	...	...	...
wantwádi	...	...	...	...	...	...	...	...	...	...	...	...	...	...	...	...	...
Total, Konkan ...	599	282	317	11	13	7	11	12	8	7	19	9	11	46	62	49	48
e Dángs	...	...	...	...	...	...	...	...	...	...	...	...	...	...	...	...	...
rgana	...	...	...	...	...	...	...	...	...	...	...	...	...	...	...	...	...
hor	271	142	129	4	5	7	1	6	5	6	3	3	1	26	15	15	18
alkot	4	2	2	...	...	...	...	...	...	...	...	...	...	...	...	...	1
tára Agency	...	...	...	...	...	...	...	...	...	...	...	...	...	...	...	...	...
Total, Deccan Group ...	275	144	131	4	5	7	1	6	5	6	3	3	1	26	15	15	19
... ...	...	...	...	...	...	...	...	...	...	...	...	...	...	...	...	...	...
lhápur	...	...	...	...	...	...	...	...	...	...	...	...	...	...	...	...	...
uthern Marátha Jaghirs ...	6	2	4	...	...	...	...	...	...	...	...	...	1	...	1	...	2
wanúr	...	...	...	...	...	...	...	...	...	...	...	...	...	...	...	...	...
Total, Karnátak Group ...	6	2	4	...	...	...	...	...	...	...	...	...	1	...	1	...	2
airpur	...	...	...	...	...	...	...	...	...	...	...	...	...	...	...	...	...
tal, Feudatory States ...	1,083	536	546	24	23	16	13	21	17	18	26	13	14	93	93	78	86

Part (J).—

State.	Total Population. Total.	Total Population. Males.	Total Population. Females.	Under 1 year. Males.	Under 1 year. Females.	1 year. Males.	1 year. Females.	2 years. Males.	2 years. Females.	3 years. Males.	3 years. Females.	4 years. Males.	4 years. Females.	Total, 0 — 4. Males.	Total, 0 — 4. Females.	5 — 9. Males.	5 — 9. Females.
tch	883	457	425	11	11	10	6	9	21	9	18	19	14	58	70	73	81
lanpur	174	89	85	3	3	1	1	1	2	7	6	4	1	16	15	10	13
hi Kántha	...	...	...	...	...	...	...	...	...	...	...	...	...	...	...	...	...
thiáwár	4	1	3	...	...	...	...	...	...	...	...	...	...	...	...	...	...
wa Kántha	64,856	32,390	32,466	1,467	1,625	508	575	1,231	1,385	1,335	1,473	1,294	1,246	5,835	6,304	5,792	5,356
mbay	...	...	...	...	...	...	...	...	...	...	...	...	...	...	...	...	...
rat Agency	...	...	...	...	...	...	...	...	...	...	...	...	...	...	...	...	...
Total, Gujarát Group ...	65,916	32,937	32,979	1,481	1,639	519	582	1,241	1,408	1,351	1,497	1,317	1,261	5,909	6,387	5,875	5,451
whár	121	58	63	1	1	2	3	4	8	1	5	3	5	11	16	12	8
jira	159	93	66	4	1	6	2	1	5	5	2	3	5	19	15	10	10
wantwádi	...	...	...	...	...	...	...	...	...	...	...	...	...	...	...	...	...
Total, Konkan Group ...	280	151	129	5	2	8	5	5	7	6	7	6	10	30	31	22	18
Dángs	11,403	5,868	5,534	151	167	34	65	121	245	215	291	261	291	782	1,059	1,092	981
rgaha	131	61	60	...	1	...	3	3	3	1	7	2	5	6	19	16	10
or	...	...	...	...	...	...	...	...	...	...	...	...	...	...	...	...	...
alkot	...	...	...	...	...	...	...	...	...	...	...	...	...	...	...	...	...
ára Agency	...	...	...	...	...	...	...	...	...	...	...	...	...	...	...	...	...
Total, Deccan Group ...	11,533	5,929	5,594	151	168	34	68	124	248	216	298	263	296	788	1,078	1,108	991
... ...	...	...	...	...	...	...	...	...	...	...	...	...	...	...	...	...	...
lhápur	...	...	...	...	...	...	...	...	...	...	...	...	...	...	...	...	...
uthern Marátha Jaghirs ...	...	...	...	...	...	...	...	...	...	...	...	...	...	...	...	...	...
wanúr	...	...	...	...	...	...	...	...	...	...	...	...	...	...	...	...	...
Total, Karnátak Group ...	...	...	...	...	...	...	...	...	...	...	...	...	...	...	...	...	...
airpur	686	389	297	8	8	6	7	16	13	13	7	20	10	63	45	69	45
tal, Feudatory States ...	78,405	39,406	38,999	1,645	1,817	557	663	1,386	1,676	1,386	1,809	1,606	1,577	6,790	7,511	7,074	6,503

Text missing in the original.

VII.

Jew.

10—14.		15—19.		20—24.		25—29.		30—34.		35—39.		40—44.		45—49.		50—54.		55—59.		60 and over.	
Males.	Females.	Males.	Females.	Males.	Females.	Males.	Females.	Males.	Females.	Males.	Females.	Males.	Females.	Males.	Females.	Males.	Females.	Males.	Females.	Males.	Females.
...	...	2	1	2	5	1	1	7	2	1	...	1	1	1	...	...	...	...	...	1	3
1	3	2	3	3	4	4	...	2	...	...	...	...	...	...	2	...	1	3	...	...	...
...	...	...	...	...	1	...	...	1	...	...	...	...	...	...	...	...	...	...	...	...	...
9	8	2	5	2	2	2	7	4	3	6	...	2	2	3	2	2	...	3	...	1	3
...	...	...	...	...	...	...	...	1	2	1	...	...	...	1	...	...	...	...	...	...	...
...	...	...	...	...	...	...	...	...	...	...	...	...	...	...	...	...	...	...	...	...	...
1	...	...	...	1	...	...	...	...	1	...	...	1	1	...	...	...	...	...	...	...	...
11	11	6	9	8	12	7	8	15	8	8	...	4	4	5	4	2	1	6	...	2	6
...	...	...	...	...	...	...	...	...	...	...	...	...	...	...	...	...	...	...	...	...	...
31	30	20	17	18	31	17	29	15	21	24	18	13	11	11	12	12	9	8	6	18	23
...	...	...	...	...	...	...	...	...	...	...	...	...	...	...	...	...	...	...	...	...	...
31	30	20	17	18	31	17	29	15	21	24	18	13	11	11	12	12	9	8	6	18	23
...	...	...	...	...	...	...	...	...	...	...	...	...	...	...	...	...	...	...	...	...	...
15	18	13	15	12	10	16	14	12	6	8	4	5	7	1	4	5	17	2	...	12	2
...	...	...	...	...	...	...	...	...	...	...	...	...	...	...	...	...	...	...	...	...	...
...	...	1	...	...	...	...	1	...	...	...	...	...	...	1	...	...	...	...	...	...	...
15	18	14	15	12	10	16	15	12	6	8	4	5	7	2	4	5	17	2	...	12	2
...	...	...	...	...	...	...	...	...	...	...	...	...	...	...	...	...	...	...	...	...	...
...	...	...	...	...	...	...	...	...	...	...	...	...	...	...	...	...	...	...	...	...	...
1	...	...	...	...	...	...	...	...	...	...	1	1	...	...	...	...	...	...	...	...	...
...	...	...	...	...	...	...	...	...	...	...	...	...	...	...	...	...	...	...	...	...	...
1	...	...	...	...	...	...	...	...	...	...	1	1	...	...	...	...	...	...	...	...	...
...	...	...	...	...	...	...	...	...	...	...	...	...	...	...	...	...	...	...	...	...	...
58	59	40	41	38	53	40	52	42	34	40	23	23	22	18	20	19	27	16	6	32	31

Animistic.

10—14.		15—19.		20—24.		25—29.		30—34.		35—39.		40—44.		45—49.		50—54.		55—59.		60 and over.	
Males.	Females.	Males.	Females.	Males.	Females.	Males.	Females.	Males.	Females.	Males.	Females.	Males.	Females.	Males.	Females.	Males.	Females.	Males.	Females.	Males.	Females.
49	36	46	31	45	38	45	41	52	29	24	17	25	29	6	15	10	18	7	2	17	17
11	9	6	6	12	7	6	10	8	7	3	3	7	3	3	3	4	3	1	2	2	6
...	...	...	...	...	...	...	...	...	...	...	...	...	...	...	...	...	...	...	...	...	...
...	...	...	...	...	...	...	1	...	...	...	...	...	1	...	1	1	...	...	...	...	...
3,188	2,546	2,376	2,257	2,712	3,193	3,220	3,142	2,722	2,906	2,273	1,842	1,582	1,819	1,103	1,197	851	988	292	281	444	635
...	...	...	...	...	...	...	...	...	...	...	...	...	...	...	...	...	...	...	...	...	...
...	...	...	...	...	...	...	...	...	...	...	...	...	...	...	...	...	...	...	...	...	...
3,248	2,591	2,428	2,294	2,769	3,238	3,271	3,194	2,782	2,942	2,300	1,862	1,614	1,852	1,112	1,216	866	1,009	300	285	463	658
1	3	3	1	1	8	4	3	4	7	2	1	3	6	8	1	4	7	...	1	5	1
5	2	7	2	6	6	10	11	9	5	9	4	5	3	6	2	2	2	2	3	3	1
...	...	...	...	...	...	...	...	...	...	...	...	...	...	...	...	...	...	...	...	...	...
6	5	10	3	7	14	14	14	13	12	11	5	8	9	14	3	6	9	2	4	8	2
769	470	420	424	420	507	583	603	465	496	501	313	259	218	195	137	173	146	56	27	153	153
5	6	8	4	1	3	3	5	6	6	4	4	7	...	...	...	2	3	...	...	3	...
...	...	...	...	...	...	...	...	...	...	...	...	...	...	...	...	...	...	...	...	...	...
...	...	...	...	...	...	...	...	...	...	...	...	...	...	...	...	...	...	...	...	...	...
...	...	...	...	...	...	...	...	...	...	...	...	...	...	...	...	...	...	...	...	...	...
774	476	428	428	421	510	586	608	471	502	505	317	266	218	195	137	175	149	56	27	156	153
...	...	...	...	...	...	...	...	...	...	...	...	...	...	...	...	...	...	...	...	...	...
...	...	...	...	...	...	...	...	...	...	...	...	...	...	...	...	...	...	...	...	...	...
...	...	...	...	...	...	...	...	...	...	...	...	...	...	...	...	...	...	...	...	...	...
...	...	...	...	...	...	...	...	...	...	...	...	...	...	...	...	...	...	...	...	...	...
...	...	...	...	...	...	...	...	...	...	...	...	...	...	...	...	...	...	...	...	...	...
35	15	31	22	30	35	18	27	41	27	18	16	18	20	8	10	14	10	9	9	35	19
4,063	3,087	2,897	2,747	3,227	3,737	3,889	3,843	3,307	3,483	2,834	2,200	1,906	2,099	1,329	1,366	1,061	1,177	367	325	662	831

TABLE VIII.

CIVIL CONDITION BY RELIGION AND AGE.

PART	A.—Total Population.	PART	F.—Jain.
"	B.—Hindu.	"	G.—Sikh.
"	C.—Mussalman.	"	H.—Pársi.
"	D.—Christian.	"	I.—Jew.
"	E.—Buddhist.	"	J.—Animistic.

(1) Unmarried. (2) Married. (3) Widowed.

Unreturned—Mahi Kántha.

Total 19,236, Males 10,579, Females 8,657.

Table VIII.

Civil Condition by Religion and Age.

TABLE

Part (A).—

(1) UN

State.	Total. Total.	Total. Males.	Total. Females.	0—4. Males.	0—4. Females.	5—9. Males.	5—9. Females.	10—14. Males.	10—14. Females.	15—19. Males.	15—19. Females.	20—24. Males.	20—24. Females.
Cutch	240,218	138,400	*101,818*	38,399	*39,442*	39,034	*38,050*	27,698	*19,539*	14,280	*3,197*	8,313	*691*
Pálanpur	280,163	165,226	*114,937*	46,127	*47,859*	49,847	*41,694*	32,471	*20,129*	17,286	*3,564*	9,784	*869*
Mahi Kántha	237,404	142,938	*94,466*	37,629	*39,048*	42,390	*34,784*	29,248	*15,916*	16,701	*2,958*	8,370	*697*
Káthiáwár	1,100,803	644,231	*456,572*	187,365	*191,795*	183,505	*167,617*	118,408	*75,552*	69,068	*14,330*	43,028	*3,158*
Rewa Kántha	338,465	193,749	*144,716*	55,546	*59,151*	58,601	*52,053*	36,076	*22,680*	20,895	*7,316*	11,312	*1,747*
Cambay	28,749	18,190	*10,559*	5,295	*5,179*	5,057	*3,646*	3,220	*1,271*	1,671	*250*	1,131	*90*
Surat Agency	88,268	48,608	*39,660*	13,606	*14,617*	14,467	*13,298*	10,018	*7,330*	5,029	*2,760*	2,751	*849*
Total, Gujarát Group ...	2,314,070	1,351,342	*962,728*	383,967	*397,091*	392,901	*351,142*	257,139	*162,417*	145,130	*34,375*	84,689	*7,600*
Jawhár	26,370	14,918	*11,452*	4,082	*4,415*	4,326	*4,153*	2,824	*1,872*	1,010	*625*	916	*160*
Janjira	33,980	19,640	*14,340*	6,536	*7,238*	6,389	*5,333*	3,717	*1,458*	1,667	*212*	599	*25*
Sáwantwádi	74,161	46,538	*27,623*	12,792	*13,848*	12,555	*9,841*	9,774	*2,096*	6,037	*321*	2,464	*240*
Total, Konkan Group ..	134,511	81,096	*53,415*	23,410	*25,501*	23,270	*19,327*	16,315	*5,426*	9,314	*1,158*	3,979	*425*
The Dángs	16,897	9,544	*7,353*	2,306	*2,769*	3,040	*2,898*	2,239	*1,211*	1,026	*311*	515	*62*
Surgana	6,321	3,576	*2,745*	974	*1,042*	1,116	*1,020*	777	*507*	346	*111*	154	*29*
Bhor	58,414	36,216	*22,198*	12,028	*12,420*	11,396	*7,964*	7,282	*1,461*	2,930	*96*	1,218	*65*
Akalkot	26,213	16,291	*9,922*	6,222	*6,156*	4,792	*2,916*	2,447	*542*	1,301	*64*	761	*58*
Sátára Agency	48,813	30,296	*18,517*	10,010	*10,445*	8,850	*6,414*	6,092	*1,250*	2,856	*97*	1,221	*60*
Total, Deccan Group ...	156,658	95,923	*60,735*	31,535	*32,831*	29,194	*21,212*	18,837	*4,971*	8,459	*679*	3,869	*274*
Jat	28,385	17,554	*10,831*	6,925	*6,852*	5,618	*3,131*	2,477	*427*	1,251	*65*	667	*69*
Kolhápur	313,437	196,719	*116,718*	66,771	*66,694*	60,219	*38,750*	39,110	*7,305*	16,300	*732*	6,839	*507*
Southern Marátha Jaghírs...	222,280	135,823	*86,457*	49,605	*48,194*	41,169	*27,510*	23,465	*5,547*	10,984	*815*	4,922	*865*
Sáwanúr	7,300	4,327	*2,973*	1,290	*1,335*	1,148	*1,025*	828	*380*	439	*69*	317	*45*
Total, Karnátak Group ...	571,402	354,423	*216,979*	124,591	*123,075*	108,154	*70,416*	65,880	*14,159*	28,974	*1,681*	12,745	*1,486*
Khairpur	58,939	38,857	*20,082*	10,980	*9,485*	10,987	*7,160*	5,701	*2,401*	3,626	*622*	2,768	*175*
Total, Feudatory States.	**3,235,580**	**1,921,641**	**1,313,939**	**574,483**	**557,983**	**564,506**	**469,257**	**363,572**	**189,374**	**195,503**	**38,515**	**108,050**	**9,960**

(2) MAR

State.	Total. Total.	Total. Males.	Total. Females.	0—4. Males.	0—4. Females.	5—9. Males.	5—9. Females.	10—14. Males.	10—14. Females.	15—19. Males.	15—19. Females.	20—24. Males.	20—24. Females.
Cutch	260,529	124,946	*135,583*	420	*646*	1,479	*2,501*	4,332	*7,869*	8,174	*17,002*	14,525	*24,478*
Pálanpur	309,574	155,598	*153,976*	792	*1,854*	3,231	*6,538*	7,184	*11,716*	11,133	*18,012*	19,216	*26,441*
Mahi Kántha	267,370	131,578	*135,792*	1,450	*3,494*	4,132	*7,755*	7,205	*12,751*	10,776	*17,815*	16,624	*23,338*
Káthiáwár	1,393,083	696,748	*696,335*	6,564	*10,752*	16,848	*24,074*	28,502	*42,173*	50,409	*83,904*	95,508	*135,725*
Rewa Kántha	340,334	168,482	*171,852*	527	*931*	1,697	*3,482*	5,152	*9,292*	11,359	*18,990*	20,654	*30,106*
Cambay	49,957	25,125	*24,832*	211	*436*	865	*1,491*	1,587	*2,359*	2,311	*3,288*	3,498	*4,333*
Surat Agency	80,832	40,140	*40,692*	91	*134*	386	*595*	950	*1,689*	2,010	*3,635*	4,222	*6,554*
Total, Gujarát Group ...	2,701,679	1,342,617	*1,359,062*	10,055	*18,247*	28,638	*46,436*	54,912	*87,349*	96,172	*162,646*	174,247	*251,025*
Jawhár	23,378	12,152	*11,226*	23	*40*	57	*104*	145	*399*	481	*1,310*	1,032	*1,752*
Janjira	39,113	18,590	*20,523*	11	*43*	85	*806*	467	*2,184*	1,124	*2,924*	1,620	*3,078*
Sáwantwádi	90,643	42,672	*47,971*	48	*168*	130	*2,026*	647	*6,396*	2,329	*6,771*	3,803	*7,326*
Total, Konkan Group ...	153,134	73,414	*79,720*	82	*251*	272	*2,936*	1,259	*8,979*	3,934	*11,005*	6,455	*12,156*
The Dángs	14,118	7,023	*7,095*	5	*20*	12	*37*	79	*287*	321	*794*	652	*1,250*
Surgana	5,483	2,770	*2,713*	13	*10*	13	*21*	43	*129*	157	*344*	242	*426*
Bhor	81,805	39,213	*42,592*	92	*294*	506	*2,778*	1,612	*5,753*	2,575	*5,450*	3,869	*6,194*
Akalkot	40,650	20,072	*20,578*	87	*423*	278	*1,877*	624	*1,928*	1,258	*2,304*	2,049	*3,260*
Sátára Agency	67,453	32,959	*34,494*	71	*200*	198	*1,919*	750	*4,071*	1,837	*4,352*	3,146	*5,266*
Total, Deccan Group ...	209,509	102,037	*107,472*	268	*947*	1,007	*6,633*	3,108	*12,168*	6,148	*13,244*	9,958	*16,396*
Jat	42,846	21,145	*21,701*	100	*503*	309	*2,486*	646	*3,044*	1,305	*2,280*	2,228	*3,211*
Kolhápur	497,163	248,644	*248,519*	771	*3,293*	3,108	*20,725*	10,822	*31,868*	17,320	*27,830*	25,786	*33,980*
Southern Marátha Jaghírs .	339,776	166,756	*173,020*	617	*2,837*	2,353	*14,115*	6,648	*18,797*	11,951	*20,007*	17,882	*25,426*
Sáwanúr	7,596	3,561	*4,035*	1	*36*	25	*216*	69	*350*	147	*486*	363	*786*
Total, Karnátak Group ...	887,381	440,106	*447,275*	1,489	*6,669*	5,795	*37,542*	18,185	*53,059*	30,723	*50,593*	46,259	*63,403*
Khairpur	61,331	29,575	*31,756*	29	*35*	70	*206*	340	*1,166*	1,174	*3,329*	2,677	*5,625*
Total, Feudatory States	**4,013,034**	**1,987,749**	**2,025,285**	**11,923**	**26,149**	**35,782**	**93,752**	**77,804**	**163,291**	**138,151**	**240,817**	**239,596**	**348,605**

Table VIII.

Civil Condition by Religion and Age.

VIII.

Total Population.

MARRIED.

25 — 29.		30 — 34.		35 — 39.		40 — 44.		45 — 49.		50 — 54.		55 — 59.		60 AND OVER.	
Males.	Females.	Males.	Females.	Males.	Females.	Males.	Females.	Males.	Females.	Males.	Females.	Males.	Females.	Males.	Females.
4,149	*288*	2,505	*254*	1,044	*132*	1,000	*133*	418	*44*	614	*66*	239	*21*	707	*61*
4,710	*330*	2,128	*249*	786	*140*	797	*172*	300	*52*	481	*74*	124	*21*	385	*84*
3,927	*377*	1,901	*291*	836	*157*	779	*178*	301	*52*	455	*64*	105	*10*	296	*34*
19,659	*1,428*	9,837	*1,094*	4,194	*482*	3,791	*511*	1,318	*144*	1,883	*210*	520	*48*	1,655	*208*
5,367	*639*	2,439	*372*	1,230	*250*	933	*188*	448	*99*	449	*111*	124	*36*	329	*74*
620	*32*	344	*31*	190	*15*	159	*20*	70	*6*	99	*11*	30	*4*	104	*4*
1,261	*307*	623	*171*	333	*117*	179	*80*	123	*54*	78	*31*	46	*13*	94	*34*
29,693	*3,398*	19,777	*2,462*	8,813	*1,293*	7,638	*1,283*	2,978	*451*	4,059	*567*	1,188	*153*	3,570	*499*
584	*83*	275	*60*	145	*24*	62	*22*	45	*11*	24	*11*	8	*6*	17	*10*
369	*15*	161	*13*	82	*13*	52	*18*	27	*2*	16	*8*	9	*1*	16	*4*
1,400	*246*	575	*236*	325	*172*	256	*163*	121	*101*	102	*152*	34	*57*	97	*150*
2,359	*344*	1,011	*309*	553	*209*	370	*203*	193	*114*	142	*171*	51	*64*	130	*164*
275	*39*	76	*26*	37	*18*	15	*10*	3	*4*	6	...	1	*2*	5	*3*
126	*11*	41	*11*	19	*7*	8	*3*	7	*2*	2	*1*	3	*1*	3	...
665	*60*	267	*54*	134	*25*	97	*23*	66	*11*	62	*7*	29	*2*	47	*10*
413	*58*	150	*41*	52	*19*	69	*38*	26	*11*	19	*11*	17	...	22	*9*
599	*66*	226	*54*	129	*31*	109	*31*	55	*17*	63	*16*	23	*14*	63	*22*
2,078	*234*	760	*186*	371	*100*	298	*105*	157	*45*	152	*35*	73	*19*	140	*44*
319	*61*	120	*74*	57	*29*	54	*65*	17	*18*	18	*24*	8	*12*	23	*14*
3,369	*565*	1,500	*490*	776	*254*	718	*338*	362	*142*	352	*182*	118	*56*	285	*203*
2,565	*804*	1,177	*776*	599	*423*	555	*522*	210	*216*	250	*348*	85	*95*	237	*342*
152	*23*	67	*33*	27	*15*	22	*12*	9	*5*	18	*14*	1	*3*	9	*14*
6,405	*1,453*	2,864	*1,373*	1,459	*721*	1,349	*937*	598	*381*	638	*568*	212	*166*	554	*573*
2,042	*78*	1,296	*50*	506	*22*	412	*30*	139	*11*	204	*11*	38	*3*	158	*34*
52,577	**5,505**	**25,708**	**4,380**	**11,501**	**2,345**	**10,067**	**2,547**	**4,065**	**1,002**	**5,195**	**1,352**	**1,562**	**405**	**4,552**	**1,314**

RIED.

25 — 29.		30 — 34.		35 — 39.		40 — 44.		45 — 49.		50 — 54.		55 — 59.		60 AND OVER.	
Males.	Females.	Males.	Females.	Males.	Females.	Males.	Females.	Males.	Females.	Males.	Females.	Males.	Females.	Males.	Females.
17,007	*21,887*	20,183	*21,001*	13,062	*11,076*	14,442	*12,847*	6,555	*4,229*	10,573	*6,465*	3,932	*1,889*	10,262	*3,693*
24,287	*25,827*	27,189	*22,944*	14,048	*11,825*	17,727	*12,933*	7,018	*5,089*	11,763	*6,165*	3,116	*1,869*	8,894	*2,763*
20,970	*22,487*	21,091	*18,459*	13,759	*11,044*	14,689	*9,427*	6,291	*3,846*	8,347	*3,366*	1,999	*891*	4,245	*1,069*
111,486	*119,575*	112,590	*103,294*	74,406	*58,392*	74,978	*56,553*	34,181	*20,827*	45,323	*23,089*	12,125	*6,318*	33,828	*11,659*
29,099	*31,016*	28,182	*27,873*	22,514	*18,206*	19,250	*15,072*	10,973	*7,539*	9,995	*6,303*	3,332	*1,820*	5,748	*2,222*
3,638	*3,618*	3,509	*3,057*	2,501	*2,090*	2,616	*1,907*	1,198	*870*	1,669	*771*	469	*261*	1,053	*351*
6,244	*7,179*	6,285	*6,505*	6,431	*5,167*	4,221	*3,613*	3,666	*2,252*	2,244	*1,527*	1,284	*785*	2,106	*1,057*
212,731	*231,589*	219,029	*203,133*	146,721	*117,800*	147,922	*112,358*	69,882	*44,652*	89,91[illegible]	*46,686*	26,257	*13,333*	66,136	*22,814*
1,927	*1,928*	1,948	*1,994*	2,291	*1,336*	1,355	*916*	1,190	*597*	678	*386*	444	*209*	581	*262*
2,819	*3,723*	2,995	*2,956*	2,507	*1,690*	2,168	*1,534*	1,495	*647*	1,345	*567*	700	*188*	1,254	*183*
6,645	*7,962*	6,455	*6,548*	4,944	*3,370*	5,056	*3,596*	3,446	*1,381*	3,788	*1,397*	1,691	*388*	3,690	*642*
11,391	*13,607*	11,398	*11,498*	9,742	*6,396*	8,579	*6,045*	6,131	*2,625*	5,811	*2,350*	2,835	*785*	5,525	*1,087*
1,299	*1,563*	1,276	*1,266*	1,290	*767*	690	*496*	549	*284*	393	*184*	147	*59*	316	*88*
503	*524*	475	*458*	417	*322*	353	*233*	235	*107*	173	*80*	41	*33*	105	*26*
6,504	*6,789*	6,024	*5,680*	4,354	*3,352*	4,477	*3,118*	2,703	*1,245*	2,986	*1,155*	1,120	*316*	2,391	*468*
3,440	*3,458*	3,165	*3,193*	2,154	*1,390*	2,598	*1,508*	1,413	*475*	1,441	*495*	523	*90*	1,042	*177*
5,429	*5,386*	5,039	*4,746*	3,594	*2,666*	4,182	*2,860*	2,358	*1,077*	2,827	*1,088*	908	*328*	2,620	*535*
17,175	*17,720*	15,979	*15,343*	11,809	*8,497*	12,300	*9,215*	7,252	*3,188*	7,820	*3,002*	2,739	*826*	6,474	*1,294*
3,455	*3,431*	3,417	*3,246*	2,325	*1,519*	2,711	*1,587*	1,319	*507*	1,611	*527*	556	*113*	1,163	*247*
37,807	*38,058*	37,239	*34,020*	27,360	*18,844*	29,248	*18,928*	17,110	*7,907*	18,438	*7,565*	6,968	*2,122*	16,577	*3,389*
25,346	*26,541*	24,938	*24,651*	18,181	*13,382*	20,723	*13,053*	10,903	*5,072*	12,215	*5,154*	4,303	*1,404*	10,746	*2,581*
569	*620*	569	*569*	434	*319*	473	*313*	235	*114*	301	*134*	115	*40*	260	*52*
67,207	*68,650*	66,163	*62,486*	48,250	*34,064*	53,155	*33,881*	29,567	*13,600*	32,565	*13,380*	11,942	*3,679*	28,746	*6,269*
3,860	*5,671*	4,938	*5,520*	3,157	*2,742*	4,230	*3,301*	2,068	*1,424*	3,101	*1,476*	891	*447*	3,031	*814*
312,433	**337,237**	**317,507**	**297,980**	**219,679**	**169,499**	**226,187**	**163,794**	**114,900**	**65,489**	**139,211**	**66,894**	**44,664**	**19,570**	**109,919**	**32,278**

Part (A).—

(3) WID

State.	Total. Total.	Total. Males.	Total. Females.	0—4. Males.	0—4. Females.	5—9. Males.	5—9. Females.	10—14. Males.	10—14. Females.	15—19. Males.	15—19. Females.
Cutch	57,668	15,095	*42,573*	1	*5*	20	*20*	73	*68*	157	*340*
Palanpur	55,789	14,763	*41,026*	26	*35*	117	*92*	264	*192*	356	*366*
Mahi Kántha	57,558	11,551	*46,007*	72	*63*	162	*147*	198	*349*	317	*560*
Káthiáwár...	258,518	75,654	*182,864*	265	*147*	422	*254*	579	*494*	1,167	*1,415*
Rewa Kántha	54,707	13,915	*40,792*	118	*137*	106	*145*	182	*233*	255	*418*
Cambay	11,016	2,916	*8,100*	9	*8*	23	*34*	58	*64*	58	*96*
Surat Agency	12,108	3,709	*8,399*	2	*1*	9	*13*	23	*21*	33	*66*
Total, Gujarát Group ...	507,364	137,603	*369,761*	493	*396*	859	*705*	1,377	*1,411*	2,343	*3,261*
Jawhar	3,083	755	*2,328*	...	*1*	1	*3*	...	*3*	8	*18*
Janjira	8,667	1,399	*7,288*	1	*3*	4	*16*	15	*50*	11	*93*
Sáwantwádi	28,144	4,310	*23,834*	3	*3*	3	*19*	9	*202*	29	*416*
Total, Konkan Group ...	39,914	6,464	*33,450*	4	*7*	8	*38*	24	*255*	48	*527*
The Dángs...	1,905	670	*1,235*	...	...	...	...	1	*4*	11	*10*
Surgana	594	199	*395*	...	...	...	*1*	1	...	5	*3*
Bhor	15,450	3,173	*12,277*	...	*3*	11	*42*	40	*135*	36	*151*
Akalkot	8,911	2,252	*6,659*	1	*12*	16	*42*	43	*49*	69	*68*
Sátára Agency	15,263	3,014	*12,249*	...	*2*	7	*34*	20	*110*	28	*204*
Total, Deccan Group ...	42,123	9,308	*32,815*	1	*17*	34	*119*	105	*298*	149	*436*
Jat	8,555	1,877	*6,678*	11	*8*	22	*64*	45	*51*	62	*63*
Kolhápur	102,531	22,209	*80,322*	12	*40*	181	*309*	532	*908*	574	*904*
Southern Marátha Jaghírs ...	77,214	17,952	*59,262*	17	*59*	155	*326*	413	*583*	512	*804*
Sáwanúr	2,080	442	*1,638*	...	...	3	*4*	3	*11*	7	*16*
Total, Karnátak Group ...	190,380	42,480	*147,900*	40	*107*	361	*703*	993	*1,553*	1,155	*1,787*
Khairpur	11,667	4,301	*7,366*	...	...	3	*3*	3	*12*	33	*53*
Total, Feudatory States...	**791,448**	**200,156**	**591,292**	**538**	**527**	**1,265**	**1,568**	**2,502**	**3,529**	**3,728**	**6,064**

Part (B).—

(1) UN

Cutch	146,347	85,474	*[illegible]0,873*	23,777	*24,065*	23,870	*23,064*	16,948	*10,961*	8,890	*1,921*
Palanpur	241,873	142,095	*99,778*	40,749	*42,096*	44,244	*36,612*	27,859	*16,743*	14,466	*2,949*
Mahi Kántha	222,431	133,876	*88,555*	35,511	*30,759*	40,030	*32,721*	27,391	*14,639*	15,651	*2,769*
Káthiáwár...	889,192	521,173	*368,019*	154,419	*157,460*	150,072	*135,750*	93,756	*57,968*	55,534	*11,135*
Rewa Kántha	293,838	169,009	*124,829*	48,121	*51,173*	51,225	*45,336*	31,702	*19,560*	18,252	*5,914*
Cambay	23,128	14,887	*8,241*	4,443	*4,263*	4,157	*2,871*	2,585	*858*	1,499	*149*
Surat Agency	85,816	47,196	*38,620*	13,237	*14,232*	14,113	*12,952*	9,715	*7,122*	4,896	*2,703*
Jawhár	26,088	14,753	*11,335*	4,043	*4,367*	4,290	*4,112*	2,797	*1,852*	1,590	*623*
Janjira	27,297	15,907	*11,390*	5,381	*6,069*	5,249	*4,253*	2,986	*908*	1,282	*102*
Sáwantwádi	69,926	44,094	*25,832*	12,114	*13,095*	11,859	*9,211*	9,268	*1,770*	5,725	*283*
The Dángs...	11,021	6,267	*4,754*	1,517	*1,710*	1,940	*1,907*	1,472	*809*	687	*208*
Surgana	6,186	3,505	*2,681*	962	*1,015*	1,090	*1,001*	766	*494*	339	*107*
Bhor	57,263	35,487	*21,776*	11,810	*12,216*	11,229	*7,817*	7,133	*1,405*	2,818	*90*
Akalkot	21,714	13,522	*8,192*	5,385	*5,284*	4,061	*2,318*	2,021	*340*	1,001	*46*
Sátára Agency	46,312	28,753	*17,559*	9,583	*10,006*	8,443	*6,064*	5,776	*1,120*	2,672	*86*
Jat	26,375	16,303	*10,072*	6,497	*6,411*	5,273	*2,877*	2,289	*387*	1,136	*57*
Kolhápur	282,651	177,029	*105,622*	60,624	*60,731*	54,440	*34,888*	34,793	*6,840*	14,577	*640*
Southern Marátha Jaghírs ...	191,889	117,337	*74,552*	43,460	*42,143*	35,762	*23,340*	20,033	*4,406*	9,296	*657*
Sáwanúr	4,909	2,950	*1,959*	893	*926*	796	*664*	576	*203*	291	*32*
Khairpur	13,746	8,500	*5,246*	2,675	*2,563*	2,542	*1,906*	1,221	*616*	743	*101*
Total, Feudatory States ...	**2,688,002**	**1,598,117**	**1,089,885**	**485,201**	**496,584**	**474,685**	**389,664**	**301,087**	**149,001**	**161,375**	**20,572**

Table VIII.

Civil Condition by Religion and Age.

VIII.

Total Population.

OWED.

20 — 24.		25 — 29.		30 — 34.		35 — 39.		40 — 44.		45 — 49.		50 — 54.		55 — 59.		60 and over.	
Males.	Females.	Males.	Females.	Males.	Females.	Males.	Females.	Males.	Females.	Males.	Females.	Males.	Females.	Males.	Females.	Males.	Females.
436	991	721	1,501	1,176	3,016	940	2,629	1,608	6,292	938	2,477	2,329	7,991	1,118	2,327	5,578	14,926
740	781	1,222	1,462	1,610	3,176	1,032	2,471	1,818	6,508	875	2,639	2,155	8,549	769	1,925	3,779	12,830
532	1,137	888	2,187	1,149	4,191	959	3,934	1,697	8,759	911	3,854	1,997	9,682	586	2,073	2,083	9,071
3,559	3,954	5,230	6,877	7,428	13,459	6,399	13,353	9,700	29,643	5,728	13,206	11,840	35,188	4,000	8,061	19,337	56,813
603	779	986	1,439	1,296	2,654	1,406	3,091	1,878	6,591	1,354	4,199	2,207	8,323	867	2,513	2,657	10,270
145	226	200	348	237	607	250	606	384	1,488	266	699	453	1,699	181	389	652	1,936
130	158	229	252	301	413	437	602	403	952	445	1,031	468	1,325	329	769	900	2,796
6,145	8,026	9,476	14,066	18,197	27,516	11,423	26,686	17,488	60,233	10,517	28,105	21,449	78,657	7,850	18,057	34,986	108,643
19	32	66	59	74	123	93	146	77	245	92	285	79	386	70	214	176	815
29	108	65	328	104	551	124	562	151	936	131	655	206	1,256	121	583	437	2,147
52	780	132	1,437	237	2,359	273	1,744	537	3,190	457	1,840	731	3,449	415	1,303	1,432	7,092
100	920	263	1,824	415	3,033	490	2,452	765	4,371	680	2,780	1,016	5,091	606	2,100	2,045	10,052
24	23	58	46	100	75	92	93	61	186	75	133	99	273	32	52	117	340
12	9	27	9	12	29	22	30	34	72	19	45	25	85	10	25	32	87
83	254	163	527	248	872	225	814	360	1,787	240	1,035	509	2,192	241	700	1,017	3,765
112	116	167	236	203	485	156	496	253	1,078	179	593	275	1,215	170	368	608	1,901
66	325	131	591	174	1,015	161	804	801	1,758	301	1,060	482	1,983	233	658	1,110	3,705
297	727	546	1,409	737	2,476	650	2,237	1,099	4,981	814	2,866	1,390	5,748	686	1,803	2,884	9,798
84	169	107	292	123	511	128	479	211	967	146	584	281	1,104	124	375	533	2,011
746	1,630	1,194	3,248	1,586	5,561	1,557	5,368	2,552	11,051	1,906	6,714	3,145	13,404	1,469	4,728	6,755	26,457
638	1,485	1,037	2,426	1,321	4,435	1,203	3,892	2,144	8,360	1,501	4,724	2,523	10,183	1,116	3,404	5,372	18,581
7	35	22	62	29	121	33	127	57	199	38	103	81	310	36	121	126	529
1,475	3,319	2,360	6,028	3,059	10,628	2,921	9,866	4,964	20,677	3,591	12,125	6,030	25,001	2,745	8,628	12,786	47,578
121	155	224	282	367	492	284	431	574	1,168	349	665	748	1,494	192	324	1,403	2,287
8,138	**13,147**	**12,869**	**23,609**	**17,775**	**44,145**	**15,774**	**41,672**	**24,800**	**91,230**	**15,951**	**46,541**	**30,633**	**109,991**	**12,079**	**30,912**	**54,104**	**178,357**

Hindu.

MARRIED.

20 — 24.		25 — 29.		30 — 34.		35 — 39.		40 — 44.		45 — 49.		50 — 54.		55 — 59.		60 and over.	
Males.	Females.	Males.	Females.	Males.	Females.	Males.	Females.	Males.	Females.	Males.	Females.	Males.	Females.	Males.	Females.	Males.	Females.
5,117	343	2,637	153	1,678	138	657	72	654	62	266	19	399	36	139	12	442	27
7,735	458	3,602	274	1,567	196	519	119	529	143	185	41	319	64	67	14	254	69
7,637	574	3,530	359	1,716	278	736	144	693	165	239	49	407	56	80	10	255	32
34,201	2,517	15,482	1,117	7,690	873	3,156	363	2,873	380	991	108	1,387	150	375	37	1,237	161
9,700	1,364	4,679	533	2,172	313	1,113	215	837	156	404	81	397	94	108	28	299	62
884	39	514	15	263	15	154	8	132	11	61	4	80	6	26	1	89	1
2,625	823	1,214	300	597	167	312	113	165	77	116	63	73	31	42	13	91	34
899	157	571	82	265	58	145	24	61	22	44	11	23	11	8	6	17	10
468	20	277	8	117	8	63	7	37	6	19	2	14	6	6		8	1
2,321	237	1,354	236	551	229	316	167	250	154	118	99	97	147	33	57	88	147
349	43	198	31	52	20	29	11	12	9	2	3	5	...	...	2	4	1
161	28	121	11	38	11	16	7	8	3	7	2	2	1	3	1	2	...
1,171	64	637	57	251	51	123	25	92	22	63	11	57	6	27	2	46	10
526	47	279	53	93	33	36	15	49	33	22	7	17	9	13	...	19	7
1,132	55	553	61	208	49	114	27	90	29	49	14	56	16	21	12	56	20
579	64	265	57	107	73	49	29	46	54	16	18	16	23	8	11	22	11
6,000	465	2,961	531	1,332	454	688	241	638	302	317	129	308	167	101	53	250	181
4,027	768	2,088	737	995	720	509	390	474	477	187	201	217	324	73	82	216	307
195	26	98	21	42	29	17	15	16	10	7	5	12	12	1	3	6	13
470	31	351	14	195	2	94	3	82	4	35	1	43	1	10	1	39	3
86,187	**8,123**	**41,411**	**4,650**	**19,929**	**3,717**	**8,846**	**1,995**	**7,738**	**2,119**	**3,148**	**858**	**3,929**	**1,160**	**1,141**	**345**	**3,440**	**1,097**

Civil Condition by Religion and Age.

TABLE

Part (B).—

(2) MAR

State.	TOTAL. Total.	TOTAL. Males.	TOTAL. Females.	0—4. Males.	0—4. Females.	5—9. Males.	5—9. Females.	10—14. Males.	10—14. Females.	15—19. Males.	15—19. Females.	20—24. Males.	20—24. Females.
Cutch	**169.326**	82,041	*87,285*	325	*507*	1,314	*2,195*	3,641	*5,995*	5,854	*10,800*	9,854	*15,506*
Pálanpur	**269.893**	135,644	*134,249*	720	*1,716*	3,027	*6,149*	6,726	*10,883*	10,052	*15,498*	16,960	*22,811*
Mahi Kántha	**250.702**	123,227	*127,475*	1,417	*3,426*	3,981	*7,480*	6,822	*12,071*	10,169	*16,677*	15,609	*21,753*
Káthiáwár	**1,176,924**	591,423	*585,501*	6,334	*10,408*	16,281	*23,136*	26,721	*38,020*	44,745	*70,162*	81,851	*112,880*
Rewa Kántha	**299.077**	147,996	*151,081*	481	*876*	1,625	*3,337*	4,856	*8,723*	10,401	*17,130*	18,198	*26,016*
Cambay	**41.791**	21,076	*20,715*	192	*415*	813	*1,426*	1,480	*2,085*	2,037	*2,750*	2,985	*3,476*
Surat Agency	**77,955**	38,682	*39,273*	84	*131*	376	*574*	919	*1,615*	1,939	*3,497*	4,050	*6,266*
Jawhár	**23.105**	11,997	*11,108*	23	*40*	57	*101*	145	*395*	475	*1,294*	1,019	*1,733*
Janjira	**32.661**	15,889	*16,772*	10	*34*	75	*754*	409	*1,962*	1,026	*2,415*	1,442	*2,508*
Sáwantwádi	**86.667**	40,840	*45,827*	46	*166*	126	*2,015*	641	*6,260*	2,278	*6,469*	3,680	*6,959*
The Dángs	**9.025**	4,536	*4,489*	5	*15*	10	*26*	66	*213*	231	469	392	*762*
Surgana	**5,360**	2,706	*2,654*	13	*10*	13	*21*	42	*126*	154	340	241	*424*
Bhor	**80,314**	38,438	*41,876*	90	*292*	504	*2,752*	1,591	*5,684*	2,538	*5,335*	3,789	*6,071*
Akalkot	**35.610**	17,582	*18,028*	84	*408*	257	*1,777*	589	*1,755*	1,172	*2,007*	1,862	*2,816*
Sátára Agency	**64.687**	31,634	*33,053*	69	*193*	192	*1,873*	732	*3,943*	1,788	*4,139*	3,034	*5,050*
Jat	**40.290**	19,855	*20,435*	90	*489*	297	*2,377*	618	*1,948*	1,255	*2,152*	2,120	*3,003*
Kolhápur	**447,596**	223,017	*224,579*	691	*3,009*	2,858	*18,950*	9,767	*28,820*	15,613	*25,185*	23,169	*30,797*
Southern Marátha Jaghírs...	**298.517**	146,489	*152,028*	552	*2,626*	2,133	*12,864*	5,963	*16,717*	10,725	*17,620*	15,914	*22,243*
Sáwanúr	**5,658**	2,685	*2,973*	...	*32*	23	*196*	59	*318*	130	*366*	300	*541*
Khairpur	**11,744**	5,814	*6,430*	6	*7*	14	*66*	106	*379*	345	*854*	586	*1,247*
Total. Feudatory States.	**3.426,902**	**1.701,071**	**1,725,831**	**11,232**	**24,800**	**33.976**	**88,069**	**71.873**	**147,912**	**122,927**	**205,159**	**207,055**	**292,862**

Part (B).—

(3) WID

State.	TOTAL. Total.	TOTAL. Males.	TOTAL. Females.	0—4. Males.	0—4. Females.	5—9. Males.	5—9. Females.	10—14. Males.	10—14. Females.	15—19. Males.	15—19. Females.	20—24. Males.	20—24. Females.
Cutch	**35.947**	9,250	*26,697*	1	*3*	16	*17*	58	*40*	121	*230*	302	*605*
Pálanpur	**46.104**	12,320	*33,784*	21	*32*	110	*82*	257	*172*	323	*315*	657	*621*
Mahi Kántha	**52.764**	10,627	*42,137*	71	*61*	152	*138*	187	*331*	297	*521*	484	*1,011*
Káthiáwár	**213.307**	63,290	*150,017*	238	*134*	394	*232*	532	*438*	1,030	*1,182*	3,112	*3,207*
Rewa Kántha	**48.896**	12,670	*36,226*	118	*137*	106	*141*	180	*227*	245	*390*	555	*705*
Cambay	**8,671**	2,388	*6,283*	9	*7*	21	*30*	55	*57*	54	*76*	126	*163*
Surat Agency	**11,527**	3,548	*7,979*	2	*1*	7	*12*	19	*19*	33	*62*	121	*150*
Jawhár	**3.039**	742	*2,297*	...	*1*	1	*3*	...	*3*	8	*17*	19	*33*
Janjira	**6.645**	1,102	*5,743*	1	*3*	4	*16*	11	*44*	7	*78*	21	*81*
Sáwantwádi	**27.156**	4,181	*22,975*	3	*3*	3	*19*	9	*201*	29	*414*	50	*768*
The Dángs	**1.297**	465	*832*	...	...	...	...	1	*4*	10	*9*	19	*18*
Surgana	**572**	186	*386*	...	...	...	*1*	1	...	4	*8*	11	*8*
Bhor	**15,139**	3,096	*12,043*	...	*3*	11	*42*	40	*130*	36	*150*	80	*249*
Akalkot	**7.710**	1,988	*5,722*	1	*12*	16	*40*	40	*46*	68	*68*	106	*102*
Sátára Agency	**14,555**	2,829	*11,726*	...	*2*	7	*34*	20	*110*	27	*193*	63	*311*
Jat	**8.025**	1,761	*6,264*	9	*8*	19	*62*	42	*49*	58	*58*	79	*157*
Kolhápur	**92.279**	19,737	*72,542*	9	*36*	170	*292*	485	*835*	527	*833*	653	*1,501*
Southern Marátha Jaghirs...	**68.063**	16,032	*52,031*	12	*56*	143	*312*	390	*534*	484	*733*	587	*1,373*
Sáwanúr	**1,541**	343	*1,198*	...	...	3	*4*	3	*11*	6	*15*	6	*27*
Khairpur	**2,724**	830	*1,894*	...	...	2	...	...	...	10	*19*	25	*35*
Total. Feudatory States.	**666.161**	**167.385**	**498,776**	**495**	**499**	**1,185**	**1,477**	**2.330**	**3.251**	**3.377**	**5.361**	**7.076**	**11.123**

Table VIII.

Civil Condition by Religion and Age.

VIII.

Hindu.

RIED.

25 — 29.		30 — 34.		35 — 39.		40 — 44.		45 — 49.		50 — 54.		55 — 59.		60 and over.	
Males.	Females.	Males.	Females.	Males.	Females.	Males.	Females.	Males.	Females.	Males.	Females.	Males.	Females.	Males.	Females.
11,114	*13,800*	13,129	*13,269*	8,338	*7,013*	9,144	*8,124*	4,003	*2,612*	6,686	*4,058*	2,450	*1,149*	6,189	*2,257*
21,320	*22,599*	23,952	*19,876*	11,819	*9,981*	15,141	*11,084*	5,736	*4,276*	10,024	*5,353*	2,551	*1,621*	7,616	*2,402*
19,671	*21,070*	19,771	*17,265*	12,767	*10,368*	13,747	*8,782*	5,782	*3,596*	7,767	*3,157*	1,816	*837*	3,908	*993*
94,763	*100,008*	95,097	*85,656*	61,940	*48,210*	61,826	*46,214*	27,847	*17,175*	37,169	*18,851*	9,635	*5,241*	27,214	*9,540*
25,208	*26,901*	24,559	*24,202*	19,475	*15,934*	16,927	*13,178*	9,522	*6,530*	8,749	*4,644*	2,887	*1,626*	5,108	*1,984*
3,035	*2,971*	2,892	*2,506*	2,057	*1,716*	2,099	*1,574*	988	*714*	1,349	*612*	367	*212*	802	*258*
6,044	*6,967*	6,071	*6,307*	6,232	*5,026*	4,072	*3,469*	3,524	*2,174*	2,144	*1,461*	1,243	*769*	1,984	*1,017*
1,907	*1,905*	1,920	*1,970*	2,270	*1,324*	1,334	*902*	1,165	*594*	669	*381*	442	*208*	571	*261*
2,482	*2,929*	2,605	*2,360*	2,138	*1,323*	1,857	*1,195*	1,243	*517*	1,089	*462*	567	*156*	946	*157*
6,372	*7,545*	6,152	*6,211*	4,718	*3,194*	4,818	*3,401*	3,293	*1,317*	3,604	*1,316*	1,609	*368*	3,503	*606*
796	*981*	850	*795*	820	*496*	450	*341*	366	*183*	257	*115*	100	*39*	193	*54*
493	*515*	464	*440*	407	*310*	339	*228*	228	*107*	170	*78*	38	*31*	104	*24*
6,383	*6,671*	5,905	*5,608*	4,275	*3,287*	4,388	*3,063*	2,644	*1,214*	2,910	*1,128*	1,097	*318*	2,324	*458*
3,064	*2,981*	2,710	*2,750*	1,852	*1,197*	2,228	*1,284*	1,194	*405*	1,237	*416*	435	*83*	898	*149*
5,310	*5,152*	4,817	*4,541*	3,449	*2,541*	4,010	*2,737*	2,262	*1,026*	2,694	*1,035*	863	*311*	2,514	*512*
3,261	*3,198*	3,171	*3,035*	2,194	*1,406*	2,525	*1,511*	1,217	*476*	1,499	*493*	522	*109*	1,086	*238*
34,129	*34,486*	33,450	*30,645*	24,408	*16,967*	26,149	*16,946*	15,336	*7,046*	16,440	*6,776*	6,230	*1,904*	14,717	*3,048*
22,358	*23,165*	21,856	*21,489*	15,860	*11,675*	18,020	*11,298*	9,568	*4,448*	10,617	*4,410*	3,783	*1,239*	9,140	*2,234*
438	*430*	408	*409*	327	*229*	351	*205*	167	*86*	214	*98*	89	*32*	179	*31*
760	*1,157*	829	*997*	546	*524*	625	*570*	377	*263*	523	*224*	191	*59*	406	*83*
268,808	**285,431**	**270,608**	**250,331**	**185,952**	**142,721**	**190,050**	**136,106**	**96,462**	**54,759**	**115,811**	**55,068**	**36,915**	**16,307**	**89,402**	**26,306**

Hindu.

OWED.

25 — 29.		30 — 34.		35 — 39.		40 — 44.		45 — 49.		50 — 54.		55 — 59.		60 and over.	
Males.	Females.	Males.	Females.	Males.	Females.	Males.	Females.	Males.	Females.	Males.	Females.	Males.	Females.	Males.	Females.
479	*883*	737	*1,876*	575	*1,644*	1,005	*4,083*	548	*1,504*	1,426	*5,185*	675	*1,474*	3,307	*9,153*
1,075	*1,164*	1,380	*2,593*	841	*1,960*	1,496	*5,333*	694	*2,062*	1,783	*7,143*	592	*1,512*	3,091	*10,795*
620	*1,964*	1,072	*3,848*	878	*3,572*	1,584	*8,023*	820	*3,484*	1,856	*8,970*	526	*1,864*	1,880	*8,350*
4,503	*5,628*	6,327	*11,090*	5,400	*10,988*	8,137	*24,554*	4,729	*10,728*	9,854	*29,086*	3,243	*6,478*	15,791	*46,272*
903	*1,282*	1,184	*2,356*	1,269	*2,735*	1,705	*5,844*	1,208	*3,599*	2,010	*7,363*	790	*2,227*	2,397	*9,220*
165	*271*	185	*461*	206	*477*	323	*1,157*	209	*530*	384	*1,293*	144	*297*	507	*1,464*
214	*234*	287	*290*	416	*574*	391	*907*	427	*991*	453	*1,264*	323	*738*	855	*2,637*
66	*56*	69	*123*	90	*144*	76	*239*	92	*280*	78	*377*	69	*211*	174	*811*
50	*264*	90	*434*	105	*443*	128	*726*	113	*492*	158	*1,005*	92	*451*	322	*1,706*
124	*1,394*	235	*2,277*	265	*1,695*	524	*3,068*	447	*1,770*	713	*3,314*	406	*1,246*	1,373	*6,806*
40	*24*	77	*51*	60	*53*	42	*120*	48	*98*	61	*192*	22	*45*	85	*218*
25	*8*	12	*29*	20	*30*	34	*72*	17	*44*	23	*80*	9	*25*	30	*86*
157	*512*	238	*856*	219	*802*	354	*1,754*	237	*1,020*	497	*2,144*	235	*684*	992	*3,697*
152	*206*	184	*407*	132	*433*	216	*933*	156	*514*	237	*1,062*	152	*320*	528	*1,584*
121	*563*	163	*968*	147	*759*	278	*1,700*	287	*1,021*	460	*1,890*	220	*632*	1,036	*3,543*
103	*283*	117	*484*	124	*450*	199	*896*	135	*541*	263	*1,022*	115	*339*	498	*1,915*
1,045	*2,972*	1,402	*5,107*	1,378	*4,868*	2,270	*10,007*	1,700	*6,027*	2,830	*12,140*	1,292	*4,226*	5,976	*23,698*
931	*2,177*	1,171	*3,959*	1,071	*3,454*	1,898	*7,354*	1,351	*4,166*	2,260	*8,915*	1,004	*2,937*	4,730	*16,062*
18	*45*	23	*87*	24	*107*	43	*141*	29	*84*	61	*231*	29	*95*	98	*351*
42	*68*	69	*114*	52	*127*	101	*828*	67	*199*	154	*399*	48	*112*	260	*497*
11,033	**19,998**	**15,022**	**37,510**	**13,272**	**35,315**	**20,804**	**77,239**	**13,314**	**39,154**	**25,561**	**93,075**	**9,986**	**25,913**	**43,930**	**148,861**

TABLE

Part (C).—

(1) UN

State.	Total. Total.	Total. Males.	Total. Females.	0—4. Males.	0—4. Females.	5—9. Males.	5—9. Females.	10—14. Males.	10—14. Females.	15—19. Males.	15—19. Females.
Cutch	**62,627**	35,605	*27,022*	9,693	*10,116*	10,214	*9,393*	7,100	*5,442*	3,840	*987*
Pálanpur	**24,722**	14,752	*9,970*	3,595	*3,857*	3,876	*3,332*	2,978	*2,043*	1,880	*477*
Mahi Kántha	**9,177**	5,534	*3,643*	1,358	*1,508*	1,564	*1,265*	1,088	*653*	616	*152*
Káthiáwár	**159,437**	91,500	*67,937*	25,554	*26,738*	25,905	*24,443*	18,148	*12,781*	9,645	*2,645*
Rewa Kántha	**10,489**	6,345	*4,144*	1,527	*1,613*	1,533	*1,345*	1,247	*744*	836	*223*
Cambay	**4,554**	2,676	*1,878*	667	*716*	717	*627*	529	*332*	322	*95*
Surat Agency	**2,161**	1,245	*916*	314	*349*	323	*286*	267	*188*	122	*53*
Jawhár	**198**	119	*79*	24	*29*	22	*30*	23	*16*	16	*1*
Janjira	**6,297**	3,503	*2,794*	1,088	*1,091*	1,078	*1,025*	685	*532*	354	*106*
Sáwantwádi	**2,036**	1,190	*846*	311	*366*	329	*343*	261	*152*	160	*8*
The Dángs	**81**	46	*35*	7	*3*	10	*19*	10	*6*	8	*3*
Surgana	**62**	37	*25*	6	*8*	10	*7*	5	*9*	3	*1*
Bhor	**826**	517	*309*	159	*144*	129	*109*	112	*43*	54	*5*
Akalkot	**4,305**	2,644	*1,661*	803	*840*	704	*575*	400	*188*	290	*18*
Sátára Agency	**1,971**	1,199	*772*	344	*373*	337	*273*	247	*91*	139	*10*
Jat	**1,902**	1,178	*724*	410	*422*	318	*240*	178	*39*	106	*8*
Kolhápur	**14,824**	9,252	*5,572*	2,834	*2,782*	2,697	*1,999*	1,902	*569*	859	*65*
Southern Marátha Jaghírs ...	**21,369**	12,666	*8,703*	4,113	*4,192*	3,662	*3,037*	2,241	*966*	1,235	*150*
Sáwanúr	**2,382**	1,371	*1,011*	396	*407*	351	*360*	251	*177*	148	*37*
Khairpur	**44,874**	30,137	*14,737*	8,243	*6,877*	8,376	*5,212*	4,446	*1,774*	2,865	*521*
Total, Feudatory States ...	**374,294**	**221,516**	**152,778**	**61,446**	**62,431**	**62,155**	**54,390**	**42,118**	**26,745**	**23,493**	**5,565**

Part (C).—

(2) MAR

State.	Total. Total.	Total. Males.	Total. Females.	0—4. Males.	0—4. Females.	5—9. Males.	5—9. Females.	10—14. Males.	10—14. Females.	15—19. Males.	15—19. Females.
Cutch	**58,280**	27,576	*30,704*	55	*88*	109	*180*	426	*1,102*	1,363	*3,712*
Pálanpur	**27,042**	13,665	*13,377*	62	*120*	185	*351*	402	*709*	678	*1,569*
Máhi Kántha	**10,958**	5,546	*5,412*	27	*58*	140	*263*	321	*559*	420	*668*
Káthiáwár	**166,360**	80,505	*85,855*	182	*265*	460	*782*	1,379	*3,155*	4,007	*10,044*
Rewa Kántha	**11,943**	6,197	*5,746*	11	*26*	37	*85*	145	*349*	309	*726*
Cambay	**6,336**	3,121	*3,215*	14	*14*	32	*52*	80	*205*	182	*423*
Surat Agency	**2,490**	1,223	*1,267*	7	*3*	10	*21*	30	*62*	62	*118*
Jawhár	**190**	106	*84*	...	...	...	*2*	...	*4*	6	*16*
Janjira	**6,061**	2,496	*3,565*	1	*9*	10	*47*	57	*207*	85	*493*
Sáwantwádi	**1,905**	856	*1,049*	2	*2*	1	*6*	3	*75*	20	*154*
The Dángs	**53**	30	*23*	...	...	...	...	...	...	1	*1*
Surgana	**61**	27	*34*	...	...	...	...	1	*1*	...	*2*
Bhor	**972**	513	*459*	1	*1*	1	*7*	6	*39*	18	*66*
Akalkot	**4,789**	2,365	*2,424*	3	*14*	17	*92*	31	*160*	80	*279*
Sátára Agency	**2,224**	1,065	*1,159*	2	*6*	6	*42*	17	*111*	46	*155*
Jat	**2,371**	1,199	*1,172*	10	*11*	9	*101*	26	*81*	42	*118*
Kolhápur	**19,566**	10,021	*9,545*	36	*79*	78	*467*	326	*972*	538	*1,068*
Southern Marátha Jaghírs ...	**25,276**	12,512	*12,764*	42	*92*	124	*534*	337	*953*	604	*1,504*
Sáwanúr	**1,934**	875	*1,059*	1	*4*	2	*20*	10	*32*	17	*120*
Khairpur	**49,264**	24,106	*25,158*	22	*28*	56	*140*	233	*783*	816	*2,454*
Total, Feudatory States ...	**398,075**	**194,004**	**204,071**	**478**	**820**	**1,277**	**3,192**	**3,830**	**9,559**	**9,294**	**23,690**

Civil Condition by Religion and Age.

Mussalman.

MARRIED.

20 — 24.		25 — 29.		30 — 34.		35 — 39.		40 — 44.		45 — 49.		50 — 54.		55 — 59.		60 and over.	
Males.	Females.	Males.	Females.	Males.	Females.	Males.	Females.	Males.	Females.	Males.	Females.	Males.	Females.	Males.	Females.	Males.	Females.
2,356	210	1,057	108	550	92	220	45	210	52	69	21	120	23	45	6	131	27
1,281	92	526	41	256	48	83	17	108	26	32	10	64	9	15	5	58	13
450	12	226	16	90	10	43	11	36	9	14	2	24	4	7	...	18	1
6,189	565	2,724	253	1,370	181	606	96	563	101	150	30	308	52	74	10	264	43
554	91	274	40	137	32	73	12	65	12	27	8	39	12	9	6	24	6
200	51	91	16	64	16	24	6	22	8	6	2	18	4	2	3	14	3
111	24	41	7	22	3	19	3	13	2	6	1	4	...	2	...	2	...
13	1	11	...	8	2	...	...	...	...	1	...	1	...	...	...	...	...
118	4	84	7	42	5	19	6	15	12	7	...	2	2	3	1	8	3
76	1	28	2	9	1	5	...	1	2	1	...	2	1	1	...	6	...
7	4	4	...	...	...	...	...	...	...	...	...	...	...	...	...	...	...
2	...	4	...	3	...	3	...	...	...	...	...	...	...	...	...	1	...
28	...	16	3	5	3	6	...	2	1	2	...	3	1	...	...	1	...
225	11	128	5	54	8	16	3	16	5	4	4	1	2	2	..	1	2
62	5	32	4	11	4	10	4	8	2	2	2	4	...	1	2	2	2
85	5	52	3	11	1	8	...	6	1	1	...	2	1	...	1	1	3
485	31	237	23	103	27	34	8	40	24	20	8	18	14	4	2	19	20
701	91	376	60	137	50	66	32	68	40	17	15	26	24	9	11	15	35
121	19	53	2	25	4	10	...	5	2	2	...	6	2	...	...	3	1
2,283	144	1,684	63	1,090	48	410	19	329	26	104	10	161	10	27	2	119	31
15,347	**1,361**	**7,648**	**652**	**3,987**	**535**	**1,655**	**262**	**1,506**	**325**	**465**	**113**	**803**	**161**	**201**	**49**	**687**	**189**

Mussalman.

RIED.

20 — 24.		25 — 29.		30 — 34.		35 — 39.		40 — 44.		45 — 49.		50 — 54.		55 — 59.		60 and over.	
Males.	Females.	Males.	Females.	Males.	Females.	Males.	Females.	Males.	Females.	Males.	Females.	Males.	Females.	Males.	Females.	Males.	Females.
2,995	5,822	3,975	5,173	4,813	5,271	3,027	2,594	3,497	3,125	1,521	913	2,414	1,494	814	373	2,567	857
1,468	2,417	2,084	2,179	2,314	2,082	1,455	1,225	1,822	1,263	747	503	1,247	650	301	160	900	249
633	966	885	929	899	806	640	415	639	408	294	144	358	124	96	29	194	43
10,278	17,697	12,853	15,324	13,777	13,981	9,430	7,936	10,241	8,071	4,484	2,712	6,348	3,377	1,813	816	5,253	1,695
735	1,142	1,039	1,031	998	857	823	594	779	444	398	200	464	174	169	44	290	74
398	678	488	524	496	443	338	270	417	261	155	110	247	126	70	38	204	71
146	268	175	189	189	169	157	131	120	125	115	65	81	62	32	16	99	38
12	12	13	13	21	16	17	10	15	6	14	3	4	1	1	1	3	...
152	533	309	754	363	570	332	348	292	328	236	122	-243	98	123	31	293	25
53	181	126	201	134	159	100	81	100	90	69	32	97	44	50	5	101	19
1	1	5	9	6	3	5	3	...	3	8	...	1	3	2	...	1	...
1	...	4	4	2	10	6	7	5	5	2	...	3	1	3	2	...	2
49	84	74	77	79	51	50	51	68	39	44	20	60	13	15	2	48	9
170	415	362	464	435	430	293	181	356	210	203	67	195	77	84	7	136	28
79	174	183	188	180	165	118	111	132	98	79	36	105	41	35	12	83	20
98	198	178	219	238	196	120	106	176	69	95	28	104	32	31	4	72	9
934	1,391	1,408	1,605	1,583	1,461	1,148	776	1,331	828	714	327	834	339	254	68	777	164
1,176	2,133	1,888	2,178	2,045	2,079	1,420	1,066	1,751	1,076	834	353	973	475	314	97	1,004	224
63	244	131	159	160	160	107	89	122	108	68	28	87	36	26	8	81	21
2,076	4,344	3,007	4,489	4,080	4,497	2,595	2,204	3,588	2,715	1,684	1,152	2,566	1,250	694	381	2,599	721
21,517	**38,700**	**29,337**	**35,739**	**32,812**	**33,406**	**22,181**	**18,198**	**25,451**	**19,272**	**11,764**	**6,815**	**16,431**	**8,317**	**4,927**	**2,094**	**14,705**	**4,269**

Part (C).–

(3) WID

State.	Total. Total.	Total. Males.	Total. Females.	0 – 4. Males.	0 – 4. Females.	5 – 9. Males.	5 – 9. Females.	10 – 14. Males.	10 – 14. Females.	15 – 19. Males.	15 – 19. Females.	20 – 24. Males.	20 – 24. Females.
Cutch	12,585	3,371	*9,214*	...	*1*	1	*3*	10	*11*	26	*52*	100	*182*
Pálanpur	5,722	1,632	*4,190*	5	*2*	7	*9*	7	*14*	18	*31*	56	*78*
Mahi Kántha	2,435	530	*1,905*	1	*2*	8	*8*	10	*13*	15	*15*	31	*52*
Káthiáwár	32,264	9,191	*23,073*	21	*7*	19	*12*	37	*39*	100	*139*	351	*451*
Rewa Kántha	2,671	560	*2,111*	...	...	...	*3*	1	*5*	4	*17*	18	*46*
Cambay	1,822	421	*1,401*	...	...	...	*2*	3	*4*	2	*15*	15	*54*
Surat Agency	508	138	*370*	...	...	2	*1*	4	*1*	...	*4*	8	*7*
Jawhár	33	10	*23*	...	...	...	...	...	...	...	*1*	...	...
Janjira	1,778	285	*1,493*	...	...	...	...	4	*5*	4	*15*	8	*27*
Sáwantwádi	514	74	*440*	...	...	...	...	...	*1*	...	*1*	1	*7*
The Dángs	17	7	*10*	...	...	...	...	...	...	...	...	...	...
Surgana	8	4	*4*	...	...	...	...	...	...	...	...	1	...
Bhor	194	44	*150*	...	...	...	...	...	*3*	...	*1*	1	*3*
Akalkot	1,136	244	*892*	...	...	...	*2*	2	*2*	...	*4*	6	*13*
Sátára Agency	479	114	*365*	...	...	...	...	...	...	1	*6*	2	*9*
Jat	491	111	*380*	2	...	3	*2*	2	*2*	3	*5*	5	*11*
Kolhápur	3,882	854	*3,028*	3	*3*	2	*7*	10	*20*	10	*23*	23	*47*
Southern Marátha Jaghírs	5,552	1,102	*4,450*	5	*2*	6	*8*	10	*20*	12	*38*	29	*57*
Sáwanúr	537	98	*439*	...	...	...	...	...	...	1	*1*	1	*8*
Khairpur	8,895	3,454	*5,441*	...	...	1	*3*	3	*12*	23	*33*	96	*119*
Total, Feudatory States.	**81,523**	**22,144**	**59,379**	**37**	**17**	**49**	**60**	**103**	**152**	**219**	**401**	**752**	**1,171**

Part (D).–

(1) UN

State.	Total. Total.	Total. Males.	Total. Females.	0 – 4. Males.	0 – 4. Females.	5 – 9. Males.	5 – 9. Females.	10 – 14. Males.	10 – 14. Females.	15 – 19. Males.	15 – 19. Females.	20 – 24. Males.	20 – 24. Females.
Cutch	63	54	*9*	10	*3*	2	*3*	2	...	4	*1*	15	*2*
Pálanpur	461	396	*65*	18	*28*	14	*21*	6	*11*	11	*4*	147	*1*
Mahi Kántha	24	21	*3*	4	*1*	...	*2*	...	...	2	...	12	...
Káthiáwár	390	252	*138*	48	*63*	31	*33*	17	*19*	38	*18*	69	*6*
Rewa Kántha	11	7	*4*	2	*2*	1	*1*	...	*1*	...	...	2	...
Cambay	5	5	...	1	...	...	...	...	...	...	...	4	...
Surat Agency	...	...	...	...	...	...	...	...	...	...	...	...	...
Jawhár	2	1	*1*	...	*1*	...	...	...	...	...	...	...	...
Janjira	7	6	*1*	1	...	2	*1*	3	...	...	...	...	...
Sáwantwádi	2,140	1,214	*926*	355	*376*	363	*312*	237	*172*	145	*30*	64	*2*
The Dángs	2	2	...	...	...	...	...	...	...	...	...	...	...
Surgana	...	...	...	...	...	...	...	...	...	...	...	...	...
Bhor	3	3	...	...	...	...	...	...	...	...	...	1	...
Akalkot	2	2	...	...	...	...	...	...	...	...	...	1	...
Sátára Agency	1	1	...	...	...	...	...	...	...	...	...		
Jat	9	4	*5*	1	*2*	...	*2*	...	...	...	...	2	...
Kolhápur	663	371	*292*	124	*129*	114	*84*	59	*46*	30	*13*	27	*5*
Southern Marátha Jaghírs	197	127	*70*	27	*21*	36	*28*	31	*18*	19	*2*	6	...
Sáwanúr	...	...	...	...	...	...	...	...	...	...	...	...	...
Khairpur	2	2	...	...	...	...	...	...	...	...	...	...	...
Total, Feudatory States.	**3,982**	**2,468**	**1,514**	**591**	**616**	**563**	**487**	**355**	**267**	**249**	**68**	**350**	**16**

Civil Condition by Religion and Ag

Mussalman.

OWED.

	25 — 29.		30 — 34.		35 — 39.		40 — 44.		45 — 49.		50 — 54.		55 — 59.		60 and over.	
	Males.	Females.	Males.	Females.	Males.	Females.	Males.	Females.	Males.	Females.	Males.	Females.	Males.	Females.	Males.	Females.
	173	*254*	312	*596*	214	*447*	374	*1,365*	198	*526*	538	*1,717*	206	*477*	1,219	*3,583*
	106	*155*	157	*329*	108	*254*	207	*680*	95	*268*	257	*885*	85	*213*	424	*1,272*
	48	*93*	49	*151*	50	*158*	60	*410*	47	*184*	75	*398*	27	*79*	109	*342*
	595	*738*	899	*1,552*	750	*1,492*	1,166	*3,553*	664	*1,605*	1,459	*4,469*	482	*1,050*	2,648	*7,966*
	32	*89*	39	*158*	56	*160*	75	*339*	56	*203*	96	*419*	47	*140*	136	*532*
	27	*60*	45	*116*	39	*96*	50	*263*	41	*128*	55	*235*	27	*58*	117	*370*
	13	*15*	13	*20*	20	*25*	12	*41*	16	*35*	11	*53*	4	*27*	35	*141*
	...	*3*	3	...	2	*2*	1	*4*	...	*3*	1	*6*	1	*2*	2	*2*
	15	*64*	14	*117*	19	*114*	23	*207*	17	*157*	45	*247*	28	*123*	108	*417*
	2	*22*	1	*32*	7	*23*	9	*57*	5	*36*	13	*74*	4	*30*	32	*157*
	...	...	...	...	3	*2*	1	*1*	1	...	...	*1*	...	...	2	*6*
	2	...	...	...	1	...	...	..	...	*1*	...	*3*	...	...	...	...
	3	*7*	6	*13*	4	*10*	4	*18*	1	*11*	6	*25*	2	*10*	17	*49*
	15	*29*	19	*75*	23	*57*	35	*140*	21	*75*	34	*145*	15	*42*	74	*308*
	6	*18*	8	*29*	8	*32*	13	*41*	7	*22*	9	*70*	7	*14*	53	*124*
	4	*8*	5	*27*	4	*29*	12	*64*	11	*38*	18	*74*	9	*31*	33	*69*
	49	*104*	67	*173*	57	*169*	94	*442*	60	*243*	125	*522*	59	*189*	295	*1,086*
	60	*151*	96	*304*	80	*263*	142	*631*	92	*362*	149	*804*	72	*275*	349	*1,536*
	4	*17*	6	*34*	9	*20*	14	*58*	9	*19*	19	*79*	7	*26*	28	*177*
	182	*213*	296	*376*	232	*302*	472	*836*	281	*465*	592	*1,087*	142	*210*	1,134	*1,785*
	1336	**2.040**	**2.035**	**4,102**	**1.686**	**3.655**	**2.764**	**9.150**	**1.622**	**4.381**	**3.502**	**11.313**	**1.224**	**2.996**	**6.815**	**10.941**

Christian.

MARRIED.

	25 — 29.		30 — 34.		35 — 39.		40 — 44.		45 — 49.		50 — 54.		55 — 59.		60 and over.	
	Males.	Females.	Males.	Females.	Males.	Females.	Males.	Females.	Males.	Females.	Males.	Females.	Males.	Females.	Males.	Females.
	11	...	4	...	3	...	2	...	1	...	...	...	...	...	...	...
	164	...	21	...	7	...	5	...	1	...	2	...	...	...	...	...
	1	...	1	...	1	...	...	...	...	...	...	...	...	...	...	...
	29	*2*	9	*4*	4	*1*	5	*2*	2	...	...	...	...	...	...	...
	...	...	...	...	2	...	...	...	..	...	...	...	...	...	...	...
	...	...	...	...	...	...	...	...	...	...	...	...	...	...	...	...
	...	...	...	...	...	...	...	...	...	...	...	...	...	...	...	...
	1	...	...	...	...	...	...	...	...	...	...	...	...	...	...	...
	...	...	...	...	...	...	...	...	...	...	...	...	...	...	...	...
	23	*8*	13	*6*	4	*4*	4	*7*	1	*2*	3	*4*	...	...	2	*3*
	2	...	...	...	...	...	...	...	...	...	...	...	...	...	...	...
	...	...	...	...	...	...	...	...	...	...	...	...	...	...	...	...
	3	...	1	...	...	...	...	...	...	...	...	...	...	...	..	...
	...	...	...	...	...	...	1	...	...	...	...	...	...	...	...	...
	...	...	...	...	...	...	...	...	...	...	...	...	...	...	...	...
	...	*1*	1	...	...	...	...	..	...	...	...	...	...	...	...	...
	11	*5*	3	*3*	1	*1*	1	*3*	...	...	1	*1*	...	...	..	*2*
	5	*1*	2	...	1	...	...	...	...	...	..	...	...	...	...	...
	...	...	...	...	...	...	...	...	...	...	...	...	...	...	...	...
	1	...	1	...	...	...	...	...	...	...	...	...	...	...	...	...
	250	**17**	**56**	**13**	**23**	**6**	**18**	**12**	**5**	**2**	**6**	**5**	...	...	**2**	**5**

Civil Condition by Religion and Age.

TABLE

Part (D).—

(2) MAR

State.	Total. Total.	Total. Males.	Total. Females.	0-4. Males.	0-4. Females.	5—9. Males.	5—9. Females.	10—14. Males.	10—14. Females.	15—19. Males.	15—19. Females.
Cutch	104	83	21	...	1	1	...	...	1	2	3
Pálanpur	134	79	55	...	...	...	...	...	...	...	4
Mahi Kantha	10	7	3	...	...	...	...	...	...	1	...
Kathiáwár	467	321	146	1	...	...	...	2	...	5	9
Rewa Kantha	25	19	6	...	...	...	...	...	...	...	1
Cambay	14	10	4	...	...	...	...	...	...	2	1
Surat Agency	1	1	...	...	...	...	...	...	...	...	...
Jawhar	4	3	1	...	...	...	...	...	...	...	...
Janjira	5	4	1	...	...	...	...	...	...	...	...
Sawantwadi	2,005	943	1,062	...	...	3	5	3	59	27	143
The Dángs	1	1	...	...	...	...	...	...	...	...	...
Surgana	...	...	...	...	...	...	...	...	...	...	...
Bhor	5	4	1	...	...	...	...	...	...	...	1
Akalkot	...	...	...	...	...	...	...	...	...	...	...
Satára Agency	...	...	...	...	...	...	...	...	...	...	...
Jat	6	3	3	...	...	...	...	...	...	...	...
Kolhápur	616	311	305	...	1	3	3	2	20	22	40
Southern Maratha Jaghírs ...	176	100	76	...	...	...	...	...	7	6	13
Sáwanúr	...	...	...	...	...	...	...	...	...	...	...
Khairpur	2	1	1	...	...	...	...	...	...	...	...
Total, Feudatory States ...	**3,575**	**1,890**	**1,685**	**1**	**2**	**7**	**8**	**7**	**87**	**65**	**215**

Part (D).—

(3) WID

State.	Total. Total.	Total. Males.	Total. Females.	0-4. Males.	0-4. Females.	5—9. Males.	5—9. Females.	10—14. Males.	10—14. Females.	15—19. Males.	15—19. Females.
Cutch	6	3	3	...	...	...	...	...	...	...	...
Palanpur	13	5	8	...	...	...	...	...	...	...	...
Mahi Kantha	1	1	...	...	...	...	...	...	...	...	...
Káthiawár	41	20	21	...	...	...	...	...	...	...	...
Rewa Kantha	...	...	...	...	...	...	...	...	...	...	...
Cambay	2	1	1	...	...	...	...	...	...	...	...
Surat Agency	...	...	...	...	...	...	...	...	...	...	...
Jawhár	1	1	...	...	...	...	...	...	...	...	...
Janjira	...	...	...	...	...	...	...	...	...	...	...
Sawantwádi	452	52	400	...	...	...	...	...	...	...	1
The Dángs	...	...	...	...	...	...	...	...	...	...	...
Surgana	...	...	...	...	...	...	...	...	...	...	...
Bhor	1	1	...	...	...	...	...	...	...	...	...
Akalkot	...	...	...	...	...	...	...	...	...	...	...
Sátara Agency	...	...	...	...	...	...	...	...	...	...	...
Jat	1	1	...	...	...	...	...	...	...	...	...
Kolhapur	134	18	116	...	...	...	...	...	...	...	...
Southern Maratha Jaghírs ...	30	6	24	...	...	...	1	...	1	...	...
Sáwanúr	...	...	...	...	...	...	...	...	...	...	...
Khairpur	...	...	...	...	...	...	...	...	...	...	...
Total, Feudatory States	**682**	**109**	**573**	...	...	...	**1**	...	**1**	...	**1**

Table VIII

Civil Condition by Religion and Age.

VIII.

Christian.

RIED.

20 — 24.		25 — 29.		30 — 34.		35 — 39.		40 — 44.		45 — 49.		50 — 54.		55 — 59.		60 and over.	
Males.	Females.	Males.	Females.	Males.	Females.	Males.	Females.	Males.	Females.	Males.	Females.	Males.	Females.	Males.	Females.	Males.	Females.
1	5	7	5	25	2	32	1	8	3	5	...	1	...	1	...	...	...
1	7	14	19	21	14	14	8	16	3	8	...	2	...	2	...	1	...
...	...	1	2	...	...	1	...	...	1	2	...	2	...	...	...	...	...
20	29	61	54	73	17	49	10	42	13	30	7	20	5	10	...	8	2
1	1	3	1	8	3	1	...	4	...	1	...	1	...	...	...	...	...
...	2	2	...	2	...	2	1	1	...	...	...	1	...	...	...	...	...
...	...	...	...	1	...	...	...	...	...	...	...	...	...	...	...	...	...
...	1	1	...	...	...	...	...	...	...	1	...	...	...	...	...	1	...
1	...	...	...	1	...	...	1	1	...	1	...	...	...	...	...	...	...
68	177	141	212	165	174	124	92	136	102	82	32	82	36	31	15	81	15
...	...	1	...	...	...	...	...	...	...	...	...	...	...	...	...	...	...
...	...	...	...	...	...	...	...	...	...	...	...	...	...	...	...	...	...
1	...	...	...	2	...	...	...	1	...	...	...	...	...	...	...	...	...
...	...	...	...	...	...	...	...	...	...	...	...	...	...	...	...	...	...
...	...	...	...	...	...	...	...	...	...	...	...	...	...	...	...	...	...
...	1	1	1	...	1	2	...	...	...	...	...	...	...	...	...	...	...
42	71	53	61	51	43	35	17	25	23	21	11	25	10	7	3	25	2
7	6	12	15	16	13	11	10	19	5	9	3	12	3	4	...	4	1
...	...	...	...	...	...	...	...	...	...	...	...	...	...	...	...	...	...
...	...	...	...	...	1	...	...	1	...	...	...	...	...	...	...	...	...
142	**300**	**297**	**370**	**365**	**268**	**271**	**140**	**254**	**150**	**160**	**53**	**146**	**54**	**55**	**18**	**120**	**20**

Christian.

OWED.

20 — 24.		25 — 29.		30 — 34.		35 — 39.		40 — 44.		45 — 49.		50 — 54.		55 — 59.		60 and over.	
Males.	Females.	Males.	Females.	Males.	Females.	Males.	Females.	Males.	Females.	Males.	Females.	Males.	Females.	Males.	Females.	Males.	Females.
...	...	...	...	1	1	1	1	1	...	...	...	...	...	...	...	...	1
...	...	...	...	...	...	1	...	1	3	...	...	1	2	1	1	1	2
...	...	...	...	...	...	...	...	1	...	...	...	...	...	...	...	...	...
1	...	...	1	5	1	1	2	1	3	2	2	2	7	2	2	6	8
...	...	...	...	...	...	...	...	...	...	...	...	...	...	...	...	...	...
...	...	...	...	...	...	...	...	...	1	...	...	...	...	1	...	...	...
...	...	...	...	...	...	...	...	...	...	...	...	...	...	...	...	...	...
...	...	...	...	...	...	1	...	...	...	...	...	...	...	...	...	...	...
...	...	...	...	...	...	...	...	...	...	...	...	...	...	...	...	...	...
1	5	6	20	1	48	1	26	4	62	5	31	5	58	4	25	25	124
...	...	...	...	...	...	...	...	...	...	...	...	...	...	...	...	...	...
...	...	...	...	...	...	...	...	...	...	...	...	...	...	...	...	...	...
...	...	...	...	...	...	...	...	...	...	...	...	1	...	...	...	...	...
...	...	...	...	...	...	...	...	...	...	...	...	...	...	...	...	...	...
...	...	...	...	...	...	...	...	...	...	...	...	...	...	...	...	...	...
...	...	...	...	...	...	...	...	...	...	...	...	...	...	...	...	1	...
...	1	...	7	...	11	2	10	2	13	...	6	5	23	2	6	7	39
...	...	...	3	...	1	...	2	2	4	...	2	1	4	1	3	2	3
...	...	...	...	...	...	...	...	...	...	...	...	...	...	...	...	...	...
...	...	...	...	...	...	...	...	...	...	...	...	...	...	...	...	...	...
2	**6**	**6**	**31**	**7**	**62**	**7**	**41**	**12**	**86**	**7**	**41**	**15**	**94**	**11**	**37**	**42**	**172**

Table VIII.

Civil Condition by Religion and Age.

TABLE

Part (E).—

(1) UN

State.	Total. Total.	Total. Males.	Total. Females.	0 – 4. Males.	0 – 4. Females.	5 – 9. Males.	5 – 9. Females.	10 – 14. Males.	10 – 14. Females.	15 – 19. Males.	15 – 19. Females.
Cutch	1	1	...	...	...	...	...	...	...	...	...

Part (F).—

(1) UN

State.	Total. Total.	Total. Males.	Total. Females.	0 – 4. Males.	0 – 4. Females.	5 – 9. Males.	5 – 9. Females.	10 – 14. Males.	10 – 14. Females.	15 – 19. Males.	15 – 19. Females.
Cutch	30,607	16,925	13,682	4,844	5,177	4,871	4,991	3,585	3,099	1,499	279
Pálanpur	12,913	7,882	5,031	1,733	1,853	1,693	1,697	1,604	1,305	916	128
Mahi Kántha	5,764	3,501	2,263	754	778	794	796	769	624	432	37
Káthiáwár...	51,290	31,023	20,267	7,283	7,475	7,417	7,332	6,437	4,733	3,815	508
Rewa Kántha	482	342	140	67	59	68	52	68	26	43	1
Cambay	997	587	410	177	193	174	139	96	71	44	2
Surat Agency	63	42	21	15	1	4	15	5	4	6	1
Jawhár	1	1	...	...	...	...	...	...	...	...	...
Janjira	39	37	2	1	1	1	1	8	...	16	...
Sáwantwádi	59	40	19	12	11	4	5	8	2	7	.
The Dángs	1	1	...	...	...	...	...	...	...	...	...
Surgana	...	...	...	...	...	...	...	...	...	...	...
Bhor	207	135	72	28	45	23	23	24	4	19	...
Akalkot	192	123	69	34	31	27	23	26	14	10	...
Sátára Agency	526	342	184	83	66	70	76	69	39	44	1
Jat	99	69	30	17	17	27	12	10	1	9	...
Kolhápur	15,286	10,061	5,225	3,189	3,049	2,966	1,778	2,354	348	833	13
Southern Marátha Jaghírs ...	8,817	5,689	3,128	2,003	1,837	1,709	1,102	1,158	157	434	6
Sáwanúr	9	6	3	1	2	1	1	1	...	...	...
Khairpur	...	...	...	...	...	...	...	...	...	...	...
Total, Feudatory States.	**127,352**	**76,806**	**50,546**	**20,241**	**20,595**	**19,849**	**18,043**	**16,222**	**10,427**	**8,127**	**976**

Part (F).—

(2) MAR

State.	Total. Total.	Total. Males.	Total. Females.	0 – 4. Males.	0 – 4. Females.	5 – 9. Males.	5 – 9. Females.	10 – 14. Males.	10 – 14. Females.	15 – 19. Males.	15 – 19. Females.
Cutch	32,334	14,980	17,354	38	49	50	122	264	766	945	2,461
Pálanpur	12,320	6,117	6,203	10	18	19	38	55	123	402	931
Mahi Kántha	5,696	2,796	2,900	6	10	11	12	62	121	186	470
Káthiáwár	48,858	24,213	24,645	47	79	107	153	398	993	1,646	3,674
Rewa Kántha	611	320	291	...	2	...	...	4	12	24	52
Cambay	1,755	888	867	5	6	20	13	47	69	89	112
Surat Agency	49	26	23	...	...	...	..	...	3	...	2
Jawhár	2	2	...	...	...	...	...	...	...	...	...
Janjira	29	24	5	...	...	...	...	..	2	1	1
Sáwantwádi	66	33	33	...	...	...	...	...	2	4	5
The Dángs	...	...	...	...	...	...	...	...	...	...	...
Surgana	...	...	...	...	...	...	...	..	...	...	...
Bhor	372	191	181	1	1	1	16	13	21	15	34
Akalkot	251	125	126	...	1	4	8	4	13	6	18
Sátára Agency	541	259	282	...	1	...	4	1	17	3	58
Jat	179	88	91	...	3	3	8	2	15	8	10
Kolhápur	29,375	15,289	14,086	44	204	169	1,305	727	2,056	1,147	1,527
Southern Marátha Jaghírs ...	15,798	7,650	8,148	23	119	96	717	347	1,120	816	870
Sáwanúr	4	1	3	...	...	...	...	...	...	...	...
Khairpur	...	...	..	...	...	...	...	...	...	...	...
Total, Feudatory States.	**148,240**	**73,002**	**75,238**	**174**	**493**	**480**	**2,396**	**1,924**	**5,333**	**5,092**	**10,225**

Table VIII.

Civil Condition by Religion and Age.

VIII.

Buddhist.

MARRIED.

20—24.		25—29.		30—34.		35—39.		40—44.		45—49.		50—54.		55—59.		60 and over.	
Males.	Females.	Males.	Females.	Males.	Females.	Males.	Females.	Males.	Females.	Males.	Females.	Males.	Females.	Males.	Females.	Males.	Females.
...	...	1	...	...	...	...	...	...	...	...	...	...	...	...	..	...	...

Jain.

MARRIED.

20—24.		25—29.		30—34.		35—39.		40—44.		45—49.		50—54.		55—59.		60 and over.	
Males.	Females.	Males.	Females.	Males.	Females.	Males.	Females.	Males.	Females.	Males.	Females.	Males.	Females.	Males.	Females.	Males.	Females.
781	*34*	429	*27*	264	*23*	159	*14*	133	*18*	82	*4*	91	*7*	55	*3*	132	*6*
610	*16*	417	*14*	284	*5*	177	*4*	155	*3*	82	*1*	96	*1*	42	*2*	73	*2*
271	*11*	169	*2*	94	*3*	55	*2*	50	*4*	48	*1*	24	*4*	18	...	23	*1*
2,529	*63*	1,415	*50*	766	*36*	426	*22*	350	*28*	175	*6*	186	*8*	71	*1*	153	*5*
23	*1*	27	...	18	...	7	*1*	7	...	5	...	4	...	3	...	2	...
43	...	15	*2*	14	...	12	*1*	5	*1*	3	...	1	*1*	2	...	1	...
5	...	1	...	2	...	2	...	1	...	...	...	1	...	...	...	..	...
1	...	...	...	...	..	...	...	...	...	...	...	...	...	...	...	...	...
6	...	4	...	1	...	...	...	...	...	...	...	...	...	...	...	...	...
3	...	1	...	2	...	...	*1*	1	...	1	...	...	...	...	...	1	...
1	...	...	...	...	...	...	...	...	...	...	...	...	...	...	...	...	...
...	...	..	...	...	...	...	...	...	...	...	...	...	...	...	...	...	...
13	...	8	...	7	...	5	...	3	...	1	...	2	...	2	...	...	...
9	...	6	...	3	...	...	*1*	3	...	...	...	1	...	2	...	2	...
26	...	14	...	7	*1*	5	...	11	...	4	*1*	3	...	1	...	5	...
1	...	2	...	1	...	...	...	2	...	...	...	...	...	...	...	...	...
327	*6*	159	*6*	62	*6*	53	*4*	39	*9*	25	*5*	25	...	13	*1*	16	...
188	*6*	96	*6*	43	*6*	23	*1*	13	*5*	6	...	7	...	3	*2*	6	...
1	...	1	...	...	...	...	...	1	...	...	...	...	...	...	...	...	...
...	...	...	...	...	...	...	...	...	...	...	...	...	...	...	...	...	...
4.838	**137**	**2.764**	**107**	**1.568**	**80**	**924**	**51**	**774**	**68**	**432**	**18**	**441**	**21**	**212**	**9**	**414**	**14**

Jain.

RIED.

20—24.		25—29.		30—34.		35—39.		40—44.		45—49.		50—54.		55—59.		60 and over.	
Males.	Females.	Males.	Females.	Males.	Females.	Males.	Females.	Males.	Females.	Males.	Females.	Males.	Females.	Males.	Females.	Males.	Females.
1,643	*3,099*	1,861	*2,861*	2,159	*2,423*	1,638	*1,458*	1,762	*1,580*	1,014	*694*	1,459	*903*	656	*365*	1,491	*573*
777	*1,187*	851	*1,018*	884	*958*	752	*601*	736	*575*	519	*306*	483	*259*	254	*84*	375	*110*
382	*667*	412	*486*	420	*388*	351	*261*	303	*236*	213	*106*	220	*86*	87	*25*	143	*33*
3,332	*5,083*	3,767	*4,151*	3,593	*3,609*	2,936	*2,217*	2,837	*2,235*	1,788	*919*	1,769	*858*	656	*259*	1,337	*420*
42	*57*	42	*48*	52	*45*	31	*24*	49	*24*	26	*10*	24	*9*	13	*2*	13	*6*
113	*172*	109	*117*	113	*104*	101	*98*	97	*70*	54	*44*	67	*32*	31	*11*	42	*19*
3	*1*	4	*4*	3	*9*	6	*4*	3	...	3	...	4	...	...	...	...	...
...	...	...	...	1	...	1	...	...	...	...	...	...	...	...	...	...	...
8	*1*	5	...	3	...	4	*1*	...	...	...	...	1	...	1	...	1	...
2	*9*	6	*4*	4	*4*	2	*3*	2	*3*	2	...	5	*1*	1	...	5	*2*
...	...	...	...	...	...	...	...	...	...	...	...	...	...	...	...	...	...
...	...	...	...	...	...	...	...	...	...	...	...	...	...	...	...	...	...
24	*30*	33	*28*	29	*17*	21	*10*	15	*12*	14	*7*	11	*3*	6	*1*	8	*1*
17	*29*	14	*13*	20	*13*	9	*12*	14	*14*	16	*3*	9	*2*	4	...	8	...
33	*42*	36	*46*	42	*40*	27	*14*	40	*25*	16	*15*	28	*12*	10	*5*	23	*3*
10	*9*	15	*13*	8	*14*	9	*7*	10	*7*	7	*3*	8	*2*	3	...	5	...
1,641	*1,721*	2,246	*1,906*	2,155	*1,870*	1,707	*1,082*	1,741	*1,130*	1,039	*523*	1,138	*440*	477	*147*	1,058	*175*
785	*1,043*	1,087	*1,182*	1,021	*1,069*	840	*630*	931	*674*	492	*268*	613	*266*	201	*68*	598	*122*
...	*1*	...	*1*	1	...	...	*1*	...	...	...	...	..	...	...	...	...	...
...	...	...	...	...	...	...	...	...	...	...	...	...	...	...	...	...	...
8,812	**13,151**	**10,488**	**11,873**	**10,508**	**10,563**	**8,435**	**6,423**	**8,540**	**6,585**	**5,203**	**2,898**	**5,839**	**2,867**	**2,400**	**967**	**5,107**	**1,464**

TABLE

Part (F).—

(3) WID

State.	Total. Total.	Total. Males.	Total. Females.	0—4. Males.	0—4. Females.	5—9. Males.	5—9. Females.	10—14. Males.	10—14. Females.	15—19. Males.	15—19. Females.
Cutch	9,047	2,450	*6,597*	...	*1*	3	...	5	*7*	9	*58*
Pálanpur	3,916	897	*3,019*	...	*1*	...	*1*	...	*6*	15	*19*
Mahi Kántha	2,358	393	*1,965*	...	...	2	*1*	1	*5*	5	*24*
Káthiáwár	12,857	3,143	*9,714*	6	*6*	9	*9*	10	*17*	37	*94*
Rewa Kántha	215	59	*156*	...	...	...	...	...	..	...	*2*
Cambay	510	103	*407*	...	*1*	2	*2*	...	*3*	2	*5*
Surat Agency	14	1	*13*	...	...	...	...	...	...	...	...
Jawhár	1	1	...	...	...	...	...	...	...	...	...
Janjira	3	1	*2*	...	...	...	...	...	...	...	...
Sáwantwádi	22	3	*19*	...	...	...	...	...	...	...	...
The Dángs	...	..	...	...	...	...	...	...	...	...	...
Surgana	...	...	...	...	...	...	...	...	...	...	...
Bhor	101	30	*71*	...	...	...	...	...	*2*	...	...
Akalkot	65	20	*45*	...	...	...	...	1	*1*	1	*1*
Sátára Agency	229	71	*158*	...	...	...	...	..	...	..	*5*
Jat	38	4	*34*	...	...	...	...	1	...	1	...
Kolhápur	6,235	1,600	*4,635*	...	*1*	9	*10*	37	*53*	37	*48*
Southern Marátha Jaghírs ...	3,568	811	*2,757*	...	*1*	6	*5*	13	*28*	16	*33*
Sáwanúr	2	1	*1*	...	...	...	...	...	...	..	...
Khairpur	...	...	...	...	...	...	...	...	...	...	...
Total, Feudatory States.	**39,181**	**9,586**	**29,593**	**6**	**11**	**31**	**28**	**68**	**122**	**123**	**289**

Part (G).—

(1) UN

State.	Total. Total.	Total. Males.	Total. Females.	0—4. Males.	0—4. Females.	5—9. Males.	5—9. Females.	10—14. Males.	10—14. Females.	15—19. Males.	15—19. Females.
Cutch	48	43	*5*	1		2	*2*	3	...	1	...

Part (G).—

(2) MAR

State.	Total. Total.	Total. Males.	Total. Females.	0—4. Males.	0—4. Females.	5—9. Males.	5—9. Females.	10—14. Males.	10—14. Females.	15—19. Males.	15—19. Females.
Cutch	42	35	*7*	...	...	..	...	..	*1*	1	*1*

Part (G).—

(3) WID

State.	Total. Total.	Total. Males.	Total. Females.	0—4. Males.	0—4. Females.	5—9. Males.	5—9. Females.	10—14. Males.	10—14. Females.	15—19. Males.	15—19. Females.
Cutch	4	3	*1*	...	...	...	...	...	...	...	...

Part (H).—

(1) UN

State.	Total. Total.	Total. Males.	Total. Females.	0—4. Males.	0—4. Females.	5—9. Males.	5—9. Females.	10—14. Males.	10—14. Females.	15—19. Males.	15—19. Females.
Cutch	64	38	*26*	11	*9*	4	*12*	12	*5*	8	...
Pálanpur	95	44	*51*	13	*10*	10	*18*	13	*16*	6	*5*
Mahi Kántha	6	4	*2*	1	*2*	1	...	...	...	...	...
Káthiáwár	430	249	*181*	53	*59*	70	*50*	41	*43*	34	*21*
Rewa Kántha	152	86	*66*	28	*26*	17	*24*	17	*11*	13	*4*
Cambay	65	35	*30*	7	*7*	9	*9*	10	*10*	6	*4*
Surat Agency	226	124	*102*	40	*84*	27	*45*	30	*16*	5	*3*
Jawhár	20	13	*7*	4	*2*	2	*4*	3	*1*	1	...
Janjira	...	...	...	...	...	...	...	...	...	...	...
Sáwantwádi	...	...	...	...	...	...	...	...	...	...	...
The Dángs	5	2	*3*	...	*2*	...	*1*	1	...	1	...
Surgana	5	1	*4*	...	...	...	*2*	1	...	...	*1*
Bhor	1	1	...	...	...	...	...	...	...	...	...
Akalkot	...	...	...	...	...	...	...	...	...	...	...
Sátára Agency	...	...	...	...	...	...	...	...	...	...	...
Jat	...	...	...	...	...	...	...	...	...	...	...
Kolhápur	13	6	*7*	...	*3*	2	*1*	2	*2*	1	*1*
Southern Marátha Jaghírs ...	4	3	*1*	2	...	...	*1*	1	...	...	...
Sáwanúr	...	...	...	...	...	...	...	..	...	...	...
Khairpur	...	...	...	...	...	...	...	...	...	...	...
Total, Feudatory States.	**1,086**	**606**	**480**	**159**	**154**	**142**	**167**	**131**	**104**	**75**	**39**

Jain.

OWED.

20—24 Males	20—24 Females	25—29 Males	25—29 Females	30—34 Males	30—34 Females	35—39 Males	35—39 Females	40—44 Males	40—44 Females	45—49 Males	45—49 Females	50—54 Males	50—54 Females	55—59 Males	55—59 Females	60 and over Males	60 and over Females
33	*204*	65	*362*	123	*541*	147	*531*	225	*829*	192	*439*	365	*1,079*	236	*375*	1,047	*2,171*
27	*81*	40	*142*	72	*254*	81	*255*	113	*489*	85	*305*	112	*516*	91	*198*	261	*752*
17	*74*	20	*130*	28	*192*	31	*204*	52	*326*	44	*186*	66	*314*	83	*130*	94	*379*
92	*296*	131	*506*	196	*815*	248	*867*	396	*1,531*	332	*866*	524	*1,619*	272	*529*	890	*2,559*
5	*3*	2	*9*	2	*13*	5	*14*	12	*26*	10	*7*	9	*30*	2	*13*	12	*39*
4	*9*	8	*17*	7	*30*	5	*32*	11	*66*	16	*40*	13	*69*	9	*34*	28	*99*
...	...	...	...	...	*2*	...	*2*	...	*1*	..	*2*	1	*3*	...	...	...	*3*
...	...	...	...	1	...	...	...	...	...	...	...	...	...	...	...	...	...
...	...	...	...	...	...	...	...	...	...	...	...	1	...	...	*1*	...	*1*
...	...	...	*1*	...	*2*	...	...	...	*3*	...	*3*	...	*3*	1	*2*	2	*5*
...	...	...	...	..	...	...	...	...	...	..	...	...	...	...	...	...	...
...	...	...	...	...	...	...	...	...	...	...	...	...	...	...	...	...	...
2	*2*	3	*7*	3	*2*	2	*2*	2	*12*	2	*4*	5	*17*	4	*6*	7	*17*
...	*1*	...	*1*	...	*3*	1	*6*	2	*5*	2	*4*	4	*8*	3	*6*	6	*9*
1	*5*	4	*10*	3	*18*	6	*13*	10	*17*	7	*17*	13	*23*	6	*12*	21	*38*
...	*1*	...	*1*	1	...	..	...	...	*7*	...	*5*	...	*8*	...	*5*	1	*7*
70	*81*	100	*165*	117	*270*	120	*320*	186	*589*	146	*438*	185	*719*	116	*307*	477	*1,634*
22	*56*	46	*95*	53	*171*	52	*173*	102	*371*	58	*194*	113	*460*	39	*189*	291	*981*
...	...	...	...	...	...	...	...	...	...	...	...	1	...	...	...	...	*1*
...	...	...	...	...	...	...	...	...	...	...	...	...	...	...	...	...	...
273	**813**	**419**	**1.446**	**606**	**2.313**	**698**	**2.419**	**1.111**	**4.272**	**894**	**2.510**	**1.412**	**4.868**	**812**	**1.807**	**3.135**	**8.695**

Sikh.

MARRIED.

20—24 Males	20—24 Females	25—29 Males	25—29 Females	30—34 Males	30—34 Females	35—39 Males	35—39 Females	40—44 Males	40—44 Females	45—49 Males	45—49 Females	50—54 Males	50—54 Females	55—59 Males	55—59 Females	60 and over Males	60 and over Females
19	*1*	7	..	2	...	3	...	...	...	...	...	4	...	...	...	1	...

Sikh.

RIED.

20—24 Males	20—24 Females	25—29 Males	25—29 Females	30—34 Males	30—34 Females	35—39 Males	35—39 Females	40—44 Males	40—44 Females	45—49 Males	45—49 Females	50—54 Males	50—54 Females	55—59 Males	55—59 Females	60 and over Males	60 and over Females
7	...	10	*2*	4	*2*	3	...	5	...	4	...	1	*1*	...	...	...	...

Sikh.

OWED.

20—24 Males	20—24 Females	25—29 Males	25—29 Females	30—34 Males	30—34 Females	35—39 Males	35—39 Females	40—44 Males	40—44 Females	45—49 Males	45—49 Females	50—54 Males	50—54 Females	55—59 Males	55—59 Females	60 and over Males	60 and over Females
1	...	2	...	..	...	...	...	...	...	...	...	...	...	...	...	...	*1*

Pársi.

MARRIED.

20—24 Males	20—24 Females	25—29 Males	25—29 Females	30—34 Males	30—34 Females	35—39 Males	35—39 Females	40—44 Males	40—44 Females	45—49 Males	45—49 Females	50—54 Males	50—54 Females	55—59 Males	55—59 Females	60 and over Males	60 and over Females
3	...	...	..	...	...	...	...	...	...	...	...	...	...	...	...	...	...
2	*1*	...	*1*	...	...	...	...	...	...	...	...	...	...	...	...	...	...
...	...	1	...	...	...	1	...	...	...	...	...	...	...	...	...	...	...
38	*7*	9	*1*	2	...	2	...	...	...	...	...	...	...	...	...	...	...
4	...	5	...	...	...	1	*1*	1	...	...	...	...	...	...	...	...	...
...	...	...	...	3	...	...	...	...	...	...	...	...	...	...	...	...	...
10	*1*	5	...	2	*1*	...	*1*	1	*1*	1	...	...	...	2	...	1	...
2	...	...	...	1	...	...	...	...	...	...	...	...	...	...	...	...	...
...	...	...	...	...	...	...	...	...	...	...	...	...	...	...	...	...	...
...	...	...	...	...	...	...	...	...	...	...	...	...	...	...	...	...	...
...	..	...	...	...	...	...	...	...	...	...	...	...	...	...	...	...	...
...	*1*	...	...	...	...	...	...	...	..	...	...	...	...	...	...	...	...
...	...	...	...	1	...	...	...	...	...	...	...	...	...	...	...	...	...
...	...	...	...	...	...	...	...	...	...	...	...	...	...	...	...	...	...
...	...	...	...	...	...	...	...	...	..	...	...	...	...	...	...	...	...
...	...	...	..	...	...	...	...	...	...	...	...	...	...	...	...	...	...
...	...	1	...	...	...	...	...	...	...	...	...	...	...	...	...	...	...
...	...	...	...	...	...	...	...	...	...	...	...	...	...	...	...	...	...
...	...	...	...	...	...	...	...	...	...	...	...	...	...	...	...	...	...
...	...	...	...	...	...	...	...	...	...	...	...	...	...	...	...	...	...
59	**10**	**21**	**2**	**9**	**1**	**4**	**2**	**2**	**1**	**1**	...	...	...	**2**	...	**1**	...

Civil Condition by Religion and Age.

TABLE

Part (H).—

(2) MAR

State.	TOTAL.			0—4.		5—9.		10—14.		15—19.	
	Total.	Males.	Females.	Males.	Females.	Males.	Females.	Males.	Females.	Males.	Females.
Cutch	53	25	*28*	...	...	...	...	...	...	...	*2*
Pálanpur	93	49	*44*	...	...	...	...	...	...	...	*2*
Mahi Kántha	2	1	*1*	...	...	...	...	...	...	...	...
Káthiáwár	439	268	*171*	...	...	...	*3*	2	*5*	6	*13*
Rewa Kántha	203	129	*74*	...	*1*	...	...	2	*1*	6	*7*
Cambay	61	30	*31*	...	*1*	...	...	...	...	1	*2*
Surat Agency	333	206	*127*	...	...	...	...	1	*9*	9	*18*
Jawhár	23	17	*6*	...	...	...	...	...	...	...	...
Janjira	...	...	...	...	...	...	...	...	...	...	...
Sáwantwádi	...	...	...	...	...	...	...	...	...	...	...
The Dángs	14	11	*3*	...	...	...	...	...	...	...	*1*
Surgana	18	15	*3*	...	...	...	...	...	...	...	...
Bhor	...	...	...	...	...	...	...	...	...	...	...
Akalkot	...	...	...	...	...	...	...	...	...	...	...
Sátára Agency	...	...	...	...	...	...	...	...	...	...	...
Jat	...	...	...	...	...	...	...	...	...	...	...
Kolhápur	10	6	*4*	...	...	...	...	...	...	...	...
Southern Marátha Jaghirs	7	4	*3*	...	...	...	...	1	...	...	...
Sáwanúr	...	...	...	...	...	...	...	...	...	...	...
Khairpur	...	...	...	...	...	...	...	...	...	...	...
Total, Feudatory States	**1,256**	**761**	**495**	...	**2**	...	**3**	**6**	**15**	**22**	**45**

Part (H).—

(3) WID

State.	Total.	Males.	Females.	0—4 Males.	0—4 Females.	5—9 Males.	5—9 Females.	10—14 Males.	10—14 Females.	15—19 Males.	15—19 Females.
Cutch	1	1	...	...	...	...	...	...	...	...	...
Pálanpur	17	3	*14*	...	...	...	...	...	...	...	*1*
Mahi Kántha	...	...	...	...	...	...	...	...	...	...	...
Káthiáwár	39	7	*32*	...	...	...	*1*	...	...	...	...
Rewa Kántha	31	13	*18*	...	...	...	...	...	...	...	...
Cambay	11	3	*8*	...	...	...	...	...	...	...	...
Surat Agency	59	22	*37*	...	...	...	...	...	*1*	...	...
Jawhár	3	1	*2*	...	...	...	...	...	...	...	...
Janjira	...	...	...	...	...	...	...	...	...	...	...
Sáwantwádi	...	...	...	...	...	...	...	...	...	...	...
The Dángs	1	1	...	...	...	...	...	...	...	...	...
Surgana	5	3	*2*	...	...	...	...	...	...	...	...
Bhor	...	...	...	...	...	...	...	...	...	...	...
Akalkot	...	...	...	...	...	...	...	...	...	...	...
Sátára Agency	...	...	...	...	...	...	...	...	...	...	...
Jat	...	...	...	...	...	...	...	...	...	...	...
Kolhápur	1	...	*1*	...	...	...	...	...	...	...	...
Southern Marátha Jaghirs	1	1	...	...	...	...	...	...	...	...	...
Sáwanúr	...	...	...	...	...	...	...	...	...	...	...
Khairpur	...	...	...	...	...	...	...	...	...	...	...
Total, Feudatory States	**169**	**55**	**114**	...	...	...	**1**	...	**1**	...	**1**

VIII.

Pársi.

RIED.

20 — 24.		25 — 29.		30 — 34.		35 — 39.		40 — 44.		45 — 49.		50 — 54.		55 — 59.		60 and over.	
Males.	Females.	Males.	Females.	Males.	Females.	Males.	Females.	Males.	Females.	Males.	Females.	Males.	Females.	Males.	Females.	Males.	Females.
...	*4*	3	*6*	4	*6*	4	...	4	*1*	1	*3*	2	*1*	4	*1*	3	*4*
4	*10*	10	*8*	9	*7*	6	*7*	6	*5*	6	*1*	3	*1*	4	*2*	1	*1*
...	*1*	1	...	...	...	...	...	...	...	...	...	...	...	...	...	...	...
27	*34*	41	*31*	46	*28*	45	*19*	30	*18*	30	*13*	16	*3*	9	*2*	16	*2*
18	*13*	17	*16*	21	*12*	20	*15*	17	*5*	12	*1*	5	...	3	*1*	8	*2*
2	*5*	4	*6*	6	*4*	3	*5*	2	*2*	1	*2*	5	*1*	1	...	5	*3*
22	*19*	21	*19*	21	*19*	36	*6*	25	*18*	24	*13*	15	*4*	9	...	23	*2*
1	...	3	*2*	3	*1*	1	*1*	4	*2*	2	...	1	...	1	...	1	...
...	...	...	...	...	...	...	...	...	...	...	...	...	...	...	...	...	...
...	...	...	...	...	...	...	...	...	...	...	...	...	...	...	...	...	...
2	...	2	...	2	*2*	1	...	2	...	1	...	1	...	...	...	...	—
...	...	4	...	3	*2*	1	*1*	2	...	5	...	...	...	...	...	...	...
...	...	...	...	...	...	...	...	...	...	...	...	...	...	...	...	...	...
...	...	...	...	...	...	...	...	...	...	...	...	...	...	...	...	...	...
...	...	...	...	...	...	...	...	...	...	...	...	...	...	...	...	...	...
...	...	...	...	...	...	...	...	...	...	...	...	...	...	...	...	...	...
...	...	1	...	...	*1*	2	*2*	2	*1*	...	...	1	...	...	...	...	...
...	*1*	1	*1*	...	*1*	...	...	1	...	...	...	...	...	1	...	...	...
...	...	...	...	...	...	...	...	...	...	...	...	...	...	...	...	...	...
...	...	...	...	...	...	...	...	...	...	...	...	...	...	...	...	...	...
76	**87**	**108**	**89**	**115**	**83**	**119**	**56**	**95**	**52**	**82**	**33**	**49**	**10**	**32**	**6**	**57**	**14**

Pársi.

OWED.

20 — 24.		25 — 29.		30 — 34.		35 — 39.		40 — 44.		45 — 49.		50 — 54.		55 — 59.		60 and over.	
Males.	Females.	Males.	Females.	Males.	Females.	Males.	Females.	Males.	Females.	Males.	Females.	Males.	Females.	Males.	Females.	Males.	Females.
...	...	...	...	...	...	...	...	...	...	...	...	...	...	1	...	...	...
...	...	...	...	...	...	...	*2*	...	*3*	...	*2*	2	*1*	...	*1*	1	*4*
...	...	...	...	...	...	...	...	...	...	...	...	...	...	...	...	...	...
3	...	...	*3*	1	*1*	...	*4*	...	*1*	...	*3*	1	*7*	...	*2*	2	*10*
2	...	1	*2*	4	...	...	...	1	*4*	2	*1*	2	*4*	...	*1*	1	*6*
...	...	...	...	...	...	...	*1*	...	*1*	...	*1*	1	*2*	...	...	2	*3*
1	*1*	2	*3*	1	*1*	1	*1*	...	*3*	2	*3*	3	*5*	2	*4*	10	*15*
...	...	...	...	1	...	...	...	...	*1*	...	*1*	...	...	...	...	...	...
...	...	...	...	...	...	...	...	...	...	...	...	...	...	...	...	...	...
...	...	...	...	...	...	...	...	...	...	...	...	...	...	...	...	...	...
...	...	1	...	...	...	...	...	...	...	...	...	...	...	...	...	...	...
...	...	...	*1*	...	...	...	...	...	...	2	...	...	...	1	...	...	*1*
...	...	...	...	...	...	...	...	...	...	...	...	...	...	...	...	...	...
...	...	...	...	...	...	...	...	...	...	...	...	...	...	...	...	...	...
...	...	...	...	...	...	...	...	...	...	...	...	...	...	...	...	...	...
...	...	...	...	...	...	...	...	...	...	...	...	...	...	...	...	...	...
...	...	...	...	...	...	...	*1*	...	...	...	...	...	...	...	...	...	...
...	...	...	...	1	...	...	...	...	...	...	...	...	...	...	...	...	...
...	...	...	...	...	...	...	...	...	...	...	...	...	...	...	...	...	...
...	...	...	...	...	...	...	...	...	...	...	...	...	...	...	...	...	...
6	**1**	**4**	**9**	**8**	**2**	**1**	**9**	**1**	**13**	**6**	**11**	**9**	**19**	**4**	**8**	**16**	**39**

Table VIII.

Civil Condition by Religion and Age.

TABLE

Part (I).—

(1) UN

State.	Total. Total	Total. Males.	Total. Females.	0—4. Males.	0—4. Females.	5—9. Males.	5—9. Females.	10—14. Males.	10—14. Females.	15—19. Males.	15—19. Females.
Cutch	23	14	*9*	7	*1*	3	*7*	...	...	2	...
Pálanpur	16	8	*8*	3	*2*	...	*1*	1	*3*	2	*1*
Mahi Kántha	2	2	...	1	...	1	...	...	...	...	...
Káthiáwár	64	34	*30*	8	*10*	10	*9*	9	*8*	2	*3*
Rewa Kántha	1	1	...	1	...	...	...	...	...	...	...
Cámbay	...	...	...	...	...	...	...	...	...	...	...
Surat Agency	2	1	*1*	...	*1*	...	...	1	...	...	...
Jawhár	...	...	...	...	...	...	...	...	...	...	...
Janjira	269	145	*124*	46	*62*	49	*43*	31	*16*	12	*3*
Sáwantwádi	...	...	...	...	...	...	...	...	...	...	...
The Dangs	...	...	...	...	...	...	...	...	...	...	...
Surgana	...	...	...	...	...	...	...	...	...	...	...
Bhor	114	73	*41*	26	*15*	15	*15*	13	*9*	9	*1*
Akalkot	...	...	...	...	...	...	...	...	...	...	...
Sátára Agency	3	1	*2*	...	...	...	*1*	...	...	1	...
Jat	...	...	...	...	...	...	...	...	...	...	...
Kolhápur	...	...	...	...	...	...	...	...	...	...	...
Southern Marátha Jaghírs ...	4	1	*3*	...	*1*	...	*2*	1	...	...	...
Sáwanúr	...	...	...	...	...	...	...	...	...	...	...
Khairpur	...	...	...	...	...	...	...	...	...	...	...
Total, Feudatory States...	**498**	**280**	**218**	**92**	**92**	**78**	**78**	**56**	**36**	**28**	**8**

Part (I).—

(2) MAR

State.	Total. Total	Total. Males.	Total. Females.	0—4. Males.	0—4. Females.	5—9. Males.	5—9. Females.	10—14. Males.	10—14. Females.	15—19. Males.	15—19. Females.
Cutch	22	12	*10*	...	...	...	...	...	...	...	*1*
Pálanpur	17	10	*7*	...	...	...	...	...	...	...	*2*
Mahi Kántha	2	1	*1*	...	...	...	...	...	...	...	...
Káthiáwár	32	17	*15*	...	...	...	...	...	...	...	*2*
Rewa Kántha	5	3	*2*	...	...	...	...	...	...	...	...
Cambay	...	...	...	...	...	...	...	...	...	...	...
Surat Agency	4	2	*2*	...	...	...	...	...	...	...	...
Jawhár	...	...	...	...	...	...	...	...	...	...	...
Janjira	274	126	*148*	...	...	...	*5*	...	*13*	8	*14*
Sáwantwádi	...	...	...	...	...	...	...	...	...	...	...
The Dangs	...	...	...	...	...	...	...	...	...	...	...
Surgana	...	...	...	...	...	...	...	...	...	...	...
Bhor	142	67	*75*	...	...	...	*3*	2	*9*	4	*14*
Akalkot	...	...	...	...	...	...	...	...	...	...	...
Sátára Agency	1	1	...	...	...	...	...	...	...	...	...
Jat	...	...	...	...	...	...	...	...	...	...	...
Kolhápur	...	...	...	...	...	...	...	...	...	...	...
Southern Marátha Jaghírs	2	1	*1*	...	...	...	...	...	...	...	...
Sáwanúr	...	...	...	...	...	...	...	...	...	...	...
Khairpur	...	...	...	...	...	...	...	...	...	...	...
Total, Feudatory States...	**501**	**240**	**261**	...	...	...	**8**	**2**	**22**	**12**	**33**

Table VIII.

Civil Condition by Religion and Age.

VIII.

Jew.

MARRIED.

20 — 24.		25 — 29.		30 — 34.		35 — 39.		40 — 44.		45 — 49.		50 — 54.		55 — 59.		60 and over.	
Males.	Females.	Males.	Females.	Males.	Females.	Males.	Females.	Males.	Females.	Males.	Females.	Males.	Females.	Males.	Females.	Males.	Females.
1	...	...	...	...	...	...	...	...	...	...	...	...	...	...	...	1	*1*
2	*1*	...	...	...	...	...	...	...	...	...	...	...	...	...	...	...	...
...	...	...	...	...	...	...	...	...	...	...	...	...	...	...	...	...	...
2	...	...	...	...	...	...	...	...	...	...	...	*2*	...	...	...	1	...
...	...	...	...	...	...	...	...	...	...	...	...	...	...	...	...	...	...
...	...	...	...	...	...	...	...	...	...	...	...	...	...	...	...	...	...
...	...	...	...	...	...	...	...	...	...	...	...	...	...	...	...	...	...
...	...	...	...	...	...	...	...	...	...	...	...	...	...	...	...	...	...
5	...	2	...	...	...	...	...	...	...	...	...	...	...	...	...	...	...
...	...	...	...	...	...	...	...	...	...	...	...	...	...	...	...	...	...
...	...	...	...	...	...	...	...	...	...	...	...	...	...	...	...	...	...
...	...	...	...	...	...	...	...	...	...	...	...	...	...	...	...	...	...
6	*1*	2	...	2	...	...	...	...	...	...	...	...	...	...	...	...	...
...	...	...	...	...	...	...	...	...	...	...	...	...	...	...	...	...	...
...	...	...	*1*	...	...	...	...	...	...	...	...	...	...	...	...	...	...
...	...	...	...	...	...	...	...	...	...	...	...	...	...	...	...	...	...
...	...	...	...	...	...	...	...	...	...	...	...	...	...	...	...	...	...
...	...	...	...	...	...	...	...	...	...	...	...	...	...	...	...	...	...
...	...	...	...	...	...	...	...	...	...	...	...	...	...	...	...	...	...
...	...	...	...	...	...	...	...	...	...	...	...	...	...	...	...	...	...
16	2	4	1	2	...	...	...	...	...	...	...	2	...	...	...	2	1

Jew.

RIED.

20 — 24. Males.	20 — 24. Females.	25 — 29. Males.	25 — 29. Females.	30 — 34. Males.	30 — 34. Females.	35 — 39. Males.	35 — 39. Females.	40 — 44. Males.	40 — 44. Females.	45 — 49. Males.	45 — 49. Females.	50 — 54. Males.	50 — 54. Females.	55 — 59. Males.	55 — 59. Females.	60 and over. Males.	60 and over. Females.
1	*6*	1	*1*	7	*2*	1	...	1	...	1	...	...	...	...	...	...	*1*
1	*3*	4	...	2	...	...	...	...	...	...	*2*	...	...	3	...	...	...
...	*1*	...	...	1	...	...	...	...	...	...	...	...	...	...	...	...	...
...	*2*	1	*6*	4	*3*	6	...	2	*1*	2	*1*	...	...	2	...	...	...
...	...	...	...	1	*2*	1	...	...	...	1	...	...	...	...	...	...	...
...	...	...	...	...	...	...	...	...	...	...	...	...	...	...	...	...	...
1	...	...	...	...	*1*	...	...	1	*1*	...	...	...	...	...	...	...	...
...	...	...	...	...	...	...	...	...	...	...	...	...	...	...	...	...	...
13	*31*	15	*29*	15	*21*	24	*13*	13	*8*	10	*6*	10	*6*	7	*1*	11	*1*
...	...	...	...	...	...	...	...	...	...	...	...	...	...	...	...	...	...
...	...	...	...	...	...	...	...	...	...	...	...	...	...	...	...	...	...
...	...	...	...	...	...	...	...	...	...	...	...	...	...	...	...	...	...
6	*9*	14	*13*	9	*4*	8	*4*	5	*4*	1	*4*	5	*11*	2	...	11	...
...	...	...	...	...	...	...	...	...	...	...	...	...	...	...	...	...	...
...	...	...	...	...	...	...	...	...	...	1	...	...	...	...	...	...	...
...	...	...	...	...	...	...	...	...	...	...	...	...	...	...	...	...	...
...	...	...	...	...	...	...	...	...	...	...	...	...	...	...	...	...	...
...	...	...	...	...	...	...	*1*	1	...	...	...	...	...	...	...	...	...
...	...	...	...	...	...	...	...	...	...	...	...	...	...	...	...	...	...
...	...	...	...	...	...	...	...	...	...	...	...	...	...	...	...	...	...
22	51	35	49	39	33	40	18	23	14	16	13	15	17	14	1	22	2

Civil Condition by Religion and Age.

TABLE

Part (I).—

(3) WID

State.	Total. Total.	Total. Males.	Total. Females.	0—4. Males.	0—4. Females.	5—9. Males.	5—9. Females.	10—14. Males.	10—14. Females.	15—19. Males.	15—19. Females.
Cutch	2	...	2	...	...	...	...	...	...	...	...
Pálanpur	1	...	1	...	...	...	...	...	...	...	...
Mahi Kántha	...	...	...	...	...	...	...	...	...	...	...
Káthiáwár	9	3	6	...	...	...	...	...	...	...	...
Rewa Kántha	...	...	...	...	...	...	...	...	...	...	...
Cambay	...	...	...	...	...	...	...	...	...	...	...
Surat Agency	...	...	...	...	...	...	...	...	...	...	...
Jawhár	...	...	...	...	...	...	...	...	...	...	...
Janjira	56	11	45	...	...	...	...	...	1	...	...
Sáwantwádi	...	...	...	...	...	...	...	...	...	...	...
The Dangs...	...	...	...	...	...	...	...	...	...	...	...
Surgana	...	...	...	...	...	...	...	...	...	...	...
Bhor	15	2	13	...	...	...	...	...	...	...	...
Akalkot	...	...	...	...	...	...	...	...	...	...	...
Sátára Agency	...	...	...	...	...	...	...	...	...	...	...
Jat	...	...	...	...	...	...	...	...	...	...	...
Kolhápur	...	...	...	...	...	...	...	...	...	...	...
Southern Marátha Jaghírs ...	...	...	...	...	...	...	...	...	...	...	...
Sáwanúr	...	...	...	...	...	...	...	...	...	...	...
Khairpur	...	...	...	...	...	...	...	...	...	...	...
Total, Feudatory States...	**83**	**16**	**67**	...	...	...	...	...	**1**	...	...

Part (J).—

(1) UN

State.	Total. Total.	Total. Males.	Total. Females.	0—4. Males.	0—4. Females.	5—9. Males.	5—9. Females.	10—14. Males.	10—14. Females.	15—19. Males.	15—19. Females.
Cutch	438	246	192	56	69	68	78	48	32	36	9
Pálanpur	83	49	34	16	13	10	13	10	8	5	...
Mahi Kántha	...	...	...	...	...	...	...	...	...	...	...
Káthiáwár	...	...	...	...	...	...	...	...	...	...	...
Rewa Kántha	33,492	17,959	15,533	5,800	6,278	5,757	5,295	3,042	2,338	1,751	1,174
Cambay	...	...	...	...	...	...	...	...	...	...	...
Surat Agency	...	...	...	...	...	...	...	...	...	...	...
Jawhár	61	31	30	11	16	12	7	1	3	3	1
Janjira	71	42	29	19	15	10	10	4	2	3	1
Sáwantwádi	...	...	...	...	...	...	...	...	...	...	...
The Dangs...	5,787	3,226	2,561	782	1,054	1,090	971	756	396	330	100
Surgana	68	33	35	6	19	16	10	5	4	4	2
Bhor	...	...	...	...	...	...	...	...	...	...	...
Akalkot	...	...	...	...	...	...	...	...	...	...	...
Sátára Agency	...	...	...	...	...	...	...	...	...	...	...
Jat	...	...	...	...	...	...	...	...	...	...	...
Kolhápur	...	...	...	...	...	...	...	...	...	...	...
Southern Marátha Jaghírs ...	...	...	...	...	...	...	...	...	...	...	...
Sáwanúr	...	...	...	...	...	...	...	...	...	...	...
Khairpur	317	218	99	62	45	69	42	34	11	18	...
Total, Feudatory States...	**40,317**	**21,804**	**18,513**	**6,752**	**7,509**	**7,032**	**6,426**	**3,900**	**2,794**	**2,150**	**1,287**

Jew.

OWED.

20 — 24.		25 — 29.		30 — 34.		35 — 39.		40 — 44.		45 — 49.		50 — 54.		55 — 59.		60 and over.	
Males.	Females.	Males.	Females.	Males.	Females.	Males.	Females.	Males.	Females.	Males.	Females.	Males.	Females.	Males.	Females.	Males.	Females.
...	...	...	...	...	...	...	...	...	*1*	...	...	...	...	...	...	...	*1*
...	...	...	...	...	...	...	...	...	...	...	...	...	*1*	...	...	...	...
...	...	...	...	...	...	...	...	...	...	...	...	...	...	...	...	...	...
...	...	1	*1*	...	...	...	...	...	*1*	1	*1*	...	...	1	...	...	*3*
...	...	...	...	...	...	...	...	...	...	...	...	...	...	...	...	...	...
...	...	...	...	...	...	...	...	...	...	...	...	...	...	...	...	...	...
...	...	...	...	...	...	...	...	...	...	...	...	...	...	...	...	...	...
...	...	...	...	...	...	...	...	...	...	...	...	...	...	...	...	...	...
...	...	...	...	...	...	...	*5*	...	*3*	1	*6*	2	*3*	1	*5*	7	...
...	...	...	...	...	...	...	...	...	...	...	...	...	...	...	...	...	...
...	...	...	...	...	...	...	...	...	...	...	...	...	...	...	...	...	...
...	...	...	...	...	...	...	...	...	...	...	...	...	...	...	...	...	...
...	...	...	*1*	1	*1*	...	...	...	*3*	...	...	...	*6*	...	...	1	*2*
...	...	...	...	...	...	...	...	...	...	...	...	...	...	...	...	...	...
...	...	...	...	...	...	...	...	...	...	...	...	...	...	...	...	...	...
...	...	...	...	...	...	...	...	...	...	...	...	...	...	...	...	...	...
...	...	...	...	...	...	...	...	...	...	...	...	...	...	...	...	...	...
...	...	...	...	...	...	...	...	...	...	...	...	...	...	...	...	...	...
...	...	...	...	...	...	...	...	...	...	...	...	...	...	...	...	...	...
...	...	...	...	...	...	...	...	...	...	...	...	...	...	...	...	...	...
...	...	**1**	**2**	**1**	**1**	...	**5**	...	**8**	**2**	**7**	**2**	**10**	**2**	**5**	**8**	**28**

Animistic.

MARRIED.

20 — 24.		25 — 29.		30 — 34.		35 — 39.		40 — 44.		45 — 49.		50 — 54.		55 — 59.		60 and over.	
Males.	Females.	Males.	Females.	Males.	Females.	Males.	Females.	Males.	Females.	Males.	Females.	Males.	Females.	Males.	Females.	Males.	Females.
21	*1*	7	...	7	*1*	2	*1*	1	*1*	...	...	...	...	...	...	...	...
7	...	1	...	...	...	...	...	...	...	...	...	...	...	...	...	...	...
...	...	...	...	...	...	...	...	...	...	...	...	...	...	...	...	...	...
...	...	...	...	...	...	...	...	...	...	...	...	...	...	...	...	...	...
1,029	*291*	382	*66*	112	*27*	34	*21*	23	*20*	12	*10*	9	*5*	4	*2*	4	*6*
...	...	...	...	...	...	...	...	...	...	...	...	...	...	...	...	...	...
...	...	...	...	...	...	...	...	...	...	...	...	...	...	...	...	...	...
1	*2*	1	*1*	1	...	...	...	1	...	...	...	...	...	...	...	...	...
2	*1*	2	...	1	...	...	...	...	...	1	...	...	...	...	...	...	...
...	...	...	...	...	...	...	...	...	...	...	...	...	...	...	...	...	...
158	*15*	71	*8*	24	*6*	8	*7*	3	*1*	1	*1*	1	...	1	...	1	*2*
1	...	1	...	...	...	...	...	...	...	...	...	...	...	...	...	...	...
...	...	...	...	...	...	...	...	...	...	...	...	...	...	...	...	...	...
...	...	...	...	...	...	...	...	...	...	...	...	...	...	...	...	...	...
...	...	...	...	...	...	...	...	...	...	...	...	...	...	...	...	...	...
...	...	...	...	...	...	...	...	...	...	...	...	...	...	...	...	...	...
...	...	...	...	...	...	...	...	...	...	...	...	...	...	...	...	...	...
...	...	...	...	...	...	...	...	...	...	...	...	...	...	...	...	...	...
...	...	...	...	...	...	...	...	...	...	...	...	...	...	...	...	...	...
15	...	6	*1*	10	...	2	...	1	...	...	...	...	...	1	...	...	...
1,234	**310**	**471**	**76**	**155**	**34**	**46**	**29**	**29**	**22**	**14**	**11**	**10**	**5**	**6**	**2**	**5**	**8**

TABLE

Part (J).—

(2) MAR

State.	Total.			0—4.		5—9.		10—14.		15—19.	
	Total.	Males.	Females.	Males.	Females.	Males.	Females.	Males.	Females.	Males.	Females.
Cutch	368	194	*174*	2	*1*	5	*4*	1	*4*	9	*22*
Pálanpur	75	34	*41*	...	...	...	...	1	*1*	1	*6*
Mahi Kántha	...	...	...	...	...	...	...	...	...	...	...
Káthiáwár	3	1	*2*	...	...	...	...	...	...	...	...
Rewa Kántha	28,470	13,818	*14,652*	35	*26*	35	*60*	145	*207*	619	*1,074*
Cambay	...	...	...	...	...	...	...	...	...	...	...
Surat Agency	...	...	...	...	...	...	...	...	...	...	...
Jawhár	54	27	*27*	...	...	...	*1*	...	...	...	...
Janjíra	83	51	*32*	...	...	...	...	1	...	4	*1*
Sáwantwádi	...	...	...	...	...	...	...	...	...	...	...
The Dangs	5,025	2,445	*2,580*	...	*5*	2	*11*	13	*74*	89	*323*
Surgana	44	22	*22*	...	...	...	...	...	*2*	3	*2*
Bhor	...	...	...	...	...	...	...	...	...	...	...
Akálkot	...	...	...	...	...	...	...	...	...	...	...
Sátára Agency	...	...	...	...	...	...	...	...	...	...	...
Jat	...	...	...	...	...	...	...	...	...	...	...
Kolhápur	...	...	...	...	...	...	...	...	...	...	...
Southern Marátha Jaghírs ..	...	...	...	...	...	...	...	...	...	...	...
Sáwanúr	...	...	...	...	...	...	...	...	...	...	...
Khairpur	321	154	*167*	1	...	...	...	1	*4*	13	*21*
Total, Feudatory States...	**34,443**	**16,746**	**17,697**	**38**	**32**	**42**	**76**	**162**	**292**	**738**	**1,449**

Part (J).—

(3) WID

State.	Total.			0—4.		5—9.		10—14.		15—19.	
	Total.	Males.	Females.	Males.	Females.	Males.	Females.	Males.	Females.	Males.	Females.
Cutch	76	17	*59*	...	...	...	...	...	...	1	...
Pálanpur	16	6	*10*	...	...	...	...	...	...	...	...
Mahi Kántha	...	...	...	...	...	...	...	...	...	...	...
Káthiáwár	1	...	*1*	...	...	...	...	...	...	...	...
Réwa Kántha	2,894	613	*2,281*	...	...	...	*1*	1	*1*	6	*9*
Cambay	...	...	...	...	...	...	...	...	...	...	...
Surat Agency	...	...	...	...	...	...	...	...	...	...	...
Jawhár	6	...	*6*	...	...	...	...	...	...	...	...
Janjíra	5	...	*5*	...	...	...	...	...	...	...	...
Sáwantwádi	...	...	...	...	...	...	...	...	...	...	...
The Dangs	590	197	*393*	...	...	...	...	...	...	1	*1*
Surganá	9	6	*3*	...	...	...	...	...	...	1	...
Bhor	...	...	...	...	...	...	...	...	...	...	...
Akálkot	...	...	...	...	...	...	...	...	...	...	...
Sátára Agency	...	...	...	...	...	...	...	...	...	...	...
Jat	...	...	...	...	...	...	...	...	...	...	...
Kolhápur	...	...	...	...	...	...	...	...	...	...	...
Southern Marátha Jaghírs	...	...	...	...	...	...	...	...	...	...	...
Sáwanúr	...	...	...	...	...	...	...	...	...	...	...
Khairpur	48	17	*31*	...	...	...	...	...	...	...	*1*
Total, Feudatory States...	**3,645**	**856**	**2,789**	...	...	...	**1**	**1**	**1**	**9**	**11**

Table VIII.

Civil Condition by Religion and Age.

VIII.

Animistic.

RIED.

20—24.		25—29.		30—34.		35—39.		40—44.		45—49.		50—54.		55—59.		60 and over.	
Males.	Females.	Males.	Females.	Males.	Females.	Males.	Females.	Males.	Females.	Males.	Females.	Males.	Females.	Males.	Females.	Males.	Females.
24	37	36	39	42	26	19	10	21	14	6	7	10	8	7	1	12	1
5	6	4	9	7	7	2	3	6	3	2	1	4	2	1	2	1	1
...	...	...	...	...	...	...	...	...	..	...	...	...	...	...	...	...	...
...	...	...	1	...	...	...	...	...	1	...	...	1	...	...	...	...	...
1,660	2,877	2,790	3,019	2,543	2,752	2,163	1,639	1,474	1,421	1,013	798	752	476	260	147	329	156
...	...	...	..	...	...	...	...	...	...	...	...	...	...	...	...	...	...
...	...	...	...	...	...	...	...	...	...	...	...	...	...	...	...	...	...
...	6	3	2	3	7	2	1	2	5	8	...	4	4	...	...	5	1
4	5	8	11	8	5	9	4	5	3	5	2	2	1	2	...	3	...
...	...	...	...	...	...	...	...	...	...	...	...	...	..	...	...	..	...
257	487	495	573	418	466	464	268	238	152	168	101	134	66	45	20	122	34
...	2	2	5	6	6	3	4	7	...	...	...	...	1	...	...	1	...
...	...	...	...	...	...	...	...	...	...	...	...	...	...	...	...	...	...
...	...	...	...	...	...	...	...	...	...	...	...	...	...	...	...	...	...
...	...	...	...	..	...	...	...	...	...	...	...	...	...	...	...	...	...
...	...	...	...	...	...	...	...	...	...	...	..	...	...	...	...	...	...
...	...	...	...	...	...	...	...	...	...	...	...	...	...	...	...	...	...
...	...	...	..	...	...	...	...	...	...	..	...	...	...	...	...	...	...
...	...	...	...	...	...	...	...	...	...	...	...	...	...	...	...	...	...
15	34	12	25	29	25	16	14	16	16	7	9	12	2	6	7	26	10
1.965	3.454	3.350	3.684	3.056	3.294	2.678	1.943	1.769	1.615	1.209	918	919	560	321	177	499	203

Animistic.

OWED.

20—24.		25—29.		30—34.		35—39.		40—44.		45—49.		50—54.		55—59.		60 and over.	
Males.	Females.	Males.	Females.	Males.	Females.	Males.	Females.	Males.	Females.	Males.	Females.	Males.	Females.	Males.	Females.	Males.	Females.
...	...	2	2	3	2	3	6	3	14	...	8	...	10	...	1	5	16
...	1	1	1	1	...	1	...	1	...	1	2	...	1	...	...	1	5
...	...	...	...	...	...	...	...	...	...	...	...	...	...	...	...	...	...
...	...	...	...	...	...	...	...	...	...	...	1	...	...	...	...	...	...
23	25	48	57	67	127	76	182	85	378	78	389	90	507	28	132	111	473
...	...	...	...	...	...	...	..	...	...	...	...	...	...	...	...	...	...
...	...	...	...	...	...	...	...	...	...	...	...	...	...	...	...	...	...
...	...	...	...	...	..	...	...	...	1	...	1	...	3	...	1	...	...
...	...	...	...	...	...	...	...	...	...	...	...	...	1	...	3	...	1
...	...	...	...	...	...	...	...	...	...	...	...	...	...	...	...	...	...
5	5	17	22	23	24	29	38	18	65	26	35	38	80	10	7	30	116
...	1	...	...	...	...	1	...	...	...	...	...	2	2	...	...	2	...
...	...	...	...	...	...	...	...	...	...	...	...	...	...	...	...	...	...
...	...	...	...	...	...	...	...	...	...	...	...	...	...	...	...	...	...
...	...	...	...	...	...	...	...	...	...	...	...	...	...	...	...	...	...
...	...	...	...	...	...	...	...	...	...	...	...	...	...	...	...	...	...
...	...	...	...	...	...	...	...	...	...	...	...	...	...	...	...	...	...
...	...	...	...	...	...	...	...	...	...	...	...	...	...	...	...	...	...
...	...	...	...	...	...	...	...	...	...	...	...	...	...	...	...	...	...
...	1	...	1	2	2	...	2	1	4	1	1	2	8	2	2	9	9
28	33	68	83	96	155	110	228	108	462	106	437	132	612	40	146	158	620

TABLE IX.

EDUCATION BY RELIGION AND AGE.

The 19,236 persons—10,579 males, 8,657 females—in Mahi Kántha, for whom Education was not returned, are excluded.

Table IX.

Education by Religion and Age.

TABLE

Part (A).—

State.	Total Population: Total.	Total Population: Males.	Total Population: Females.	Total by Education: Learning: Males.	Learning: Females.	Literate: Males.	Literate: Females.	Illiterate: Males.	Illiterate: Females.	0—14: Total: Males.	Total: Females.	Learning: Males.	Learning: Females.	Literate: Males.	Literate: Females.
Cutch	558,415	278,441	279,974	9,117	706	34,821	2,233	234,503	277,035	111,456	108,130	8,502	664	2,404	240
Pálanpur	645,526	335,587	309,939	4,380	228	21,054	675	310,153	309,086	140,059	130,109	3,928	205	1,166	86
Mahi Kántha	562,332	286,067	276,265	5,206	178	18,182	303	262,679	275,784	122,486	114,307	4,607	164	1,351	47
Káthiáwár	2,752,404	1,416,633	1,335,771	44,293	2,565	176,318	6,911	1,196,022	1,326,295	542,458	512,858	39,707	2,335	14,703	1,231
Rewa Kántha	733,506	376,146	357,360	5,925	340	19,788	907	350,433	356,113	158,005	148,104	5,182	313	1,123	115
Cambay	89,722	46,231	43,491	1,418	133	7,161	643	37,667	42,816	16,325	14,488	1,287	112	422	80
Surat Agency	181,208	92,457	88,751	1,485	197	3,844	288	87,128	88,266	39,552	37,698	1,361	196	256	79
Total, Gujarát Group ...	5,523,113	2,831,562	2,691,551	71,819	4,346	281,158	11,860	2,478,585	2,675,345	1,130,341	1,065,694	64,574	3,989	21,425	1,969
Jawhár	52,831	27,825	25,006	154	5	554	18	27,117	24,983	11,458	10,990	142	4	22	6
Janjira	81,780	39,629	42,151	1,567	183	3,005	184	35,057	41,784	17,225	17,131	1,343	178	174	29
Sáwantwádi	192,948	93,520	99,428	3,855	170	9,862	227	79,803	99,031	35,961	34,599	3,141	165	319	42
Total, Konkan Group ...	327,559	160,974	166,585	5,576	358	13,421	429	141,977	165,798	64,644	62,720	4,620	347	465	76
The Dángs	32,920	17,237	15,683	...	...	35	...	17,202	15,683	7,682	7,286	...	...	...	...
Surgana	12,398	6,545	5,853	17	...	61	2	6,467	5,851	2,937	2,730	16	...	2	...
Bhor	155,669	78,602	77,067	1,283	54	3,432	55	73,887	76,958	32,962	30,850	1,070	49	74	11
Akalkot	75,774	38,615	37,159	981	29	1,742	14	35,892	37,116	14,610	13,944	787	24	57	3
Sátára Agency	131,529	66,269	65,260	1,817	53	3,454	44	61,498	65,163	25,998	24,445	1,049	47	79	12
Total, Deccan Group ...	408,290	207,268	201,022	3,598	136	8,724	115	194,946	200,771	84,089	79,195	2,922	120	212	26
Jat	79,786	40,576	39,210	708	13	2,080	8	37,788	39,189	16,163	15,566	595	12	55	...
Kolhápur	913,131	467,572	445,559	11,850	558	26,193	502	429,529	444,499	181,526	170,392	9,368	519	536	76
Southern Marátha Jaghirs ...	639,270	320,531	318,739	10,655	407	24,499	418	285,377	317,914	124,442	117,968	8,598	369	672	73
Sáwanúr	16,976	8,330	8,646	435	35	880	45	7,015	8,566	3,367	3,357	400	34	32	7
Total, Karnátak Group ...	1,649,163	837,009	812,154	23,648	1,013	53,652	973	759,709	810,168	325,488	307,283	18,961	934	1,295	156
Khairpur	131,937	72,733	59,204	904	2	5,689	27	66,140	59,175	28,113	20,468	823	1	269	3
Total, Feudatory States ...	8,040,063	4,109,546	3,930,516	105,545	5,855	362,644	13,404	3,641,357	3,911,257	1,632,675	1,535,360	91,906	5,391	28,666	2,130

Part (B).—

State.	Total Population: Total.	Total Population: Males.	Total Population: Females.	Total by Education: Learning: Males.	Learning: Females.	Literate: Males.	Literate: Females.	Illiterate: Males.	Illiterate: Females.	0—14: Total: Males.	Total: Females.	Learning: Males.	Learning: Females.	Literate: Males.	Literate: Females.
Cutch	351,620	176,765	174,855	5,134	482	20,744	1,341	150,887	173,092	69,950	66,847	4,733	403	1,382	102
Pálanpur	557,870	290,059	267,811	1,615	52	8,236	193	280,208	267,567	123,713	114,485	1,391	48	454	20
Mahi Kántha	525,897	267,730	258,167	3,922	135	12,359	233	251,449	257,799	115,562	107,620	3,445	125	928	35
Káthiáwár	2,279,423	1,175,886	1,103,537	28,244	1,643	114,021	4,820	1,033,621	1,097,074	448,747	423,546	25,034	1,513	9,273	815
Rewa Kántha	641,811	329,675	312,136	5,190	267	16,707	503	307,778	311,366	138,414	129,510	4,544	245	926	72
Cambay	73,590	38,351	35,239	961	34	5,040	140	32,350	35,065	13,735	12,012	873	25	285	34
Surat Agency	175,298	89,426	85,872	1,290	150	3,052	178	85,084	85,544	38,472	36,658	1,185	150	219	50
Total, Gujarát Group ...	4,605,509	2,367,892	2,257,617	46,356	2,703	180,159	7,407	2,141,377	2,237,507	948,593	890,684	41,205	2,503	13,467	1,223
Jawhár	52,232	27,492	24,740	132	5	474	18	20,880	24,722	11,356	10,874	125	4	18	4
Janjira	66,803	32,898	33,905	815	17	1,969	23	30,114	33,846	14,126	14,043	688	16	66	4
Sáwantwádi	183,749	89,115	94,634	2,548	142	9,330	211	76,237	94,281	34,069	33,740	2,898	137	299	37
Total, Konkan Group ...	302,784	149,505	153,279	4,495	164	11,773	247	133,237	152,868	59,551	57,657	3,711	157	383	45
The Dángs	21,343	11,268	10,075	...	...	20	...	11,248	10,075	5,011	4,684	...	...	...	...
Surgana	12,118	6,397	5,721	13	...	36	...	6,348	5,721	2,887	2,668	12	...	1	...
Bhor	152,716	77,021	75,695	1,225	53	3,218	60	72,583	75,698	32,408	30,341	1,021	48	70	10
Akalkot	65,034	33,092	31,942	831	23	1,629	12	30,732	31,907	12,454	11,980	666	20	41	3
Sátára Agency	125,554	63,216	62,338	1,138	44	2,922	33	59,156	62,261	24,822	23,345	888	40	63	10
Total, Deccan Group ...	376,765	190,994	185,771	3,207	120	7,720	95	180,067	185,556	77,582	73,018	2,587	108	175	13
Jat	74,690	37,919	36,771	648	10	1,930	6	35,341	36,756	15,134	14,608	548	10	48	...
Kolhápur	823,526	419,783	401,743	9,736	433	21,515	373	388,532	401,937	163,837	154,401	7,613	405	404	65
Southern Marátha Jaghirs ...	558,469	279,858	278,611	9,291	343	21,719	335	248,848	277,933	108,448	102,998	7,449	310	580	64
Sáwanúr	12,108	5,978	6,130	331	25	672	18	4,975	6,087	2,353	2,354	310	25	19	6
Total, Karnátak Group ...	1,467,793	743,538	724,255	20,006	811	45,836	738	677,696	722,713	289,772	274,361	15,020	750	1,031	135
Khairpur	28,214	14,644	13,570	729	1	5,085	21	8,830	13,548	6,566	5,657	675	1	253	3
Total, Feudatory States ...	6,781,055	3,466,573	3,314,492	74,793	3,799	250,578	8,503	3,141,207	3,303,191	1,382,034	1,301,257	64,098	3,519	15,309	1,434

Table IX.

IX. Education by Religion and Age.

Total Population.

Illiterate.		15—24.								25 and over.							
		Total.		Learning.		Literate.		Illiterate.		Total.		Learning.		Literate.		Illiterate.	
Males.	Females.	Males.	Females.	Males.	Females.	Males.	Females.	Males.	Females.	Males.	Females.	Males.	Females.	Males.	Females.	Males.	Females.
100,550	107,196	45,885	46,599	536	20	8,607	745	36,742	45,834	121,100	125,246	79	22	23,810	1,148	97,211	124,075
134,965	129,818	58,515	49,733	393	14	5,601	203	52,521	49,516	137,018	130,097	59	9	14,287	386	122,667	129,702
116,528	114,096	53,320	46,455	529	9	5,087	104	47,704	46,342	110,261	115,503	70	6	11,744	152	98,447	115,346
488,048	509,292	262,739	248,486	4,025	135	49,704	2,501	209,010	239,850	611,436	580,427	661	95	111,011	3,179	498,964	577,153
151,700	147,676	65,078	59,356	650	22	5,424	336	59,004	58,998	153,063	149,900	93	6	13,241	456	139,729	149,439
14,616	14,296	9,014	8,283	217	10	1,750	155	7,147	8,118	20,892	20,720	9	10	4,979	308	15,904	20,402
37,935	37,432	14,175	14,021	120	1	1,124	116	12,931	13,904	38,730	37,032	4	...	2,464	102	36,262	36,930
1,044,342	1,059,736	608,726	466,933	6,370	211	77,297	4,160	425,059	462,562	1,192,495	1,158,924	875	146	182,430	5,731	1,009,184	1,153,047
11,294	10,981	4,066	3,897	9	1	129	18	3,928	3,884	12,301	10,119	3	...	403	1	11,895	10,119
15,768	16,984	5,050	6,440	185	4	704	55	4,161	6,381	17,354	18,580	89	1	2,177	100	15,138	18,479
32,501	34,398	14,714	15,854	695	5	2,144	82	11,875	15,767	42,845	48,975	19	...	7,399	103	35,427	48,872
59,553	62,297	23,830	26,191	889	10	2,977	149	19,964	26,032	72,500	77,674	61	1	9,979	204	62,460	77,469
7,682	7,226	2,549	2,450	...	...	6	...	2,543	2,450	7,006	6,007	...	...	29	...	6,977	6,007
2,919	2,730	916	922	1	...	6	...	909	922	2,692	2,201	...	...	53	2	2,639	2,199
31,818	30,790	10,711	12,210	204	4	634	12	9,873	12,194	34,929	34,007	9	1	2,724	33	32,196	33,974
13,666	13,917	5,550	5,870	168	1	346	4	5,046	5,865	18,555	17,345	36	4	1,339	7	17,180	17,334
24,870	24,386	9,154	10,304	231	5	671	16	8,252	10,283	31,117	30,511	37	1	2,704	16	28,376	30,494
80,955	79,049	28,880	31,756	594	10	1,663	32	26,623	31,714	94,299	90,071	82	6	6,849	57	87,368	90,008
15,503	15,654	5,597	5,857	111	...	440	2	5,046	5,855	18,826	17,787	2	1	1,585	6	17,239	17,780
171,622	169,797	67,565	65,673	2,274	24	5,619	198	59,672	65,351	218,481	209,594	208	15	20,038	228	198,235	209,351
115,172	117,526	46,889	49,403	1,863	18	5,306	173	39,720	49,211	149,200	151,369	104	20	18,521	172	130,485	151,177
2,935	3,316	1,280	1,437	31	1	173	19	1,076	1,417	3,683	3,852	4	...	675	19	3,004	3,833
305,232	306,193	121,381	122,269	4,279	43	11,538	392	105,514	121,834	390,190	382,602	408	36	40,819	425	348,963	382,141
27,021	20,464	10,399	9,959	79	...	1,185	8	9,135	9,951	34,221	28,777	2	1	4,235	16	29,984	28,760
1.517.103	1.527.739	693.166	657.108	12.211	274	94.660	4.741	586.295	652.093	1.783.705	1.738.048	1.428	190	244.318	6.433	1.537.959	1.731.425

Hindu.

Illiterate.		15—24.								25 and over.							
		Total.		Learning.		Literate.		Illiterate.		Total.		Learning.		Literate.		Illiterate.	
Males.	Females.	Males.	Females.	Males.	Females.	Males.	Females.	Males.	Females.	Males.	Females.	Males.	Females.	Males.	Females.	Males.	Females.
63,835	66,242	30,138	29,405	357	9	5,201	438	24,580	28,908	76,677	78,603	44	10	14,161	651	62,472	77,943
121,868	114,425	60,193	42,652	190	6	2,204	66	47,799	42,580	116,153	110,674	34	4	[illegible],578	106	110,541	110,664
111,189	107,466	49,647	43,306	430	8	3,439	78	45,978	43,219	102,321	107,236	47	2	7,992	120	94,282	107,114
414,440	421,218	220,473	201,083	2,840	80	32,561	1,816	185,072	119,187	506,666	478,908	370	50	72,187	2,189	434,109	476,669
132,944	129,193	57,851	51,519	569	17	4,689	205	52,193	51,297	133,910	131,107	77	5	11,192	226	122,641	130,876
12,677	11,953	7,585	6,653	83	5	1,253	44	6,249	6,604	17,031	16,574	5	4	3,502	62	13,524	16,508
37,068	36,458	13,664	13,501	101	...	915	80	12,648	13,421	37,290	35,713	4	...	1,918	49	35,368	35,665
893,921	886,953	429,251	388,118	4,570	125	50,162	2,777	374,510	385,216	990,048	958,816	581	75	116,530	3,402	872,937	955,338
11,213	10,866	4,010	3,856	7	1	107	8	3,896	3,847	12,126	10,010	...	...	349	1	11,777	10,009
13,872	14,023	4,246	5,204	104	1	491	10	3,651	5,193	14,526	14,659	23	...	1,412	9	13,091	14,649
30,872	32,566	14,083	15,150	638	6	2,015	78	11,435	15,047	40,963	46,764	17	...	7,016	96	33,930	46,668
55,457	57,455	22,339	24,190	744	7	2,613	96	18,982	24,087	67,615	71,452	40	...	8,777	106	58,798	71,326
5,011	4,684	1,688	1,509	...	...	4	...	1,684	1,509	4,569	3,882	...	...	16	...	4,553	3,882
2,874	2,668	900	910	1	...	5	...	894	910	2,610	2,143	...	...	30	...	2,580	2,143
31,817	30,283	10,462	11,959	196	4	592	10	9,674	11,945	34,151	33,395	8	1	2,551	30	31,592	33,364
11,747	11,957	4,735	5,081	133	1	306	3	4,296	5,077	15,903	14,881	32	2	1,182	6	14,689	14,873
23,871	23,295	8,716	9,834	215	4	560	9	7,941	9,821	29,678	29,159	35	...	2,299	14	27,344	29,145
74,820	72,887	26,501	29,295	545	9	1,467	22	24,489	29,262	80,911	83,460	75	3	6,078	60	80,758	83,407
14,638	14,598	5,227	5,491	98	...	402	2	4,727	5,489	17,558	16,672	2	...	1,480	4	16,076	16,668
155,820	153,931	60,539	59,481	1,945	10	4,553	148	54,041	59,254	195,407	188,921	178	9	16,558	160	178,671	188,752
100,439	102,624	41,033	43,395	1,684	17	4,615	149	34,734	43,228	130,877	132,220	158	16	16,544	183	113,675	132,081
2,024	2,323	928	1,007	19	...	140	9	769	998	2,697	2,769	2	...	518	3	2,182	2,766
272,921	273,476	107,727	109,318	3,746	36	9,710	307	94,271	108,969	346,039	340,582	340	25	35,095	290	310,604	340,267
5,638	6,633	2,179	2,287	54	...	1,073	6	1,052	2,281	6,899	5,746	...	...	3,759	12	2,140	5,734
1.302.657	1,296.304	587.997	553.200	9.659	177	65.025	3.203	518.313	649.815	1.496.512	1.460.035	1.036	103	170.239	3.860	1.325.237	[illegible]

Part (C).—

State.	Total Population. Total.	Males.	Females.	Total by Education. Learning. Males.	Learning. Females.	Literate. Males.	Literate. Females.	Illiterate. Males.	Illiterate. Females.	0–14. Total. Males.	Total. Females.	Learning. Males.	Learning. Females.
Cutch	133,492	66,552	*66,940*	1,487	*191*	4,961	*561*	60,104	*66,188*	27,608	*26,836*	1,370	*178*
Pálanpur	57,486	29,949	*27,537*	717	*98*	2,701	*245*	26,531	*27,194*	11,117	*10,437*	619	*91*
Mahi Kántha	22,570	11,610	*10,960*	338	*10*	1,644	*22*	9,628	*10,928*	4,517	*4,329*	293	*66*
Káthiáwár	358,061	181,196	*176,865*	7,961	*372*	28,539	*983*	144,696	*175,510*	71,705	*68,222*	7,333	*317*
Rewa Kántha	25,103	13,102	*12,001*	574	*53*	2,367	*351*	10,161	*11,597*	4,501	*4,170*	497	*50*
Cambay	12,712	6,218	*6,494*	235	*66*	1,047	*362*	4,936	*6,066*	2,042	*1,952*	211	*61*
Surat Agency	5,159	2,606	*2,553*	148	*14*	504	*19*	1,954	*2,520*	957	*911*	133	*14*
Total, Gujarát Group ...	614,583	311,233	*303,350*	11,460	*804*	41,763	*2,645*	258,010	*300,005*	122,447	*116,957*	10,456	*711*
Jawhár	421	235	*186*	22	...	52	*4*	161	*182*	69	*81*	17	...
Janjira	14,136	6,284	*7,852*	726	*165*	929	*157*	4,629	*7,530*	2,923	*2,916*	629	*161*
Sáwantwádi	4,455	2,120	*2,335*	229	*25*	364	*11*	1,527	*2,299*	907	*915*	184	*25*
Total, Konkan Group ...	19,012	8,639	*10,373*	977	*190*	1,345	*172*	6,317	*10,011*	3,899	*3,912*	830	*186*
The Dángs...	151	83	*68*	...	...	2	...	81	*68*	27	*28*	...	...
Surgana	131	68	*63*	4	...	8	*1*	56	*62*	22	*25*	4	...
Bhor	1,992	1,074	*918*	43	*1*	81	*3*	950	*914*	408	*346*	36	*1*
Akalkot	10,230	5,253	*4,977*	112	*3*	131	...	5,010	*4,974*	1,960	*1,878*	89	*3*
Sátára Agency	4,674	2,378	*2,296*	80	*4*	154	*8*	2,144	*2,284*	953	*896*	69	*3*
Total, Deccan Group ...	17,178	8,856	*8,322*	239	*8*	376	*12*	8,241	*8,302*	3,370	*3,168*	198	*7*
Jat	4,764	2,488	*2,276*	44	*3*	110	...	2,334	*2,273*	958	*898*	34	*2*
Kolhápur	38,272	20,127	*18,145*	764	*75*	1,146	*56*	18,217	*18,014*	7,888	*6,898*	617	*69*
Southern Marátha Jaghírs ...	52,197	26,280	*25,917*	810	*53*	1,297	*51*	24,173	*25,813*	10,540	*9,804*	699	*49*
Sáwanúr	4,853	2,344	*2,509*	103	*10*	206	*27*	2,035	*2,472*	1,011	*1,000*	89	*9*
Total, Karnátak Group ..	100,086	51,239	*48,847*	1,721	*141*	2,759	*134*	46,759	*48,572*	20,397	*18,600*	1,439	*129*
Khairpur	103,033	57,697	*45,336*	175	*1*	602	*5*	56,920	*45,330*	21,380	*14,829*	148	...
Total, Feudatory States...	**853,892**	**437,664**	**416,228**	**14,572**	**1,144**	**46,845**	**2,866**	**376,247**	**412,218**	**171,493**	**157,366**	**13,071**	**1,039**

Part (D).—

State.	Total.	Males.	Females.	Learning Males.	Learning Females.	Literate Males.	Literate Females.	Illiterate Males.	Illiterate Females.	0–14 Total Males.	Total Females.	Learning Males.	Learning Females.
Cutch	173	140	*33*	3	*3*	84	*12*	53	*18*	15	*8*	3	*3*
Pálanpur	608	480	*128*	19	*22*	404	*46*	57	*60*	38	*60*	18	*22*
Mahi Kántha	35	29	*6*	...	...	20	*3*	9	*3*	4	*3*	...	...
Káthiáwár	898	593	*305*	36	*31*	366	*129*	191	*145*	99	*105*	28	*29*
Rewa Kántha	36	26	*10*	2	*3*	13	*4*	11	*3*	3	*4*	2	*3*
Cambay	21	16	*5*	...	...	9	*2*	7	*3*	1	...	...	...
Surat Agency	1	1	...	...	...	1	...	...	...	...	...	...	...
Total, Gujarát Group ...	1,773	1,286	*487*	60	*59*	897	*196*	328	*232*	160	*180*	61	*57*
Jawhár	7	5	*2*	...	...	2	...	3	*2*	...	*1*	...	...
Janjira	12	10	*2*	1	...	2	...	7	*2*	6	*1*	1	...
Sáwantwádi	4,597	2,209	*2,388*	71	*2*	140	*5*	1,998	*2,381*	961	*924*	54	*2*
Total, Konkan Group ...	4,616	2,224	*2,398*	72	*2*	144	*5*	2,008	*2,385*	967	*926*	55	*2*
The Dángs...	3	3	...	...	...	1	...	2	...	...	...	...	...
Surgana	...	...	...	...	...	...	...	...	...	...	...	...	...
Bhor	9	8	*1*	...	...	3	...	5	*1*	...	...	...	...
Akalkot	2	2	...	...	...	1	...	1	...	...	...	...	...
Sátára Agency	1	1	...	...	...	1	...	...	...	...	...	...	...
Total, Deccan Group ...	15	14	*1*	...	...	6	...	8	*1*	...	...	...	...
Jat	16	8	*8*	...	...	5	*2*	3	*6*	1	*4*	...	...
Kolhápur	1,413	700	*713*	37	*26*	93	*49*	570	*638*	302	*283*	29	*23*
Southern Marátha Jaghírs ...	403	233	*170*	32	*5*	44	*13*	157	*152*	94	*76*	25	*5*
Sáwanúr	...	...	...	...	...	...	...	...	...	...	...	...	...
Total, Karnátak Group ...	1,832	941	*891*	69	*31*	142	*64*	730	*796*	397	*363*	54	*28*
Khairpur	4	3	*1*	...	...	2	*1*	1	...	...	...	...	...
Total, Feudatory States...	**8,239**	**4,467**	**3,772**	**201**	**92**	**1,191**	**266**	**3,075**	**3,414**	**1,524**	**1,469**	**160**	**87**

Part (E).—

State.	Total.	Males.	Females.	Learning Males.	Learning Females.	Literate Males.	Literate Females.	Illiterate Males.	Illiterate Females.	0–14 Total Males.	Total Females.	Learning Males.	Learning Females.
Cutch	1	1	...	...	...	1	...	...	...	...	...	...	...

Table IX.

Education by Religion and Age.

IX.

Mussalmán.

Literate.		Illiterate.		15 — 24. Total.		15 — 24. Learning.		15 — 24. Literate.		15 — 24. Illiterate.		25 and over. Total.		25 and over. Learning.		25 and over. Literate.		25 and over. Illiterate.	
Males.	Females.	Males.	Females.	Males.	Females.	Males.	Females.	Males.	Females.	Males.	Females.	Males.	Females.	Males.	Females.	Males.	Females.	Males.	Females.
363	88	25,875	26,670	10,680	10,965	93	6	1,291	182	9,296	10,777	28,264	29,139	24	7	3,307	291	24,933	28,841
142	32	10,356	10,314	5,381	4,663	83	4	783	74	4,515	4,586	13,451	12,436	15	3	1,776	139	11,660	12,294
125	4	4,099	4,319	2,165	1,865	36	1	518	7	1,611	1,857	4,928	4,766	9	3	1,001	11	3,918	4,752
2,912	316	61,460	67,689	30,570	31,541	506	27	7,872	322	22,192	31,192	78,921	77,102	122	28	17,755	445	61,044	76,629
156	41	3,848	4,079	2,456	2,245	63	3	664	115	1,729	2,127	6,145	5,586	14	...	1,547	195	4,584	5,391
59	38	1,772	1,853	1,119	1,316	21	4	226	97	872	1,215	3,057	3,226	3	1	762	227	2,292	2,998
24	4	800	893	449	474	15	...	153	8	281	466	1,200	1,168	...	...	327	7	873	1,161
3,781	433	108,210	115,717	52,820	53,070	817	45	11,507	805	40,496	52,220	135,966	133,423	187	42	26,475	1,315	109,304	132,066
2	...	50	81	47	31	2	...	17	4	28	27	119	74	3	...	33	...	83	74
51	24	2,243	2,731	721	1,178	81	3	167	44	473	1,131	2,640	3,758	16	1	711	89	1,913	3,668
13	4	710	886	310	352	43	...	86	3	181	349	903	1,068	2	...	265	4	636	1,064
66	28	3,003	3,698	1,078	1,561	126	3	270	51	682	1,507	3,662	4,900	21	1	1,009	93	2,632	4,806
...	...	27	28	17	9	...	...	...	...	17	9	39	31	...	...	2	...	37	31
...	...	18	25	7	3	...	...	1	...	6	3	39	35	...	...	7	1	32	34
...	1	372	344	150	159	6	...	14	2	130	157	516	413	1	...	67	...	448	413
9	...	1,862	1,870	771	740	21	...	24	...	726	740	2,522	2,364	2	...	98	...	2,422	2,364
7	...	877	893	329	359	9	1	32	6	288	352	1,096	1,041	2	...	115	2	979	1,039
16	1	3,156	3,160	1,274	1,270	36	1	71	8	1,167	1,261	4,212	3,884	5	...	289	3	3,918	3,881
3	...	921	896	339	345	10	...	30	...	299	345	1,191	1,033	...	1	77	...	1,114	1,032
41	6	7,230	6,823	2,849	2,625	137	1	270	21	2,442	2,603	9,390	8,622	10	5	835	29	8,545	8,588
60	7	9,781	9,748	3,757	3,973	91	1	354	17	3,312	3,955	11,983	12,140	20	3	883	27	11,080	12,110
13	1	909	990	351	429	12	1	32	10	307	418	982	1,080	2	...	161	16	819	1,064
117	14	18,841	18,457	7,296	7,372	250	5	686	48	6,360	7,321	23,546	22,875	32	9	1,956	72	21,558	22,794
16	...	21,216	14,829	8,159	7,615	25	...	112	2	8,022	7,613	28,158	22,892	2	1	474	3	27,682	22,888
3,996	**466**	**154,426**	**155.861**	**70,627**	**70,888**	**1.254**	**52**	**12.646**	**914**	**56.727**	**69.922**	**195.544**	**167.974**	**247**	**53**	**30.203**	**1.486**	**165.094**	**186.435**

Christian.

Literate. Males.	Literate. Females.	Illiterate. Males.	Illiterate. Females.	15 — 24. Total. Males.	15 — 24. Total. Females.	15 — 24. Learning. Males.	15 — 24. Learning. Females.	15 — 24. Literate. Males.	15 — 24. Literate. Females.	15 — 24. Illiterate. Males.	15 — 24. Illiterate. Females.	25 and over. Total. Males.	25 and over. Total. Females.	25 and over. Learning. Males.	25 and over. Learning. Females.	25 and over. Literate. Males.	25 and over. Literate. Females.	25 and over. Illiterate. Males.	25 and over. Illiterate. Females.
2	...	10	5	22	11	...	...	17	4	5	7	103	14	...	...	65	8	38	6
5	6	15	32	159	16	1	...	146	8	12	8	283	52	...	...	253	32	80	20
1	...	3	3	15	...	...	...	13	...	2	...	10	3	...	...	6	3	4	...
15	10	56	66	133	62	5	1	83	44	45	17	361	138	3	1	268	75	90	62
...	...	1	1	3	2	...	...	1	1	2	1	20	4	...	...	12	3	8	1
...	...	1	...	6	3	...	...	4	1	2	2	9	2	...	...	5	1	4	1
...	...	...	...	...	...	...	...	...	...	...	...	1	...	...	...	1	...	...	...
23	16	86	107	338	94	6	1	264	58	68	35	787	213	3	1	610	122	174	90
...	...	...	1	...	1	...	...	...	...	...	1	5	...	...	...	2	...	3	...
...	...	5	1	1	...	...	...	...	...	1	...	3	1	...	...	2	...	1	1
7	1	900	921	305	358	17	...	37	1	251	357	943	1,106	...	...	96	3	847	1,103
7	1	905	923	306	359	17	...	37	1	252	358	951	1,107	...	...	100	3	851	1,104
...	...	...	...	...	...	...	...	...	...	...	...	3	...	...	...	1	...	2	...
...	...	...	...	...	...	...	...	...	...	...	...	...	...	...	...	...	...	...	...
...	...	...	...	1	1	...	...	...	...	1	1	7	...	...	...	3	...	4	...
...	...	...	...	1	...	...	...	...	...	1	...	1	...	...	...	1	...	...	...
...	...	...	...	1	...	...	...	1	...	...	...	...	...	...	...	...	...	...	...
...	...	...	...	3	1	...	...	1	...	2	1	11	...	...	...	5	...	6	...
...	...	1	4	2	1	...	...	1	...	1	1	5	3	...	...	4	2	1	1
2	2	271	258	121	130	5	3	25	22	91	105	277	300	3	...	66	25	208	275
2	...	67	71	38	21	7	...	14	3	17	18	101	73	...	...	28	10	73	63
...	...	...	...	...	...	...	...	...	...	...	...	...	...	...	...	...	...	...	...
4	2	339	333	161	152	12	3	40	25	109	124	383	376	3	..	98	37	282	339
...	...	...	...	...	...	...	...	...	...	...	...	3	1	...	...	2	1	1	...
34	**19**	**1,330**	**1.363**	**808**	**606**	**35**	**4**	**342**	**84**	**431**	**518**	**2.135**	**1,697**	**6**	**1**	**815**	**163**	**1,314**	**1,533**

Buddhist.

Literate. Males.	Literate. Females.	Illiterate. Males.	Illiterate. Females.	15 — 24. Total. Males.	15 — 24. Total. Females.	15 — 24. Learning. Males.	15 — 24. Learning. Females.	15 — 24. Literate. Males.	15 — 24. Literate. Females.	15 — 24. Illiterate. Males.	15 — 24. Illiterate. Females.	25 and over. Total. Males.	25 and over. Total. Females.	25 and over. Learning. Males.	25 and over. Learning. Females.	25 and over. Literate. Males.	25 and over. Literate. Females.	25 and over. Illiterate. Males.	25 and over. Illiterate. Females.
...	...	...	...	...	...	...	...	...	...	...	...	1	...	...	...	1	...	...	...

Education by Religion and Age.

Part (F).—

State.	Total Population. Total.	Males.	Females.	Total by Education. Learning. Males.	Learning. Females.	Literate. Males.	Literate. Females.	Illiterate. Males.	Illiterate. Females.	0–14. Total. Males.	Total. Females.	Learning. Males.	Learning. Females.
Cutch	71,988	34,355	37,633	2,483	77	8,925	280	22,947	37,276	13,660	14,212	2,389	68
Pálanpur	29,149	14,896	14,253	2,011	44	9,635	132	8,250	14,077	5,114	5,042	1,882	40
Mahi Kántha	13,818	6,690	7,128	945	33	4,154	43	1,591	7,052	2,399	2,347	868	33
Káthiáwár	113,005	58,379	54,626	7,917	453	33,024	787	17,438	53,386	21,714	20,797	7,206	420
Rewa Kántha	1,308	721	587	75	3	481	8	165	576	207	151	70	3
Cambay	3,262	1,578	1,684	202	25	1,020	26	356	1,634	521	497	188	19
Surat Agency	126	69	57	7	2	44	3	18	52	24	23	7	2
Total, Gujarát Group	232,656	116,688	115,968	13,640	637	57,283	1,278	45,765	114,053	43,639	43,069	12,610	583
Jawhár	4	4	...	...	...	4	...	...	...	...	...	...	...
Janjira	71	62	9	1	...	51	...	10	...	10	4	1	...
Sáwantwádi	147	76	71	7	1	28	...	41	70	24	20	5	1
Total, Konkan Group	222	142	80	8	1	83	...	51	79	34	24	6	1
The Dángs	1	1	...	...	...	...	...	1	...	...	...	...	...
Surgana	...	...	...	...	...	...	...	...	...	...	...	...	...
Bhor	680	356	324	8	...	120	...	228	324	90	112	8	...
Akalkot	508	268	240	38	3	81	2	149	235	96	91	32	1
Sátára Agency	1,296	672	624	99	5	375	3	198	616	223	203	92	4
Total, Deccan Group	2,485	1,297	1,188	145	8	576	5	576	1,175	409	406	132	5
Jat	316	161	155	16	...	35	...	110	155	60	56	13	...
Kolhápur	50,896	26,950	23,946	1,309	22	3,431	18	22,210	23,906	9,495	8,804	1,106	21
Southern Marátha Jaghírs	28,183	14,150	14,033	521	6	1,438	18	12,191	14,009	5,355	5,086	424	5
Sáwanúr	15	8	7	1	...	2	...	5	7	3	3	1	...
Total, Karnátak Group	79,410	41,269	38,141	1,847	28	4,906	36	34,516	38,077	14,913	13,949	1,544	26
Khairpur	...	...	...	...	...	...	...	...	...	...	...	...	...
Total, Feudatory States	**314,773**	**159,396**	**155,377**	**15,640**	**674**	**62,848**	**1,319**	**80,908**	**153,384**	**58,995**	**57,448**	**14,292**	**617**

Part (G).—

State.	Total.	Males.	Females.	Learning Males.	Learning Females.	Literate Males.	Literate Females.	Illiterate Males.	Illiterate Females.	0–14 Total Males.	Total Females.	Learning Males.	Learning Females.
Cutch	94	81	13	...	...	39	...	42	13	6	5	...	...

Part (H).—

State.	Total.	Males.	Females.	Learning Males.	Learning Females.	Literate Males.	Literate Females.	Illiterate Males.	Illiterate Females.	0–14 Total Males.	Total Females.	Learning Males.	Learning Females.
Cutch	118	64	54	10	7	45	34	9	13	27	26	7	7
Pálanpur	205	96	109	17	8	66	68	13	43	36	44	17	8
Mahi Kántha	8	5	3	1	...	4	1	...	2	2	2	1	...
Káthiáwár	908	524	384	116	60	343	175	65	149	166	161	89	50
Rewa Kántha	386	228	158	28	12	145	41	55	105	64	63	22	11
Cambay	137	68	69	15	7	85	14	18	48	26	27	15	7
Surat Agency	618	352	266	38	31	242	88	72	147	98	105	35	30
Total, Gujarát Group	2,380	1,337	1,043	225	125	880	411	232	507	419	428	186	113
Jawhár	46	31	15	...	...	22	1	9	14	9	7	...	...
Janjira	...	...	...	...	...	...	...	...	...	...	...	...	...
Sáwantwádi	...	...	...	...	...	...	...	...	...	...	...	...	...
Total, Konkan Group	46	31	15	...	...	22	1	9	14	9	7	...	...
The Dángs	20	14	6	...	...	12	...	2	6	1	3	...	...
Surgana	28	19	9	...	...	17	1	2	8	1	2	...	...
Bhor	1	1	...	...	...	...	...	1	...	...	...	...	...
Akalkot	...	...	...	...	...	...	...	...	...	...	...	...	...
Sátára Agency	...	...	...	...	...	...	...	...	...	...	...	...	...
Total, Deccan Group	49	34	15	...	...	29	1	5	14	2	5	...	...
Jat	...	...	...	...	...	...	...	...	...	...	...	...	...
Kolhápur	24	12	12	4	2	8	6	...	4	4	6	3	1
Southern Marátha Jaghírs	12	8	4	...	...	1	1	7	3	4	1	...	...
Sáwanúr	...	...	...	...	...	...	...	...	...	...	...	...	...
Total, Karnátak Group	36	20	16	4	2	9	7	7	7	8	7	3	1
Khairpur	...	...	...	...	...	...	...	...	...	...	...	...	...
Total, Feudatory States	**2,511**	**1,422**	**1,089**	**229**	**127**	**940**	**420**	**253**	**542**	**438**	**447**	**189**	**114**

IX.

Jain.

				15—24.								25 and over.							
Literate.		Illiterate.		Total.		Learning.		Literate.		Illiterate.		Total.		Learning.		Literate.		Illiterate.	
Males.	Females.	Males.	Females.	Males.	Females.	Males.	Females.	Males.	Females.	Males.	Females.	Males.	Females.	Males.	Females.	Males.	Females.	Males.	Females.
646	40	10,625	14,104	4,910	6,135	83	4	2,074	63	2,753	6,068	15,785	17,286	11	5	6,205	177	9,569	17,104
558	15	2,674	4,987	2,747	2,362	119	2	2,452	37	176	2,323	7,035	6,849	10	2	6,625	80	400	6,767
296	8	1.235	2,306	1,293	1,283	63	...	1.117	17	143	1,266	2,998	3,498	14	..	2,741	18	243	3,480
2,475	156	12,033	20,221	11,451	9,718	646	21	9,105	260	1,700	9,437	25,214	24,111	65	12	21,444	371	3,705	23,728
28	...	109	148	137	116	4	...	116	1	17	115	377	320	1	...	337	7	39	313
76	4	257	474	295	300	13	1	260	7	22	292	762	887	1	5	684	14	77	868
...	...	17	21	14	4	...	...	14	1	...	3	31	30	...	...	30	2	1	28
4,079	223	20,950	42,261	20,847	19,918	928	28	15,188	386	4,781	19,504	52,202	52,951	102	24	38,066	669	14,034	52,288
...	...	..	...	1	...	...	...	1	...	...	...	3	...	...	...	3	...	...	...
5	...	4	4	31	2	...	...	29	...	2	2	21	3	...	...	17	...	4	3
...	...	19	19	16	14	2	...	6	...	8	14	36	37	...	...	22	...	14	37
5	...	23	23	48	16	2	...	36	...	10	16	60	40	...	...	42	...	18	40
...	...	...	...	1	...	...	...	...	...	1	...	...	...	...	...	...	...	...	...
...	...	...	...	...	...	...	...	...	...	...	...	...	...	...	...	...	...	...	...
4	...	78	112	73	66	...	...	27	...	46	66	193	146	...	...	89	...	104	146
7	...	57	90	43	49	4	...	16	1	23	48	129	100	2	2	58	1	69	97
9	2	122	197	107	111	7	...	77	1	23	110	342	310	...	1	289	...	53	309
20	2	257	399	224	226	11	...	120	2	93	224	664	556	2	3	436	1	226	552
4	...	43	56	29	20	3	...	7	...	19	20	72	79	...	...	24	...	48	79
88	1	8,301	8,782	4,055	3,396	186	...	771	7	3,098	3,389	13,400	11,746	17	1	2.572	10	10,811	11,785
50	2	4,881	5,079	2,061	2,014	81	...	323	5	1,657	2,009	6,734	6,933	16	1	1,065	11	5,653	6,921
...	...	2	3	1	1	...	...	1	...	...	1	4	3	...	...	1	...	3	3
142	3	13,227	13,920	6,146	5,431	270	...	1,102	12	4,774	5,419	20,210	18,761	33	2	3,662	21	16,515	18,788
...	...	...	...	...	...	...	...	...	...	...	...	...	...	...	...	...	..	...	...
4,246	**228**	**40.457**	**56,603**	**27,265**	**25.591**	**1.211**	**28**	**16.396**	**400**	**9.658**	**25,163**	**73,136**	**72,338**	**137**	**29**	**42,206**	**691**	**30,793**	**71,618**
Sikh.																			
...	...	6	5	29	2	...	...	12	...	17	2	46	6	...	...	27	...	19	6
Pársi.																			
11	10	9	9	11	6	3	...	8	6	...	...	26	22	...	...	26	18	...	4
7	12	12	24	12	19	...	...	11	17	1	2	48	46	...	...	48	29	...	17
1	...	...	2	...	1	...	...	...	1	...	...	3	...	...	...	3	...	...	...
27	28	50	83	108	75	27	6	80	54	1	15	250	148	...	4	236	93	14	51
6	2	36	50	43	24	6	1	32	14	5	9	121	71	...	...	107	25	14	46
2	4	9	16	9	11	...	...	7	6	2	5	33	31	...	...	26	4	7	27
13	16	50	59	47	42	3	1	42	27	2	14	207	119	...	...	187	45	20	74
67	72	166	243	230	178	39	8	180	125	11	45	688	437	...	4	633	214	56	219
2	1	7	6	4	...	...	...	4	...	...	...	18	8	...	...	16	...	2	8
...	...	...	...	...	...	...	...	...	...	...	...	...	...	...	...	...	...	...	...
...	...	...	...	...	...	...	...	...	...	...	...	...	...	...	...	...	...	...	...
2	1	7	6	4	...	...	...	4	...	...	...	18	8	...	...	16	...	2	8
1	...	1	3	3	1	...	...	2	...	1	1	10	2	...	...	10	...	...	2
...	...	...	2	...	2	...	...	...	...	...	2	18	5	...	...	16	1	2	4
...	...	...	...	...	...	...	...	...	...	...	...	1	...	...	...	...	...	1	...
...	...	...	...	...	...	...	...	...	...	...	...	...	...	...	...	...	...	...	...
...	...	...	...	...	...	...	...	...	...	...	...	..	...	...	...	...	...	...	..
1	...	1	5	3	3	...	...	2	...	1	3	29	7	...	...	26	1	3	6
...	...	...	...	...	...	...	...	...	...	...	...	...	...	...	...	...	...	...	...
1	2	...	3	1	1	1	1	...	...	...	...	7	5	...	...	7	4	...	1
...	...	4	1	...	1	...	...	...	...	...	1	4	2	..	...	1	1	3	1
...	...	...	...	...	...	...	...	...	...	...	...	...	...	...	...	...	...	...	...
1	2	4	4	1	2	1	1	...	...	...	1	11	7	...	...	8	5	3	2
...	...	...	...	...	...	...	...	...	...	...	...	...	...	...	...	...	...	...	...
71	**75**	**178**	**258**	**238**	**183**	**40**	**9**	**186**	**125**	**12**	**49**	**746**	**459**	...	**4**	**683**	**220**	**63**	**235**

Education by Religion and Age.

TABLE

Part (I).—

State.	Total Population: Total.	Total Population: Males.	Total Population: Females.	Total by Education: Learning, Males.	Learning, Females.	Literate, Males.	Literate, Females.	Illiterate, Males.	Illiterate, Females.	0–14: Total, Males.	Total, Females.	Learning, Males.	Learning, Females.
Cutch	47	26	21	...	6	15	5	11	10	10	8	...	5
Pálanpur	34	18	16	1	4	12	2	5	10	4	6	1	2
Mahi Kántha	4	3	1	...	...	1	1	2	...	2	...	...	...
Káthiáwár	105	54	51	19	6	25	17	10	28	27	27	17	6
Rewa Kántha	6	4	2	...	...	3	...	1	2	1	...	...	...
Cambay	...	...	...	...	...	...	...	...	...	...	...	...	...
Surat Agency	6	3	3	2	...	1	...	...	3	1	1	1	...
Total, Gujarát Group	202	108	94	22	16	57	25	29	53	45	42	19	13
Jawhár	...	...	...	...	...	...	...	...	...	...	...	...	...
Janjira	599	282	317	24	1	54	4	204	312	126	140	24	1
Sáwantwádi	...	...	...	...	...	...	...	...	...	...	...	...	...
Total, Konkan Group	599	282	317	24	1	54	4	204	312	126	140	24	1
The Dángs	...	...	...	...	...	...	...	...	...	...	...	...	...
Surgana	...	...	...	...	...	...	...	...	...	...	...	...	...
Bhor	271	142	129	7	...	15	2	120	127	56	51	5	...
Akalkot	...	...	...	...	...	...	...	...	...	...	...	...	...
Sátára Agency	4	2	2	...	...	2	...	...	2	...	1	...	...
Total, Deccan Group	275	144	131	7	...	17	2	120	129	56	52	5	...
Jat	...	...	...	...	...	...	...	...	...	...	...	...	...
Kolhápur	...	...	...	...	...	...	...	...	...	...	...	...	...
Southern Marátha Jaghírs	6	2	4	1	...	...	...	1	4	1	3	1	...
Sáwanúr	...	...	...	...	...	...	...	...	...	...	...	...	...
Total, Karnátak Group	6	2	4	1	...	...	...	1	4	1	3	1	...
Khairpur	...	...	...	...	...	...	...	...	...	...	...	...	...
Total, Feudatory States	**1,082**	**536**	**546**	**54**	**17**	**128**	**31**	**354**	**498**	**228**	**237**	**49**	**14**

Part (J).—

State.	Total Population: Total.	Total Population: Males.	Total Population: Females.	Total by Education: Learning, Males.	Learning, Females.	Literate, Males.	Literate, Females.	Illiterate, Males.	Illiterate, Females.	0–14: Total, Males.	Total, Females.	Learning, Males.	Learning, Females.
Cutch	882	457	425	...	...	7	...	450	425	180	188	...	...
Pálanpur	174	89	85	...	...	...	...	89	85	37	35	...	...
Mahi Kántha	...	...	...	...	...	...	...	...	...	...	...	...	...
Káthiáwár	4	1	3	...	...	...	...	1	3	...	...	...	...
Rewa Kántha	64,856	32,390	32,466	56	2	72	...	32,262	32,464	14,815	14,206	47	1
Cambay	...	...	...	...	...	...	...	...	...	...	...	...	...
Surat Agency	...	...	...	...	...	...	...	...	...	...	...	...	...
Total, Gujarát Group	65,916	32,937	32,979	56	2	79	...	32,802	32,977	15,032	14,429	47	1
Jawhár	121	58	63	...	...	...	...	58	63	24	27	...	...
Janjira	159	93	66	...	...	...	...	93	66	34	27	...	...
Sáwantwádi	...	...	...	...	...	...	...	...	...	...	...	...	...
Total, Konkan Group	280	151	129	...	...	...	...	151	129	58	54	...	...
The Dángs	11,402	5,868	5,534	...	...	...	...	5,868	5,534	2,643	2,511	...	...
Surgana	121	61	60	...	...	...	...	61	60	27	35	...	...
Bhor	...	...	...	...	...	...	...	...	...	...	...	...	...
Akalkot	...	...	...	...	...	...	...	...	...	...	...	...	...
Sátára Agency	...	...	...	...	...	...	...	...	...	...	...	...	...
Total, Deccan Group	11,523	5,929	5,594	...	...	...	...	5,929	5,594	2,670	2,546	...	...
Jat	...	...	...	...	...	...	...	...	...	...	...	...	...
Kolhápur	...	...	...	...	...	...	...	...	...	...	...	...	...
Southern Marátha Jaghírs	...	...	...	...	...	...	...	...	...	...	...	...	...
Sáwanúr	...	...	...	...	...	...	...	...	...	...	...	...	...
Total, Karnátak Group	...	...	...	...	...	...	...	...	...	...	...	...	...
Khairpur	686	389	297	...	...	...	...	389	297	167	102	...	...
Total, Feudatory States	**78,405**	**39,406**	**38,999**	**56**	**2**	**79**	**...**	**39,271**	**38,997**	**17,927**	**17,131**	**47**	**1**

Table IX.

Education by Religion and Age.

IX.

Jew.

Literate.		Illiterate.		15 — 24.								25 and over.							
				Total.		Learning.		Literate.		Illiterate.		Total.		Learning.		Literate.		Illiterate.	
Males.	Females.	Males.	Females.	Males.	Females.	Males.	Females.	Males.	Females.	Males.	Females.	Males.	Females.	Males.	Females.	Males.	Females.	Males.	Females.
...	...	10	3	4	6	...	1	4	2	...	3	12	7	...	...	11	3	1	4
...	1	3	3	5	7	...	2	5	1	...	4	9	3	...	...	7	...	2	3
...	...	2	...	...	1	...	...	...	1	...	...	1	...	...	...	1	...	...	...
1	6	9	15	4	7	1	...	3	5	...	2	23	17	1	...	21	6	1	11
...	...	1	...	...	...	...	...	...	...	...	...	3	2	...	...	3	...	...	2
...	...	...	...	...	...	...	...	...	...	...	...	...	...	...	...	...	...	...	...
...	...	...	1	1	...	1	...	...	...	...	...	1	2	...	...	1	...	...	2
1	7	25	22	14	21	2	3	12	9	...	9	49	31	1	...	44	9	4	22
...	...	...	...	...	...	...	...	...	...	...	...	...	...	...	...	...	...	...	...
2	1	100	138	38	48	...	...	17	1	21	47	118	129	...	...	35	2	83	127
...	...	...	...	...	...	...	...	...	...	...	...	...	...	...	...	...	...	...	...
2	1	100	138	38	48	...	...	17	1	21	47	118	129	...	...	35	2	83	127
...	...	...	...	...	...	...	...	...	...	...	...	...	...	...	...	...	...	...	...
...	...	...	...	...	...	...	...	...	...	...	...	...	...	...	...	...	...	...	...
...	...	51	51	25	25	2	...	1	...	22	25	61	53	...	...	14	2	47	51
...	...	...	...	...	...	...	...	...	...	...	...	...	...	...	...	...	...	...	...
...	...	...	1	1	...	...	...	1	...	...	...	1	1	...	...	1	...	...	1
...	...	51	52	26	25	2	...	2	...	22	25	62	54	...	...	15	2	47	52
...	...	...	...	...	...	...	...	...	...	...	...	...	...	...	...	...	...	...	...
...	...	...	...	...	...	...	...	...	...	...	...	...	...	...	...	...	...	...	...
...	...	...	3	...	...	...	...	...	...	...	...	1	1	...	...	...	...	1	1
...	...	...	...	...	...	...	...	...	...	...	...	...	...	...	...	...	...	...	...
...	...	...	3	...	...	...	...	...	...	...	...	1	1	...	...	...	...	1	1
...	...	...	...	...	...	...	...	...	...	...	...	...	...	...	...	...	...	...	...
3	8	176	215	78	94	4	3	31	10	43	81	230	215	1	...	94	13	135	202

Animistic.

Literate.		Illiterate.		15 — 24.								25 and over.							
				Total.		Learning.		Literate.		Illiterate.		Total.		Learning.		Literate.		Illiterate.	
Males.	Females.	Males.	Females.	Males.	Females.	Males.	Females.	Males.	Females.	Males.	Females.	Males.	Females.	Males.	Females.	Males.	Females.	Males.	Females.
...	...	180	188	91	69	...	...	...	...	91	69	186	168	...	...	7	...	179	168
...	...	37	35	18	13	...	...	...	...	18	13	34	37	...	...	...	...	34	37
...	...	...	...	...	...	...	...	...	...	...	...	...	...	...	...	...	...	...	...
...	...	...	...	...	...	...	...	...	...	...	...	1	3	...	...	...	...	1	3
7	...	14,761	14,206	5,088	5,450	8	1	22	...	5,058	5,449	12,487	12,810	1	...	43	...	12,443	12,810
...	...	...	...	...	...	...	...	...	...	...	...	...	...	...	...	...	...	...	...
...	...	...	...	...	...	...	...	...	...	...	...	...	...	...	...	...	...	...	...
7	...	14,078	14,428	5,197	5,533	8	1	22	...	5,167	5,531	12,708	13,018	1	...	50	...	12,657	13,018
...	...	24	27	4	9	...	...	...	...	4	9	30	27	...	...	...	...	30	27
...	...	34	27	13	8	...	...	...	...	13	8	46	31	...	...	...	...	46	31
...	...	...	...	...	...	...	...	...	...	...	...	...	...	...	...	...	...	...	...
...	...	58	54	17	17	...	...	...	...	17	17	76	58	...	...	...	...	76	58
...	...	2,643	2,511	840	931	...	...	...	...	840	931	2,385	2,092	...	...	...	...	2,385	2,092
...	...	27	35	9	7	...	...	...	...	9	7	25	18	...	...	...	...	25	18
...	...	...	...	...	...	...	...	...	...	...	...	...	...	...	...	...	...	...	...
...	...	...	...	...	...	...	...	...	...	...	...	...	...	...	...	...	...	...	...
...	...	...	...	...	...	...	...	...	...	...	...	...	...	...	...	...	...	...	...
...	...	2,670	2,546	849	938	...	...	...	...	849	938	2,410	2,110	...	...	...	...	2,410	2,110
...	...	...	...	...	...	...	...	...	...	...	...	...	...	...	...	...	...	...	...
...	...	...	...	...	...	...	...	...	...	...	...	...	...	...	...	...	...	...	...
...	...	...	...	...	...	...	...	...	...	...	...	...	...	...	...	...	...	...	...
...	...	...	...	...	...	...	...	...	...	...	...	...	...	...	...	...	...	...	...
...	...	...	...	...	...	...	...	...	...	...	...	...	...	...	...	...	...	...	...
...	...	167	102	61	57	...	...	...	...	61	57	161	138	...	...	...	...	161	138
7	...	17,873	17,130	6,124	6,544	8	1	22	...	6,094	6,543	15,355	15,324	1	...	50	...	15,304	15,324

TABLE X.

PARENT-TONGUE.

Detail of Languages shown under "Others" :—

Language.	Feudatories.			Language.	Feudatories.		
	Total.	Males.	Females.		Total.	Males.	Females.
A.—Kashmiri ...	1	1	...	B.—Abyssinian ...	4	3	1
Malay	132	67	65	Turki	25	14	11
Nepáli	23	14	9	Zanzibári ...	34	17	17
Sanskrit	14	13	1	C.—Italian	2	2	...
Uriya	9	5		Swedish... ...	1	1	...
				Total ...	245	137	108

A.—IN

State.	Gujaráti. Total.	Gujaráti. Males.	Gujaráti. Females.	Cutchi. Total.	Cutchi. Males.	Cutchi. Females.	Bhil. Total.	Bhil. Males.	Bhil. Females.	Maráthi. Total.	Maráthi. Males.	Maráthi. Females.
Cutch	236,909	116,172	120,737	311,078	155,659	155,419	...	...	...	904	631	273
Pálanpur	581,841	301,219	280,622	...	...	...	...	...	...	1,508	995	513
Mahi Kántha...	548,124	278,155	269,969	8	5	3	...	...	...	251	141	110
Káthiáwár	2,571,052	1,323,562	1,247,490	64,434	28,396	36,038	...	...	...	3,898	2,330	1,568
Rewa Kántha...	707,651	362,598	345,053	...	...	...	10,653	5,543	5,110	690	438	252
Cambay	84,710	43,892	40,818	32	18	14	...	...	...	32	18	14
Surat Agency	70,079	35,544	34,535	...	...	...	...	...	...	108,418	55,435	52,983
Jawhár	1,333	1,082	251	27	18	9	...	...	...	51,049	26,483	24,566
Janjira	490	423	67	6	4	2	...	...	...	68,018	33,214	34,804
Sáwantwádi	13	11	2	...	...	...	...	...	...	183,634	88,969	94,665
The Dángs	69	60	9	...	...	...	969	526	443	31,702	16,550	15,152
Surgana	58	39	19	...	...	...	...	...	...	12,198	6,429	5,769
Bhor	508	343	165	...	...	...	...	...	...	152,726	76,913	75,813
Akalkot	245	131	114	...	...	...	...	...	...	26,197	13,163	13,034
Sátára Agency	1,185	625	560	...	...	...	...	...	...	118,469	59,632	58,837
Jat	269	126	143	...	...	...	...	...	...	42,736	21,740	20,996
Kolhápur	2,131	1,211	920	...	...	...	...	...	...	709,582	360,919	348,663
Southern Marátha Jaghírs...	3,352	1,825	1,527	...	...	...	...	...	...	246,206	123,946	122,260
Sáwanúr	56	23	33	...	...	...	...	...	...	810	377	433
Khairpur	...	...	...	...	...	...	...	...	...	...	...	...
Grand Total ...	4,810,075	2,467,041	2,343,034	375,585	184,100	191,485	11,622	6,069	5,553	1,759,028	888,323	870,705

A.—IN

State.	Urdu. Total.	Urdu. Males.	Urdu. Females.	Hindi. Total.	Hindi. Males.	Hindi. Females.	Gipsy dialects. Total.	Gipsy dialects. Males.	Gipsy dialects. Females.	Marwádi. Total.	Marwádi. Males.	Marwádi. Females.	Panjábi. Total.	Panjábi. Males.	Panjábi. Females.
Cutch	3,189	2,327	862	20	15	5	...	...	...	4,018	2,225	1,793	232	192	40
Pálanpur	24,149	12,936	11,213	...	...	...	...	...	...	35,187	18,639	16,548	254	221	33
Mahi Kántha...	31,338	17,243	14,095	...	...	...	...	...	...	1,740	1,014	726	5	5	...
Káthiáwár	56,573	34,452	22,121	183	119	64	...	...	...	3,018	1,740	1,278	240	193	47
Rewa Kántha...	12,812	6,619	6,193	332	272	60	87	71	16	434	204	230	176	20	156
Cambay	4,830	2,228	2,602	...	...	...	...	...	...	25	17	8	1	1	...
Surat Agency	2,481	1,331	1,150	2	...	2	...	...	...	28	20	8	...	...	...
Jawhár	330	192	138	...	...	...	...	...	...	87	47	40	...	...	...
Janjira	1,711	879	832	...	...	...	...	...	...	65	53	12	...	...	...
Sáwantwádi	4,463	2,123	2,340	...	...	...	...	...	...	2	2	...	5	5	...
The Dángs	173	97	76	...	...	...	...	...	...	...	...	...	...	...	...
Surgana	137	72	65	...	...	...	2	2	...	...	...	...	...	...	...
Bhor	1,836	994	842	16	13	3	6	4	2	122	87	35	...	...	...
Akalkot	9,858	5,033	4,825	...	...	...	206	124	82	22	14	8	2	2	...
Sátára Agency	4,556	2,338	2,218	13	10	3	417	231	186	211	108	103	...	...	...
Jat	5,111	2,927	2,184	4	1	3	282	143	139	55	32	23	...	...	...
Kolhápur	36,810	19,444	17,366	...	...	...	219	117	102	353	227	126	...	...	...
Southern Marátha Jaghírs...	48,932	24,650	24,282	...	...	...	18	9	9	804	518	286	...	...	...
Sáwanúr	4,965	2,410	2,555	...	...	...	116	60	56	2	2	...	...	...	...
Khairpur	28	26	2	...	...	...	...	...	...	1,119	661	458	457	308	149
Grand Total ...	1254,282	138,321	115,961	570	430	140	1,353	761	592	47,292	25,610	21,682	1,372	947	425

X.

DIAN.

Konkani.			Goanese.			Kanarese.			Sindhi.			Baluchi.		
Total.	Males.	Females.	Total.	Males.	Females.	Total.	Males.	Females.	Total.	Males.	Females.	Total.	Males.	Females.
...	...	...	84	71	*13*	4	3	*1*	1,353	763	*590*	4	4	...
24	15	*9*	53	39	*14*	8	4	*4*	1,481	804	*677*	294	170	*124*
4	...	*4*	14	14	...	...	...	...	2	2	...	23	17	*6*
28	25	*3*	291	235	*56*	30	23	*7*	45,982	21,845	*24,137*	1,583	914	*669*
3	3	...	3	2	*1*	6	3	*3*	13	8	*5*	164	84	*80*
...	...	...	2	2	...	...	...	...	31	18	*13*	...	...	...
10	...	*10*	1	1	...	56	32	*24*	...	...	...	1	1	...
...	...	...	1	1	...	...	...	...	...	...	...	...	...	...
11,437	5,025	*6,412*	25	8	*17*	...	...	...	...	...	...	...	...	...
4,594	2,207	*2,387*	...	...	...	200	167	*33*	...	...	...	...	...	...
...	...	...	2	2	...	...	...	...	...	...	...	...	...	...
...	...	...	...	...	...	...	...	...	...	...	...	...	...	...
...	...	...	7	6	*1*	28	16	*12*	...	...	...	...	...	...
...	...	...	...	...	...	38,061	19,582	*18,479*	...	...	...	...	...	...
...	...	...	...	...	...	5,971	2,962	*3,009*	...	...	...	...	...	...
...	...	...	2	2	...	30,187	15,011	*15,176*	...	...	...	...	...	...
...	...	...	22	20	*2*	159,262	83.247	*76,015*	2	2	...	...	...	...
39	38	*1*	...	...	...	330,881	164,890	*165,991*	...	...	...	...	...	...
2	2	...	...	...	...	10,822	8,346	*5,476*	...	...	...	...	...	...
...	...	...	...	...	...	...	...	...	128,478	70,660	*57,818*	1,803	1,028	*775*
16,141	7,315	8,826	507	403	104	575,516	291,286	284,230	177,342	94,102	83,240	3,872	2,218	1,654

DIAN.

Bengali.			Tamil.			Telagu.			Patnuli.			Malyalam.			Pashtu.		
Total.	Males.	Females.	Total.	Males.	Females.	Total.	Males.	Females.	Total.	Males.	Females.	Total.	Males.	Females.	Total.	Males.	Females.
7	5	*2*	14	9	*5*	12	8	*4*	...	...	...	...	...	...	111	76	*35*
1	1	...	61	7	*54*	23	12	*11*	...	...	...	...	...	...	144	117	*27*
...	...	...	...	...	...	1	1	...	...	...	...	...	...	...	28	27	*1*
52	19	*33*	51	32	*19*	50	25	*25*	...	...	...	2	2	...	968	550	*418*
...	...	...	...	...	...	1	1	...	...	...	...	...	...	...	62	47	*15*
...	...	...	...	...	...	...	...	...	...	...	...	...	...	...	17	11	*6*
1	1	...	...	...	...	1	1	...	...	...	...	...	...	...	3	3	...
...	...	...	...	...	...	1	1	...	...	...	...	...	...	...	...	...	...
...	...	...	...	...	...	19	14	*5*	...	...	...	...	...	...	...	...	...
...	...	...	...	...	...	34	34	...	...	...	...	...	...	...	...	...	...
...	...	...	...	...	...	...	...	...	...	...	...	...	...	...	...	...	...
...	...	...	...	...	...	...	...	...	...	...	...	...	...	...	...	...	...
...	...	...	...	...	...	408	217	*191*	...	...	...	...	...	...	...	...	...
...	...	...	39	27	*12*	1,029	516	*513*	...	...	...	...	...	...	71	1	*70*
...	...	...	...	...	...	662	350	*312*	...	...	...	...	...	...	11	...	*11*
...	...	...	...	...	...	882	456	*426*	...	...	...	...	...	...	149	77	*72*
...	...	...	1,473	631	*842*	3.156	1,686	*1,470*	...	...	...	26	19	7	...	...	...
...	...	...	866	426	*440*	7,535	3,869	*3,666*	301	164	*137*	3	3	...	...	...	...
...	...	...	...	...	...	192	106	*86*	...	...	...	...	...	...	5	2	*3*
...	...	...	...	...	...	...	...	...	...	...	...	...	...	...	43	42	*1*
61	26	35	2,504	1,132	1,372	14,006	7,297	6,709	301	164	137	31	24	7	1,612	953	659

State.	A.—INDIAN.											
	Coorgi.			Kathodi.			Nemadi.			Rangdi.		
	Total.	Males.	Females.	Total.	Males.	Females.	Total.	Males.	Females.	Total.	Males.	Females.
Cutch	...	...	...	...	...	...	...	...	...	...	...	...
Pálanpur...	...	...	...	...	...	...	...	...	...	...	...	...
Mahi Kántha	...	...	...	...	...	...	...	...	...	...	...	...
Káthiáwár	...	...	...	...	...	...	6	5	*1*	...	...	...
Rewa Kántha	...	...	...	...	...	...	71	45	*26*	1	1	...
Cambay	...	...	...	...	...	...	...	...	...	...	...	...
Surat Agency	...	...	...	...	...	...	...	...	...	...	...	...
Jawhár	...	...	...	...	...	...	...	...	...	...	...	...
Janjira	...	...	...	3	3	...	...	...	...	...	...	...
Sáwantwádi	...	...	...	...	...	...	...	...	...	...	...	...
The Dángs	...	...	...	...	...	...	...	...	...	...	...	...
Surgana	...	...	...	...	...	...	...	...	...	...	...	...
Bhor	...	...	...	6	5	*1*	...	...	...	...	...	...
Akalkot	...	...	...	...	...	...	...	...	...	...	...	...
Sátára Agency	...	...	...	...	...	...	...	...	...	...	...	...
Jat	...	...	...	...	...	...	...	...	...	1	1	...
Kolhápur	19	11	*8*	...	...	...	...	...	...	...	...	...
Southern Marátha Jagbírs ...	...	...	...	...	...	...	...	...	...	...	...	...
Sáwanúr	...	...	...	...	...	...	...	...	...	...	...	...
Khairpur...	...	...	...	...	...	...	...	...	...	...	...	...
Grand Total ...	**19**	**11**	**8**	**9**	**8**	**1**	**77**	**50**	**27**	**2**	**2**	...

State.	C.—EUROPEAN.					
	English.			Irish.		
	Total.	Males.	Females.	Total.	Males.	Females.
Cutch	42	28	*14*	......	......	...
Pálanpur	477	396	*81*	1	1	...
Mahi Kántha	4	3	*1*	......	......	...
Káthiáwár	297	172	*125*	......	......	...
Rewa Kántha...	16	8	*8*	......	......	...
Cambay	9	7	*2*	......	......	...
Surat Agency...	......	......	......	......	......	...
Jawhár	3	1	*2*	......	......	...
Janjira...	......	......	......	......	......	...
Sáwantwádi	3	2	*1*	......	......	...
The Dángs	1	1	......	......	......	...
Surgana	......	......	......	......	......	...
Bhor	2	2	......	......	......	...
Akalkot	......	......	......	......	......	...
Sátára Agency	......	......	......	......	......	...
Jat	8	4	*4*	......	......	...
Kolhápur	58	28	*30*	......	......	...
Southern Marátha Jagbírs ...	47	27	*20*	......	......	...
Sáwanúr	......	......	......	......	......	...
Khairpur	3	2	*1*	......	......	...
Grand Total ...	**970**	**681**	**289**	**1**	**1**	...

B.—ASIATIC AND AFRICAN.

Persian.			Arabic.			Hebrew.			Chinese.			Negro dialects.		
Total.	Males.	Females.	Total.	Males.	Females.	Total.	Males.	Females.	Total.	Males.	Females.	Total.	Males.	Females.
15	12	*3*	373	218	*155*	...	...	...	1	1	...	1	...	*1*
9	5	*4*	5	2	*3*	...	...	...	...	...	...	...	...	...
12	11	*1*	6	...	*6*	...	...	...	...	...	...	...	...	...
1,838	971	*867*	1.757	981	*776*	6	4	*2*	...	...	...	9	4	*5*
12	7	*5*	185	103	*82*	...	...	...	...	...	...	...	...	...
4	4	...	4	3	*1*	...	...	...	...	...	...	...	...	...
1	1	...	124	85	*39*	...	...	...	...	...	...	...	...	...
...	...	...	...	...	...	...	...	...	...	...	...	...	...	...
...	...	...	5	5	...	...	...	...	...	...	...	...	...	...
...	...	...	...	...	...	...	...	...	...	...	...	...	...	...
4	1	*3*	...	...	...	...	...	...	...	...	...	...	...	...
3	3	...	...	...	...	...	...	...	...	...	...	...	...	...
...	...	...	...	...	...	4	2	*2*	...	...	...	...	...	...
...	...	...	...	...	...	...	...	...	...	...	...	...	...	...
...	...	...	...	...	...	...	...	...	...	...	...	...	...	...
4	1	*3*	9	8	*1*	...	...	...	...	...	...	...	...	...
2	1	*1*	16	9	*7*	...	...	...	...	...	...	...	...	...
...	...	...	280	163	*117*	...	...	...	...	...	...	...	...	...
...	...	...	...	...	...	...	...	...	...	...	...	...	...	...
6	6	...	...	...	...	...	...	...	...	...	...	...	...	...
1.910	**1.023**	**887**	**2.764**	**1.577**	**1.187**	**10**	**6**	**4**	**1**	**1**	...	**10**	**4**	**6**

German.			Others.			Unreturned.		
Total.	Males.	Females.	Total.	Males.	Females.	Total.	Males.	Females.
1	...	*1*	43	22	*21*	......	......	...
1	1	...	2	2	......	3	1	*2*
...	...	...	8	8	......	......	......	...
...	...	...	40	26	*14*	16	8	*8*
...	...	...	134	69	*65*	......	......	...
...	...	...	2	1	*1*	23	11	*12*
...	...	...	2	2	......	......	......	...
...	...	...	......	......	......	...	......	...
...	...	...	......	......	......	1	1	...
...	...	...	......	......	......	......	......	...
...	...	...	......	......	......	......	......	...
...	...	...	......	......	......	......	......	...
...	...	...	......	......	......	......	......	...
...	...	...	8	4	*4*	36	18	*18*
...	...	...	......	......	......	34	13	*21*
...	...	...	......	......	......	87	47	*40*
...	...	...	......	......	......	......	......	...
...	...	...	6	3	*3*	......	......	...
...	...	...	......	......	......	6	2	*4*
...	...	...	......	......	......	......	......	...
2	**1**	**1**	**245**	**137**	**108**	**206**	**101**	**105**

TABLE XI.

BIRTH-PLACE.

Civil Condition by Religion and Age.

TABLE

Part (H).—

(3) WID

District.	Total. Total.	Total. Males.	Total. Females.	0 — 4. Males.	0 — 4. Females.	5 — 9. Males.	5 — 9. Females.	10 — 14. Males.	10 — 14. Females.	15 — 19. Males.	15 — 19. Females.	20 — 24. Males.	20 — 24. Females.
Bombay City	4,153	810	3,343	2	1	3	...	3	...	4	21	17	48
Ahmedabad	52	12	40	...	...	...	...	...	...	...	1	...	...
Kaira	7	...	7	...	...	...	...	...	...	...	...	...	1
Panch Mahàls	6	3	3	...	...	...	...	...	...	...	...	...	...
Broach	329	70	259	...	...	...	...	...	...	3	1	1	6
Surat	1,423	266	1,157	...	1	1	...	...	2	...	5	4	26
Thána	412	78	334	...	...	...	...	...	...	...	6	1	6
Kolába	16	7	9	...	...	...	...	...	...	...	...	...	...
Ratnágiri	...	...	...	...	...	...	...	...	...	...	...	...	...
Kánara	1	1	...	...	...	...	...	...	...	...	...	...	...
Khándesh	18	10	8	...	...	...	...	...	...	...	...	1	...
Násik	20	6	14	...	...	...	...	...	...	...	...	...	...
Ahmednagar	15	5	10	...	...	...	...	...	...	...	...	...	...
Poona	140	42	98	...	...	...	...	...	...	...	...	1	...
Sholápur	11	3	8	...	...	...	...	...	...	...	...	...	...
Sátára	9	1	8	...	...	...	...	...	...	...	...	...	...
Belgaum	4	1	3	...	...	...	...	...	...	...	...	...	...
Dhárwár	4	2	2	...	...	...	...	...	...	...	...	...	...
Bijápur	3	1	2	...	...	...	...	...	...	...	...	...	...
Total, Presidency Proper ...	6,623	1,318	5,304	2	2	4	...	3	2	7	34	25	87
Karáchi	91	26	65	...	...	...	...	...	...	...	...	1	...
Hyderabad	...	...	...	...	...	...	...	...	...	...	...	...	...
Shikárpur	3	1	2	...	...	...	...	...	...	...	...	...	...
Thar and Párkar	...	...	...	...	...	...	...	...	...	...	...	...	...
Upper Sind Frontier	1	1	...	...	...	...	...	...	...	...	...	...	...
Total, Sind ...	95	28	67	...	...	...	...	...	...	...	...	1	...
Total, British Territory ...	**6,717**	**1,346**	**5,371**	**2**	**2**	**4**	...	**3**	**2**	**7**	**34**	**26**	**87**
Total, Feudatories ...	**169**	**55**	**114**	...	...	...	**1**	...	**1**	...	**1**	**6**	**1**
Grand Total ...	**6,886**	**1,401**	**5,485**	**2**	**2**	**4**	**1**	**3**	**3**	**7**	**35**	**32**	**88**
Aden	15	8	7	...	...	...	...	...	...	...	...	...	...

Part (I).—

(1) UN

District.	Total. Total.	Total. Males.	Total. Females.	0 — 4. Males.	0 — 4. Females.	5 — 9. Males.	5 — 9. Females.	10 — 14. Males.	10 — 14. Females.	15 — 19. Males.	15 — 19. Females.	20 — 24. Males.	20 — 24. Females.
Bombay City	2,464	1,458	1,006	329	309	291	307	321	238	250	75	150	40
Ahmedabad	118	62	56	17	24	14	18	12	12	10	...	9	...
Kaira	7	4	3	1	1	2	1	1	1	...	...	...	...
Panch Mahàls	...	...	...	...	...	...	...	...	...	...	...	...	...
Broach	15	9	6	3	3	3	2	3	1	...	...	...	...
Surat	19	13	6	5	2	1	3	5	...	1	1	1	...
Thána	222	135	87	33	31	37	31	32	19	15	3	14	2
Kolába	1,052	561	491	167	162	198	194	116	111	51	17	23	2
Ratnágiri	...	...	...	...	...	...	...	...	...	...	...	...	...
Kánara	5	4	1	2	1	2	...	...	...	...	...	...	...
Khándesh	49	27	22	4	15	7	6	8	...	5	1	1	...
Násik	55	33	22	5	4	8	10	11	6	6	2	2	...
Ahmednagar	23	14	9	7	3	2	6	2	1	3	...	...	...
Poona	480	251	229	63	58	54	84	64	67	41	16	18	7
Sholápur	9	5	4	1	1	2	2	...	1	1	...	...	...
Sátára	41	29	12	8	7	10	4	6	1	4	...	1	...
Belgaum	...	...	...	...	...	...	...	...	...	...	...	...	...
Dhárwár	15	9	6	4	2	1	1	1	1	...	2	3	...
Bijápur	5	1	4	...	...	1	1	...	3	...	...	...	...
Total, Presidency Proper ...	4,579	2,615	1,964	639	623	633	669	582	462	387	117	222	45
Karáchi	74	34	40	10	13	11	13	3	10	6	1	2	...
Hyderabad	16	10	6	2	2	2	3	1	1	3	...	...	...
Shikárpur	17	8	9	2	2	4	4	...	3	2	...	...	...
Thar and Párkar	...	...	...	...	...	...	...	...	...	...	...	...	...
Upper Sind Frontier	2	1	1	1	...	...	1	...	...	...	...	...	...
Total, Sind ...	109	53	56	15	17	17	21	4	14	11	1	2	...
Total, British Territory ...	**4,688**	**2,668**	**2,030**	**654**	**640**	**650**	**690**	**586**	**476**	**398**	**118**	**224**	**45**
Total, Feudatories ...	**498**	**280**	**218**	**92**	**93**	**78**	**78**	**56**	**36**	**28**	**8**	**16**	**2**
Grand Total ...	**5,186**	**2,948**	**2,238**	**746**	**733**	**728**	**768**	**642**	**512**	**426**	**126**	**240**	**47**
Aden	1,528	835	693	167	206	171	178	187	163	137	89	89	37

Table VIII.

Civil Condition by Religion and Age.

VIII.

Pársi.

OWED.

25—29. Males.	25—29. Females.	30—34. Males.	30—34. Females.	35—39. Males.	35—39. Females.	40—44. Males.	40—44. Females.	45—49. Males.	45—49. Females.	50—54. Males.	50—54. Females.	55—59. Males.	55—59. Females.	60 and over. Males.	60 and over. Females.
23	88	60	145	76	172	86	357	63	315	99	565	96	412	278	1,218
...	1	...	...	...	1	1	9	...	4	...	3	1	5	10	16
...	...	...	...	...	1	...	...	...	...	...	3	...	...	...	2
...	...	...	...	...	1	1	...	...	...	1	...	1	...	...	9
...	7	4	4	7	10	7	20	5	13	7	41	6	22	30	135
10	27	4	41	7	59	17	98	16	90	28	147	25	95	155	566
5	6	4	10	7	20	7	48	8	52	10	47	8	33	28	127
...	...	1	...	...	...	2	1	...	1	1	6	...	1	3	4
...	...	...	...	...	...	...	...	...	...	...	...	...	...	...	...
...	...	...	...	...	...	...	...	1	...	...	...	...	...	...	...
...	...	1	3	...	...	1	...	...	...	1	2	...	1	6	2
1	1	...	1	...	...	...	2	2	...	1	2	1	2	1	6
...	...	...	...	1	2	...	1	...	2	...	1	2	1	2	3
1	...	2	8	2	10	3	11	6	10	6	8	2	9	20	42
...	...	1	...	...	1	...	...	1	1	...	...	...	...	1	6
...	1	...	...	...	...	...	1	...	...	...	3	...	1	1	2
...	...	...	...	...	1	...	1	...	...	...	...	1	...	...	1
...	...	...	...	...	...	...	1	...	...	...	...	1	...	1	1
...	...	...	...	...	...	...	1	...	...	...	1	1	...	...	...
40	130	77	212	100	278	125	551	101	468	153	825	145	582	538	2,133
2	2	1	5	2	1	3	8	2	5	5	10	1	8	9	26
...	...	...	...	...	...	...	...	...	...	...	...	...	...	...	...
...	...	...	...	...	1	...	...	...	...	1	...	...	...	...	1
1	...	...	...	...	...	...	...	...	...	...	...	...	...	...	...
3	2	1	5	2	2	3	8	2	5	6	10	1	8	9	27
43	**133**	**78**	**217**	**103**	**230**	**128**	**559**	**103**	**473**	**159**	**835**	**146**	**590**	**545**	**2.160**
4	**9**	**8**	**2**	**1**	**9**	**1**	**13**	**6**	**11**	**9**	**19**	**4**	**8**	**16**	**39**
47	**141**	**86**	**219**	**103**	**289**	**129**	**572**	**109**	**484**	**168**	**851**	**150**	**598**	**561**	**2.199**
...	2	2	...	...	1	1	1	...	1	2	...	1	...	2	2

Jew.

MARRIED.

25—29. Males.	25—29. Females.	30—34. Males.	30—34. Females.	35—39. Males.	35—39. Females.	40—44. Males.	40—44. Females.	45—49. Males.	45—49. Females.	50—54. Males.	50—54. Females.	55—59. Males.	55—59. Females.	60 and over. Males.	60 and over. Females.
53	20	35	4	16	6	7	2	3	3	3	1	...	...	...	1
...	...	...	2	...	...	...	...	...	...	...	...	...	...	...	...
...	...	...	...	...	...	...	...	...	...	...	...	...	...	...	...
...	...	...	...	...	...	...	...	...	...	...	...	...	...	...	...
...	...	...	...	...	...	...	...	...	...	...	...	...	...	...	...
...	...	...	...	...	...	...	...	...	...	...	...	...	...	...	...
2	...	1	...	...	...	1	...	...	...	...	...	...	...	...	1
10	1	3	2	...	2	1	...	...	...	1	...	...	...	1	...
...	...	...	...	...	...	...	...	...	...	...	...	...	...	...	...
...	...	...	...	...	...	...	...	...	...	...	...	...	...	...	...
1	...	...	...	1	...	...	...	...	...	...	...	...	...	...	...
1	...	...	...	...	...	...	...	...	...	...	...	...	...	...	...
...	...	...	...	...	...	...	...	...	...	...	...	...	...	...	...
7	2	2	...	...	1	...	...	...	...	1	...	...	...	1	...
...	...	...	...	...	...	...	...	...	...	...	...	...	...	1	...
...	...	...	...	...	...	...	...	...	...	...	...	...	...	...	...
...	...	...	...	...	...	...	...	...	...	...	...	...	...	...	...
...	...	...	...	...	...	...	...	...	...	...	...	...	...	...	...
...	...	...	...	...	...	...	...	...	...	...	...	...	...	...	...
74	23	41	8	17	9	9	2	3	3	6	1	...	...	3	2
1	2	...	...	1	...	...	...	...	1	...	...	...	...	...	...
1	...	...	...	...	...	1	...	...	...	...	...	...	...	...	...
...	...	...	...	...	...	...	...	...	...	...	...	...	...	...	...
...	...	...	...	...	...	...	...	...	...	...	...	...	...	...	...
...	...	...	...	...	...	...	...	...	...	...	...	...	...	...	...
2	2	...	...	1	...	1	...	...	1	...	...	...	...	...	...
76	**25**	**41**	**8**	**18**	**9**	**10**	**2**	**3**	**4**	**5**	**1**	...	...	**3**	**3**
4	**1**	**3**	...	...	...	...	...	...	...	**2**	...	...	...	**3**	**1**
80	**26**	**34**	**8**	**18**	**9**	**10**	**2**	**3**	**4**	**7**	**1**	...	...	**6**	**3**
35	13	30	6	11	3	7	2	...	1	1	1	...	...	...	...

Table VIII.

Civil Condition by Religion and Age.

TABLE

Part (I).—

(2) MAR

District.	Total. Total.	Total. Males.	Total. Females.	0—4. Males.	0—4. Females	5—9. Males.	5—9. Females.	10—14. Males.	10—14. Females.	15—19. Males.	15—19. Females.	20—24. Males.	20—24. Females.
Bombay City	2,159	1,075	1,084	2	...	3	4	4	40	21	165	127	222
Ahmedabad	77	37	40	...	...	...	...	...	...	2	10	5	9
Kaira	2	1	1	...	...	...	...	...	...	...	...	...	...
Panch Mahâls	...	...	...	...	...	...	...	...	...	...	...	...	...
Broach	5	2	3	...	...	...	...	...	...	...	...	...	1
Surat	17	10	7	...	...	...	...	...	1	...	1	2	...
Thâna	191	98	93	...	...	1	...	1	4	1	14	12	22
Kolâba	1,040	479	561	...	1	2	3	11	37	16	85	45	91
Ratnâgiri	...	...	...	...	...	...	...	...	...	...	...	...	...
Kânara	5	3	2	...	...	...	...	...	...	...	1	...	...
Khândesh	43	23	20	2	...	...	...	...	...	...	4	3	5
Nâsik	47	22	25	...	...	...	...	...	1	...	6	4	6
Ahmednagar	11	4	7	...	...	...	...	...	...	...	3	1	1
Poona	373	180	193	...	1	...	2	1	10	3	22	20	23
Sholâpur	10	6	4	...	...	...	...	...	...	...	...	1	...
Sâtâra	35	17	19	...	...	...	...	...	2	1	3	1	5
Belgaum	...	...	...	...	...	...	...	...	...	...	...	...	...
Dhârwâr	8	4	4	...	...	...	...	...	...	...	2	...	1
Bijâpur	2	1	1	...	...	...	...	...	...	...	...	...	1
Total, Presidency Proper	4,026	1,962	2,064	4	2	6	9	17	95	44	315	221	[illegible]
Karâchi	66	34	32	...	...	...	...	1	1	1	6	5	9
Hyderabad	11	7	7	...	...	...	...	...	1	...	1	1	1
Shikârpur	8	4	4	...	...	...	...	...	...	...	...	...	2
Thar and Pârkar	...	...	...	...	...	...	...	...	...	...	...	...	...
Upper Sind Frontier	2	1	1	...	...	...	...	...	...	...	1	...	...
Total, Sind	90	46	44	...	...	...	...	1	2	1	8	6	19
Total, British Territory	4,115	2,008	2,108	4	2	6	9	18	97	45	323	227	407
Total, Feudatories	501	240	261	...	...	...	8	2	22	13	33	22	51
Grand Total	4,617	2,248	2,369	4	2	6	17	20	119	57	356	249	458
Aden	1,050	588	[illegible]	...	...	...	...	2	17	16	54	68	110

Part (I).—

(3) WID

District.	Total. Total.	Total. Males.	Total. Females.	0—4. Males.	0—4. Females	5—9. Males.	5—9. Females.	10—14. Males.	10—14. Females.	15—19. Males.	15—19. Females.	20—24. Males.	20—24. Females.
Bombay City	398	57	341	...	...	...	...	...	...	...	3	1	8
Ahmedabad	12	2	10	...	...	...	...	...	...	...	...	...	1
Kaira	...	...	...	...	...	...	...	...	...	...	...	...	...
Panch Mahâls	...	...	...	...	...	...	...	...	...	...	...	...	...
Broach	3	2	1	...	...	...	...	...	...	...	...	...	1
Surat	...	...	...	...	...	...	...	...	...	...	...	...	...
Thâna	47	7	[illegible]	...	...	...	...	...	...	...	...	...	1
Kolâba	256	45	211	...	...	...	...	...	...	...	4	2	1
Ratnâgiri	...	...	...	...	...	...	...	...	...	...	...	...	...
Kânara	2	...	2	...	...	...	...	...	...	...	...	...	1
Khândesh	7	1	6	...	...	...	...	...	...	...	1	...	...
Nâsik	6	1	5	...	...	...	...	...	...	...	1	...	1
Ahmednagar	5	2	3	...	...	...	...	...	...	...	...	...	1
Poona	77	12	65	...	...	...	...	...	...	...	...	1	4
Sholâpur	1	...	1	...	...	...	...	...	...	...	...	...	...
Sâtâra	5	1	4	...	...	...	1	...	...	...	...	...	...
Belgaum	...	...	...	...	...	...	...	...	...	...	...	...	...
Dhârwâr	4	1	3	...	...	...	...	...	...	...	...	...	...
Bijâpur	1	...	1	...	...	...	...	...	...	...	...	...	...
Total, Presidency Proper	824	131	693	...	...	...	1	...	...	...	9	4	20
Karâchi	7	2	5	...	...	...	...	...	...	...	...	...	...
Hyderabad	2	...	2	...	...	...	...	...	...	...	...	...	...
Shikârpur	2	1	1	...	...	...	...	...	...	...	...	...	...
Thar and Pârkar	...	...	...	...	...	...	...	...	...	...	...	...	...
Upper Sind Frontier	...	...	...	...	...	...	...	...	...	...	...	...	...
Total, Sind	11	3	8	...	...	...	...	...	...	...	...	...	...
Total, British Territory	835	131	701	...	...	...	1	...	...	...	9	4	20
Total, Feudatories	83	16	67	...	...	...	...	...	1	...	...	...	...
Grand Total	918	150	768	...	...	...	1	...	1	...	9	4	20
Aden	248	33	215	...	...	...	...	...	...	...	1	1	4

Civil Condition by Religion and Age.

VIII.

Jew.

RIED.

25 — 29.		30 — 34.		35 — 39.		40 — 44.		45 — 49.		50 — 54.		55 — 59.		60 and over.	
Males.	Females.	Males.	Females.	Males.	Females.	Males.	Females.	Males.	Females.	Males.	Females.	Males.	Females.	Males.	Females.
179	186	158	147	132	102	130	90	95	49	86	44	47	8	91	27
2	6	11	2	6	2	4	5	1	3	1	...	1	...	4	3
...	1	1	...	...	...	...	...	...	...	...	...	...	...	...	...
...	...	...	...	...	...	...	...	...	...	...	...	...	...	...	...
1	1	1	1	...	...	...	...	...	...	...	...	...	...	...	...
...	...	2	2	3	1	1	2	1	...	1	...	...	...	...	...
14	17	18	10	10	6	8	8	5	4	8	2	7	1	13	6
55	91	66	68	60	58	57	55	34	23	42	24	23	9	68	16
...	...	...	...	...	...	...	...	...	...	...	...	...	...	...	...
1	1	1	...	...	...	...	...	...	...	...	...	1	...	...	...
4	3	3	3	2	2	3	2	3	...	2	1	...	...	1	...
5	4	1	1	2	2	2	3	3	1	1	2	3	...	1	1
2	1	1	1	...	1	...	...	...	...	...	...	...	...	...	...
22	36	17	35	33	12	19	18	15	9	14	8	9	4	27	4
...	...	...	3	2	1	1	...	1	...	...	...	1	...	...	...
1	5	5	2	5	1	1	...	...	...	1	...	...	1	3	...
...	...	...	...	...	...	...	...	...	...	...	...	...	...	...	...
1	1	1	...	2	...	...	...	...	...	...	...	...	...	...	...
...	...	...	...	...	...	...	...	...	...	1	...	...	...	...	...
287	353	286	275	257	188	226	183	158	89	157	81	92	23	207	56
5	6	6	3	7	4	2	3	4	...	3	...	...	...	...	...
1	2	...	1	3	...	1	1	...	...	1	...	...	...	...	...
...	...	1	1	...	1	3	...	...	...	...	...	...	...	...	...
...	...	...	...	...	...	...	...	...	...	...	...	...	...	...	...
1	...	...	...	...	...	...	...	...	...	...	...	...	...	...	...
7	8	7	5	10	5	6	4	4	...	4	...	...	...	...	...
294	**361**	**293**	**280**	**267**	**193**	**232**	**187**	**162**	**89**	**161**	**81**	**92**	**23**	**207**	**56**
35	**49**	**39**	**33**	**40**	**18**	**23**	**14**	**16**	**13**	**15**	**17**	**14**	**1**	**22**	**2**
329	**410**	**332**	**313**	**307**	**211**	**255**	**201**	**178**	**102**	**176**	**98**	**106**	**24**	**229**	**58**
100	77	109	90	76	38	91	38	39	18	42	13	13	2	32	5

Jew.

OWED.

25 — 29.		30 — 34.		35 — 39.		40 — 44.		45 — 49.		50 — 54.		55 — 59.		60 and over.	
Males.	Females.	Males.	Females.	Males.	Females.	Males.	Females.	Males.	Females.	Males.	Females.	Males.	Females.	Males.	Females.
6	16	6	28	4	30	3	48	6	36	5	63	4	19	22	91
...	2	1	...	...	3	...	...	...	1	...	2	...	2	1	...
...	...	...	...	...	...	...	...	...	...	...	...	...	...	...	...
...	...	...	...	...	...	...	...	...	...	...	...	...	...	...	...
1	...	...	...	...	...	...	...	...	...	...	...	...	...	1	...
...	...	...	...	...	...	...	...	...	...	...	...	...	...	...	...
...	3	...	5	...	1	...	6	...	3	3	8	...	1	4	11
1	6	3	16	4	14	5	33	5	19	3	29	4	21	18	68
...	...	...	...	...	...	...	...	...	...	...	...	...	...	...	...
...	...	...	...	...	...	...	...	...	...	...	...	...	1	...	...
...	...	...	1	...	...	...	...	...	1	...	1	...	2	1	...
...	...	...	...	...	...	...	...	...	...	...	1	...	...	1	2
...	...	...	...	...	...	...	1	...	...	...	...	...	...	2	1
...	3	...	9	...	3	2	13	1	1	...	4	1	3	7	24
...	...	...	...	...	...	...	...	...	...	...	...	...	...	...	1
...	...	...	...	1	...	...	...	...	...	...	1	...	...	...	2
...	...	...	...	...	...	...	...	...	...	...	...	...	...	...	...
...	...	...	...	...	...	...	...	...	...	...	1	...	1	1	1
...	...	...	...	...	1	...	...	...	...	...	...	...	...	...	...
8	30	10	59	9	52	10	101	12	61	11	109	9	50	58	201
1	...	...	...	...	...	...	2	...	1	...	...	...	1	1	1
...	...	...	...	...	...	...	...	...	1	...	...	...	...	...	1
...	...	...	...	...	...	...	...	...	...	...	...	...	...	1	1
...	...	...	...	...	...	...	...	...	...	...	...	...	...	...	...
...	...	...	...	...	...	...	...	...	...	...	...	...	...	...	...
1	...	...	...	...	...	...	2	...	2	...	...	...	1	2	3
9	**30**	**10**	**59**	**9**	**52**	**10**	**103**	**12**	**63**	**11**	**109**	**9**	**51**	**60**	**204**
1	**2**	**1**	**1**	...	**5**	...	**8**	**2**	**7**	**2**	**10**	**2**	**5**	**8**	**28**
10	**32**	**11**	**60**	**9**	**57**	**10**	**111**	**14**	**70**	**13**	**119**	**11**	**56**	**68**	**232**
1	8	7	24	1	14	6	28	3	9	1	45	2	19	11	62

B 1072—20 ap

Civil Condition by Religion and Age.

TABL

Part (I).-

(1) U

District.	TOTAL. Total.	Males.	Females.	0—4. Males.	Females.	5—9. Males.	Females.	10—14. Males.	Females.	15—19. Males.	Females.	20—24. Males.	Females.
Bombay City	......	...	...	...	...	...	...	...	...	...	...	...	...
Ahmedabad	75	33	42	10	16	13	17	4	6	4	2	2	...
Kaira	...	...	...	...	...	...	...	...	...	...	...	...	...
Panch Mahâls	5,784	3,082	2,702	984	1,130	1,025	953	579	425	327	141	103	37
Broach	8,428	4,538	3,890	1,430	1,600	1,416	1,370	952	664	448	184	104	34
Surat	......	...	...	...	...	...	...	...	...	...	...	...	...
Thána	3,041	1,665	1,376	561	609	524	509	250	169	102	67	80	11
Kolába	272	133	139	48	82	40	40	25	12	11	5	4	...
Ratnágiri	......	...	...	...	...	...	...	...	...	...	...	...	...
Kánara	......	...	...	...	...	...	...	...	...	...	...	...	...
Khándesh	43,931	23,866	20,065	7,564	8,431	7,681	7,383	5,117	3,201	2,000	701	855	147
Násik	6,065	3,437	2,628	1,065	1,243	1,127	974	741	384	318	42	107	17
Ahmednagar	147	72	75	23	32	17	27	18	14	3	...	5	1
Poona	......	...	...	...	...	...	...	...	...	...	...	...	...
Sholápur	......	...	...	...	...	...	...	...	...	...	...	...	...
Sátára	......	...	...	...	...	...	...	...	...	...	...	...	...
Belgaum	......	...	...	...	...	...	...	...	...	...	...	...	...
Dhárwár	11	8	3	2	1	...	1	...	1	...	...	6	...
Bijápur	......	...	...	...	...	...	...	...	...	...	...	...	...
Total, Presidency Proper...	67,754	36,834	30,920	11,687	13,143	11,843	11,274	7,695	4,816	3,273	1,142	1,356	237
Karáchi	1,593	915	678	281	285	272	274	172	91	83	19	49	3
Hyderabad	10,519	6,341	4,178	1,818	1,789	1,876	1,514	1,072	666	571	137	463	33
Shikárpur	1,481	827	654	299	256	265	201	137	77	83	11	67	3
Thar and Párkar	30,074	17,786	12,288	5,444	5,198	5,352	4,681	3,085	1,92[illegible]	1,675	337	1,174	73
Upper Sind Frontier... ...	101	67	34	15	14	14	11	8	7	4	2	3	...
Total, Sind ...	43,768	26,036	17,732	7,857	7,548	7,779	6,681	4,474	2,766	2,416	506	1,758	112
Total, British Territory	111,522	62,870	48,652	19,544	20,685	19,622	17,955	12,169	7,582	5,689	1,648	3,114	349
Total, Feudatories ...	40,317	21,804	18,513	6,752	7,509	7,032	6,426	3,900	2,794	2,150	1,287	1,234	310
Grand Total ...	151,839	84,674	67,165	26,296	28,194	26,654	24,331	16,069	10,376	7,839	2,935	4,348	659
Aden	......	...	...	...	...	...	...	...	...	...	...	...	...

Part (J).—

(2) MAR

District.	TOTAL. Total.	Males.	Females.	0—4. Males.	Females.	5—9. Males.	Females.	10—14. Males.	Females.	15—19. Males.	Females.	20—24. Males.	Females.
Bombay City	......	...	...	...	...	...	...	...	...	...	...	...	...
Ahmedabad	91	45	46	...	...	...	1	...	4	2	5	4	8
Kaira	...	...	...	...	...	...	...	...	...	...	...	...	...
Panch Mahâls	4,870	2,402	2,468	11	10	8	6	30	57	107	239	306	491
Broach	8,335	4,178	4,157	6	12	18	12	48	113	199	404	575	886
Surat	......	...	...	...	...	...	...	...	...	...	...	...	...
Thána	2,948	1,489	1,459	8	7	7	25	19	78	70	171	128	244
Kolába	313	165	148	...	...	...	3	...	15	10	25	23	24
Ratnágiri	......	...	...	...	...	...	...	...	...	...	...	...	...
Kánara	......	...	...	...	...	...	...	...	...	...	...	...	...
Khándesh	37,924	18,481	19,443	32	41	53	188	243	1,114	892	2,639	2,192	3,540
Násik	5,825	2,767	3,058	9	16	9	61	41	261	127	445	205	671
Ahmednagar	146	67	79	2	...	...	1	...	6	1	10	5	17
Poona	......	...	...	...	...	...	...	...	...	...	...	...	...
Sholápur	......	...	...	...	...	...	...	...	...	...	...	...	...
Sátára	......	...	...	...	...	...	...	...	...	...	...	...	...
Belgaum	......	...	...	...	...	...	...	...	...	...	...	...	...
Dhárwár	19	14	5	...	...	...	1	...	...	...	...	6	2
Bijápur	1	1	...	...	...	...	...	...	...	...	...	...	...
Total, Presidency Proper...	60,472	29,609	30,863	68	85	95	293	381	1,647	1,408	3,997	3,534	5,793
Karáchi	1,260	647	613	1	1	...	3	5	19	30	58	75	128
Hyderabad	7,194	3,576	3,618	2	2	6	18	25	181	103	354	320	778
Shikárpur	1,198	627	571	...	...	2	6	8	18	21	45	61	88
Thar and Párkar	19,068	9,326	9,742	11	13	21	38	40	169	212	839	775	1,762
Upper Sind Frontier	103	60	43	...	1	...	...	1	1	1	6	10	8
Total, Sind ...	28,822	14,236	14,586	14	17	28	65	79	388	367	1,301	1,250	2,758
Total, British Territory	89,294	43,845	45,449	82	102	123	357	460	1,975	1,775	5,298	4,783	8,541
Total, Feudatories ...	34,443	16,746	17,697	38	32	42	76	162	262	738	1,449	1,965	3,454
Grand Total ...	123,737	60,591	63,146	120	134	165	433	622	2,237	2,513	6,747	6,749	11,995
Aden	......	...	...	...	...	...	...	...	...	...	...	...	...

VIII.

Animistic.

MARRIED.

25 — 29.		30 — 34.		35 — 39.		40 — 44.		45 — 49.		50 — 54.		55 — 59.		60 and over.	
Males.	Females.	Males.	Females.	Males.	Females.	Males.	Females.	Males.	Females.	Males.	Females.	Males.	Females.	Males.	Females.
...	...	...	...	...	...	...	...	...	...	...	...	...	...	...	...
...	...	...	1	...	...	...	...	...	...	...	...	...	...	...	...
...	...	...	...	...	...	...	...	...	...	...	...	...	...	...	...
39	10	12	3	6	1	8	5	2	3	1	3	...	...	1	1
54	6	19	10	9	7	10	6	1	2	2	5	2	...	1	2
...	...	...	...	...	...	...	...	...	...	...	...	...	...	...	...
54	6	15	1	6	2	2	1	2	...	...	...	1	...	...	1
3	...	...	...	...	...	2	...	...	...	...	...	...	...	...	...
...	...	...	...	...	...	...	...	...	...	...	...	...	...	...	...
...	...	...	...	...	...	...	...	...	...	...	...	...	...	...	...
367	69	159	55	41	53	47	22	8	10	16	6	2	4	9	4
50	6	12	5	10	4	2	4	1	4	2	...	...	2	2	4
4	...	1	...	...	...	...	1	...	...	...	...	...	...	1	...
...	...	...	...	...	...	...	...	...	...	...	...	...	...	...	...
...	...	...	...	...	...	...	...	...	...	...	...	...	...	...	...
...	...	...	...	...	...	...	...	...	...	...	...	...	...	...	...
...	...	...	...	...	...	...	...	...	...	...	...	...	...	...	...
...	...	...	...	...	...	...	...	...	...	...	...	...	...	...	...
...	...	...	...	...	...	...	...	...	...	...	...	...	...	...	...
571	97	218	75	71	47	66	39	14	19	21	14	5	6	14	12
32	2	12	2	7	1	3	...	1	...	2	...	1	...	...	1
268	11	152	14	60	4	37	4	8	...	13	1	...	...	11	3
34	1	25	3	10	...	1	2	1	...	3	...	1	...	1	...
589	32	298	12	66	4	57	10	7	2	12	4	5	...	22	1
9	...	7	...	5	...	...	...	1	...	1	...	...	...	...	...
932	46	494	51	138	9	98	16	18	2	31	5	7	...	34	1
1.503	143	712	106	209	56	164	51	33	21	52	19	12	6	48	28
471	76	155	34	45	29	29	22	14	11	10	5	6	2	5	8
1.974	219	867	140	255	85	193	76	46	32	63	24	18	8	53	35
...	...	...	...	...	...	...	...	...	...	...	...	...	...	...	...

Animistic.

RIED.

25 — 29.		30 — 34.		35 — 39.		40 — 44.		45 — 49.		50 — 54.		55 — 59.		60 and over.	
Males.	Females.	Males.	Females.	Males.	Females.	Males.	Females.	Males.	Females.	Males.	Females.	Males.	Females.	Males.	Females.
...	...	...	...	...	...	...	...	...	...	...	...	...	...	...	...
9	7	12	13	4	1	4	4	1	1	5	2	...	...	4	...
...	...	...	...	...	...	...	...	...	...	...	...	...	...	...	...
436	479	432	373	317	300	279	207	173	187	161	107	60	37	82	[illegible]
797	818	740	608	527	447	451	336	271	193	277	140	96	71	173	[illegible]
...	...	...	...	...	...	...	...	...	...	...	...	...	...	...	...
288	317	272	242	248	148	165	97	112	67	66	41	52	17	54	[illegible]
26	29	34	13	22	19	24	12	11	5	9	2	5	...	1	1
...	...	...	...	...	...	...	...	...	...	...	...	...	...	...	...
...	...	...	...	...	...	...	...	...	...	...	...	...	...	...	...
3,147	3,540	3,408	3,132	2,467	2,021	2,327	1,480	1,230	721	1,199	543	380	190	911	261
554	538	404	441	379	286	307	194	202	107	158	77	68	21	154	41
15	16	17	9	6	7	9	7	4	1	4	3	...	1	4	2
...	...	...	...	...	...	...	...	...	...	...	...	...	...	...	...
...	...	...	...	...	...	...	...	...	...	...	...	...	...	...	...
...	...	...	...	...	...	...	...	...	...	...	...	...	...	...	...
...	...	...	...	...	...	...	...	...	...	...	...	...	...	...	...
4	1	2	1	1	...	1	...	...	...	...	...	...	...	...	...
...	...	...	...	1	...	...	...	...	...	...	...	...	...	...	...
5,276	5,745	5,381	4,832	3,072	3,229	3,567	2,337	2,004	1,211	1,879	915	661	337	1,383	403
113	136	136	102	78	54	81	65	24	9	50	23	13	3	41	12
525	708	837	760	355	231	569	336	182	85	299	150	63	26	282	55
89	102	126	129	72	45	103	62	31	18	44	33	5	6	64	20
1,352	1,860	1,968	1,961	1,016	736	1,397	1,097	443	381	891	564	240	116	900	266
6	5	17	11	4	3	8	4	4	1	7	2	...	...	2	1
2,085	2,811	3,084	2,963	1,526	1,069	2,168	1,564	684	494	1,291	771	321	151	1,349	354
7.331	8.556	8.465	7.845	5.498	4.298	5.725	3.901	2.683	1.645	3.170	1.686	982	488	2,733	757
3.359	3.684	3.056	3.294	2.678	1.943	1.769	1.615	1.209	918	919	560	321	177	499	203
10.711	12.240	11.521	11.139	8.176	6.241	7.494	5.516	3.897	2.563	4.089	2.246	1,303	665	3.231	960
...	...	...	...	...	...	...	...	...	...	...	...	...	...	...	...

Table VIII.

Civil Condition by Religion and Age.

TABLE

Part (J).—

(3) WID

District.	Total. Total.	Total. Males.	Total. Females.	0—4. Males.	0—4. Females.	5—9. Males.	5—9. Females.	10—14. Males.	10—14. Females.	15—19. Males.	15—19. Females.	20—24. Males.	20—24. Females.
Bombay City	...	...	...	...	...	...	...	...	...	...	...	...	...
Ahmedabad	9	2	7	...	...	...	...	...	...	...	...	...	...
Kaira	...	...	...	...	...	...	...	...	...	...	...	...	...
Panch Mahâls	432	120	312	...	...	...	...	...	...	3	1	5	6
Broach	1,042	338	704	...	...	...	1	2	3	7	4	27	20
Surat	...	...	...	...	...	...	...	...	...	...	...	...	...
Thána	379	80	299	...	...	...	1	...	1	...	[illegible]	2	3
Kolâba	25	3	23	...	...	...	...	...	...	...	...	1	...
Ratnágiri	...	...	...	...	...	...	...	...	...	...	...	...	...
Kânara	...	...	...	...	...	...	...	...	...	...	...	...	...
Khândesh	4,813	1,203	3,610	...	1	1	1	6	8	13	38	43	78
Násik	722	162	560	...	...	...	...	1	3	2	4	9	16
Ahmednagar	33	16	17	...	...	1	...	12	8	2	...	...	...
Poona	...	...	...	...	...	...	...	...	...	...	...	...	...
Sholâpur	...	...	...	...	...	...	...	...	...	...	...	...	...
Sâtâra	...	...	...	...	...	...	...	...	...	...	...	...	...
Belgaum	...	...	...	...	...	...	...	...	...	...	...	...	...
Dhârwâr	2	...	2	...	...	...	...	...	...	...	...	...	...
Bijâpur	...	...	...	...	...	...	...	...	...	...	...	...	...
Total, Presidency Proper	7,457	1,923	5,534	...	1	2	3	21	23	27	49	87	123
Karâchi	189	68	121	...	...	...	...	...	...	...	4	3	4
Hyderabad	1,447	421	1,026	...	...	2	2	1	2	3	3	13	27
Shikârpur	229	66	163	...	...	...	...	1	...	2	...	1	3
Thar and Pârkar	3,473	957	2,516	1	...	1	...	...	6	11	43	37	101
Upper Sind Frontier	7	6	1	...	...	...	...	...	1	1	...	2	...
Total, Sind	5,345	1,518	3,827	1	...	3	2	2	8	17	50	56	135
Total, British Territory	12,802	3,441	9,361	1	1	5	5	23	31	44	99	143	258
Total, Feudatories	3,645	856	2,789	...	...	...	1	1	1	9	11	28	33
Grand Total	16,447	4,297	12,150	1	1	5	6	24	32	53	110	171	291
Aden	...	...	...	...	...	...	...	...	...	...	...	...	...

Part (K).—

(1) UN

District.	Total. Total.	Total. Males.	Total. Females.	0—4. Males.	0—4. Females.	5—9. Males.	5—9. Females.	10—14. Males.	10—14. Females.	15—19. Males.	15—19. Females.	20—24. Males.	20—24. Females.
Bombay City	18	13	5	...	1	3	2	2	...	2	...	3	1
Ahmedabad	3	3	...	2	...	...	...	...	...	...	...	...	...
Kaira	...	...	...	...	...	...	...	...	...	...	...	...	...
Panch Mahâls	...	...	...	...	...	...	...	...	...	...	...	...	...
Broach	...	...	...	...	...	...	...	...	...	...	...	...	...
Surat	...	...	...	...	...	...	...	...	...	...	...	...	...
Thâna	1	1	...	...	...	...	...	...	...	...	...	...	...
Kolâba	...	...	...	...	...	...	...	...	...	...	...	...	...
Ratnágiri	...	...	...	...	...	...	...	...	...	...	...	...	...
Kânara	...	...	...	...	...	...	...	...	...	...	...	...	...
Khândesh	...	...	...	...	...	...	...	...	...	...	...	...	...
Násik	...	...	...	...	...	...	...	...	...	...	...	...	...
Ahmednagar	...	...	...	...	...	...	...	...	...	...	...	...	...
Poona	5	2	3	...	...	1	1	...	1	...	1	...	...
Sholâpur	1	1	...	...	...	...	...	...	...	...	...	1	...
Sâtâra	...	...	...	...	...	...	...	...	...	...	...	...	...
Belgaum	...	...	...	...	...	...	...	...	...	...	...	...	...
Dhârwâr	...	...	...	...	...	...	...	...	...	...	...	...	...
Bijâpur	...	...	...	...	...	...	...	...	...	...	...	...	...
Total, Presidency Proper	28	20	8	2	1	4	3	2	1	2	1	4	1
Karâchi	1	1	...	...	...	...	...	...	...	...	...	...	...
Hyderabad	1	1	...	...	...	...	...	...	...	...	...	...	...
Shikârpur	...	...	...	...	...	...	...	...	...	...	...	...	...
Thar and Pârkar	...	...	...	...	...	...	...	...	...	...	...	...	...
Upper Sind Frontier	...	...	...	...	...	...	...	...	...	...	...	...	...
Total, Sind	2	2	...	...	...	...	...	...	...	...	...	...	...
Total British Territory	30	22	8	2	1	4	3	2	1	2	1	4	1
Total, Feudatories	...	...	...	...	...	...	...	...	...	...	...	...	...
Grand Total	30	22	8	2	1	4	3	2	1	2	1	4	1
Aden	...	...	...	...	...	...	...	...	...	...	...	...	...

VIII.

Animistic.

OWED.

25—29.		30—34.		35—39.		40—44.		45—49.		50—54.		55—59.		60 and over.	
Males.	Females.	Males.	Females.	Males.	Females.	Males.	Females.	Males.	Females.	Males.	Females.	Males.	Females.	Males.	Females.
...	...	...	...	...	...	...	...	...	...	...	...	...	...	...	...
1	...	...	1	...	...	1	2	...	...	...	3	...	...	...	7
6	11	10	15	10	20	21	51	15	25	21	65	2	19	27	99
27	24	31	42	23	50	35	100	33	83	55	144	18	40	80	194
...	...	...	...	...	...	...	...	...	...	...	...	...	...	...	...
12	11	5	11	7	22	9	42	9	49	8	47	10	27	18	83
...	...	...	1	...	5	1	4	1	...	...	5	...	7	...	3
...	...	...	...	...	...	...	...	...	...	...	...	...	...	...	...
...	...	...	...	...	...	...	...	...	...	...	...	...	...	...	...
64	116	114	233	125	[illegible]	153	648	97	362	157	679	101	188	329	1,076
18	16	12	38	7	40	14	77	12	69	23	104	10	30	48	163
...	1	...	2	...	1	...	...	...	2	...	...	...	...	...	3
...	...	...	...	...	...	...	...	...	...	...	...	...	...	...	...
...	...	...	...	...	...	...	...	...	...	...	...	...	...	...	...
...	...	...	...	...	...	...	...	...	...	...	...	...	...	...	...
...	...	...	...	...	...	...	1	...	1	...	...	...	...	...	...
...	...	...	...	...	...	...	...	...	...	...	...	...	...	...	...
...	...	...	...	...	...	...	...	...	...	...	...	...	...	...	...
128	179	172	513	172	418	234	825	167	590	264	1,046	147	311	502	1,623
8	6	8	8	6	9	10	20	1	11	12	17	2	3	19	40
20	71	52	125	27	62	62	125	27	63	50	[illegible]	10	23	142	296
6	5	11	9	7	1	8	39	2	4	7	41	1	3	21	58
88	130	136	228	52	113	117	308	59	116	107	430	56	111	292	878
...	...	1	...	...	...	...	...	...	...	1	...	...	...	1	...
127	211	208	364	91	184	197	623	89	194	177	645	76	140	475	[illegible]
255	**390**	**380**	**707**	**263**	**603**	**431**	**1.447**	**256**	**784**	**441**	**1.691**	**222**	**451**	**977**	**2.895**
68	**83**	**96**	**155**	**110**	**228**	**108**	**452**	**106**	**437**	**122**	**613**	**40**	**146**	**158**	**620**
323	**473**	**476**	**862**	**373**	**820**	**539**	**1.909**	**362**	**1.221**	**573**	**2.303**	**262**	**597**	**1.135**	**3.515**
...	...	...	...	...	...	...	...	...	...	...	...	...	...	...	...

Others.

MARRIED.

25—29. Males.	25—29. Females.	30—34. Males.	30—34. Females.	35—39. Males.	35—39. Females.	40—44. Males.	40—44. Females.	45—49. Males.	45—49. Females.	50—54. Males.	50—54. Females.	55—59. Males.	55—59. Females.	60 and over. Males.	60 and over. Females.
2	...	...	...	...	...	...	...	1	...	...	1	...	...	...	...
...	...	...	...	...	...	1	...	...	...	...	...	...	...	...	...
...	...	...	...	...	...	...	...	...	...	...	...	...	...	...	...
...	...	...	...	...	...	...	...	...	...	...	...	...	...	...	...
...	...	...	...	...	...	...	...	...	...	...	...	...	...	...	...
...	...	...	...	...	...	...	...	...	...	...	...	...	...	...	...
...	...	...	...	...	...	...	...	1	...	...	...	...	...	...	...
...	...	...	...	...	...	...	...	...	...	...	...	...	...	...	...
...	...	...	...	...	...	...	...	...	...	...	...	...	...	...	...
...	...	...	...	...	...	...	...	...	...	...	...	...	...	...	...
...	...	...	...	...	...	...	...	...	...	...	...	...	...	...	...
...	...	...	...	...	...	...	...	...	...	...	...	...	...	...	...
...	...	...	...	...	...	...	...	...	...	...	...	...	...	...	...
...	...	1	...	...	...	...	...	...	...	...	...	...	...	...	...
...	...	...	...	...	...	...	...	...	...	...	...	...	...	...	...
...	...	...	...	...	...	...	...	...	...	...	...	...	...	...	...
...	...	...	...	...	...	...	...	...	...	...	...	...	...	...	...
...	...	...	...	...	...	...	...	...	...	...	...	...	...	...	...
...	...	...	...	...	...	...	...	...	...	...	...	...	...	...	...
2	...	1	...	...	...	1	...	2	...	...	1	...	...	...	...
1	...	...	...	...	...	...	...	...	...	...	...	...	...	...	...
...	...	1	...	...	...	...	...	...	...	...	...	...	...	...	...
...	...	...	...	...	...	...	...	...	...	...	...	...	...	...	...
...	...	...	...	...	...	...	...	...	...	...	...	...	...	...	...
...	...	...	...	...	...	...	...	...	...	...	...	...	...	...	...
1	...	1	...	...	...	...	...	...	...	...	...	...	...	...	...
3	...	**2**	...	...	...	**1**	...	**2**	...	...	**1**	...	...	...	...
...	...	...	...	...	...	...	...	...	...	...	...	...	...	...	...
3	...	**2**	...	...	...	**1**	...	**2**	...	...	**1**	...	...	...	...
...	...	...	...	...	...	...	...	...	...	...	...	...	...	...	...

Civil Condition by Religion and Age.

TABI

Part (K)

(2) M

District.	Total. Total.	Total. Males.	Total. Females.	0—4. Males.	0—4. Females.	5—9. Males.	5—9. Females.	10—14. Males.	10—14. Females.	15—19. Males.	15—19. Females.	20—24. Males.	20—24. Females.
Bombay City	17	12	5	..	..	..	..	1	..	..	..	..	..
Ahmedabad	2	1	1	..	..	..	..	..	..	..	1	..	..
Kaira	..	..	..	..	..	..	..	..	..	..	..	..	..
Panch Mahals	..	..	..	..	..	..	..	..	..	..	..	..	..
Broach	..	..	..	..	..	..	..	..	..	..	..	..	..
Surat	..	..	..	..	..	..	..	..	..	..	..	..	..
Thana	..	..	..	..	..	..	..	..	..	..	..	..	..
Kolaba	..	..	..	..	..	..	..	..	..	..	..	..	..
Ratnagiri	..	..	..	..	..	..	..	..	..	..	..	..	..
Kanara	..	..	..	..	..	..	..	..	..	..	..	..	..
Khandesh	..	..	..	..	..	..	..	..	..	..	..	..	..
Nasik	..	..	..	..	..	..	..	..	..	..	..	..	..
Ahmednagar	..	..	..	..	..	..	..	..	..	..	..	..	..
Poona	7	4	3	..	..	..	..	..	..	..	1	1	..
Sholapur	..	..	..	..	..	..	..	..	..	..	..	..	..
Satara	..	..	..	..	..	..	..	..	..	..	..	..	..
Belgaum	..	..	..	..	..	..	..	..	..	..	..	..	..
Dharwar	..	..	..	..	..	..	..	..	..	..	..	..	..
Bijapur	..	..	..	..	..	..	..	..	..	..	..	..	..
Total, Presidency Proper	26	17	9	..	..	..	..	1	..	..	2	1	..
Karachi	..	..	..	..	..	..	..	..	..	..	..	..	..
Hyderabad	1	1	..	..	..	..	..	..	..	..	..	..	..
Shikarpur	..	..	..	..	..	..	..	..	..	..	..	..	..
Thar and Parkar	..	..	..	..	..	..	..	..	..	..	..	..	..
Upper Sind Frontier	..	..	..	..	..	..	..	..	..	..	..	..	..
Total, Sind	1	1	..	..	..	..	..	..	..	..	..	..	..
Total, British Territory	27	18	9	..	..	..	..	1	..	..	2	1	..
Total, Feudatories	..	..	..	..	..	..	..	..	..	..	..	..	..
Grand Total	27	18	9	..	..	..	..	1	..	..	2	1	..
Aden	..	..	..	..	..	..	..	..	..	..	..	..	..

Part (K).-

(3) WI

District.	Total. Total.	Total. Males.	Total. Females.	0—4. Males.	0—4. Females.	5—9. Males.	5—9. Females.	10—14. Males.	10—14. Females.	15—19. Males.	15—19. Females.	20—24. Males.	20—24. Females.
Bombay City	2	2	..	..	..	..	..	..	..	..	..	..	..
Ahmedabad	..	..	..	..	..	..	..	..	..	..	..	..	..
Kaira	..	..	..	..	..	..	..	..	..	..	..	..	..
Panch Mahals	..	..	..	..	..	..	..	..	..	..	..	..	..
Broach	..	..	..	..	..	..	..	..	..	..	..	..	..
Surat	..	..	..	..	..	..	..	..	..	..	..	..	..
Thana	..	..	..	..	..	..	..	..	..	..	..	..	..
Kolaba	..	..	..	..	..	..	..	..	..	..	..	..	..
Ratnagiri	..	..	..	..	..	..	..	..	..	..	..	..	..
Kanara	..	..	..	..	..	..	..	..	..	..	..	..	..
Khandesh	..	..	..	..	..	..	..	..	..	..	..	..	..
Nasik	..	..	..	..	..	..	..	..	..	..	..	..	..
Ahmednagar	..	..	..	..	..	..	..	..	..	..	..	..	..
Poona	2	1	1	..	..	..	..	..	1	..	..	..	..
Sholapur	..	..	..	..	..	..	..	..	..	..	..	..	..
Satara	..	..	..	..	..	..	..	..	..	..	..	..	..
Belgaum	..	..	..	..	..	..	..	..	..	..	..	..	..
Dharwar	..	..	..	..	..	..	..	..	..	..	..	..	..
Bijapur	..	..	..	..	..	..	..	..	..	..	..	..	..
Total, Presidency Proper	4	3	1	..	..	..	..	..	1	..	..	..	..
Karachi	..	..	..	..	..	..	..	..	..	..	..	..	..
Hyderabad	..	..	..	..	..	..	..	..	..	..	..	..	..
Shikarpur	..	..	..	..	..	..	..	..	..	..	..	..	..
Thar and Parkar	..	..	..	..	..	..	..	..	..	..	..	..	..
Upper Sind Frontier	..	..	..	..	..	..	..	..	..	..	..	..	..
Total, Sind	..	..	..	..	..	..	..	..	..	..	..	..	..
Total, British Territory	4	3	1	..	..	..	..	..	1	..	..	..	..
Total, Feudatories	..	..	..	..	..	..	..	..	..	..	..	..	..
Grand Total	4	3	1	..	..	..	..	..	1	..	..	..	..
Aden	..	..	..	..	..	..	..	..	..	..	..	..	..

VIII.

Others.

RIED.

25 — 29.		30 — 34.		35 — 39.		40 — 44.		45 — 49.		50 — 54.		55 — 59.		60 and over.	
Males.	Females.	Males.	Females.	Males.	Females.	Males.	Females.	Males.	Females.	Males.	Females.	Males.	Females.	Males.	Females.
1	..	1	1	2	2	1	1	2	..	..	..	4	..	..	..
1	..	..	..	..	..	..	..	..	..	..	..	..	..	..	..
..	..	..	..	..	..	..	..	..	..	..	..	..	..	..	..
..	..	..	..	..	..	..	..	..	..	..	..	..	..	..	..
..	..	..	..	..	..	..	..	..	..	..	..	..	..	..	..
..	..	..	..	..	..	..	..	..	..	..	..	..	..	..	..
..	..	..	..	..	..	..	..	..	..	..	..	..	..	..	..
..	..	..	..	..	..	..	..	..	..	..	..	..	..	..	..
..	..	..	..	..	..	..	..	..	..	..	..	..	..	..	..
..	..	..	..	..	..	..	..	..	..	..	..	..	..	..	..
2	..	..	..	..	..	..	..	..	1	1	..	..	..	..	..
..	..	..	..	..	..	..	..	..	..	..	..	..	..	..	..
..	..	..	..	..	..	..	..	..	..	..	..	..	..	..	..
..	..	..	..	..	..	..	..	..	..	..	..	..	..	..	..
..	..	..	..	..	..	..	..	..	..	..	..	..	..	..	..
4	..	1	1	2	2	1	1	3	1	1	..	4	..	..	..
..	..	..	..	..	..	1	..	..	..	..	..	..	..	..	..
..	..	..	..	..	..	..	..	..	..	..	..	..	..	..	..
..	..	..	..	..	..	..	..	..	..	..	..	..	..	..	..
..	..	..	..	..	..	..	..	..	..	..	..	..	..	..	..
..	..	..	..	..	..	1	..	..	..	..	..	..	..	..	..
4	..	1	1	2	2	2	1	3	1	1	..	4	..	..	..
..	..	..	..	..	..	..	..	..	..	..	..	..	..	..	..
4	..	1	1	3	3	2	1	2	1	1	..	4	..	..	..
..	..	..	..	..	..	..	..	..	..	..	..	..	..	..	..

Others.

OWED.

25 — 29.		30 — 34.		35 — 39.		40 — 44.		45 — 49.		50 — 54.		55 — 59.		60 and over.	
Males.	Females.	Males.	Females.	Males.	Females.	Males.	Females.	Males.	Females.	Males.	Females.	Males.	Females.	Males.	Females.
1	..	..	..	..	..	1	..	..	..	..	..	..	..	..	..
..	..	..	..	..	..	..	..	..	..	..	..	..	..	..	..
..	..	..	..	..	..	..	..	..	..	..	..	..	..	..	..
..	..	..	..	..	..	..	..	..	..	..	..	..	..	..	..
..	..	..	..	..	..	..	..	..	..	..	..	..	..	..	..
..	..	..	..	..	..	..	..	..	..	..	..	..	..	..	..
..	..	..	..	..	..	..	..	..	..	..	..	..	..	..	..
..	..	..	..	..	..	..	..	..	..	..	..	..	..	..	..
..	..	..	..	..	..	..	..	..	..	..	..	..	..	..	..
..	..	..	..	..	..	..	..	..	..	..	..	..	..	..	..
..	..	..	..	..	..	..	..	..	..	..	..	..	..	1	..
..	..	..	..	..	..	..	..	..	..	..	..	..	..	..	..
..	..	..	..	..	..	..	..	..	..	..	..	..	..	..	..
..	..	..	..	..	..	..	..	..	..	..	..	..	..	..	..
..	..	..	..	..	..	..	..	..	..	..	..	..	..	..	..
1	..	..	..	..	..	1	..	..	..	..	..	..	..	1	..
..	..	..	..	..	..	..	..	..	..	..	..	..	..	..	..
..	..	..	..	..	..	..	..	..	..	..	..	..	..	..	..
..	..	..	..	..	..	..	..	..	..	..	..	..	..	..	..
..	..	..	..	..	..	..	..	..	..	..	..	..	..	..	..
..	..	..	..	..	..	..	..	..	..	..	..	..	..	..	..
1	..	..	..	..	..	1	..	..	..	..	..	..	..	1	..
..	..	..	..	..	..	..	..	..	..	..	..	..	..	..	..
1	..	..	..	..	..	1	..	..	..	..	..	..	..	1	..
..	..	..	..	..	..	..	..	..	..	..	..	..	..	..	..

TABLE IX.

EDUCATION BY RELIGION AND AGE.

PART A.—Total Population.
,, B.—Hindu.
,, C.—Mussalman.
,, D.—Christian.
,, E.—Buddhist.
,, F.—Jain.
PART G.—Sikh.
,, H.—Pársi.
,, I.—Jew.
,, J.—Animistic.
,, K.—Others.

The 19,236 persons—10,579 males, 8,657 females—in Feudatories, for whom Education was not returned, are excluded.

B 1072—22 ap

Education by Religion and Age.

TABLE

Part (A).—

District.	Total Population: Total.	Total Population: Males.	Total Population: Females.	Total by Education: Learning: Males.	Learning: Females.	Literate: Males.	Literate: Females.	Illiterate: Males.	Illiterate: Females.	0—14: Total: Males.	Total: Females.	Learning: Males.	Learning: Females.	Literate: Males.	Literate: Females.
Bombay City	831.764	518,093	308,671	21,319	5,421	144,190	26,496	352,584	271,754	113,940	96,033	15,567	4,826	13,367	5,128
Ahmedabad	921.712	473,563	448,149	17,773	1,403	60,952	2,537	394,838	444,209	178,866	162,642	14,835	1,334	3,325	315
Kaira	871.589	460,610	410,979	18,361	1,053	48,598	1,157	393,651	408,769	177,904	147,451	16,176	991	2,157	175
Panch Mahâls	313.417	162,101	151,316	4,078	254	10,320	287	147,703	150,775	67,992	63,926	3,571	240	463	64
Broach	341.490	174,964	166,526	10,619	720	38,054	1,335	126,291	164,471	61,062	58,236	9,616	697	1,648	105
Surat	649.989	321,625	328,364	19,888	2,195	58,754	3,801	242,983	322,368	129,252	124,812	17,517	2,053	3,352	156
Total, Gujarát	3.098.197	1,592,863	1,505,334	70,719	5,625	216,678	9,117	1,305,466	1,490,592	615,076	557,067	61,715	5,314	10,950	1,437
Thána	904.868	471,669	433,199	13,059	1,336	33,815	1,613	424,795	430,250	185,199	175,654	11,319	1,218	1,395	163
Kolába	509.584	255,064	254,520	9,604	604	21,873	590	223,587	253,536	107,270	101,513	8,258	565	1,000	131
Ratnágiri	1.105.926	513,616	592,310	21,016	598	44,300	752	448,300	590,960	226,715	220,622	18,026	566	1,335	141
Kánara	446.351	234,356	211,995	11,143	1,067	25,535	1,181	197,678	209,747	83,456	78,633	9,488	1,041	940	107
Total, Konkan	2,966.729	1,474,705	1,492,024	54,822	3,605	125,523	4,136	1,294,360	1,484,283	602,640	576,322	47,091	3,390	4,670	738
Khándesh	1.460.851	745,847	715,004	24,634	396	53,866	706	667,347	713,902	307,800	298,034	21,751	334	1,792	113
Násik	843.582	432,338	411,244	12,924	407	32,541	853	386,873	409,984	176,390	166,744	11,093	559	980	129
Ahmednagar	888.755	451,825	436,930	14,069	936	32,096	875	405,660	435,119	175,151	169,244	11,752	879	828	105
Poona	1.067.800	545,494	522,306	24,453	2,136	52,194	3,394	468,847	516,776	210,485	199,272	18,472	1,894	1,381	473
Sholápur	750.689	381,400	369,289	11,040	486	27,689	650	342,671	368,153	143,723	137,625	9,122	452	851	111
Sátára	1.225.989	613,852	612,137	16,876	438	37,659	628	559,317	611,071	251,360	230,403	13,867	394	1,172	95
Total, Deccan	6.237.666	3,170,756	3,066,910	103,996	4,799	236,045	7,106	2,830,715	3,055,005	1,264,909	1,201,322	86,057	4,502	7,004	1,081
Belgaum	1.013.261	511,885	501,376	15,659	642	37,240	941	458,986	499,793	202,025	191,715	13,094	598	1,325	186
Dhárwár	1.051.314	528,071	523,243	25,154	1,727	57,528	1,802	445,391	519,714	204,960	198,408	21,891	1,671	2,247	224
Bijápur	796.339	398,104	398,235	12,509	582	25,851	378	359,744	397,275	151,629	146,946	10,939	571	642	54
Total, Karnátak	2.860.914	1,438,060	1,422,854	53,320	2,951	120,619	3,121	1,264,121	1,416,782	558,614	537,067	45,924	2,840	4,214	566
Total, Presidency Proper	15.985.270	8,194,477	7,790,793	304,176	22,401	843,055	49,976	7,047,246	7,718,416	3,155,179	2,967,811	256,354	20,472	40,205	8,919
Karáchi	564.830	313,152	251,728	6,986	1,048	27,282	1,884	278,884	248,796	124,008	104,221	5,921	953	1,321	210
Hyderabad	918.646	500,068	418,578	9,351	823	25,709	1,599	465,008	416,156	208,906	172,856	7,993	783	1,078	144
Shikárpur	915.497	493,872	421,625	10,349	470	37,509	687	446,114	420,468	199,423	166,506	8,830	415	1,463	81
Thar and Párkar	298.203	165,225	132,978	1,352	44	6,919	118	156,954	132,816	72,322	59,921	1,222	40	365	14
Upper Sind Frontier	174.548	96,273	78,275	1,701	104	5,551	74	89,021	78,097	39,800	32,493	1,492	92	242	9
Total, Sind	2.871.774	1,568,590	1,303,184	29,639	2,489	102,970	4,362	1,435,981	1,296,333	644,459	535,977	25,458	2,286	4,454	558
Total, British Territory	18.887.044	9.793.037	9.093.977	333.815	24.890	946.025	54.338	8.483.227	9.014.749	3.799.633	3.503.788	281.812	22.858	44.659	9,470
Total, Feudatories	8.040.052	4.109.543	3.930.516	105.545	5.855	362.644	13.404	3.641.357	3,911,257	1.632.675	1.535.330	91.906	5.391	23.666	2,230
Grand Total	26.897.103	13.873.613	13.024.493	439.360	30.745	1.308.669	67.742	12.124.584	12.926.006	5.432.313	5.039.148	373.718	28.249	68.325	11,700
Aden	44.079	30,914	13,165	955	91	6,147	561	23,812	12,713	6,387	4,445	810	84	234	45

Table IX.

Education by Religion and Age.

IX.

Total Population.

Illiterate.		15 — 24.								25 and over.							
		Total.		Learning.		Literate.		Illiterate.		Total.		Learning.		Literate.		Illiterate.	
Males.	Females.	Males.	Females.	Males.	Females.	Males.	Females.	Males.	Females.	Males.	Females.	Males.	Females.	Males.	Females.	Males.	Females.
85,006	86,049	131,341	71,083	5,443	516	44,382	9,001	81,516	61,566	272,812	136,555	309	79	86,441	12,337	186,062	124,139
160,706	151,023	91,531	82,413	2,484	85	16,230	951	73,811	81,377	203,166	203,094	454	84	41,391	1,201	161,321	201,809
159,571	146,381	86,720	73,883	2,008	39	12,912	446	71,800	73,398	195,986	189,645	177	23	33,529	532	162,280	189,090
63,953	63,628	29,325	25,988	452	12	2,902	101	25,971	25,875	64,784	61,402	55	3	6,950	122	57,779	61,278
49,798	57,334	34,137	31,030	951	18	10,652	547	22,634	31,065	79,765	76,660	52	5	25,754	583	53,959	76,073
108,383	128,764	53,241	55,172	2,080	82	15,076	1,433	35,085	53,658	140,132	148,380	291	61	40,326	1,773	99,515	146,646
542,411	550,424	293,954	269,086	7,975	236	67,778	3,477	228,201	265,373	683,833	679,181	1,029	176	147,950	4,211	534,854	674,795
172,465	174,176	75,127	76,071	1,065	104	8,447	652	65,015	75,345	211,843	181,474	75	14	23,973	731	187,295	180,729
98,012	100,817	37,322	42,062	1,256	24	5,241	207	30,825	42,431	110,472	110,345	90	15	15,632	258	94,750	110,078
207,354	210,910	67,214	92,003	2,946	20	9,734	300	54,534	91,683	219,687	279,695	44	12	33,231	306	186,412	279,367
73,028	77,391	42,459	39,796	1,583	20	7,211	542	33,665	39,234	108,441	93,606	72	6	17,384	438	90,985	93,222
550,879	572,194	221,122	250,532	7,450	168	30,633	1,671	184,039	248,693	649,943	665,170	281	47	90,220	1,727	559,442	663,396
284,257	297,582	113,680	124,806	2,699	34	13,632	252	97,349	124,610	824,367	298,074	184	23	38,442	336	285,741	291,710
164,317	166,265	65,784	73,674	1,740	33	7,495	254	56,549	73,388	190,164	170,826	91	16	24,066	479	166,007	170,331
162,571	168,262	68,724	76,174	2,241	49	7,440	298	59,043	75,837	207,950	191,513	76	8	23,828	474	184,046	191,030
190,632	196,906	85,482	87,679	5,603	205	12,775	1,154	67,104	86,320	249,527	235,355	378	37	38,038	1,768	211,111	233,550
133,750	137,060	58,154	62,024	1,688	23	6,469	213	49,997	61,789	179,523	169,640	230	18	20,369	384	158,924	169,304
236,331	229,924	80,031	93,674	2,703	29	8,131	183	75,197	93,463	276,461	229,060	306	25	28,356	350	247,799	228,685
1,171,848	1,195,999	477,855	517,131	16,674	371	55,942	2,354	405,239	514,396	1,427,992	1,348,467	1,265	126	173,099	3,731	1,253,628	1,344,610
187,606	190,930	79,644	78,856	2,248	28	9,012	348	68,384	78,480	230,216	230,807	317	16	26,903	407	202,996	230,384
180,822	196,411	90,724	93,509	2,885	33	16,127	829	71,712	92,642	232,387	231,326	376	18	39,154	647	192,857	230,661
140,048	146,321	64,823	68,001	1,480	1	6,202	153	57,141	67,847	181,652	183,288	90	10	19,007	171	162,555	183,107
508,476	533,661	235,191	240,366	6,613	67	31,341	1,330	197,237	238,969	644,255	645,421	783	44	85,064	1,22[illegible]	558,408	644,152
2,859,620	2,908,337	1,360,463	1,348,188	44,155	1,358	220,076	17,833	1,096,232	1,328,997	3,678,835	3,474,794	3,067	471	582,774	23,231	3,093,894	3,451,092
116,706	103,055	47,711	39,486	963	55	7,157	678	39,591	38,753	141,433	108,021	102	37	18,804	996	122,527	106,988
190,855	171,809	74,794	65,752	1,245	23	5,717	496	67,832	65,333	210,368	179,990	113	17	18,034	859	197,321	179,114
189,125	166,010	69,793	59,458	1,169	29	7,945	182	60,679	59,247	224,656	195,661	250	26	28,096	434	196,310	195,211
70,735	59,867	24,757	17,402	107	1	1,686	31	22,964	17,370	68,146	55,656	23	3	4,868	73	63,255	55,579
38,066	42,392	13,158	10,461	169	6	1,296	19	11,693	10,436	43,315	35,321	40	6	4,013	46	39,262	35,269
614,547	553,133	230,283	192,659	3,653	114	23,801	1,406	202,759	191,039	693,918	574,648	528	89	74,715	2,398	618,675	572,161
3.473.167	**3.471.460**	**1.590.676**	**1.540.747**	**47.808**	**1.472**	**243.877**	**19.239**	**1.298.991**	**1.520.033**	**4.372.753**	**4.049.442**	**4.195**	**560**	**657.489**	**25.629**	**3.711.069**	**4.023.253**
1.517.103	**1.527.739**	**693.166**	**657.108**	**12.211**	**274**	**94.660**	**4.741**	**586.295**	**652.093**	**1.783.705**	**1.738.048**	**1.428**	**190**	**244.318**	**6.433**	**1.537.959**	**1.731.425**
4.990.270	**4.999.199**	**2.283.842**	**2.197.855**	**60.019**	**1.746**	**338.537**	**23.980**	**1.885.286**	**2.172.129**	**6.156.458**	**5.787.490**	**5.623**	**750**	**901.807**	**32.062**	**5.249.028**	**5.754.678**
5,343	4,316	8,195	2,582	120	5	1,811	109	6,255	2,468	16,332	6,138	16	2	4,102	307	12,214	3,929

TABLE

Part (B).—

District.	Total Population.			Total by Education.						0—14.					
				Learning.		Literate.		Illiterate.		Total.		Learning.		Literate.	
	Total.	Males.	Females.	Males.	Females.	Males.	Females.	Males.	Females.	Males.	Females.	Males.	Females.	Males.	Females.
Bombay City	543,276	345,815	197,461	10,708	1,868	76,812	6,454	258,295	189,739	72,722	61,234	7,937	1,179	6,453	1,425
Ahmedabad	788,718	406,563	382,155	12,717	890	40,907	1,442	352,939	379,823	155,208	140,697	10,475	775	2,132	215
Kaira	782,448	414,496	367,952	15,683	835	41,022	922	357,791	366,195	159,803	138,289	13,815	790	1,743	160
Panch Maháls	281,750	146,146	135,604	3,337	213	7,796	206	135,013	135,185	61,201	57,302	2,931	200	351	48
Broach	245,422	126,225	119,197	6,994	367	26,687	646	92,544	118,184	42,697	40,955	6,298	351	1,074	117
Surat	572,916	284,054	288,862	15,369	1,061	46,263	1,390	222,422	286,411	115,036	110,990	13,631	987	2,693	255
Total, Gujarát ...	2,671,254	1,377,484	1,293,770	54,100	3,366	162,675	4,606	1,160,709	1,285,798	533,945	483,211	47,150	3,106	7,903	795
Thána	808,217	420,172	388,045	9,824	430	25,617	523	384,731	387,102	166,618	158,079	8,515	394	917	103
Kolába	479,024	239,079	239,945	8,292	356	18,574	359	212,213	239,231	101,268	96,100	7,101	339	812	86
Ratnágiri	1,019,943	475,449	544,494	18,273	427	39,828	588	417,348	543,479	208,040	202,641	15,628	414	1,164	111
Kánara	402,644	211,905	190,739	9,547	764	22,986	853	179,372	189,122	75,002	70,340	8,120	751	861	152
Total, Konkan ...	2,709,828	1,346,605	1,363,223	45,936	1,966	107,005	2,323	1,193,664	1,358,934	550,928	527,160	39,364	1,898	3,754	452
Khándesh	1,249,132	636,677	612,455	21,931	255	45,944	364	568,802	611,836	261,967	254,296	19,354	200	1,473	66
Násik	776,824	396,102	380,722	10,882	186	25,208	319	360,012	380,217	163,426	154,619	9,821	161	729	52
Ahmednagar	818,585	414,768	403,817	10,805	404	23,845	401	380,118	403,012	161,812	156,558	9,080	396	601	63
Poona	989,799	501,883	487,916	20,223	997	38,047	1,269	443,613	485,650	196,534	186,333	15,087	887	908	131
Sholápur	686,945	348,567	338,378	9,493	346	23,536	337	315,538	337,695	181,894	186,154	7,828	319	688	69
Sátára	1,163,606	581,998	581,608	15,012	342	33,230	423	533,756	580,843	238,961	218,698	12,275	294	957	61
Total, Deccan ...	5,684,891	2,879,995	2,804,896	88,340	2,530	189,810	3,113	2,601,839	2,799,253	1,154,094	1,096,637	72,945	2,257	5,356	522
Belgaum	873,051	439,981	433,070	12,796	469	29,750	516	397,435	432,092	174,495	165,549	10,652	423	1,057	110
Dhárwár	903,739	453,112	450,627	21,861	1,361	50,772	1,112	380,479	448,154	174,750	169,578	18,994	1,322	1,911	235
Bijápur	703,604	351,668	351,936	11,063	497	23,493	267	317,112	351,172	133,492	129,381	9,661	489	553	42
Total, Karnátak ...	2,480,394	1,244,761	1,235,633	45,720	2,330	104,016	1,895	1,095,026	1,231,418	482,737	464,501	39,807	2,244	3,521	387
Total, Presidency Proper ...	14,089,643	7,194,660	6,894,983	244,810	11,450	640,317	18,391	6,309,533	6,865,142	2,794,426	2,631,743	206,703	10,634	27,077	3,531
Karáchi	100,547	57,051	43,896	3,504	121	17,630	250	36,517	43,525	19,432	16,925	2,991	113	857	40
Hyderabad	185,625	100,449	85,176	5,407	268	19,258	807	75,784	84,101	42,447	36,173	4,627	253	741	134
Shikárpur	183,905	98,658	84,247	6,015	67	30,806	257	61,837	83,933	39,741	34,838	5,373	44	1,193	38
Thar and Párkar	79,853	44,569	35,284	794	15	5,202	34	38,573	35,235	19,331	15,883	741	15	267	...
Upper Sind Frontier	18,606	10,739	7,867	609	3	4,222	12	5,908	7,852	3,653	3,296	567	3	198	1
Total, Sind ...	567,536	312,066	255,470	16,329	464	77,118	1,360	218,619	253,646	124,604	107,114	14,290	428	3,256	213
Total, British Territory.	14,657,179	7,506,726	7,150,453	261,139	11,914	717,435	19,751	6,528,152	7,118,788	2,919,030	2,738,857	221,003	11,112	30,333	3,794
Total, Feudatories ...	6,781,065	3,466,573	3,314,492	74,793	3,799	250,573	8,502	3,141,207	3,302,191	1,382,064	1,301,257	64,098	3,519	15,309	1,434
Grand Total ...	21,438,244	10,973,299	10,464,945	335,932	15,713	968,008	28,253	9,669,359	10,420,979	4,301,094	4,040,114	285,100	14,631	45,642	5,228
Aden	2,713	2,108	605	111	1	946	13	1,052	591	270	237	60	1	20	—

Table IX.

Education by Religion and Age.

IX.

Hindu.

Illiterate.		15 — 24. Total.		15 — 24. Learning.		15 — 24. Literate.		15 — 24. Illiterate.		25 and over. Total.		25 and over. Learning.		25 and over. Literate.		25 and over. Illiterate.	
Males.	Females.	Males.	Females.	Males.	Females.	Males.	Females.	Males.	Females.	Males.	Females.	Males.	Females.	Males.	Females.	Males.	Females.
58,332	58,630	89,109	48,503	2,602	69	23,629	2,375	62,878	46,060	183,984	87,724	169	21	46,730	2,654	137,085	85,049
142,601	139,704	79,045	70,412	1,906	49	10,959	562	66,160	69,801	172,310	171,046	336	63	27,816	665	144,158	170,318
144,245	131,339	77,982	66,094	1,728	25	10,774	346	65,480	65,713	176,711	169,579	140	20	28,505	416	148,066	169,143
57,919	57,054	26,670	25,218	366	11	2,205	76	24,099	25,131	58,275	55,084	40	2	5,240	82	52,995	55,000
35,325	40,465	25,143	22,972	662	12	7,434	267	17,047	22,693	58,385	65,292	84	4	18,179	262	40,172	65,020
98,712	109,748	46,067	48,063	1,512	34	12,149	513	32,406	47,516	122,951	129,809	226	40	31,421	622	91,304	129,147
478,802	478,310	254,907	250,749	6,174	131	43,521	1,764	205,212	228,854	588,632	580,810	776	129	111,161	2,047	476,695	578,634
157,186	157,582	66,917	69,230	1,262	20	6,427	214	59,228	67,996	186,637	161,736	47	6	18,273	206	168,317	161,524
93,355	95,675	34,781	40,083	1,112	9	4,457	129	29,212	39,945	103,030	103,762	79	7	13,305	144	89,646	103,611
191,249	202,116	62,756	84,421	2,610	6	8,869	258	51,277	84,177	204,653	257,438	35	7	29,795	239	174,823	257,196
66,021	69,437	36,518	35,897	1,372	8	6,509	406	30,637	35,483	98,385	84,502	56	5	15,616	295	82,714	84,202
507,810	524,810	202,972	228,631	6,856	43	26,262	987	170,354	227,601	592,705	607,432	216	25	76,989	884	515,500	606,523
241,140	254,030	97,095	107,136	2,420	29	11,589	122	83,066	106,985	277,615	251,623	157	26	32,862	176	244,576	250,821
153,376	154,406	60,215	68,210	1,491	11	5,808	89	52,916	68,110	172,461	157,893	70	14	18,671	178	153,720	157,701
152,131	156,099	62,467	70,508	1,674	4	5,241	130	55,552	70,374	190,489	176,751	61	4	18,003	208	172,435	176,539
180,539	185,224	76,677	81,511	4,820	83	3,539	450	63,318	80,978	228,672	220,073	316	27	28,600	598	199,756	219,448
122,878	125,756	53,009	56,791	1,484	19	5,446	107	46,079	56,665	164,164	155,453	181	8	17,402	171	146,581	155,274
225,729	218,343	81,163	88,063	2,467	28	6,965	126	71,730	87,909	261,875	274,847	270	20	25,308	236	236,297	274,591
1,075,793	1,093,858	430,625	472,219	14,356	174	43,588	1,014	372,681	471,021	1,295,276	1,236,040	1,045	99	140,866	1,567	1,153,365	1,234,374
162,786	164,999	68,052	68,290	1,903	18	6,954	197	59,195	68,075	197,434	199,238	241	11	21,739	209	175,464	199,018
153,845	168,021	78,076	80,604	2,529	25	14,082	538	61,465	80,041	200,286	200,445	338	14	34,779	339	165,169	200,092
123,278	128,850	57,498	60,318	1,323	1	5,586	103	50,589	60,214	160,678	162,237	79	7	17,354	122	143,245	162,108
439,909	461,870	203,626	209,212	5,755	44	26,622	838	171,249	208,330	558,398	561,920	658	32	78,872	670	483,868	561,218
2,560,646	2,617,478	1,181,239	1,189,314	35,243	460	163,622	6,988	982,374	1,181,866	3,218,995	3,073,926	2,864	306	449,618	7,822	2,706,513	3,065,798
15,584	16,772	11,202	7,934	492	5	4,394	96	6,316	7,833	27,017	18,037	21	3	12,379	114	14,617	17,920
37,079	35,786	16,707	13,778	770	10	4,198	311	11,739	13,457	41,295	35,236	10	5	14,319	362	26,966	34,958
33,176	34,756	16,033	13,046	611		6,538	66	8,884	12,974	42,884	36,363	31	7	23,075	153	19,778	36,203
18,323	15,867	7,385	4,568	47	...	1,289	9	6,049	4,559	17,853	14,834	6	...	3,640	25	14,201	14,809
2,888	3,292	1,879	1,323	38	...	910	5	931	1,318	5,207	3,248	4	...	3,114	6	2,089	3,243
107,049	106,473	53,206	40,649	1,958	21	17,329	497	32,919	40,141	134,256	107,707	72	15	56,533	660	77,651	107,032
2.667.695	2.723.951	1.234.445	1.229.963	37.201	481	180.951	7.475	1.015.293	1.222.007	3.353.251	3.181.633	2.935	321	506.151	8.482	2.844.164	3.172.830
1.302.657	1.296.304	587.997	553.200	9.659	177	65.025	3.208	513.313	549.815	1.496.512	1.460.035	1.036	103	170.239	3.860	1.325.237	1.456.072
3.970.352	4.020.255	1.822.442	1.783.163	46.860	658	245.976	10.683	1.529.606	1.771.822	4.849.763	4.641.668	3.972	424	676.390	12.342	4.169.401	4.628.902
181	286	548	166	43	...	258	10	247	156	1,290	203	8	...	658	3	624	199

District.	Total Population. Total.	Males.	Females.	Total by Education. Learning. Males.	Learning. Females.	Literate. Males.	Literate. Females.	Illiterate. Males.	Illiterate. Females.	0—14. Total. Males.	Total. Females.	Learning. Males.	Learning. Females.	Literate. Males.	Literate. Females.
Bombay City	155.247	95,065	60,182	3,082	752	21,774	3,344	70,209	56,086	22,429	19,944	2,431	694	2,112	83
Ahmedabad...	90.487	45,811	44,676	1,875	77	6,978	177	36,958	44,422	16,628	15,430	1,575	67	398	[illegible]
Kaira	77.443	40,053	37,390	1,741	67	4,333	40	33,979	37,283	15,971	15,346	1,523	62	241	[illegible]
Panch Mahâls	18.651	9,352	9,299	581	21	1,825	50	6,946	9,225	3,858	3,735	508	20	78	7
Broach	71.263	36,178	35,085	2,852	93	9,158	113	24,168	34,879	13,348	13,461	2,653	89	507	[illegible]
Surat	52.307	25,251	27,056	1,912	229	5,734	411	17,605	26,416	9,683	9,672	1,066	206	321	[illegible]
Total, Gujarât ..	310.151	156,645	153,506	8,961	487	28,028	791	119,656	152,228	59,488	54,645	7,925	444	1,545	119
Thána...	40.293	22,225	18,067	1,067	185	3,374	134	17,784	17,748	7,547	6,841	958	177	117	31
Kolába	25.328	12,922	12,406	1,034	179	1,930	140	9,958	12,087	5,024	4,532	902	163	76	11
Ratnágiri	79.673	35,074	44,599	2,524	141	4,019	116	28,531	44,342	17,433	16,726	2,215	134	159	[illegible]
Kánara	26.460	13,180	13,280	1,105	205	1,738	169	10,337	12,906	5,207	5,002	951	198	51	31
Total, Konkan ...	171.753	83,401	88,352	5,730	710	11,061	559	66,610	87,083	35,211	33,101	5,026	672	402	109
Khándesh	112.049	58,094	53,955	1,915	83	3,747	81	52,432	53,790	22,915	21,377	1,680	78	129	[illegible]
Násik	42.059	22,330	19,729	1,244	42	2,291	66	18,795	19,621	8,204	7,580	1,000	39	88	8
Ahmednagar	47.071	24,239	22,832	1,100	45	1,931	46	21,208	22,741	9,144	8,649	916	42	57	5
Poona...	51.200	26,955	24,245	1,909	201	3,928	188	21,118	23,856	9,697	9,060	1,479	186	123	[illegible]
Sholápur	53.971	27,590	26,381	857	46	1,640	55	25,093	26,280	10,552	9,848	684	42	68	7
Sátára	43.256	21,796	21,460	1,021	39	1,827	45	18,948	21,376	8,800	8,340	844	35	113	13
Total, Deccan ...	249.606	181,004	168,602	8,046	456	15,364	482	157,594	167,664	69,312	64,847	6,693	422	578	[illegible]
Belgaum	80.484	40,810	39,674	1,576	109	2,886	164	36,348	39,411	16,584	15,532	1,351	100	110	27
Dhárwár	131.000	66,273	64,727	2,764	194	4,360	250	59,149	64,283	27,316	25,947	2,435	180	211	41
Bijápur	88.522	44,194	44,328	1,260	71	1,644	55	41,290	44,202	17,421	16,823	1,114	68	62	7
Total, Karnátak ...	300.006	151,277	148,729	5,600	374	8,890	459	136,787	147,896	61,321	58,302	4,900	357	383	75
Total, Presidency Proper ...	1.286.763	667,392	619,371	31,419	2,779	85,117	5,635	550,856	610,957	247,761	230,837	26,975	2,580	6,020	1,213
Karáchi	453.188	248,378	204,810	2,868	503	6,070	496	239,440	203,811	102,751	85,633	2,449	456	370	77
Hyderabad	713.009	388,603	324,397	3,925	546	5,896	712	378,782	323,139	161,587	132,481	3,353	521	304	101
Shikárpur	728.661	392,923	335,738	4,176	378	6,375	288	382,372	335,072	158,827	130,987	3,408	358	204	27
Thar and Párkar	164.890	92,127	72,763	494	29	1,382	77	90,251	72,657	38,899	31,832	421	25	84	14
Upper Sind Frontier	155.408	85,133	70,275	1,082	96	1,215	35	82,836	70,144	36,069	29,145	917	85	42	5
Total, Sind ...	2.215.147	1,207,164	1,007,983	12,545	1,552	20,938	1,608	1,173,681	1,004,823	498,153	410,079	10,548	1,425	1,061	[illegible]
Total, British Territory ...	3.501.910	1.874.556	1.627.354	43.964	4.331	106.055	7.243	1.724.537	1.615.780	745.914	640.916	37.523	4.014	6.081	1.437
Total, Feudatories ...	853.893	437.664	416.228	14.572	1.144	46.845	2.850	373.247	412.218	171.493	157,356	13.071	1.039	3.998	466
Grand Total ...	4.355.802	2.312.220	2.043.582	58.536	5.475	152.900	10.109	2.100.781	2.027.998	917.407	798.282	50.591	5.053	10.080	1.903
Aden...	35.193	24,436	10,757	581	56	2,482	83	21,373	10,619	5,427	3,510	507	49	162	6

Table IX.

Education by Religion and Age.

IX.

Mussalman.

		15 — 24.								25 and over.							
Illiterate.		Total.		Learning.		Literate.		Illiterate.		Total.		Learning.		Literate.		Illiterate.	
Males.	Females.	Males.	Females.	Males.	Females.	Males.	Females.	Males.	Females.	Males.	Females.	Males.	Females.	Males.	Females.	Males.	Females.
17,886	18,427	20,507	12,379	578	29	5,965	1,157	13,964	11,193	52,129	27,859	73	29	13,697	1,364	38,359	26,466
14,655	15,341	8,338	8,092	247	5	1,886	67	6,205	8,010	20,845	21,164	58	5	4,694	88	16,098	21,071
14,207	13,280	7,580	6,774	192	2	1,309	12	6,079	6,760	16,502	17,271	26	2	2,783	25	13,693	17,243
3,272	3,708	1,620	1,699	70	1	530	22	1,020	1,676	3,874	3,865	3	...	1,217	21	2,654	3,844
10,188	12,348	6,916	6,429	187	3	2,709	39	4,020	6,283	15,914	16,195	12	1	5,942	51	9,960	16,143
7,696	9,403	4,111	4,909	209	15	1,427	135	2,475	4,759	11,457	12,475	37	8	3,986	213	7,434	12,254
50,018	54,080	28,565	27,893	905	26	7,861	274	19,799	27,593	68,592	70,970	131	17	18,622	398	49,839	70,555
6,472	6,633	3,523	2,997	90	5	821	51	2,612	2,941	11,155	8,229	19	3	2,436	52	8,700	8,174
4,047	4,348	1,927	2,206	125	12	397	48	1,405	2,146	5,971	6,668	7	4	1,458	71	4,506	5,593
15,059	16,566	3,951	7,060	301	4	739	40	2,911	7,022	13,690	20,807	8	3	3,121	60	10,561	20,754
4,205	4,773	2,273	2,429	140	6	477	63	1,656	2,359	5,700	5,550	14	1	1,210	75	4,476	5,774
29,783	32,320	11,674	14,607	656	27	2,434	202	8,584	14,468	36,516	40,554	48	11	8,225	248	28,243	40,295
21,106	21,279	9,169	9,492	212	3	1,019	37	7,938	9,452	26,010	23,086	23	2	2,599	26	23,388	23,039
7,026	7,533	3,351	3,435	146	3	620	18	2,585	3,414	10,775	8,714	8	...	1,583	40	9,184	8,674
8,171	8,595	3,701	3,765	175	2	500	14	3,026	3,749	11,394	10,425	9	1	1,374	27	10,011	10,397
8,095	8,840	4,609	4,130	383	13	994	63	3,232	4,064	12,840	11,055	47	2	2,811	91	9,791	10,962
9,800	9,799	4,204	4,414	133	1	391	27	3,680	4,386	12,834	12,119	40	3	1,181	21	11,613	12,095
7,843	8,892	3,211	3,190	151	...	475	13	2,585	3,177	9,785	9,930	26	4	1,239	19	8,520	9,907
62,041	64,388	28,245	28,426	1,200	22	3,999	172	23,046	28,232	83,447	75,329	153	12	10,787	223	72,607	75,094
15,123	15,405	6,262	6,145	184	6	718	60	5,300	6,079	17,964	17,997	41	3	2,058	67	15,865	17,927
24,670	25,717	10,809	11,358	207	3	1,287	93	9,274	11,262	28,149	27,422	32	2	2,912	116	25,205	27,304
16,245	16,748	6,886	7,316	135	...	408	21	6,343	7,295	19,887	20,189	11	3	1,174	27	18,702	20,159
56,038	57,870	23,956	24,819	616	9	1,363	174	20,077	24,636	66,000	65,608	84	8	6,144	210	59,772	65,390
215,766	227,035	112,947	108,214	3,055	113	22,622	1,979	86,370	106,123	306,684	280,320	489	77	57,475	2,443	248,720	277,800
99,932	85,100	34,023	30,729	340	20	1,434	151	32,654	30,558	110,999	88,449	79	27	4,266	268	106,654	88,153
157,930	131,860	56,339	50,619	469	13	1,280	171	54,590	50,435	170,677	141,296	103	12	4,312	440	166,262	140,844
155,155	130,622	53,383	46,174	550	21	1,340	73	51,493	46,080	180,713	158,577	218	19	4,771	188	175,724	158,370
38,394	31,793	13,410	9,620	56	1	324	19	13,030	9,600	39,818	31,311	17	3	974	44	38,827	31,264
35,120	29,055	11,135	9,112	129	5	329	10	10,677	9,097	37,909	31,018	36	6	844	20	37,029	31,902
486,541	409,430	168,895	146,254	1,544	60	4,707	434	162,644	145,770	540,116	451,650	453	67	15,167	969	524,496	450,683
702.307	635.465	231.812	254.438	5.199	173	27.339	2.493	219.011	251.892	816.800	731.970	942	141	72.642	3.403	773.216	728.423
154.428	155.851	70.627	70.888	1.254	52	12.645	914	56.727	69.922	195.544	187.974	247	53	30.203	1.483	165.094	186.435
856.783	791.326	352.469	325.350	6.753	225	39.975	3.317	305.741	321.811	1.042.344	919.944	1.189	197	102.845	4.889	938.310	914.858
4,758	3,465	6,499	2,034	68	5	732	32	5,699	1,997	12,510	5,213	6	2	1,588	44	10,916	5,167

District.	Total Population.			Total by Education.						0—14.					
				Learning.		Literate.		Illiterate.		Total.		Learning.		Literate.	
	Total.	Males.	Females.	Males.	Females.	Males.	Females.	Males.	Females.	Males.	Females.	Males.	Females.	Males.	Females.
Bombay City	45,310	30,437	14,873	2,370	1,114	14,486	4,954	13,581	8,805	5,810	4,563	1,504	967	918	713
Ahmedabad	1,592	1,043	549	87	61	660	258	296	230	263	253	70	60	42	45
Kaira	2,282	1,256	1,026	111	79	278	112	867	835	507	413	96	68	24	6
Panch Mahâls	84	67	17	...	...	36	4	31	13	6	2	...	...	...	...
Broach	128	90	38	3	3	54	14	33	21	8	14	3	3	...	...
Surat	540	271	269	41	64	149	94	81	111	77	126	36	56	2	10
Total, Gujarát ...	4,626	2,727	1,899	242	207	1,177	482	1,308	1,210	861	783	205	177	68	60
Thána	43,295	22,008	2[illegible]287	1,556	518	2,426	498	18,026	20,271	8,413	8,362	1,339	450	213	61
Koláha	823	479	344	21	7	93	23	365	314	152	132	16	7	4	3
Ratnágiri	4,206	2,054	2,152	110	26	215	36	1,729	2,090	867	878	89	16	6	7
Kánara	15,639	8,407	7,232	463	97	666	151	7,278	6,984	2,981	2,955	393	91	21	17
Total, Konkan ...	63,963	32,948	31,015	2,150	648	3,400	708	27,398	29,659	12,413	12,327	1,837	564	244	88
Khándesh	1,174	686	488	41	40	381	167	264	281	198	195	35	40	24	19
Násik	3,683	2,728	955	209	142	2,017	377	502	436	391	307	158	126	28	48
Ahmednagar	6,333	3,737	2,596	714	442	1,288	346	1,735	1,808	1,218	1,130	77	398	39	23
Poona	11,252	7,537	3,725	777	639	4,688	1,394	2,072	1,692	1,400	1,471	603	555	117	150
Sholápur	1,081	604	477	85	45	316	169	203	263	197	205	74	44	11	24
Sátára	903	629	274	53	33	390	113	186	1[illegible]8	127	107	42	32	10	15
Total, Deccan ...	24,436	15,921	8,515	1,879	1,341	9,080	2,566	4,962	4,608	3,591	3,505	1,389	1,195	229	277
Belgaum	7,617	4,494	3,123	158	56	1,654	251	2,682	2,816	1,124	1,213	130	51	49	46
Dhárwár	4,222	2,303	1,919	186	138	915	397	1,202	1,384	749	760	157	127	34	41
Bijápur	827	431	396	19	4	91	45	321	347	170	171	17	4	...	6
Total, Karnátak ...	12,666	7,228	5,438	363	198	2,660	693	4,205	4,547	2,043	2,134	304	182	83	93
Total, Presidency Proper ...	151,001	89,261	61,740	7,004	3,509	30,803	9,403	51,454	48,829	24,718	23,312	5,239	3,085	1,542	1,230
Karáchi	6,314	4,493	1,821	382	307	3,066	854	1,045	660	770	681	316	283	68	63
Hyderabad	778	628	150	9	8	506	70	113	72	53	60	8	8	11	8
Shikárpur...	522	327	195	41	33	214	117	72	45	82	76	38	31	4	12
Thar and Párkar...	21	14	7	...	...	8	5	6	2	...	2	...	...	...	...
Upper Sind Frontier	129	81	48	9	5	49	27	23	16	15	16	8		2	3
Total, Sind ...	7,764	5,548	2,221	441	353	3,843	1,073	1,259	795	920	835	370	316	85	91
Total, British Territory.	**158,765**	**94,804**	**63,961**	**7,445**	**3,861**	**34,646**	**10,476**	**53,713**	**49,624**	**25,638**	**24,137**	**5,609**	**3,411**	**1,627**	**1,321**
Total, Feudatories ...	**8,239**	**4,467**	**3,772**	**201**	**92**	**1,191**	**266**	**3,075**	**3,414**	**1,524**	**1,469**	**160**	**87**	**34**	**19**
Grand Total ...	**167,004**	**99,271**	**67,733**	**7,646**	**3,953**	**35,837**	**10,742**	**55,788**	**53,038**	**27,162**	**25,606**	**5,769**	**3,498**	**1,661**	**1,340**
Aden	3,005	2,657	348	41	23	2,226	221	390	104	121	107	34	23	30	37

Table IX.

Education by Religion and Age.

IX.

Christian.

Illiterate.		15 — 24.								25 and over.							
		Total.		Learning.		Literate.		Illiterate.		Total.		Learning.		Literate.		Illiterate.	
Males.	Females.	Males.	Females.	Males.	Females.	Males.	Females.	Males.	Females.	Males.	Females.	Males.	Females.	Males.	Females.	Males.	Females.
3,388	2,883	9,156	3,166	840	139	5,074	1,506	3,242	1,521	15,471	7,144	26	9	8,494	2,735	6,951	4,400
151	133	278	124	14	9	228	93	36	22	502	197	3	3	390	120	109	74
387	340	247	208	13	11	81	51	153	146	502	405	2	...	173	56	327	349
6	2	25	6	...	...	15	1	10	5	36	9	...	...	21	3	15	6
5	11	21	7	...	...	12	4	9	3	61	17	...	...	42	10	19	7
39	60	46	56	5	8	31	35	10	13	148	87	...	...	116	49	32	38
588	546	617	401	32	28	367	184	218	189	1,249	715	5	3	742	238	502	474
6,861	7,851	3,376	3,825	212	68	572	183	2,592	3,574	10,219	9,100	5	...	1,641	254	8,573	8,846
132	122	88	65	5	...	20	9	63	56	239	147		...	69	11	170	136
772	855	342	351	20	10	50	16	272	325	845	923	1	...	159	13	685	910
2,567	2,847	1,481	1,314	67	6	180	68	1,234	1,240	3,945	2,963	3	...	465	66	3,477	2,897
10,332	11,675	5,287	5,555	304	84	822	276	4,161	5,195	15,248	13,133	9	...	2,334	344	12,905	12,789
139	136	117	108	6	...	81	64	30	44	371	135	...	...	276	34	95	101
205	233	379	182	41	16	279	121	59	44	1,958	377	10	...	1,710	208	238	169
702	709	945	455	224	41	519	131	202	283	1,574	1,011	13	3	730	192	831	816
740	766	2,266	788	169	80	1,777	448	320	260	3,811	1,466	5	4	2,794	796	1,012	666
112	137	119	89	11	1	89	57	19	51	288	183	...	...	216	88	72	95
75	62	180	35		...	148	23	25	12	322	132	4	1	232	77	86	54
1,973	2,033	4,006	1,656	458	138	2,893	844	655	674	8,324	3,354	32	8	5,958	1,445	2,334	1,901
945	1,116	1,110	580	21	3	642	85	477	493	2,230	1,330	7	2	963	120	1,260	1,208
658	582	509	438	27	10	285	178	197	250	1,045	731	2	1	596	178	447	552
153	162	53	88	2	...	15	25	36	63	208	137	...	...	76	15	132	122
1,656	1,860	1,702	1,106	50	13	942	288	710	805	3,483	2,198	9	3	1,635	313	1,839	1,882
17,937	18,997	20,768	11,854	1,684	401	10,098	3,098	8,986	8,385	43,775	26,544	81	24	19,163	5,075	24,531	21,445
386	330	1,419	434	64	21	1,207	314	148	99	2,304	706	2	3	1,791	472	511	231
34	34	256	26	1	...	232	13	23	13	319	74	...	...	263	49	56	25
40	33	58	41	2	2	49	33	7	6	187	78	1	...	161	72	25	6
...	2	2	2	...	...	...	2	2	...	12	3	...	...	8	3	4	...
5	9	10	7	1	1	7	4	2	2	56	25	...	...	40	20	16	5
465	408	1,745	510	68	24	1,495	366	182	120	2,878	886	3	3	2,263	616	612	267
18,402	**19.405**	**22.513**	**12.394**	**1.752**	**425**	**11.593**	**3.464**	**9.168**	**8.505**	**46.653**	**27.430**	**84**	**25**	**21.426**	**5.691**	**25.143**	**21.714**
1,330	**1.363**	**808**	**606**	**35**	**4**	**342**	**84**	**431**	**518**	**2.135**	**1.697**	**6**	**1**	**815**	**163**	**1.314**	**1.533**
19.732	**20.768**	**23.321**	**13,000**	**1.787**	**429**	**11.935**	**3.548**	**9,599**	**9.023**	**48.788**	**29.127**	**90**	**26**	**22.241**	**5.854**	**26.457**	**23.247**
57	47	780	67	7	...	686	46	87	21	1,766	174	...	...	1,510	138	246	36

D 1072—24 *ap*

Education by Religion and Age.

TABLE

Part (E).—

District.	Total Population.			Total by Education.						0 — 14					
				Learning.		Literate.		Illiterate.		Total.		Learning.		Literate.	
	Total.	Males.	Females.	Males.	Females.	Males.	Females.	Males.	Females.	Males.	Females.	Males.	Females.	Males.	Females.
Bombay City	190	137	53	2	...	66	5	69	48	8	14	1	...	1	...
Ahmedabad	32	32	...	...	...	24	...	8	...	...	...	...	...	...	...
Kaira	...	...	...	...	...	...	...	...	...	...	...	...	...	...	...
Panch Maháls	...	...	...	...	...	...	...	...	...	...	...	...	...	...	...
Broach	...	...	...	...	...	...	...	...	...	...	...	...	...	...	...
Surat	1	1	...	...	...	1	...	...	...	...	...	...	...	...	...
Total, Gujarát ...	33	33	...	...	...	25	...	8	...	...	...	...	...	...	...
Thána	47	41	6	...	...	30	...	11	6	3	4	...	...	...	...
Kolába	1	1	...	...	...	...	...	1	...	...	...	...	...	...	...
Ratnágiri	35	11	24	...	...	1	8	10	16	3	9	...	...	...	1
Kánara	22	16	6	...	...	1	...	15	6	5	2	...	...	...	...
Total, Konkan ...	105	69	36	...	...	32	8	37	28	11	15	...	...	...	1
Khándesh	11	8	3	...	...	2	...	6	3	3	2	...	...	...	...
Násik	...	...	...	...	...	...	...	...	...	...	...	...	...	...	...
Ahmednagar	1	1	...	...	...	...	...	1	...	...	...	...	...	...	...
Poona	56	55	1	1	...	28	...	26	1	1	...	1	...	...	...
Sholápur	...	...	...	...	...	...	...	...	...	...	...	...	...	...	...
Sátára	68	40	28	3	...	4	...	33	28	15	12	3	...	...	...
Total, Deccan ...	136	104	32	4	...	34	...	66	32	19	14	4	...	...	...
Belgaum	207	106	101	4	...	13	...	89	101	47	37	4	...	1	...
Dhárwár	...	...	...	...	...	...	...	...	...	...	...	...	...	...	...
Bijápur	...	...	...	...	...	...	...	...	...	...	...	...	...	...	...
Total, Karnátak ...	207	106	101	4	...	13	...	89	101	47	37	4	...	1	...
Total, Presidency Proper ...	671	449	222	10	...	170	13	269	209	85	80	9	...	2	1
Karáchi	2	2	...	...	...	2	...	...	...	...	...	...	...	...	...
Hyderabad	...	...	...	...	...	...	...	...	...	...	...	...	...	...	...
Shikárpur	...	...	...	...	...	...	...	...	...	...	...	...	...	...	...
Thar and Párkar	...	...	...	...	...	...	...	...	...	...	...	...	...	...	...
Upper Sind Frontier	...	...	...	...	...	...	...	...	...	...	...	...	...	...	...
Total, Sind ...	2	2	...	...	...	2	...	...	...	...	...	...	...	...	...
Total, British Territory	**673**	**451**	**222**	**10**	...	**172**	**13**	**269**	**209**	**85**	**80**	**9**	...	**2**	**1**
Total, Feudatories ...	**1**	**1**	...	...	...	**1**	...	...	...	...	...	...	...	...	...
Grand Total ...	**674**	**452**	**222**	**10**	...	**173**	**13**	**269**	**209**	**85**	**80**	**9**	...	**2**	**1**
Aden	24	23	1	...	...	15	...	8	1	2	...	...	...	1	...

IX.

Buddhist.

Illiterate.		15 — 24.								25 and over.							
		Total.		Learning.		Literate.		Illiterate.		Total.		Learning.		Literate.		Illiterate.	
Males.	Females.	Males.	Females.	Males.	Females.	Males.	Females.	Males.	Females.	Males.	Females.	Males.	Females.	Males.	Females.	Males.	Females.
6	14	32	24	...	...	24	5	8	19	97	15	1	...	41	...	55	15
...	...	2	...	...	...	1	...	1	...	30	...	...	...	23	...	7	...
...	...	...	...	...	...	...	...	...	...	...	...	...	...	...	...	...	...
...	...	...	...	...	...	...	...	...	...	...	...	...	...	...	...	...	...
...	...	...	...	...	...	...	...	...	...	...	...	...	...	...	...	...	...
...	...	1	...	...	...	1	...	...	...	...	...	...	...	...	...	...	...
...	...	3	...	...	...	2	...	1	...	30	...	...	...	23	...	7	...
3	4	3	...	...	...	2	...	1	...	35	2	...	...	28	...	7	2
...	...	...	...	...	...	...	...	...	...	1	...	...	...	...	...	1	...
3	8	1	5	...	...	...	4	1	1	7	10	...	...	1	3	6	7
5	2	2	3	...	...	...	...	2	3	9	1	...	...	1	...	8	1
11	14	6	8	...	...	2	4	4	4	52	13	...	...	30	3	22	10
3	2	...	1	...	...	...	...	...	1	5	...	...	...	2	...	3	...
...	...	...	...	...	...	...	...	...	...	...	...	...	...	...	...	...	...
...	...	...	...	...	...	...	...	...	...	1	...	...	...	...	...	1	...
...	...	2	...	...	...	...	...	2	...	52	1	...	...	28	...	24	1
...	...	...	...	...	...	...	...	...	...	...	...	...	...	...	...	...	...
12	12	1	3	...	...	...	...	1	3	24	13	...	...	4	...	20	13
15	14	3	4	...	...	...	...	3	4	82	14	...	...	34	...	48	14
42	37	11	14	...	...	3	...	8	14	48	50	...	...	9	...	39	50
...	...	...	...	...	...	...	...	...	...	...	...	...	...	...	...	...	...
...	...	...	...	...	...	...	...	...	...	...	...	...	...	...	...	...	...
42	37	11	14	...	...	3	...	8	14	48	50	...	...	9	...	39	50
74	79	56	50	...	...	31	9	24	41	309	92	1	...	137	3	171	89
...	...	2	...	...	...	2	...	...	...	...	...	...	...	...	...	...	...
...	...	...	...	...	...	...	...	...	...	...	...	...	...	...	...	...	...
...	...	...	...	...	...	...	...	...	...	...	...	...	...	...	...	...	...
...	...	...	...	...	...	...	...	...	...	...	...	...	...	...	...	...	...
...	...	...	...	...	...	...	...	...	...	...	...	...	...	...	...	...	...
...	...	2	...	...	...	2	...	...	...	...	...	...	...	...	...	...	...
74	79	57	50	...	...	33	9	24	41	309	92	1	...	137	3	171	89
...	...	...	...	...	...	...	...	...	...	1	...	...	...	1	...	...	...
74	79	57	50	...	...	33	9	24	41	310	92	1	...	138	3	171	89
1	...	7	...	...	...	7	...	...	...	14	1	...	...	7	...	7	1

Education by Religion and Age.

District.	Total Population.			Total by Education.						0 – 14.					
				Learning.		Literate.		Illiterate.		Total.		Learning.		Literate.	
	Total.	Males.	Females.	Males.	Females.	Males.	Females.	Males.	Females.	Males.	Females.	Males.	Females.	Males.	Females.
Bombay City	25,225	19,317	5,908	885	67	14,439	322	3,993	5,519	3,760	1,845	743	65	1,764	85
Ahmedabad	39,661	19,484	20,177	2,951	314	12,069	445	4,464	19,418	6,545	6,059	2,608	284	740	63
Kaira	9,254	4,712	4,542	797	61	2,914	60	1,001	4,421	1,583	1,373	717	60	145	7
Panch Mahals	1.738	855	883	119	14	583	13	153	856	268	293	113	14	34	7
Broach	3.576	1,878	1,698	265	34	1,319	36	294	1,628	518	443	237	34	41	6
Surat	11.432	6,172	5,260	1,033	114	3,815	84	1,324	5,062	2,042	1,785	925	106	248	10
Total, Gujarát ...	65.661	33,101	32,560	5,165	537	20,700	638	7,236	31,385	10,956	9,951	4,600	498	1,208	108
Thána	2,264	1,821	443	143	8	1,288	3	390	432	388	170	129	7	102	...
Kolába	1.282	1,100	182	73	1	911	...	116	181	205	63	71	1	80	...
Ratnágiri	2.054	1,018	1,036	107	3	230	1	681	1,032	369	366	92	1	6	1
Kánara	1,564	831	733	26	1	131	6	674	727	257	233	22	1	7	1
Total, Konkan ...	7.164	4,770	2,394	349	13	2,560	9	1,861	2,372	1,219	832	314	10	195	2
Khándesh	11.209	6,452	4,757	680	9	3,475	16	2,297	4,732	1,937	1,713	625	8	160	1
Násik	7.889	4,515	3,374	621	8	2,853	26	1,141	3,340	1,269	1,180	466	6	131	...
Ahmednagar	16,203	8,802	7,400	1,400	18	4,972	27	2,430	7,355	2,859	2,786	1,245	17	128	4
Poona	12,437	7,476	4,961	1,106	22	4,759	30	1,611	4,909	2,188	1,880	989	20	203	7
Sholápur	8.439	4,503	3,936	576	29	2,125	39	1,802	3,868	1,526	1,382	615	29	82	12
Sátára	17,934	9,274	8,660	772	17	2,145	9	6,357	8,634	3,413	3,198	689	17	83	...
Total, Deccan ...	74.110	41,022	33,088	5,055	103	20,329	147	15,638	32,838	13,192	12,079	4,529	97	787	25
Belgaum	51.841	26,454	25,387	1,122	14	2,908	10	22,424	25,363	9,706	9,385	955	13	107	1
Dhárwár	12,159	6,268	5,891	337	25	1,417	17	4,514	5,849	2,118	2,103	302	25	89	6
Bijápur	3,353	1,794	1,559	166	6	611	5	1,017	1,548	541	565	147	6	25	...
Total, Karnátak ...	67.353	34,516	32,837	1,625	45	4,936	33	27,955	32,760	12,425	12,050	1,404	44	221	8
Total, Presidency Proper ...	239.513	132,726	106,787	13,079	765	62,964	1,148	56,683	104,874	41,552	36,737	11,590	714	4,175	198
Karáchi	99	65	34	7	...	39	...	19	34	16	17	5	...	3	...
Hyderabad	...	...	...	...	...	...	...	...	...	...	...	...	...	...	...
Shikárpur	1	1	...	...	...	1	...	...	...	...	...	...	...	...	...
Thar and Párkar	823	445	378	60	...	269	...	116	378	137	176	56	...	13	...
Upper Sind Frontier	...	...	...	...	...	...	...	...	...	...	...	...	...	...	...
Total, Sind ...	923	511	412	67	...	309	...	135	412	153	193	61	...	16	...
Total, British Territory ...	**240.436**	**133.237**	**107.199**	**13,146**	**765**	**63,273**	**1,148**	**56,818**	**105,286**	**41.705**	**36,930**	**11,651**	**714**	**4.191**	**228**
Total, Feudatories ...	**314.773**	**159.396**	**155.377**	**15,640**	**674**	**62,848**	**1,319**	**80,908**	**153,384**	**58.995**	**57,448**	**14,292**	**617**	**4.246**	**228**
Grand Total ...	**555.209**	**292.633**	**262.576**	**28,786**	**1.439**	**126,121**	**2.467**	**137.726**	**258,670**	**100.700**	**94.378**	**25,943**	**1.331**	**8.437**	**456**
Aden	...	...	...	...	...	...	...	...	...	...	...	...	...	...	...

IX

Jain.

Illiterate.		15 — 24. Total.		Learning.		Literate.		Illiterate.		25 and over. Total.		Learning.		Literarte.		Illiterate.	
Males.	Females.	Males.	Females.	Males.	Females.	Males.	Females.	Males.	Females.	Males.	Females.	Males.	Females.	Males.	Females.	Males.	Females.
1,253	1,695	6,474	1,812	131	1	5,425	115	918	1,696	9,083	8,251	11	1	7,250	122	1,822	8,128
197	5,687	3,744	3,677	285	19	3,085	154	374	3,504	9,195	10,461	58	11	8,244	223	893	10,227
721	1,506	901	809	71	1	743	31	87	777	2,228	2,360	9	...	2,026	23	193	2,337
121	278	147	155	6	...	135	...	6	155	440	435	...	...	414	6	26	429
246	403	370	323	26	...	333	14	11	309	990	933	2	...	945	16	43	917
809	1,657	1,130	885	98	4	927	28	111	853	2,094	2,598	10	4	2,040	36	344	2,558
5,148	9,325	6,298	6,849	486	24	5,223	227	589	6,597	15,847	16,781	79	15	14,269	303	1,499	16,463
157	163	498	85	14	...	403	2	81	83	935	198	...	1	783	1	152	196
54	62	321	40	2	...	301	...	18	40	574	79	...	...	530	...	44	79
271	364	162	158	15	...	74	...	73	158	487	512	...	2	150	...	337	510
228	231	184	152	4	...	44	3	136	149	390	348	...	...	80	1	310	347
710	820	1,165	435	35	...	822	6	308	430	2,386	1,127	...	3	1,543	2	843	1,122
1,152	1,705	1,238	964	51	1	882	7	305	956	3,277	2,080	4	...	2,433	7	840	2,073
672	1,174	928	710	52	...	745	7	131	703	2,318	1,484	3	2	1,977	19	338	1,463
1,486	2,765	1,569	1,394	152	1	1,169	5	248	1,388	4,374	3,220	3	...	3,675	18	696	3,202
996	1,793	1,615	972	113	...	1,315	3	187	969	3,673	2,169	4	2	3,241	20	428	2,147
929	1,341	800	714	53	...	529	8	218	706	2,177	1,840	8	...	1,514	19	655	1,821
2,641	5,181	1,458	1,359	77	...	528	6	853	1,353	4,403	4,103	6	...	1,534	3	2,863	4,100
7,876	11,957	7,608	6,113	498	2	5,168	36	1,942	6,075	20,222	14,896	28	4	14,374	86	5,820	14,806
8,704	9,870	4,173	3,822	139	1	690	3	3,344	3,818	12,515	12,180	28	...	2,111	5	10,376	12,175
1,727	2,071	1,200	1,086	31	...	506	7	762	1,079	2,851	2,703	4	...	822	4	2,025	2,699
369	557	383	276	19	...	191	1	173	275	870	720	...	...	395	4	475	716
10,800	11,998	5,855	5,184	189	1	1,397	11	4,279	5,173	16,236	15,603	32	...	3,328	13	12,876	15,590
25,787	35,795	27,400	19,392	1,339	28	18,025	394	8,036	18,970	63,774	50,658	150	23	40,764	586	22,860	50,109
8	17	15	5	2	...	9	...	4	5	34	12	...	...	27	...	7	12
...	...	...	...	...	...	...	...	...	...	...	...	...	...	...	...	...	...
...	...	...	...	...	...	...	...	...	...	1	...	...	...	1	...	...	...
68	176	75	57	4	...	60	...	11	57	233	145	...	...	196	...	37	145
...	...	...	...	...	...	...	...	...	...	...	...	...	...	...	...	...	...
76	193	90	62	6	...	69	...	15	62	268	157	...	...	224	...	44	157
25.863	35.988	27.490	19.454	1.345	28	18.094	394	8.051	19.032	64.042	50.815	150	23	40.938	526	23.904	50.266
40.457	56.603	27.255	25.591	1.211	28	16.393	400	9.658	25.163	73.136	73.338	137	29	43.70[illegible]	691	30.793	71.618
66.320	92.591	54.755	45.045	2.556	56	34.490	794	17.709	44.195	137.178	123.153	287	52	83.1[illegible]	1,217	53.697	121.884
...	...	...	...	...	...	...	...	...	...	...	...	...	...	...	...	...	...

District.	Total Population.			Total by Education.						0—14.					
				Learning.		Literate.		Illiterate.		Total.		Learning.		Literate.	
	Total.	Males.	Females.	Males.	Females.	Males.	Females.	Males.	Females.	Males.	Females.	Males.	Females.	Males.	Females.
Bombay City	...	...	...	...	...	...	...	...	...	...	...	...	...	...	...
Ahmedabad	...	...	...	...	...	...	...	...	...	...	...	...	...	...	...
Kaira	...	...	...	...	...	...	...	...	...	...	...	...	...	...	...
Panch Mahals	...	...	...	...	...	...	...	...	...	...	...	...	...	...	...
Broach	...	...	...	...	...	...	...	...	...	...	...	...	...	...	...
Surat	...	...	...	...	...	...	...	...	...	...	...	...	...	...	...
Total, Gujarát ...	...	...	...	...	...	...	...	...	...	...	...	...	...	...	...
Thána...	4	3	1	...	...	2	...	1	1	...	...	...	...	...	...
Kolaba	...	...	...	...	...	...	...	...	...	...	...	...	...	...	...
Ratnágiri	...	...	...	...	...	...	...	...	...	...	...	...	...	...	...
Kánara	...	...	...	...	...	...	...	...	...	...	...	...	...	...	...
Total, Konkan ...	4	3	1	...	...	2	...	1	1	...	...	...	...	...	...
Khándesh	1	1	...	...	...	...	...	1	...	...	...	...	...	...	...
Násik	...	...	...	...	...	...	...	...	...	...	...	...	...	...	...
Ahmednagar	11	7	4	1	...	4	...	2	4	3	...	1	...	...	...
Poona	76	72	4	1	...	41	...	30	4	1	2	1	...	...	...
Sholápur	...	...	...	...	...	...	...	...	...	...	...	...	...	...	...
Sátára...	6	6	...	...	...	1	...	5	...	...	...	...	...	...	...
Total, Deccan ...	94	86	8	2	...	46	...	38	8	4	2	2	...	...	...
Belgaum	...	...	...	...	...	...	...	...	...	...	...	...	...	...	...
Dhárwár	...	...	...	...	...	...	...	...	...	...	...	...	...	...	...
Bijápur	...	...	...	...	...	...	...	...	...	...	...	...	...	...	...
Total, Karnátak ...	...	...	...	...	...	...	...	...	...	...	...	...	...	...	...
Total, Presidency Proper ...	98	89	9	2	...	48	...	39	9	4	2	2	...	...	...
Karáchi	132	102	30	...	1	39	...	63	29	9	8	...	1	...	...
Hyderabad	3	3	...	...	...	1	...	2	...	2	...	...	...	...	...
Shikárpur	402	282	120	6	...	68	1	208	119	45	30	6	...	3	...
Thar and Párkar	...	...	...	...	...	...	...	...	...	...	...	...	...	...	...
Upper Sind Frontier	183	179	4	...	...	57	...	122	4	4	...	...	...	...	...
Total, Sind ...	720	566	154	6	1	165	1	395	152	60	38	6	1	3	...
Total, British Territory ...	818	655	163	8	1	213	1	434	161	64	40	8	1	3	...
Total, Feudatories ...	94	81	13	...	...	39	...	42	13	6	5	...	...	...	...
Grand Total ...	912	735	176	8	1	252	1	476	174	70	45	8	1	3	...
Aden	...	...	...	...	...	...	...	...	...	...	...	...	...	...	...

Table IX.

Education by Religion and Age.

IX.

Sikh.

Illiterate.		15 — 24. Total.		15 — 24. Learning.		15 — 24. Literate.		15 — 24. Illiterate.		25 and over. Total.		25 and over. Learning.		25 and over. Literate.		25 and over. Illiterate.	
Males.	Females.	Males.	Females.	Males.	Females.	Males.	Females.	Males.	Females.	Males.	Females.	Males.	Females.	Males.	Females.	Males.	Females.
...	...	...	...	...	...	...	...	...	...	...	...	...	...	...	...	...	...
...	...	...	...	...	...	...	...	...	...	...	...	...	...	...	...	...	...
...	...	...	...	...	...	...	...	...	...	...	...	...	...	...	...	...	...
...	...	...	...	...	...	...	...	...	...	...	...	...	...	...	...	...	...
...	...	...	...	...	...	...	...	...	...	...	...	...	...	...	...	...	...
...	...	...	...	...	...	...	...	...	...	...	...	...	...	...	...	...	...
...	...	...	...	...	...	...	...	...	...	...	...	...	...	...	...	...	...
...	...	1	...	...	...	...	...	1	...	2	*1*	...	...	2	...	...	*1*
...	...	...	...	...	...	...	...	...	...	...	...	...	...	...	...	...	...
...	...	...	...	...	...	...	...	...	...	...	...	...	...	...	...	...	...
...	...	...	...	...	...	...	...	...	...	...	...	...	...	...	...	...	...
...	...	1	...	...	...	...	...	1	...	2	*1*	...	...	2	...	...	*1*
...	...	...	...	...	...	...	...	...	...	1	...	...	...	...	...	1	...
...	...	...	...	...	...	...	...	...	...	...	...	...	...	...	...	...	...
2	...	2	*2*	...	...	2	...	...	*2*	2	*2*	...	...	2	...	...	*2*
...	*2*	45	*2*	...	...	25	...	20	*2*	26	...	...	...	16	...	10	...
...	...	...	...	...	...	...	...	...	...	...	...	...	...	...	...	...	...
...	...	...	...	...	...	...	...	...	...	6	...	...	...	1	...	5	...
2	*2*	47	*4*	...	...	27	...	20	*4*	35	*2*	...	...	19	...	16	*2*
...	...	...	...	...	...	...	...	...	...	...	...	...	...	...	...	...	...
...	...	...	...	...	...	...	...	...	...	...	...	...	...	...	...	...	...
...	...	...	...	...	...	...	...	...	...	...	...	...	...	...	...	...	...
...	...	...	...	...	...	...	...	...	...	...	...	...	...	...	...	...	...
2	*2*	48	*4*	...	...	27	...	21	*4*	37	*3*	...	...	21	...	16	*3*
9	*7*	17	*13*	...	...	7	...	10	*13*	76	*9*	...	...	32	...	44	*9*
2	...	...	...	...	...	...	...	...	...	1	...	...	...	1	...	...	...
36	*30*	73	*40*	...	...	13	*1*	60	*39*	104	*50*	...	...	52	...	112	*50*
...	...	...	...	...	...	...	...	...	...	...	...	...	...	...	...	...	...
4	...	111	*2*	...	...	48	...	63	*2*	64	*2*	...	...	9	...	55	*2*
51	*37*	201	*55*	...	...	68	*1*	133	*54*	305	*61*	...	...	94	...	211	*61*
53	**39**	**249**	**59**	...	...	**95**	**1**	**154**	**58**	**342**	**64**	...	...	**115**	...	**227**	**64**
6	**5**	**39**	**2**	...	...	**12**	...	**17**	**2**	**45**	**6**	...	...	**27**	...	**19**	**6**
59	**44**	**278**	**61**	...	...	**107**	**1**	**171**	**60**	**388**	**70**	...	...	**142**	...	**243**	**70**
...	...	...	...	...	...	...	...	...	...	...	...	...	...	...	...	...	...

Table IX.

Education by Religion and Age.

TABLE

Part (H).–

District.	Total Population. Total.	Total Population. Males.	Total Population. Females.	Total by Education. Learning. Males.	Learning. Females.	Literate. Males.	Literate. Females.	Illiterate. Males.	Illiterate. Females.	0–14. Total. Males.	Total. Females.	Learning. Males.	Learning. Females.	Literate. Males.	Literate. Females.
Bombay City	47.458	24,705	22,753	3,991	2,068	15,341	10,841	5,373	9,850	8,255	7,533	2,710	1,777	1,952	1,943
Ahmedabad	835	445	390	117	47	251	185	77	158	150	150	86	41	10	29
Kaira	153	88	65	25	9	50	33	13	33	36	28	21	9	4	4
Panch Mahâls	108	77	31	12	6	55	14	10	11	22	13	9	6	3	2
Broach	3.273	1,526	1,747	402	218	776	521	348	1,008	610	604	324	215	17	58
Surat	12.757	5,853	6,904	1,527	727	2,781	1,818	1,545	4,359	2,403	2,235	1,254	697	88	248
Total, Gujarât ...	17.126	7,989	9,137	2,083	1,007	3,913	2,561	1,993	5,569	3,221	3,030	1,694	968	122	341
Thâna...	3.920	1,924	1,996	423	192	1,003	439	498	1,365	748	714	337	178	41	62
Kolâba	167	97	70	19	9	59	17	19	44	24	26	14	8	1	1
Ratnâgiri	15	10	5	2	1	7	3	1	1	3	2	2	1	...	...
Kânara	10	10	...	...	...	10	...	...	...	...	...	...	...	...	...
Total, Konkan ...	4.112	2,041	2,071	444	202	1,079	459	518	1,410	775	742	353	187	42	63
Khândesh	508	328	180	19	9	245	74	64	97	2	68	13	8	3	11
Nâsik	407	241	166	43	23	147	60	51	83	83	67	35	21	4	10
Ahmednagar	188	97	91	26	13	50	50	21	28	31	32	15	12	3	8
Poona...	2,036	1,066	960	317	175	515	399	234	386	421	362	222	150	22	37
Sholâpur	233	124	108	28	20	65	49	31	39	51	52	20	18	2	11
Sâtâra...	134	62	72	9	7	40	33	13	32	20	33	8	6	5	7
Total, Deccan ...	3.495	1,918	1,577	442	247	1,062	665	414	665	668	614	313	215	39	84
Belgaum	61	40	21	3	1	29	10	8	10	9	4	2	1	1	1
Dhârwâr	135	79	56	4	8	56	26	19	22	19	23	3	7	...	3
Bijâpur	24	14	10	1	...	10	4	3	6	4	4	...	...	1	...
Total, Karnâtak ...	220	133	87	8	9	95	40	30	38	82	31	5	8	2	4
Total, Presidency Proper ...	72.411	36,786	35,625	6,968	3,527	21,400	14,566	8,328	17,552	12,051	11,949	5,075	3,155	2,157	2,435
Karâchi	1,408	760	648	218	108	389	273	153	267	274	247	154	98	13	24
Hyderabad	46	28	18	3	...	16	6	9	12	11	10	2	...	1	...
Shikârpur	71	48	23	8	...	36	15	4	8	10	8	4	...	2	2
Thar and Pârkar	1	1	...	...	...	1	...	...	...	...	...	...	...	...	...
Upper Sind Frontier	8	6	2	1	...	5	...	...	2	...	...	...	...	...	...
Total, Sind ...	1.534	843	691	230	108	447	294	166	289	295	265	160	98	16	26
Total, British Territory ...	73.945	37.629	36,316	7.198	3.635	21.937	14.860	8.494	17.831	12.346	12.214	5.235	3.253	2.173	2.461
Total, Feudatories ...	2.511	1.422	1.089	229	127	940	420	253	542	438	447	189	114	71	75
Grand Total ...	76.456	39.051	37.405	7.427	3.762	22.877	15.280	8.747	18.363	12.684	12.661	5.424	3.367	2.244	2.536
Aden	318	234	84	13	4	181	27	40	53	40	33	13	4	5	1

Table IX.

Education by Religion and Age.

IX.

Pársi.

Illiterate.		15 — 24. Total.		Learning.		Literate.		Illiterate.		25 and over. Total.		Learning.		Literate.		Illiterate.	
Males.	Females.	Males.	Females.	Males.	Females.	Males.	Females.	Males.	Females.	Males.	Females.	Males.	Females.	Males.	Females.	Males.	Females.
3,503	3,812	5,509	[illegible]	1,254	267	3,899	3,658	356	765	10,941	10,537	27	18	9,490	5,246	1,424	5,273
54	80	86	82	28	3	53	64	5	15	209	158	3	3	188	92	18	63
11	15	10	8	4	...	5	6	1	2	42	29	...	...	41	13	1	16
10	5	12	5	3	...	9	2	...	3	43	13	...	...	43	10	...	3
269	351	237	306	75	3	145	222	17	81	679	837	3	...	614	241	62	596
1,061	1,290	876	1,257	256	21	637	719	83	517	2,574	3,412	17	9	2,156	851	401	2,552
1,405	1,721	1,221	1,658	366	27	749	1,013	106	618	3,547	4,449	23	12	3,042	1,207	482	3,230
370	474	325	394	82	10	207	165	36	219	851	888	4	4	755	212	92	672
9	17	19	14	5	1	11	10	3	3	54	30	...	...	47	6	7	24
1	1	2	2	...	...	2	2	...	...	5	1	...	...	5	1	...	...
...	...	1	...	...	...	1	...	...	...	9	...	...	...	9	...	...	...
380	492	347	410	87	11	221	177	39	222	919	919	4	4	816	219	99	696
46	49	57	42	6	3	46	21	5	20	209	70	...	...	196	42	13	28
44	36	41	29	8	2	32	16	1	11	117	70	...	...	111	34	6	36
13	12	20	17	11	1	8	15	1	1	46	42	...	...	39	27	7	15
177	175	184	197	90	23	85	150	9	24	461	401	5	2	408	212	48	187
29	23	19	16	7	1	11	14	1	1	54	40	1	1	52	24	1	15
7	20	12	16	1	1	10	13	1	2	30	23	...	...	25	13	5	10
316	315	333	317	123	29	192	229	18	59	917	646	6	3	831	352	80	291
6	2	6	5	1	...	5	3	...	2	25	12	...	...	23	6	2	6
16	13	17	16	1	...	15	13	1	3	43	17	...	1	41	10	2	6
3	4	3	2	1	...	2	2	...	...	7	4	...	...	7	2	...	2
25	19	26	23	3	...	22	18	1	5	75	33	...	1	71	18	4	14
5,719	6,359	7,436	7,092	1,833	334	5,083	5,089	520	1,669	16,399	16,584	60	38	14,250	7,042	2,089	9,504
107	125	174	139	64	8	93	111	17	20	312	262	...	2	283	138	29	122
8	10	4	1	1	...	3	...	...	1	13	7	...	...	12	6	1	1
4	6	9	5	4	...	5	5	...	...	20	10	...	...	29	8	...	2
...	...	1	...	...	...	1	...	...	...	...	...	...	...	...	...	...	...
...	...	2	1	1	...	1	...	...	1	4	1	...	...	4	...	...	1
119	141	190	146	70	8	103	116	17	22	358	280	...	2	328	152	30	126
5.838	6.500	7.626	7.238	1.903	343	5.186	5.205	537	1.691	16.757	16.864	60	40	14.578	7.194	2.119	9.630
178	258	238	183	40	9	186	125	12	49	746	459	...	4	683	220	63	235
6.016	6.758	7,854	7.421	1.943	351	5.372	5.330	549	1.740	17.503	17,323	60	44	15.261	7.414	2.182	9.865
22	28	50	19	...	...	40	12	4	7	144	33	...	...	130	14	14	19

Education by Religion and Age.

TABI[illegible]

Part (I)

District.	Total Population. Total.	Males.	Females.	Total by Education. Learning. Males.	Females.	Literate. Males.	Females.	Illiterate. Males.	Females.	0 — 14. Total. Males.	Females.	Learning. Males.	Females.	Literate. Males.	Females.
Bombay City	5,031	2,590	2,431	276	156	1,253	570	1,061	1,705	950	898	237	142	167	[illegible]
Ahmedabad	207	101	106	26	14	63	29	23	63	43	64	21	14	3	
Kaira	9	5	4	4	2	1	...	...	2	4	3	4	2	...	...
Panch Mahâls	...	...	...	...	...	...	...	...	...	...	...	...	...	...	...
Broach	23	13	10	6	3	4	4	3	3	9	6	6	3	...	...
Surat	36	23	13	6	...	11	4	6	9	11	6	5	...	...	...
Total, Gujarât	275	142	133	42	19	69	37	31	77	67	69	36	19	3	
Thâna	460	240	220	46	13	74	16	120	191	104	85	41	12	5	
Kolaba	2,348	1,085	1,263	165	53	306	51	614	1,159	484	508	154	47	28	
Ratnagiri	...	...	...	...	...	...	...	...	...	...	...	...	...	...	...
Kanara	12	7	5	2	...	2	3	2	2	4	1	2	...	...	...
Total, Konkan	2,820	1,332	1,488	213	66	383	70	736	1,352	692	594	197	59	33	[illegible]
Khandesh	99	51	48	6	...	18	2	27	46	21	21	5	...	1	...
Nasik	108	56	52	15	6	10	5	25	41	24	21	14	6	...	
Ahmednagar	39	20	19	8	6	6	5	6	8	11	9	5	6	...	...
Poona	930	443	487	119	97	183	112	141	278	182	222	90	93	8	[illegible]
Sholapur	20	11	9	1	...	6	1	4	8	3	4	1	...	...	...
Satara	82	47	35	6	...	22	5	19	30	24	15	6	...	4	
Total, Deccan	1,278	628	650	155	109	251	130	222	411	265	293	121	105	13	[illegible]
Belgaum	...	...	...	...	...	...	...	...	...	...	...	...	...	...	...
Dharwar	27	14	13	...	1	7	...	7	12	6	4	...	1	1	...
Bijapur	8	2	6	...	4	2	2	...	...	1	4	...	4	1	...
Total, Karnatak	35	16	19	...	5	9	2	7	13	7	8	...	5	2	...
Total, Presidency Proper	9,429	4,708	4,721	686	355	1,965	809	2,067	3,557	1,881	1,831	591	330	218	223
Karachi	147	70	77	6	8	35	11	20	58	25	37	5	5	1	1
Hyderabad	33	17	16	6	1	8	4	3	10	5	7	3	1	...	1
Shikarpur	27	13	14	3	2	7	6	3	6	6	9	1	2	2	[illegible]
Thar and Parkar	...	...	...	...	...	...	...	...	...	...	...	...	...	...	...
Upper Sind Frontier	4	2	2	...	...	1	...	1	2	1	1	...	...	...	...
Total, Sind	210	102	108	15	11	51	21	36	76	37	54	9	8	3	4
Total, British Territory	**9,639**	**4,810**	**4,829**	**701**	**366**	**2,016**	**830**	**2,093**	**3,633**	**1,918**	**1,915**	**600**	**333**	**221**	**227**
Total, Feudatories	**1,032**	**536**	**546**	**54**	**17**	**128**	**31**	**354**	**498**	**228**	**237**	**49**	**14**	**3**	**8**
Grand Total	**10,731**	**5,346**	**5,375**	**755**	**383**	**2,144**	**861**	**2,447**	**4,131**	**2,116**	**2,152**	**649**	**353**	**224**	**235**
Aden	2,826	1,456	1,370	209	7	298	18	949	1,345	527	568	106	7	7	1

Table IX.

Education by Religion and Age.

IX.

Jew.

Illiterate.		15 — 24.								25 and over.							
		Total.		Learning.		Literate.		Illiterate.		Total.		Learning.		Literate.		Illiterate.	
Males.	Females.	Males.	Females.	Males.	Females.	Males.	Females.	Males.	Females.	Males.	Females.	Males.	Females.	Males.	Females.	Males.	Females.
546	588	549	513	38	13	361	189	150	311	1,091	1,020	1	1	725	213	365	806
19	34	26	20	4	...	21	10	1	10	82	32	1	...	29	13	2	19
...	1	...	...	...	...	...	...	...	...	1	1	...	...	1	...	...	1
...	...	...	...	...	...	...	...	...	...	...	...	...	...	...	...	...	...
3	3	...	2	...	...	...	2	...	...	4	2	...	...	4	2	...	...
6	6	4	2	...	...	4	2	...	...	8	5	1	...	7	2	...	3
28	44	30	24	4	...	25	14	1	10	45	40	2	...	41	17	2	[illegible]
58	70	42	42	5	1	15	7	22	34	94	93	...	...	54	6	40	87
302	441	137	200	7	2	55	11	75	187	464	555	4	4	223	20	237	[illegible]
...	...	...	...	...	...	...	...	...	...	...	...	...	...	...	...	...	...
2	1	...	2	...	...	...	2	...	...	3	2	...	...	3	1	...	1
302	512	179	244	12	3	70	20	97	221	561	650	4	4	280	27	277	[illegible]
15	21	9	11	1	...	5	1	3	10	21	16	...	...	12	1	9	15
10	13	12	14	1	...	8	3	3	11	20	17	...	...	8	...	12	17
6	3	4	5	3	...	1	3	...	2	5	5	...	...	5	2	...	3
84	106	83	76	28	4	39	30	16	33	178	189	1	...	136	50	41	[illegible]
2	4	2	...	...	...	2	...	...	...	6	5	...	...	4	1	2	4
14	14	7	8	...	...	5	2	2	6	16	12	...	...	13	2	3	10
131	161	117	114	83	4	60	48	24	62	246	244	1	...	178	56	67	158
...	...	...	...	...	...	...	...	...	...	...	...	...	...	...	...	...	...
5	3	3	5	...	...	2	...	1	5	5	4	...	...	4	...	1	4
...	...	...	1	...	...	...	1	...	...	1	1	...	...	1	1	...	...
5	3	3	6	...	...	2	1	1	5	6	5	...	...	5	1	1	4
1,072	1,308	878	901	87	20	518	272	273	609	1,949	1,939	8	5	1,220	314	712	1,640
19	31	14	16	1	1	11	6	2	9	81	24	...	2	23	4	8	18
2	5	4	2	3	...	1	1	...	1	8	6	...	...	7	2	1	4
3	5	2	2	2	...	...	2	...	...	5	3	...	...	5	2	...	1
...	...	...	...	...	...	...	...	...	...	...	...	...	...	...	...	...	...
1	1	...	1	...	...	...	...	...	1	1	...	...	...	1	...	...	...
25	42	20	21	6	1	12	9	2	11	45	33	...	2	36	8	9	23
1,097	**1,350**	**898**	**922**	**93**	**21**	**530**	**281**	**275**	**620**	**1,994**	**1,993**	**8**	**7**	**1,265**	**322**	**721**	**1,663**
176	**215**	**78**	**94**	**4**	**3**	**31**	**10**	**43**	**81**	**230**	**215**	**1**	...	**94**	**13**	**135**	**202**
1,273	**1,535**	**976**	**1,016**	**97**	**24**	**561**	**291**	**318**	**701**	**2,224**	**2,207**	**9**	**7**	**1,359**	**335**	**856**	**1,865**
324	550	311	296	11	...	82	9	218	287	618	516	2	...	209	8	407	568

Table IX.

Education by Religion and Age.

TABLE

Part (J).–

District.	Total Population.			Total by Education.						0 — 14.					
				Learning.		Literate.		Illiterate.		Total.		Learning.		Literate.	
	Total.	Males.	Females.	Males.	Females.	Males.	Females.	Males.	Females.	Males.	Females.	Males.	Females.	Males.	Females.
Bombay City	...	...	...	...	...	...	...	...	...	...	...	...	...	...	...
Ahmedabad...	175	80	95	...	...	9	...	71	95	27	44	...	...	...	...
Kaira...	...	...	...	...	...	...	...	...	...	...	...	...	...	...	...
Panch Mahâls	11,086	5,604	5,482	29	...	25	...	5,550	5,482	2,037	2,581	10	...	2	...
Broach	17,805	9,054	8,751	97	2	56	1	8,901	8,749	3,872	3,775	95	2	9	...
Surat...	...	...	...	...	...	...	...	...	...	...	...	...	...	...	...
Total, Gujarát ...	29.056	14,738	14,318	126	2	90	1	14,522	14,325	6,556	6,400	105	2	11	...
Thána	6,368	3,234	3,134	...	...	...	...	3,234	3,134	1,378	1,399	...	...	...	...
Kolába	611	301	310	...	...	...	...	301	310	113	152	...	...	...	...
Ratnágiri	...	...	...	...	...	...	...	...	...	...	...	...	...	...	...
Kánara	...	...	...	...	...	...	...	...	...	...	...	...	...	...	...
Total, Konkan ...	6.979	3,535	3,444	...	...	...	...	3,535	3,444	1,401	1,551	...	...	...	...
Khándesh	86.668	43,550	43,118	42	...	54	1	43,454	43,117	20,697	20,368	39	...	2	...
Násik...	12.612	6,366	6,246	10	...	9	...	6,347	6,246	2,903	2,880	9	...	...	...
Ahmednagar	325	154	171	15	6	...	...	139	165	73	87	13	6	...	...
Poona...	...	...	...	...	...	...	...	...	...	...	...	...	...	...	...
Sholápur	...	...	...	...	...	...	...	...	...	...	...	...	...	...	...
Sátára	...	...	...	...	...	...	...	...	...	...	...	...	...	...	...
Total, Deccan ...	99.605	50,070	49,535	67	6	63	1	49,940	49,526	23,763	23,329	61	6	2	...
Belgaum	...	...	...	...	...	...	...	...	...	...	...	...	...	...	...
Dhárwár	32	22	10	...	...	1	...	21	10	2	4	...	...	1	...
Bijápur	1	1	...	...	...	...	...	1	...	...	...	...	...	...	...
Total, Karnátak ...	33	23	10	...	...	1	...	22	10	2	4	...	...	1	...
Total, Presidency Proper ...	135,683	68,366	67,317	193	10	154	2	68,019	67,305	31,792	31,284	166	10	14	...
Karáchi	3.043	1,630	1,412	1	...	11	...	1,618	1,412	731	673	1	...	9	...
Hyderabad	19.160	10,338	8,822	1	...	22	...	10,315	8,822	4,801	4,114	...	...	1	—
Shikárpur	2.908	1,620	1,288	...	...	2	3	1,618	1,285	712	558	...	...	...	...
Thar and Párkar	52.615	28,069	24,546	4	...	57	2	28,008	24,544	13,956	12,020	4	...	1	...
Upper Sind Frontier	210	133	77	...	...	2	...	131	77	38	35	...	...	...	...
Total, Sind ...	77.935	41,790	36,145	6	...	94	5	41,690	36,140	20,237	17,409	5	...	11	...
Total, British Territory ...	213.618	110.156	103.462	199	10	248	7	109,709	103,445	52,029	48,693	171	10	25	...
Total, Feudatories ...	78.405	39.406	38.999	56	2	79	.	39,271	38,997	17,927	17,131	47	1	7	...
Grand Total ...	292.023	149.562	142.461	255	12	327	.7	148.980	142,442	69,956	65,824	218	11	33	...
Aden	...	...	...	...	...	...	...	...	...	...	...	...	...	...	...

Table IX.

Education by Religion and Age.

IX.

Animistic.

Illiterate.		15 — 24.								25 and over.							
		Total.		Learning.		Literate.		Illiterate.		Total.		Learning.		Literate.		Illiterate.	
Males.	Females.	Males.	Females.	Males.	Females.	Males.	Females.	Males.	Females.	Males.	Females.	Males.	Females.	Males.	Females.	Males.	Females.
...	...	...	...	...	...	...	...	...	...	...	...	...	...	...	...	...	...
17	44	12	15	...	...	3	...	9	15	41	36	...	...	6	...	35	36
...	...	...	...	...	...	...	...	...	...	...	...	...	...	...	...	...	...
2,625	2,581	851	906	7	...	8	...	838	905	2,116	1,996	12	...	15	...	2,089	1,996
3,763	3,773	1,450	1,599	1	...	19	...	1,430	1,599	3,732	3,384	1	...	28	1	3,703	3,383
...	...	...	...	...	...	...	...	...	...	...	...	...	...	...	...	...	...
6,420	6,398	2,313	2,518	8	...	30	...	2,275	2,518	5,889	6,416	13	...	49	1	5,827	6,415
1,278	1,299	442	498	...	...	...	...	442	498	1,414	1,237	...	...	...	...	1,414	1,237
113	252	49	54	...	...	...	...	49	54	139	104	...	...	...	...	139	104
...	...	...	...	...	...	...	...	...	...	...	...	...	...	...	...	...	...
...	...	...	...	...	...	...	...	...	...	...	...	...	...	...	...	...	...
1,491	1,551	491	552	...	...	...	...	491	552	1,553	1,341	...	...	...	...	1,553	1,341
20,636	20,363	5,995	7,142	3	...	10	...	5,982	7,142	16,858	15,614	...	...	42	1	16,816	15,613
2,984	2,880	858	1,095	1	...	3	...	854	1,095	2,515	2,271	...	...	6	...	2,509	2,271
60	79	16	28	2	...	...	...	14	28	65	56	...	...	...	...	65	56
...	...	...	...	...	...	...	...	...	...	...	...	...	...	...	...	...	...
...	...	...	...	...	...	...	...	...	...	...	...	...	...	...	...	...	...
...	...	...	...	...	...	...	...	...	...	...	...	...	...	...	...	...	...
23,700	23,321	6,869	8,265	6	...	13	...	6,850	8,265	19,438	17,941	...	...	48	1	19,390	17,940
...	...	...	...	...	...	...	...	...	...	...	...	...	...	...	...	...	...
1	4	12	2	...	...	...	...	12	2	8	4	...	...	...	...	8	4
...	...	...	...	...	...	...	...	...	...	1	...	...	...	...	...	1	...
1	4	12	2	...	...	...	...	12	2	9	4	...	...	...	...	9	4
31,612	31,274	9,685	11,331	14	...	43	...	9,628	11,331	26,889	24,702	13	...	97	2	26,779	24,700
721	673	240	216	...	...	...	...	240	216	659	593	...	...	3	...	657	593
4,800	4,114	1,484	1,326	1	...	3	...	1,480	1,326	4,053	3,683	...	...	18	...	4,035	3,386
712	558	235	150	...	...	...	2	235	148	673	580	...	...	2	1	671	579
13,950	12,029	3,884	3,155	...	...	12	1	3,872	3,154	10,230	9,362	...	...	44	1	10,186	9,361
38	35	21	15	...	...	1	...	20	15	74	87	...	...	1	...	73	87
20,221	17,409	5,864	4,862	1	...	16	3	5,847	4,859	15,689	13,874	...	...	67	2	15,622	13,872
51,833	48,683	15,549	16,193	15	...	59	3	15,475	16,190	42,578	38,576	13	...	164	4	42,401	38,573
17,873	17,130	6,124	6,544	8	1	22	...	6,094	6,543	15,355	15,324	1	...	50	...	15,304	15,324
69,706	65,813	21,673	22,737	23	1	81	3	21,569	22,733	57,933	53,900	14	...	214	4	57,705	53,896
...	...	...	...	...	...	...	...	...	...	...	...	...	...	...	...	...	...

Education by Religion and Age.

TABLE

Part (K).—

District.	Total Population. Total.	Males.	Females.	Total by Education. Learning. Males.	Learning. Females.	Literate. Males.	Literate. Females.	Illiterate. Males.	Illiterate. Females.	0 — 14. Total. Males.	Total. Females.	Learning. Males.	Learning. Females.	Literate. Males.	Literate. Females.
Bombay City	37	27	10	5	2	19	6	3	2	6	3	4	2	...	1
Ahmedabad	5	4	1	...	...	1	1	3	...	2	...	...	...	...	...
Kaira	...	...	...	...	...	...	...	...	...	...	...	...	...	...	...
Panch Maháls	...	...	...	...	...	...	...	...	...	...	...	...	...	...	...
Broach	...	...	...	...	...	...	...	...	...	...	...	...	...	...	...
Surat	...	...	...	...	...	...	...	...	...	...	...	...	...	...	...
Total, Gujarát ...	5	4	1	...	...	1	1	3	...	2	...	...	...	...	...
Thána	1	1	...	...	...	1	...	...	...	...	...	...	...	...	...
Kolába	...	...	...	...	...	...	...	...	...	...	...	...	...	...	...
Ratnágiri	...	...	...	...	...	...	...	...	...	...	...	...	...	...	...
Kánara	...	...	...	...	...	...	...	...	...	...	...	...	...	...	...
Total, Konkan ...	1	1	...	...	...	1	...	...	...	...	...	...	...	...	...
Khándesh...	...	...	...	...	...	...	...	...	...	...	...	...	...	...	...
Násik	...	...	...	...	...	...	...	...	...	...	...	...	...	...	...
Ahmednagar	...	...	...	...	...	...	...	...	...	...	...	...	...	...	...
Poona	14	7	7	...	5	5	2	2	...	1	3	...	3	...	...
Sholápur	1	1	...	...	...	1	...	...	...	...	...	...	...	...	...
Sátára	...	...	...	...	...	...	...	...	...	...	...	...	...	...	...
Total, Deccan ...	15	8	7	...	5	6	2	2	...	1	3	...	3	...	...
Belgaum	...	...	...	...	...	...	...	...	...	...	...	...	...	...	...
Dhárwár	...	...	...	...	...	...	...	...	...	...	...	...	...	...	...
Bijápur	...	...	...	...	...	...	...	...	...	...	...	...	...	...	...
Total, Karnátak ...	...	...	...	...	...	...	...	...	...	...	...	...	...	...	...
Total, Presidency Proper ...	58	40	18	5	7	27	9	8	2	9	6	4	5	...	1
Karáchi	1	1	...	...	...	1	...	...	...	...	...	...	...	...	...
Hyderabad	2	2	...	...	...	2	...	...	...	...	...	...	...	...	...
Shikárpur	...	...	...	...	...	...	...	...	...	...	...	...	...	...	...
Thar and Párkar...	...	...	...	...	...	...	...	...	...	...	...	...	...	...	...
Upper Sind Frontier	...	...	...	...	...	...	...	...	...	...	...	...	...	...	...
Total, Sind ...	3	3	...	...	...	3	...	...	...	...	...	...	...	...	...
Total, British Territory ...	61	43	18	5	7	30	9	8	2	9	6	4	5	...	1
Total, Feudatories ...	...	...	...	...	...	...	...	...	...	...	...	...	...	...	...
Grand Total ...	61	43	18	5	7	30	9	8	2	9	6	4	5	...	1
Aden	...	...	...	...	...	...	...	...	...	...	...	...	...	...	...

IX. **Education by Religion and Age.**

Others.

Illiterate.		15 — 24.								25 and over.							
		Total.		Learning.		Literate.		Illiterate.		Total.		Learning.		Literate.		Illiterate.	
Males.	Females.	Males.	Females.	Males.	Females.	Males.	Females.	Males.	Females.	Males.	Females.	Males.	Females.	Males.	Females.	Males.	Females.
2	...	5	2	...	...	5	2	...	...	16	5	1	...	14	3	1	2
2	...	...	1	...	...	...	1	...	...	2	...	...	...	1	...	1	...
...	...	...	...	...	...	...	...	...	...	...	...	...	...	...	...	...	...
...	...	...	...	...	...	...	...	...	...	...	...	...	...	...	...	...	...
...	...	...	...	...	...	...	...	...	...	...	...	...	...	...	...	...	...
...	...	...	...	...	...	...	...	...	...	...	...	...	...	...	...	...	...
2	...	...	1	...	...	...	1	...	...	2	...	...	...	1	...	1	...
...	...	...	...	...	...	...	...	...	...	1	...	...	...	1	...	...	...
...	...	...	...	...	...	...	...	...	...	...	...	...	...	...	...	...	...
...	...	...	...	...	...	...	...	...	...	...	...	...	...	...	...	...	...
...	...	...	...	...	...	...	...	...	...	...	...	...	...	...	...	...	...
...	...	...	...	...	...	...	...	...	...	1	...	...	...	1	...	...	...
...	...	...	...	...	...	...	...	...	...	...	...	...	...	...	...	...	...
...	...	...	...	...	...	...	...	...	...	...	...	...	...	...	...	...	...
...	...	...	...	...	...	...	...	...	...	...	...	...	...	...	...	...	...
1	...	1	3	...	2	1	1	...	...	5	1	...	...	4	1	1	...
...	...	1	...	...	...	1	...	...	...	...	...	...	...	...	...	...	...
...	...	...	...	...	...	...	...	...	...	...	...	...	...	...	...	...	...
1	...	2	3	...	2	2	1	...	...	5	1	...	...	4	1	1	...
...	...	...	...	...	...	...	...	...	...	...	...	...	...	...	...	...	...
...	...	...	...	...	...	...	...	...	...	...	...	...	...	...	...	...	...
...	...	...	...	...	...	...	...	...	...	...	...	...	...	...	...	...	...
...	...	...	...	...	...	...	...	...	...	...	...	...	...	...	...	...	...
5	...	7	6	...	2	7	4	...	...	24	6	1	...	20	4	3	2
...	...	...	...	...	...	...	...	...	...	1	...	...	...	1	...	...	...
...	...	...	...	...	...	...	...	...	...	2	...	...	...	2	...	...	...
...	...	...	...	...	...	...	...	...	...	...	...	...	...	...	...	...	...
...	...	...	...	...	...	...	...	...	...	...	...	...	...	...	...	...	...
...	...	...	...	...	...	...	...	...	...	...	...	...	...	...	...	...	...
...	...	...	...	...	...	...	...	...	...	3	...	...	...	3	...	...	...
5	...	7	6	...	2	7	4	...	...	27	6	1	...	23	4	3	2
...	...	...	...	...	...	...	...	...	...	...	...	...	...	...	...	...	...
5	...	7	6	...	2	7	4	...	...	27	6	1	...	23	4	3	2
...	...	...	...	...	...	...	...	...	...	...	...	...	...	...	...	...	...

TABLE X.

PARENT-TONGUE.

Detail of Languages shown under "Others":—

Language.	Bombay City and Aden.			Districts.		
	Total.	Males.	Females.	Total.	Males.	Females.
A.						
Assamese ...	**5**	5	...	...	...	...
Bhoti	**4**	4	...	...	...	...
Javanese... ...	**18**	11	*7*	...	...	...
Kashmiri ...	**151**	108	*43*	**33**	27	*6*
Malay	**103**	56	*47*	**6**	3	*3*
Multáni	**5**	1	*4*	...	...	...
Nepáli	**4**	4	...	**1**	1	...
Sanskrit	**25**	21	*4*	**43**	36	*7*
Shám	...	...	...	**1**	...	*1*
Siamese	...	...	...	**4**	3	*1*
Singhalese	**41**	39	*2*	**6**	6	...
Uriya	...	...	...	**68**	40	*28*
B.						
Abyssinian ...	**165**	86	*79*	...	...	...
Armenian ...	**46**	32	*14*	**3**	...	*3*
Japanese	**31**	10	*21*	...	...	...
Syrian	**4**	4	...	...	...	...
Turki	**166**	132	*34*	**36**	28	*8*
C.						
Bulgarian ...	**2**	2	...	...	...	...
Danish	**20**	13	*7*	**1**	1	...
Dutch	**25**	22	*3*	**4**	3	*1*
Gaelic	...	...	...	**1**	1	...
Greek	**116**	96	*20*	**24**	23	*1*
Hungarian ...	**17**	12	*5*	...	...	...
Italian	**216**	171	*45*	**21**	10	*11*
Maltese	**26**	23	*3*	...	...	...
Polish	**22**	10	*12*	...	...	...
Romanian ...	**5**	2	*3*	...	...	...
Russian... ...	**42**	26	*16*	...	...	...
Slavonic ...	**47**	47	...	...	...	...
Spanish... ...	**77**	48	*29*	**5**	2	*3*
Swedish... ...	**60**	60	...	**2**	1	*1*
Total ...	**1,443**	1,045	*398*	**259**	185	*74*

B 1072—28 *ap*

A.—IN

District.	Gujara'ti.			Cutchi.			Bhil.		
	Total.	Males.	Females.	Total.	Males.	Females.	Total.	Males.	Females.
Bombay City	**175,833**	109,116	*66,717*	**45.148**	26,095	*19,053*	...	...	...
Ahmedabad	**876,223**	449,159	*427,064*	**207**	127	*80*	**1**	1	...
Kaira	**839.727**	443,707	*396,020*	**188**	116	*72*	...	...	...
Panch Maháls	**306.475**	158,202	*148,273*	**11**	8	*3*	**14**	5	*9*
Broach	**316.695**	162,049	*154,646*	**50**	47	*3*	**3.116**	1,594	*1,522*
Surat	**624.278**	308,325	*315,953*	**235**	147	*88*	...	...	...
Thána	**64.872**	36,199	*28,673*	**927**	547	*380*	...	...	...
Kolába	**4.392**	3,039	*1,353*	**272**	-169	*103*	...	...	...
Ratnágiri...	**1.163**	731	*432*	**230**	163	*67*	...	...	...
Kánara	**682**	401	*281*	**36**	24	*12*	...	...	...
Khándesh	**65.132**	33,817	*31,315*	**1.262**	781	*481*	**110,689**	56,259	*54,430*
Násik	**5.535**	3,088	*2,447*	**104**	67	*37*	**53**	27	*26*
Ahmédnagar	**2.815**	1,656	*1,159*	**59**	47	*12*	**1**	1	...
Poona	**13.228**	7,583	*5,645*	**334**	179	*155*	...	...	...
Sholápur	**4.303**	2,318	*1,985*	**82**	51	*31*	...	...	...
Sátára	**4.405**	2,459	*1,946*	**70**	42	*28*	...	...	...
Belgaum	**2.264**	1,422	*842*	**20**	7	*13*	...	...	...
Dhárwár	**8.821**	4,568	*4,253*	**32**	21	*11*	...	...	...
Bijápur	**6.986**	3,932	*3,054*	**7**	5	*2*	...	...	...
Karáchi	**31.954**	18,166	*13,788*	...	...	...	...	...	...
Hyderábád	**11.470**	6,334	*5,136*	...	...	...	...	...	...
Shikárpur	**562**	313	*249*	...	...	...	...	...	...
Thar and Párkar ...	**30,556**	16,004	*14,552*	...	..	...	...	...	...
Upper Sind Frontier ...	**27**	17	*10*	...	...	...	...	...	...
British Territory ...	3.398.398	1.772,605	1.625.793	49,274	28,643	20,631	113.874	57,887	55,987
Feudatoriés	4,810,075	2,467,041	2.343.034	375,585	184,100	191.485	11.622	6.069	5.553
Grand Total ...	8.208.473	4.239.646	3,968.827	424.859	212.743	212.116	125.496	63.956	61.540
Aden	**1.606**	1,212	*394*	**279**	170	*109*	...	...	...

A.—IN

District.	Sindhi.			Baluchi.			Brahui.		
	Total.	Males.	Females.	Total.	Males.	Females.	Total.	Males.	Females.
Bombay City	**2,855**	1,831	*1,024*	**221**	212	*9*	...	...	...
Ahmedabad	**790**	401	*389*	**11**	7	*4*	...	...	...
Kaira	**28**	18	*10*	...	...	...	...	...	...
Panch Mahâls	**8**	6	*2*	**12**	7	*5*	...	...	...
Broach	**44**	43	*1*	**1**	1	...	...	...	...
Surat	**27**	22	*5*	**1**	1	...	...	...	...
Thána	**42**	36	*6*	**6**	3	*3*	...	...	...
Kolába	...	...	...	...	...	...	...	...	...
Ratnágiri	...	...	...	...	...	...	...	...	...
Kánara	**3**	2	*1*	...	...	...	...	...	...
Khándesh...	...	...	...	**21**	11	*10*	...	...	...
Násik	...	...	...	...	...	...	...	...	...
Ahmednagar	**5**	5	...	**4**	2	*2*	...	...	...
Poona	**34**	24	*10*	**3**	2	*1*	...	...	...
Sholápur	...	...	...	...	...	...	...	...	...
Sátára	**4**	4	...	...	...	...	...	...	...
Belgaum	**2**	2	...	...	...	...	...	...	...
Dhárwár	...	...	...	...	...	...	...	...	...
Bijápur	...	...	...	...	...	...	...	...	...
Karáchi	**441.627**	240,973	*200,654*	**45.170**	24,605	*20,505*	**10.690**	5,739	*4,951*
Hyderabad	**821.086**	445,218	*375,868*	**44.721**	24,685	*20,036*	**373**	216	*157*
Shikárpur	**834.237**	447,180	*387,057*	**42.976**	23,264	*19,712*	**10.817**	5,778	*5,039*
Thar and Párkar ...	**166.130**	93,563	*72,567*	**7.547**	4,139	*3,408*	**381**	220	*161*
Upper Sind Frontier ...	**120.581**	65,877	*54,704*	**37.932**	20,757	*17,235*	**6.723**	3,581	*3,142*
British Territory ...	2,387,503	1.295,205	1.092,298	178,636	97,756	80.930	28.984	15.534	13.450
Feudatories	177,342	94,102	83.240	3.872	2.218	1.654	...	...	...
Grand Total ...	2.564.345	1.389.307	1.175.538	182.558	99.974	82.584	28.984	15.534	13,450
Aden	**51**	42	*9*	**4**	4	...	...	...	...

X.

DIAN.

Marathi.			Konkani.			Goanese.			Kanarese.		
Total.	Males.	Females.	Total.	Males.	Females.	Total.	Males.	Females.	Total.	Males.	Females.
414.148	254,438	159,710	7.056	4.967	2,089	10.855	8,124	2,731	1.396	1,093	303
3,328	1,831	1,497	...	...	...	180	135	45	20	16	4
594	316	278	...	...	...	26	21	5	4	4	...
778	410	368	...	...	...	17	16	1	...	...	...
1.754	1,041	713	...		...	47	40	7	2	2	...
5.511	3,047	2,464	...	...	...	84	58	26	1	1	...
806.078	415,312	390,766	5	2	3	2.682	1,487	1,195	344	198	146
495.282	246,111	249,171	596	318	278	253	148	105	258	133	125
1.074.581	498,856	575,725	761	389	372	2.284	1,113	1,171	658	366	292
37.483	20,271	17,212	125.038	63,228	61,810	214	115	99	258.464	137,163	121,301
1.120.614	567,315	553,299	1.110	561	549	200	136	64	663	347	316
770.613	391,893	378,720	...	...	...	451	324	127	189	106	83
803.930	406,724	397,206	5	5	...	327	118	209	603	378	225
959.054	484,211	474,843	46	39	7	2.676	1,930	746	940	569	371
613.069	310,826	302,243	...	...	...	127	85	42	50.332	25,610	24,722
1.158.675	579,161	579,514	57	40	17	166	119	47	14.526	7,342	7,184
257.083	130,749	126,334	2.035	1,001	1,034	687	404	283	655.298	328,921	326,377
48.407	24,718	23,689	1.715	1,017	698	386	310	76	861.020	425,390	435,630
31.915	16,143	15,772	403	196	207	14	12	2	648.183	322,899	325,284
8,559	5,485	3,074	...	...		1.548	1,155	393	33	16	17
480	276	204	...	...	...	73	53	20	...	...	...
107	72	35	...	...	...	40	35	5	3	3	...
8	7	1	...	...	...	5	5	...	...	...	...
109	57	52	...	...	...	28	26	2	...	...	...
8.612.160	4.359.270	4.252.890	138.827	71.763	67.064	23,370	15.969	7,401	2.492.937	1.250.557	1.242.380
1.759.028	888.323	870.705	16.141	7.315	8.826	507	403	104	575.516	291.286	284.230
10.371.188	5.247.593	5.123.595	154.968	79.078	75.890	23.877	16.372	7.505	3.068.453	1.541.843	1.526.610
1.441	1,036	405	...	...		479	464	15	20	17	

DIAN.

Urdu.			Hindi.			Gipsy dialects.			Marwadi.		
Total.	Males.	Females.	Total.	Males.	Females.	Total.	Males.	Females.	Total.	Males.	Females.
94.431	63,592	30,839	7.241	4.918	2,323	16	16	...	13.337	11,943	1,394
30.671	16,103	14,568	217	169	48	19	11	8	8.665	4,639	4,026
29.771	15,675	14,096	39	35	4	...	...		961	542	419
5.366	2,974	2,392	160	104	56	50	36	14	450	271	179
19.108	9,691	9,417	68	53	15	...	...	...	375	254	121
19.275	9,645	9,630	64	37	27	1	1		164	128	36
24.821	14,649	10,172	86	56	30	24	16	8	2.527	1,844	683
5.932	3,297	2,635	340	187	153	119	54	65	1.383	1,184	199
25.867	11,754	14,113	5	3	2	...	...	...	79	72	7
18.627	9,877	8,750	545	244	301	470	314	156	12	10	2
117.844	61.901	55,943	4.949	2,796	2,153	11.611	6,257	5,354	18.895	11,412	7,483
47.977	25,769	22,208	1.079	564	515	180	82	98	11.314	6,452	4,862
48.847	25,204	23,643	967	434	533	450	243	207	19.714	10,834	8,880
57.669	30.859	26,810	2.474	1,573	901	574	297	277	8.322	5,098	3,224
56.669	28,882	27,787	28	14	14	1.280	630	650	2.512	1,486	1,026
40.781	20,724	20,057	122	80	42	814	397	417	1.123	672	451
76.950	39.040	37,910	117	61	56	2.343	1.178	1,165	204	151	53
101.216	56,708	44,508	60	22	38	4.354	2,234	2,120	923	452	471
79.999	40,147	39,852	182	59	123	6.412	3,259	3,153	1.221	839	382
7.949	5,280	2,669	439	339	100	...			2.977	1,647	1,330
2.368	1,637	731	148	83	65	...		...	34.241	18,898	15,343
4.163	2,892	1,271	97	70	27	...		...	6.333	2,812	3,521
488	392	96	3	2	1	...	...		92.430	50,414	42,016
3,041	2,050	991	...	...	...	...			636	355	281
919.830	498.742	421.088	19.430	11.903	7.527	28.717	15.025	13.692	228.798	132.409	96,389
254.282	138.321	115.961	570	430	140	1,353	761	592	47.292	25.610	21.682
1.174.112	637.063	537.049	20.000	12.333	7.667	30.070	15.786	14.284	276.090	158.019	118.071
4.222	2,642	1,580	...	...			...	...	34	28	

TABLE XVII.

OCCUPATION.

PART A.—PROVINCIAL SUMMARY.
PART B.—TERRITORIAL DISTRIBUTION.
PART C.—SUMMARY OF COMBINED OCCUPATIONS.

Classification.

Class A.—Government Service.
,, B.—Pasture and Agriculture.
,, C.—Personal and Household Services.
,, D.—Preparation and Supply of Material Substances.
,, E.—Commerce, Transport and Storage.
,, F.—Learned and Artistic Professions.
,, G.—Indefinite and Independent.

Occupation and Class.				Total.				Provincial … Ma…	
Class.	Order.	Sub-order and Group.	Occupation.	Total.	0 — 4.	5 — 14.	15 and over.	Total.	0 — 4.
A.—Government Service.	I. Administration.	1 Service of the Imperial and Provincial Governments.	1 Viceroy, Governors, Chiefs, &c.	847	89	182	576	379	47
			2 Officers	3,853	431	815	2,107	1,789	222
			3 Office Supts., Clerks, &c.	54,973	7,256	12,088	35,632	29,886	3,606
			4 Messengers, constables, menials, &c.	118,901	15,040	24,099	79,763	66,545	7,433
			Total, Sub-order 1 ...	178,077	22,816	37,184	118,077	98,599	11,314
		2 Service of Local and Municipal Bodies.	5 Inspecting and supervising officials	103	19	19	70	49	8
			6 Clerical establishments	854	128	229	497	555	87
			7 Menials	2,065	314	405	1,346	1,062	131
			Total, Sub-order 2 ...	3,027	461	653	1,913	1,666	227
		3 Village Service	8 Headmen, not agriculturists	15,572	2,038	3,274	10,260	8,662	973
			9 Accountants	6,311	851	1,258	4,202	3,478	416
			11 Watchmen and other menials	83,501	13,242	19,500	50,759	46,624	6,613
			Total, Sub-order 3 ...	105,384	16,131	24,032	65,221	58,759	8,007
	Total, Order I ...		......	286,488	39,403	61,869	185,211	159,024	19,548
	II. Defence ...	4 Army	12 Officers	313	50	41	222	119	20
			13 Non-commissioned officers and privates ...	16,528	2,026	2,974	11,628	10,231	1,030
			14 Followers	2,828	328	568	1,932	1,773	190
			15 Administrative establishments	138	14	34	90	63	3
			Total, Sub-order 4 ...	19,907	2,418	3,617	13,872	12,186	1,243
		5 Navy and Marine... ...	16 Officers	23	2	6	15	4	...
			17 Engineers, seamen, &c.	40	10	8	22	25	6
			18 Administrative staff	12	3	2	7	...	...
			Total, Sub-order 5 ...	75	15	16	44	29	6
	Total, Order II ...		......	19,982	2,433	3,633	13,916	12,215	1,249
	III. Foreign and Feudatory State Service.	6 Administrative service ...	19 Chiefs, Consuls, and officers	427	61	112	254	232	31
			20 Clerical establishments	1,028	140	243	645	534	51
			21 Menials, &c.	7,191	1,023	1,600	4,568	4,018	526
			Total, Sub-order 6 ...	8,646	1,224	1,956	5,467	4,784	608
		7 Army and Marine ...	22 Officers	18	4	4	10	9	4
			23 Privates and seamen, &c.	195	31	36	128	79	13
			Total, Sub-order 7 ...	213	35	40	138	88	17
	Total, Order III ...		......	8,859	1,259	1,095	5,605	4,872	625
Total, Class A ...	......		......	315,329	43,100	67,497	204,732	176,111	21,422
B.—Pasture and Agriculture.	IV. Live Stock .	8 Stock breeding and dealing. (a) Horses and horned cattle.	24 Horse breeders and dealers	659	128	152	379	425	90
			25 Cattle breeders and dealers	19,928	2,487	6,981	10,460	11,925	1,307
			26 Herdsmen	143,412	18,850	40,916	83,646	79,895	9,457
			27 Buffalo breeders and dealers	913	125	255	538	516	58
			Total ...	164,911	21,585	48,304	95,022	92,761	10,912
		(b) Other draught, &c., animals.	28 Elephant catchers and breeders	34	2	10	22	10	1
			29 Camel breeders and dealers	990	94	224	672	693	45
			30 Ass and Mule breeders and dealers	229	16	34	170	128	8
			Total ...	1,253	112	268	873	840	54
		(c) Small stock.	31 Sheep and Goat breeders and dealers	41,854	6,011	10,672	25,171	23,409	3,206
			31a Shepherds	2,650	381	739	1,530	1,453	183
			32 Pig breeders and dealers	170	27	45	98	55	8
			Total ...	44,674	6,419	11,456	26,799	24,917	3,397
			Total, Sub-order 8 ...	210,833	28,116	60,028	122,694	118,518	14,363

TOTAL.

...le.		Female.			
5—14.	15 and over.	Total.	0—4.	5—14.	15 and over.
85	247	468	42	97	329
441	1,126	1,564	209	374	981
6,433	19,847	25,090	3,650	5,655	15,785
12,896	46,210	52,356	7,601	11,203	33,552
19,855	67,430	79,478	11,502	17,329	50,647
11	30	59	11	8	40
153	315	299	41	76	182
216	714	1,003	182	189	632
380	1,059	1,361	234	273	854
1,720	5,964	6,910	1,060	1,554	4,296
640	2,417	2,838	435	618	1,785
10,803	29,208	36,877	6,629	8,697	21,551
13,163	37,589	46,625	8,124	10,869	27,632
35,398	106,078	127,464	19,860	28,471	79,133
19	80	194	30	22	142
1,635	7,566	6,397	996	1,339	4,062
322	1,261	1,055	138	246	671
19	41	75	11	15	49
1,995	8,948	7,721	1,175	1,622	4,924
...	4	19	2	6	11
6	13	15	4	2	9
...	...	12	3	2	7
6	17	46	9	10	27
2,001	8,965	7,767	1,184	1,632	4,951
68	133	195	30	44	121
127	356	494	89	116	289
860	2,632	3,173	497	740	1,936
1,055	3,121	3,862	616	900	2,346
...	5	9	...	4	5
13	63	116	18	23	75
13	68	125	18	27	80
1,068	3,179	3,987	634	927	2,426
36,467	118,222	139,218	21,678	31,030	86,510
111	224	234	38	41	155
4,767	5,851	7,997	1,175	2,214	4,608
24,856	45,582	63,517	9,398	16,060	38,064
150	308	402	67	105	230
29,884	51,965	72,150	10,678	18,420	43,057
6	12	15	1	4	10
160	488	297	49	64	184
20	100	101	8	14	79
186	600	413	58	82	273
6,209	13,994	18,445	2,805	4,463	11,177
482	788	1,197	198	257	742
19	28	115	19	26	70
6,710	14,810	19,757	3,022	4,746	11,989
38,780	67,375	92,320	13,753	23,248	55,319

Town.							
Total.				Male.			
Total.	0 — 4.	5 — 14.	15 and over.	Total.	0 — 4.	5 — 14.	15 and over.
705	75	151	479	329	40	76	213
2,013	249	522	1,242	1,029	131	281	617
30,748	4,196	7,136	19,416	15,810	2,140	3,915	9,755
66,145	8,702	13,863	43,580	34,936	4,288	7,285	23,363
99,611	13,222	21,672	64,717	52,104	6,599	11,5[illegible]7	33,948
78	12	15	51	46	8	11	27
538	76	143	319	316	45	86	185
1,784	277	352	1,155	920	116	189	615
2,400	365	510	1,525	1,282	169	286	827
909	105	211	593	460	55	111	294
1,385	200	318	867	688	101	188	399
4,317	565	893	2,8[illegible]	2,499	294	523	1,682
6,611	870	1,422	4,319	3,647	450	822	2,375
108,622	14,457	23,604	70,561	57,0[illegible]	7,218	12,665	37,150
54	10	10	34	33	8	7	18
9,712	1,193	1,655	6,864	5,817	620	895	4,302
1,359	138	299	922	874	84	177	613
25	1	6	18	14	...	3	11
11,150	1,342	1,970	7,838	6,738	712	1,082	4,944
...	...	...	...	...	...	...	......
39	10	8	21	24	6	6	12
...	...	...	...	...	...	...	......
39	10	8	21	24	6	6	12
11,189	1,352	1,978	7,859	6,762	718	1,088	4,956
180	21	49	110	108	12	34	62
429	69	107	253	210	23	56	140
2,584	363	559	1,662	1,380	189	281	910
3,193	453	715	2,025	1,707	224	371	1,112
1	...	...	1	1	...	...	1
35	7	6	22	25	6	4	15
36	7	6	23	26	6	4	16
3,229	460	721	2,048	1,733	230	375	1,128
123,040	16,269	26,303	80,468	65,628	8,166	14,128	43,234
224	32	45	147	35	3	10	22
1,622	219	508	895	915	121	333	461
8,958	1,122	2,340	5,496	5,092	565	1,426	3,101
52	7	13	32	19	2	6	11
10,856	1,380	2,906	6,570	6,061	691	1,775	3,595
...	...	...	...	...	...	...	...
192	25	32	135	117	13	20	84
89	6	10	73	19	2	2	15
281	31	42	208	136	15	22	99
1,990	294	511	1,185	1,132	160	313	659
36	5	10	21	21	1	9	11
46	8	11	27	23	3	7	13
2,072	307	532	1,233	1,176	164	329	683
13,209	1,718	3,480	8,011	7,373	870	2,120	4,377

XVII.

Table XVII-A.

Occupation.

Female.				Country. Total.				Country. Male.				Country. Female.			
Total.	0—4.	5—14.	15 and over.	Total.	0—4.	5—14.	15 and over.	Total.	0—4.	5—14.	15 and over.	Total.	0—4.	5—14.	15 and over.
376	35	75	266	142	14	31	97	50	7	9	34	92	7	22	63
984	118	241	625	1,340	182	293	865	760	91	160	509	580	91	133	356
14,938	2,056	3,221	9,661	24,228	3,060	4,952	16,216	14,076	1,466	2,518	10,002	10,152	1,594	2,434	6,124
31,309	4,414	6,578	20,317	52,756	6,338	10,236	36,182	31,609	3,151	5,611	22,847	21,147	3,187	4,625	13,335
47,607	6,623	10,115	30,769	78,466	9,594	15,512	53,360	46,495	4,715	8,298	33,482	31,971	4,879	7,214	19,878
33	4	4	24	30	7	4	19	3	...	...	3	27	7	4	16
222	31	57	134	316	52	86	178	239	42	67	130	77	10	19	48
854	161	103	540	281	37	53	191	142	16	27	99	139	21	26	92
1,118	196	224	698	627	96	143	388	384	53	94	232	243	38	49	156
449	50	100	299	14,663	1,933	3,063	9,667	8,202	923	1,609	5,670	6,461	1,010	1,454	3,997
697	99	130	468	4,926	651	940	3,335	2,785	315	452	2,018	2,141	336	488	1,317
1,818	271	370	1,177	79,184	12,677	18,607	47,900	44,125	6,319	10,280	27,526	35,059	6,358	8,327	20,374
2,964	420	600	1,914	98,773	15,261	22,610	60,902	55,112	7,557	12,341	35,214	43,661	7,704	10,269	25,688
51,589	7,239	10,939	33,411	177,865	24,951	38,265	114,650	101,991	13,330	20,733	68,928	75,875	12,621	17,532	45,722
21	2	3	16	259	40	31	188	86	12	12	62	173	28	19	126
3,895	573	760	2,562	6,916	833	1,319	4,764	4,414	410	740	3,264	2,502	423	579	1,500
485	54	122	309	1,469	190	269	1,010	899	106	145	618	570	84	124	362
11	1	3	7	113	13	28	72	49	3	16	30	64	10	12	42
4,412	630	888	2,894	8,757	1,076	1,647	6,034	5,448	531	913	4,004	3,309	545	734	2,030
...	...	...	...	23	2	6	15	4	...	...	4	19	2	6	11
15	4	2	9	1	...	...	1	1	...	...	1	...	...	...	...
...	...	...	...	12	3	2	7	...	...	...	...	12	3	2	7
15	4	2	9	36	5	8	23	5	...	...	5	31	5	8	18
4,427	634	890	2,903	8,793	1,081	1,655	6,057	5,453	531	913	4,009	3,340	550	742	2,048
72	9	15	48	247	40	63	144	124	19	34	71	123	21	29	73
210	46	51	113	599	71	136	392	315	28	71	216	284	43	65	176
1,204	174	278	752	4,607	660	1,041	2,906	2,638	337	579	1,722	1,969	323	462	1,184
1,486	229	344	913	5,453	771	1,240	3,442	3,077	384	684	2,009	2,376	387	556	1,433
...	...	...	...	17	4	4	9	8	4	...	4	9	...	4	5
10	1	2	7	160	24	30	106	54	7	9	38	106	17	21	68
10	1	2	7	177	28	34	115	62	11	9	42	115	17	25	73
1,496	230	346	920	5,630	799	1,274	3,557	3,139	395	693	2,051	2,491	404	581	1,506
57,518	8,103	12,175	37,234	193,289	26,831	41,194	124,264	110,583	13,256	22,339	74,988	81,706	13,575	18,855	49,276
189	29	35	125	435	96	107	232	390	87	101	202	45	9	6	30
707	98	175	434	18,300	2,263	6,473	9,564	11,010	1,186	4,434	5,390	7,290	1,077	2,039	4,174
3,856	657	914	2,835	134,451	17,728	38,676	78,150	74,803	8,892	23,430	42,481	59,651	8,836	15,146	35,669
33	5	7	21	866	118	242	506	497	56	144	297	369	62	98	209
4,795	689	1,131	2,975	154,055	20,205	45,398	88,452	86,700	10,221	28,109	48,370	67,355	9,984	17,289	40,082
...	...	...	...	34	2	10	22	19	1	6	12	15	1	4	10
75	12	12	51	798	69	192	537	576	32	140	404	222	37	52	133
70	4	8	58	140	10	24	106	109	6	18	85	31	4	6	21
145	16	20	109	972	81	226	665	704	39	164	501	268	42	62	164
858	134	198	526	39,864	5,717	10,161	23,986	22,277	3,046	5,896	13,335	17,587	2,671	4,265	10,651
15	4	1	10	2,611	376	729	1,509	1,432	182	473	777	1,183	194	256	732
23	5	4	14	124	19	34	71	32	5	12	15	92	14	22	56
896	143	203	550	42,673	6,112	10,924	25,566	23,741	3,233	6,381	14,127	18,882	2,879	4,543	11,459
5,836	848	1,354	3,634	197,629	26,393	56,548	114,683	111,145	13,493	34,654	62,998	85,484	12,905	21,894	51,685

Occupation and Class.				Total.				PROVINCIAL Males	
Class.	Order.	Sub-order and Group.	Occupation.	Total.	0 – 4.	5 — 14.	15 and over.	Total.	0 – 4.
B.—Pasture and Agriculture—*continued.*	IV. Live Stock—*contd.*	9 Subsidiary services to stock. (a) Training & doctoring live stock.	33 Veterinary Surgeons and assistants	83	7	19	57	48	6
			34 Farriers and gelders	586	79	153	354	321	46
			35 Horse and elephant breakers & trainers, &c....	670	86	143	441	377	19
			Total ...	1,339	172	315	852	746	161
		(b) Vermin destroying.	36 Rat, monkey, &c., catchers	46	9	6	31	12	3
			Total, Sub-order 9 ...	1,385	181	321	883	758	104
		Total, Order IV ...	......	212,223	28,207	60,349	123,577	119,276	14,457
	V. Agriculture..	10 Interest in land.. ...	37 Land occupants, not cultivating	127,336	17,101	30,492	79,748	64,010	8,527
			38 Land occupants, cultivating	1,519,426	237,946	373,429	908,051	776,217	115,654
			39 Lessees of villages, &c.	3,571	415	752	2,404	2,023	253
			40 Tenants, not cultivating	8,817	1,316	2,047	5,454	4,378	543
			41 Tenants and sharers, cultivating	2,446,744	382,869	631,264	1,432,611	1,259,417	186,813
			Total, Sub-order 10 ...	4,105,894	639,647	1,037,984	2,428,263	2,105,745	312,094
		11 Agricultural labourers..	42 Farm servants	138,474	19,340	29,398	89,736	71,653	8,678
			43 Field labourers and crop-watchers ...	364,709	55,924	84,153	224,632	180,540	871
			Total, Sub-order 11 ...	503,183	75,264	113,551	314,368	252,193	36,549
		12 Growers of special products and trees.	44 Tea, coffee & cinchona planters	43	8	10	25	25	6
			45 Cocoanut growers	49	4	10	35	24	1
			46 Betel-vine & areca-nut growers...	624	146	169	309	317	74
			47 Waternut growers	3,281	581	866	1,834	1,700	275
			48 Cardamom & pepper growers	37	5	5	27	21	1
			49 Indigo planters, managers, &c....	1,053	128	235	690	992	124
			50 Fruit growers	30	1	8	21	21	—
			51 Market gardeners (vegetable growers) ...	1,038	175	267	596	554	58
			52 Gardeners, seedsmen, &c.	3,289	421	744	2,124	1,794	227
			53 Manure preparers and sellers	237	33	56	148	65	13
			54 Forest officers	106	16	17	73	49	5
			55 Forest rangers, guards and peons	1,199	163	205	831	671	73
			Total, Sub-order 12 ...	10,986	1,681	2,592	6,713	6,233	684
		13 Agricultural training and supervision.	56 Directors of Agriculture	44	5	9	30	28	2
			57 Model-farm managers, &c.	10	1	1	8	8	—
			58 Estate agents and managers	587	71	123	393	220	24
			Total, Sub-order 13 ...	641	77	133	431	261	26
		Total, Order V ...	......	4,620,704	716,669	1,154,260	2,749,775	2,364,422	349,553
	Total, Class B...	......	......	4,832,927	744,966	1,214,609	2,873,352	2,483,698	364,020
C.—Personal and Household Services.	VI. Personal and Household Services.	14 Personal and domestic services.	59 Barbers	75,252	10,938	18,595	45,719	40,205	5,481
			60 Ear-pickers	81	11	20	50	47	6
			61 Tattooers	86	8	29	49	42	3
			62 Caste-mark appliers	17	4	1	12	9	2
			63 Washermen	27,967	3,469	5,705	18,793	11,720	1,722
			64 Water-carriers	5,586	687	1,271	3,628	2,514	334
			65 Cooks	5,256	563	1,027	3,666	2,613	240
			66 In-door servants	52,220	5,939	10,777	35,504	22,965	2,461
			67 Grooms, coachmen, dogboys, &c.	6,498	865	1,394	4,239	3,810	429
			68 Door-keepers, &c.	1,822	192	396	1,234	1,136	103
			Total, Sub-order 14 ...	169,785	22,676	39,215	107,894	85,061	10,711

Total.					
...le.		Female.			
5 — 14.	15 and over.	Total.	0 — 4.	5 — 14.	15 and over.
11	31	36	1	8	28
85	190	265	83	68	164
64	264	293	37	79	177
160	485	593	71	155	367
1	8	34	6	5	23
161	493	627	77	160	390
36,941	67,808	92,947	13,83[illegible]	23,4[illegible]8	55,709
16,817	38,366	63,32[illegible]	8,274	13,075	41,377
197,861	402,899	743,209	122,292	175,765	445,152
394	1,877	1,548	163	358	1,027
1,071	2,759	4,43[illegible]	765	976	2,695
335,569	786,735	1,187,627	196,056	295,695	695,876
551,515	1,242,136	2,000,149	327,553	486,469	1,180,127
14,759	48,216	66,821	10,662	14,639	41,520
45,078	107,5[illegible]	184,169	28,053	39,075	117,041
59,837	155,807	250,9[illegible]	38,715	53,714	158,561
6	15	18	4	4	10
2	21	25	3	8	14
78	165	307	72	91	144
467	958	1,581	306	399	876
5	15	16	4	...	12
214	654	61	4	21	36
7	14	9	1	1	7
150	316	484	87	117	280
381	1,166	1,495	194	363	938
22	31	172	21	34	117
11	33	57	11	6	40
107	491	528	90	98	340
1,450	3,809	4,753	797	1,142	2,814
4	22	16	3	5	8
...	3	7	1	1	5
41	155	337	47	82	238
45	180	390	51	88	251
612,847	1,402,022	2,2[illegible]6,282	367,116	541,413	1,347,753
649,788	1,469,890	2,34[illegible],[illegible]	380,946	564,821	1,403,462
10,083	24,691	35,0[illegible]	5,507	8,512	21,028
12	30	34	6	8	20
9	30	44	5	20	19
...	7	8	2	1	5
2,942	7,056	11,247	1,747	2,763	6,737
673	1,517	3,072	363	598	2,111
548	1,825	2,643	323	479	1,841
5,159	15,340	29,255	3,478	5,619	20,158
830	2,570	2,688	445	574	1,669
245	788	683	89	151	443
20,400	53,860	84,724	11,965	18,725	54,0[illegible]

Total.				Town.			
				Male.			
Total.	0—4.	5—14.	15 and over.	Total.	0—4.	5—14.	15 and over.
27	4	4	19	18	3	3	12
330	42	83	205	184	24	45	115
483	64	104	315	274	41	49	184
840	110	191	539	476	68	97	311
14	3	1	10	7	1	1	6
854	113	192	549	483	69	98	316
14,053	1,831	3,672	8,560	7,856	939	2,224	4,693
25,091	3,121	5,939	16,031	12,548	1,651	3,238	7,659
76,161	10,985	17,152	48,024	38,811	5,450	9,104	24,257
685	85	184	416	395	63	57	275
4,449	656	935	2,858	2,208	223	472	1,513
91,990	13,417	21,391	57,182	48,438	6,570	11,155	30,707
193,376	28,264	45,601	124,511	102,390	13,953	24,026	64,411
13,902	1,793	3,020	9,089	7,129	865	1,586	4,678
29,606	4,312	6,170	19,124	14,095	2,124	3,101	8,870
43,503	6,105	9,190	28,213	21,224	2,989	4,687	13,549
5	2	...	3	5	2	...	3
10	1	2	7	6	...	...	6
492	121	142	229	233	56	65	112
632	83	172	367	331	47	90	194
6	...	1	5	6	...	1	5
...	...	...	...	...	...	...	
11	...	6	5	10	...	6	4
198	32	51	115	112	12	32	68
1,729	208	381	1,140	879	111	181	587
3	...	...	2	1	...	...	1
47	10	11	26	19	3	7	9
428	68	86	274	203	27	50	126
3,550	525	852	2,173	1,805	258	432	1,115
7	1	2	4	1	...	...	1
5	...	1	4	3	...	...	3
248	35	51	162	129	15	27	87
260	36	54	17	133	15	27	91
245,694	34,930	55,697	155,067	125,552	17,215	29,172	79,165
259,757	36,761	59,369	163,627	133,408	18,154	31,396	83,858
11,328	1,532	2,679	7,117	6,097	782	1,440	3,875
10	2	1	7	6	1	1	4
5	...	1	4	1	...	...	1
...	...	...	...	...	...	...	...
6,265	921	1,491	3,853	3,224	444	809	1,971
2,502	282	554	1,666	1,222	142	328	752
3,198	300	584	2,314	1,766	139	352	1,275
19,099	2,190	3,773	13,136	8,586	992	1,832	5,762
3,906	560	791	2,555	2,115	281	422	1,412
482	52	96	334	290	32	59	199
46,795	5,839	9,970	30,986	23,307	2,813	5,243	15,251

Table XVII.-A.

Occupation.

XVII.

Female.				Country. Total.				Male.				Female.			
Total	0–4.	5–14.	15 and over.	Total.	0–4.	5–14.	15 and over.	Total.	0–4.	5–14.	15 and over.	Total.	0–4.	5–14.	15 and over.
9	1	1	7	56	3	15	38	30	3	8	19	26	...	7	19
141	18	33	90	256	37	70	149	137	22	40	75	119	15	30	74
219	23	65	131	187	22	39	126	103	8	15	80	84	14	24	46
369	42	94	228	499	62	124	313	270	33	63	174	229	29	61	139
7	2	...	5	32	6	5	21	5	2	...	3	27	4	5	18
371	44	94	233	531	68	129	334	275	35	63	177	256	33	66	157
6,207	692	1,448	3,867	198.160	20,466	56,677	115,017	111,420	13,528	34,717	63,175	86,740	12,938	21,960	51,842
12,543	1,470	2,701	8,372	103.245	13,980	24,553	63,712	51,462	7,176	13,579	30,707	50,783	6,804	10,974	33,005
37,350	5,535	8,048	23,767	1,443.255	226,961	356,277	860,027	737,406	110,204	189,560	438,642	705,859	116,757	167,717	421,385
300	32	127	141	2.886	330	568	1,988	1,638	199	337	1,102	1,248	131	231	886
2,241	433	463	1,345	4.368	660	1,112	2,596	2,170	325	599	1,246	2,198	335	513	1,350
43,552	6,841	10,236	26,475	2.354.754	369,452	609,873	1,375,429	1,210,679	180,237	324,414	706,028	1,144,075	189,215	285,459	669,401
95,986	14,311	21,675	60,100	3.907.518	611,383	992,383	2,303,752	2,003,355	298,141	527,489	1,177,725	1,904,163	313,242	464,894	1,126,027
6,773	928	1,434	4,411	124.572	17,547	26,378	80,647	64,524	7,813	13,173	43,538	60,048	9,734	13,205	37,109
15,511	2,188	3,069	10,254	335.103	51,612	77,983	205,508	166,445	25,747	41,977	98,721	168,658	25,865	36,006	106,787
22,284	3,116	4,503	14,665	459.675	69,159	104,361	286,155	230,969	33,560	55,150	142,259	228,706	35,599	49,211	143,896
...	...	...	...	38	6	10	22	20	2	6	12	18	4	4	10
4	1	2	1	39	3	8	28	18	1	2	15	21	2	6	13
259	65	77	117	133	25	27	80	84	18	13	53	48	7	14	27
291	36	82	173	2.659	498	694	1,467	1,369	228	377	764	1,290	270	317	703
...	...	...	...	31	5	4	22	15	1	4	10	16	4	...	12
...	...	...	...	1.053	128	235	690	992	124	214	654	61	4	21	36
1	...	...	1	19	1	2	16	11	...	1	10	8	1	1	6
86	20	19	47	840	143	216	481	442	76	118	248	398	67	98	233
850	97	200	553	1.560	213	363	984	915	116	200	599	645	97	163	385
1	...	...	1	235	33	56	146	64	12	22	30	171	21	34	116
28	7	4	17	59	6	6	47	30	2	4	24	29	4	2	23
225	41	36	148	771	95	119	557	468	46	57	365	303	49	62	192
1,745	267	420	1,058	7.436	1,156	1,740	4,540	4,428	626	1,018	2,784	3,008	530	722	1,756
6	1	2	3	37	4	7	26	27	2	4	21	10	2	3	5
2	...	1	1	5	1	...	4	...	...	...	...	5	1	...	4
119	20	24	75	339	36	72	231	91	9	14	68	248	27	58	163
127	21	27	79	383	41	79	261	118	11	18	89	263	30	61	172
120,148	17,715	26,525	75,902	4.375.010	681,739	1,098,563	2,594,708	2,238,870	332,338	588,675	1,322,857	2,136,140	349,401	514,888	1,271,851
126,349	18,607	27,973	79,769	4.573.170	708,205	1,155,240	2,709,725	2,350,290	345,866	618,392	1,386,032	2,222,830	362,839	536,848	1,323,693
5,231	750	1,239	3,242	63.924	9,406	15,916	38,602	34,108	4,649	8,643	20,816	29,816	4,757	7,273	17,786
4	1	...	3	71	9	19	43	41	4	11	26	30	5	8	17
4	...	1	3	81	8	28	45	41	3	9	29	40	5	19	16
...	...	...	...	17	4	1	12	9	2	...	7	8	2	1	5
3,041	477	682	1,882	16.702	2,548	4,214	9,940	8,496	1,278	2,133	5,085	8,206	1,270	2,081	4,855
1,280	140	226	914	3.084	405	717	1,962	1,292	182	345	765	1,792	223	372	1,197
1,432	161	232	1,039	2.058	263	443	1,352	847	101	196	550	1,211	162	217	802
10,513	1,198	1,041	7,874	33.121	3,749	7,004	22,368	14,379	1,469	3,326	9,584	18,742	2,280	3,678	12,784
1,791	279	369	1,143	2.592	305	603	1,684	1,695	139	398	1,158	897	166	205	526
102	20	87	135	1.310	140	300	900	840	71	186	589	494	69	114	311
23,488	3,026	4,727	15,735	122,990	16,887	29,245	76,908	61,754	7,898	15,247	38,609	61,236	8,939	13,998	38,299

Occupation and Class.				Total.				PROVINCIAL ... Ma...	
Class.	Order.	Sub-order and Group.	Occupation.	Total.	0—4.	5—14	15 and over.	Total.	0—4.
C.—Personal and House-hold Services—*continued.*	VI. Personal and Household Services—*continued.*	15 Non-domestic establishment.	69 Hotel, Bar-keepers, &c.	610	78	136	396	253	33
			70 Rest-house owners and managers	14	3	2	9	6	1
			71 Club secretaries, managers, &c.	29	2	5	22	16	2
			Total, Sub-order 15 ...	653	83	143	427	275	36
		16 Sanitation...	72 Sanitary Officers of Government	104	19	21	64	62	8
			73 Sanitary Inspectors, &c., Local & Municipal .	661	118	155	388	323	67
			74 Sweepers and scavengers	18,030	2,670	4,597	10,793	9,120	1,292
			75 Dust and sweepings contractors	34	4	3	27	23	1
			Total, Sub-order 16 ...	18,359	2,811	4,776	11,272	9,5[illegible]3	1,358
	Total, Order VI ...		......	189,297	25,570	44,134	119,593	94,869	12,105
Total, Class C ...		......	......	189,2[illegible]7	25,570	44,134	119,593	94,869	12,105
D.—Preparation and Supply of Material Substances.	VII. Food and Drink.	17 Animal Food	76 Cow-keepers and butter-sellers...	24,958	3,539	6,347	15,072	12,502	1,756
			77 Ghee preparers and sellers	12,885	1,874	3,344	7,667	6,526	918
			78 Cheese makers and sellers	12	1	4	7	......	......
			79 Butchers	4,799	694	1,213	2,892	2,506	349
			80 Fowl and egg dealers	872	66	111	695	431	9
			81 Fishermen and fish-curers	10,807	1,922	2,698	6,187	5,725	946
			82 Fish dealers...	6,427	1,125	1,635	3,667	2,925	535
			Total, Sub-order 17 ...	60,760	9,221	15,352	36,187	30,015	4,513
		18 Vegetable Food	83 Grain dealers	112,744	16,158	26,943	69,643	60,237	8,396
			84 Grain parchers	2,164	340	505	1,319	1,115	177
			85 Pulse and flour preparers, &c.	28,153	3,379	6,745	18,032	12,572	1,648
			86 Flour-mill service	36	5	9	22	21	2
			87 Bakers	369	46	93	230	198	29
			88 Bran sellers	19	3	5	11	5	......
			89 Vegetable sellers	34,214	5,235	8,724	20,255	16,903	2,580
			90 Fruit sellers...	5,284	794	1,247	3,243	2,571	384
			91 Cocoanut dealers	329	51	83	195	192	32
			92 Confectioners	10,292	1,366	2,376	6,550	5,536	671
			93 Sweetmeat pedlars	102	10	18	74	57	6
			Total, Sub-order 18 ...	193,709	27,387	46,748	119,574	99,406	13,888
		19 Drink, condiments and narcotics.	94 Ice manufacturers and sellers...	29	3	9	17	15	1
			95 Sodawater, &c., makers and sellers	37	6	12	19	17	4
			96 Sharbat preparers and sellers	45	8	8	29	21	5
			97 Country spirits distillers, &c.	6,403	861	1,521	4,024	3,392	445
			98 Toddy drawers and sellers	1,398	256	328	814	816	141
			99 Foreign wine and spirit dealers	105	22	30	53	51	8
			100 Brewers	389	43	109	237	189	18
			101 Tea sellers and tasters	58	8	14	36	37	6
			102 Coffee preparers and sellers	60	8	16	36	38	6
			103 Sugar makers and sellers	449	66	107	276	224	31
			104 Molasses makers and sellers	2,477	356	634	1,487	1,195	168
			105 Salt preparers and sellers	4,571	704	1,017	2,850	2,377	344
			106 Assafœtida, &c., sellers	1,085	117	264	704	686	64
			107 Vinegar makers and sellers	49	9	14	26	6	2
			108 Pickle makers and sellers	2	......	1	1	1	......
			109 Grocers	38,790	5,299	9,038	24,453	20,339	2,634
			110 Cardomom dealers	16	4	4	8	5	1
			111 Betel-leaf, &c., sellers	3,892	543	854	2,495	1,918	245
			112 Tobacco and snuff dealers	8,358	1,180	1,901	5,277	4,376	570
			113 Prepared hukka pedlars	22	6	7	9	12	3
			114 Opium, &c., makers and sellers	523	72	126	325	273	34
			115 Bháng, gánja, &c., dealers	559	74	134	351	331	45
			Total, Sub-order 19 ...	69,330	9,645	16,148	43,527	36,213	4,775
	Total, Order VII ...		......	323,789	46,253	78,248	199,288	166,234	23,176

TOTAL.

...le.		Female.			
5—14.	15 and over.	Total.	0—4.	5—14.	15 and over.
60	160	357	45	76	236
	5	8	2	2	4
1	13	13	......	4	9
61	178	378	47	82	249
17	37	42	11	4	27
77	194	333	61	78	194
2,480	5,348	8,940	1,378	2,117	5,445
3	19	11	3	......	8
2,577	5,598	9,326	1,453	2,199	5,674
23,128	59,636	94,428	13,465	21,006	59,957
23,128	59,636	94,428	13,465	21,006	59,957
3,360	7,386	12,456	1,783	2,987	7,686
1,752	3,856	6,359	956	1,592	3,811
......	......	12	1	4	7
672	1,485	2,293	345	541	1,407
26	396	441	57	85	299
1,513	3,266	5,082	976	1,185	2,921
871	1,519	3,502	590	764	2,148
8,194	17,908	30,145	4,708	7,158	18,279
14,971	36,870	52,507	7,762	11,972	32,773
279	659	1,049	163	226	660
3,299	7,625	15,584	1,731	3,446	10,407
5	14	15	3	4	8
47	122	171	17	46	108
1	4	14	3	4	7
4,532	9,831	17,312	2,696	4,192	10,424
636	1,551	2,713	410	611	1,692
42	114	137	15	41	81
1,276	3,589	4,756	695	1,100	2,961
8	43	45	4	10	31
25,096	60,422	94,303	13,499	21,652	59,152
6	8	14	2	3	9
5	8	20	2	7	11
8	13	24	8	5	16
810	2,137	3,014	416	711	1,887
169	506	583	115	159	308
14	29	54	14	16	24
61	110	200	25	48	127
11	20	21	2	3	
9	23	22	2	7	
51	142	225	35	56	134
284	743	1,282	188	350	744
524	1,509	2,194	360	493	1,341
141	381	499	53	123	323
1	3	43	7	13	23
......	1	1	......	1	......
4,752	12,953	18,451	2,665	4,286	11,500
......	4	11	3	4	4
446	1,221	1,980	298	408	1,274
1,016	2,790	3,982	610	885	2,487
4	5	10	3	3	4
67	172	250	38	59	153
79	207	228	29	55	144
8,453	22,985	33,107	4,870	7,695	20,542
41,743	101,915	157,555	28,077	36,505	97,973

Towns.							
Total.				Male.			
Total.	0—4.	5—14.	15 and over.	Total.	0—4.	5—14.	15 and over.
481	58	109	314	204	28	50	126
6	2	...	4	3	1	...	2
14	...	3	11	6	...	...	6
501	60	112	329	213	29	50	134
48	9	9	30	30	4	9	17
495	90	105	300	247	44	57	146
4,917	703	1,143	3,071	2,456	343	628	1,485
14	3	1	10	4	...	1	3
5,474	805	1,258	3,411	2,737	391	695	1,651
52,770	6,704	11,340	34,726	26,257	3,233	5,988	17,036
52,770	6,704	11,340	34,726	26,257	3,233	5,988	17,036
4,324	613	951	2,650	1,866	292	479	1,095
2,335	314	567	1,384	1,151	165	309	677
......	...	...	...	......	...	...	...
3,149	465	799	1,885	1,625	233	444	948
424	3	5	416	211	1	3	207
3,480	685	912	1,883	1,900	341	525	1,034
1,366	213	308	845	665	103	173	389
14,908	2,293	3,542	9,073	7,418	1,135	1,933	4,350
27,503	3,953	6,864	16,686	13,675	1,951	3,664	8,060
1,210	197	289	724	659	113	162	384
6,349	581	1,422	4,346	2,227	261	679	1,287
......	...	...	...	......	...	...	...
210	27	48	135	114	16	28	70
......	...	...	...	......	...	...	...
11,648	1,721	2,932	6,995	5,481	808	1,484	3,189
2,576	371	612	1,593	1,238	185	308	745
217	31	54	132	118	21	26	71
6,702	864	1,521	4,317	3,581	426	817	2,338
74	7	10	57	44	4	5	35
56,489	7,752	13,752	34,985	27,137	3,785	7,173	16,179
27	3	9	15	14	1	6	7
6	...	2	4	......	...	...	...
16	3	2	11	9	2	1	6
845	100	172	573	463	51	95	317
445	80	92	273	285	50	59	176
59	10	19	30	30	3	7	20
14	2	2	10	8	2	1	5
40	5	9	26	25	4	7	14
58	8	15	35	36	6	8	22
233	38	51	144	115	16	26	73
779	125	195	459	334	49	87	198
1,015	159	249	607	468	76	121	271
289	22	68	199	143	10	31	102
10	3	4	3	......	...	...	...
1	...	1	...	......	...	..	...
13,543	1,914	3,257	8,372	6,878	947	1,730	4,201
4	2	1	1	1	1	...	...
1,894	234	439	1,221	907	100	212	586
4,870	649	1,066	3,155	2,609	338	575	1,696
15	5	4	6	7	2	2	3
182	17	50	115	103	8	27	68
276	40	64	172	52	11	11	30
24,681	3,419	5,771	15,481	12,487	1,686	3,006	7,795
96,018	13,464	23,065	59,489	47,042	6,606	12,112	28,324

XVII.

Table XVII.-A.

Occupation.

Female.				Country. Total.				Country. Male.				Country. Female.			
Total.	0—4.	5—14.	15 and over.	Total.	0—4.	5—14.	15 and over.	Total.	0—4.	5—14.	15 and over.	Total.	0—4.	5—14.	15 and over.
277	30	59	188	129	20	27	82	49	5	10	34	80	15	17	48
3	1	...	2	8	1	2	5	3	...	...	3	5	1	2	2
8	...	3	5	15	2	2	11	10	2	1	7	5	...	1	4
288	31	62	195	152	23	31	98	62	7	11	44	90	16	20	54
13	5	...	13	56	10	12	34	32	4	8	20	24	6	4	14
248	46	48	154	163	28	50	88	81	13	20	48	85	15	30	40
2,461	360	515	1,586	13,143	1,967	3,454	7,722	6,664	949	1,852	3,863	6,479	1,018	1,602	3,859
10	3	...	7	20	1	2	17	19	1	2	16	1	...	...	1
2,737	414	563	1,760	13,385	2,006	3,518	7,861	6,796	967	1,882	3,947	6,589	1,039	1,636	3,914
26,513	3,471	5,352	17,690	136,527	18,866	32,794	84,867	68,612	8,872	17,140	42,600	67,915	9,994	15,654	42,267
26,513	3,471	5,352	17,690	136,527	18,866	32,794	84,867	68,612	8,872	17,140	42,600	67,915	9,994	15,654	42,267
2,358	321	472	1,565	20,734	2,926	5,396	12,412	10,636	1,464	2,881	6,291	10,098	1,462	2,515	6,121
1,114	149	258	707	10,620	1,560	2,777	6,283	5,375	753	1,443	3,179	5,245	807	1,334	3,104
...	...	...	...	12	1	4	7	......	...	...	...	12	1	4	7
1,524	232	355	937	1,650	229	414	1,007	881	116	228	537	769	113	186	470
213	2	2	209	448	63	106	279	220	8	23	189	228	55	83	90
1,580	344	387	849	7,327	1,237	1,786	4,304	3,825	605	988	2,232	3,502	632	798	2,072
701	110	135	456	5,061	912	1,327	2,822	2,260	432	698	1,130	2,801	480	629	1,692
7,490	1,158	1,609	4,723	45,852	6,928	11,810	27,114	23,197	3,378	6,261	13,558	22,655	3,550	5,549	13,556
13,828	2,002	3,200	8,626	85,241	12,205	20,079	52,957	46,562	6,445	11,307	28,810	38,679	5,760	8,772	24,147
551	84	127	340	954	143	216	595	456	64	117	275	498	79	99	320
4,122	320	743	3,059	21,807	2,798	5,323	13,686	10,345	1,387	2,620	6,338	11,462	1,411	2,703	7,348
...	...	...	...	36	5	9	22	21	2	5	14	15	3	4	8
96	11	20	65	159	19	45	95	84	13	19	52	75	6	26	43
...	...	...	...	19	3	5	11	5	...	1	4	14	3	4	7
6,167	913	1,448	3,806	22,566	3,514	5,792	13,260	11,421	1,731	3,048	6,642	11,145	1,783	2,744	6,618
1,338	186	304	848	2,708	423	635	1,650	1,333	199	328	806	1,375	224	307	844
99	10	28	61	113	20	20	63	74	15	16	43	38	5	13	20
3,121	438	704	1,979	3,590	502	855	2,233	1,955	245	459	1,251	1,635	257	396	982
30	3	5	22	28	3	8	17	13	2	3	8	15	1	5	9
29,352	3,967	6,570	18,806	137,220	19,636	32,996	84,589	72,269	10,103	17,923	44,243	64,951	9,532	15,073	40,346
13	2	3	8	2	...	......	2	1	...	...	1	1	...	...	1
6	...	2	4	31	6	10	15	17	4	5	8	14	2	5	7
7	1	1	5	29	5	6	18	12	3	2	7	17	2	4	11
382	49	77	256	5,561	761	1,349	3,451	2,929	394	716	1,820	2,632	367	634	1,631
160	30	33	97	953	170	236	541	531	91	110	330	422	85	126	211
29	7	12	10	46	12	11	23	21	5	7	9	25	7	4	14
6	...	1	5	375	41	107	227	181	16	60	105	194	25	47	122
15	1	2	12	18	3	5	10	12	2	4	6	6	1	1	4
22	2	7	13	2	...	1	1	2	...	1	1	...	...	...	...
116	22	25	71	216	28	56	132	109	15	25	69	107	13	31	63
445	76	108	261	1,698	231	439	1,028	861	119	197	545	837	112	242	483
547	83	128	336	3,556	545	768	2,243	1,909	268	403	1,238	1,647	277	365	1,005
146	12	37	97	798	95	198	505	443	54	110	279	355	41	88	226
10	3	4	3	39	6	10	23	6	2	1	3	33	4	9	20
1	...	1	...	1	...	......	1	1	...	...	1	...	...	...	...
6,665	967	1,527	4,171	25,247	3,385	5,781	16,081	13,461	1,687	3,022	8,752	11,786	1,698	2,759	7,329
3	1	1	1	12	2	3	7	4	...	...	4	8	2	3	3
987	125	227	635	1,998	309	415	1,274	1,005	186	234	585	993	173	181	639
2,261	311	491	1,459	3,488	531	835	2,122	1,707	232	441	1,034	1,781	299	394	1,028
8	3	2	3	7	1	3	3	5	1	2	2	2	...	1	1
79	9	23	47	341	55	76	210	170	26	40	104	171	29	36	106
224	29	53	142	283	34	70	179	279	34	68	177	4	...	2	2
12,134	1,793	2,765	7,636	44,699	6,226	10,377	28,096	23,726	3,089	5,447	15,190	20,973	3,137	4,930	12,906
48,970	6,858	10,953	31,165	227,771	32,789	55,188	139,799	119,192	16,570	29,631	72,991	108,579	16,219	25,552	66,808

TABLE

Occupation and Class.				Total.				PROVINCIAL Ma[les]	
Class.	Order.	Sub-order and Group.	Occupation.	Total.	0—4.	5—14.	15 and over.	Total.	0—4
D.—Preparation and Supply of Material Substances—*continued*.	VIII. Light, Firing and Forage.	20 Lighting ...	116 Oil pressers and sellers ...	33,831	5,606	9,780	23,439	20,007	2,722
			117 Oil and salt sellers	2,330	337	577	1,416	1,202	167
			118 Oilcake dealers	388	59	111	218	196	28
			119 Candle makers and sellers	5	......	1	4	2	......
			120 Torch makers and sellers	142	22	31	89	67	10
			121 Kerosine oil dealers	61	9	13	39	29	5
			122 Matches makers and sellers	4	......	......	4	2	......
			123 Lamp makers and sellers	215	33	41	141	133	19
			124 Gas workers	......	......	......	......	......	......
			Total, Sub-order 20 ...	41,979	6,066	10,563	25,350	21,638	2,951
		21 Fuel and Forage ...	125 Firewood and grass gatherers...	69,110	10,356	16,769	41,985	31,276	4,791
			126 Firewood dealers ...	1,459	315	395	749	793	158
			127 Coal miners, &c. ...	......	......	......	......	......	......
			128 Coal dealers	104	11	23	70	55	3
			129 Charcoal burners and dealers ...	590	99	147	344	326	41
			130 Cowdung-fuel preparers...	4,327	686	980	2,661	1,217	252
			131 Hay, &c., contractors and dealers	5,805	855	1,461	3,489	2,662	423
			Total, Sub-order 21 ...	81,295	12,222	19,775	49,298	36,329	5,668
		Total, Order VIII ...	....	123,274	18,288	30,338	74,648	57,967	8,619
	IX. Buildings...	22 Building materials ...	132 Brick and tile burners ...	3,371	551	955	1,865	1,811	275
			133 Lime, &c., burners	3,352	485	797	2,070	1,596	202
			134 Stone-quarry owners and dealers	2,242	424	534	1,284	929	171
			135 Thatch dealers and thatchers...	283	36	55	192	145	24
			Total, Sub-order 22 ...	9,248	1,496	2,341	5,411	4,481	672
		23 Artificers in building ...	136 Building contractors	414	53	102	2[illegible]0	194	28
			137 Stone and marble workers	6,417	970	1,461	3,986	3,467	476
			138 Masons	35,668	5,295	8,445	21,928	18,570	2,615
			139 Builders and joiners	511	61	125	325	281	28
			140 Plasterers and house painters...	704	99	165	440	353	51
			141 Mud wall and roof builders	1,332	231	326	775	687	103
			142 Plumbers and glaziers ...	2	......	......	2	2	......
			143 Tilers and tile-turners ...	610	106	145	359	505	86
			Total, Sub-order 23 ...	45,658	6,815	10,769	28,074	24,059	3,387
		Total, Order IX ...	....	54,906	8,311	13,110	33,485	28,540	4,059
	X. Vehicles and Vessels.	24 Railway plant ...	144 Railway mechanics	185	29	47	109	109	17
			145 Railway permanent-way men...	606	96	69	441	396	53
			Total, Sub-order 24 ...	791	125	116	550	505	70
		25 Carts, carriages, &c. ...	146 Cart makers and sellers...	673	92	163	418	390	52
			147 Pálki, &c., makers and sellers	11	1	2	8	9	1
			147a Carriage painters	......	......	......	......	......	......
			Total, Sub-order 25 ...	684	93	165	426	399	53
		26 Ships and boats... ...	148 Shipwrights, boat-builders, &c.	258	47	63	148	129	25
			149 Ship painters, &c.	29	3	10	16	13	2
			150 Sail makers	21	2	5	14	8	......
			151 Wicker-boat makers, &c.	......	......	......	......	......	......
			152 Ship chandlers	......	......	......	......	......	......
			Total, Sub-order 26 ...	308	52	78	178	150	27
		Total, Order X ...	....	1,783	270	359	1,154	1,054	150
	XI. Supplementary requirements.	27 Paper, &c. ...	153 Paper makers	240	32	54	154	130	21
			154 Stationers ...	347	43	76	228	165	16
			155 Waste paper dealers	60	11	13	36	42	6
			156 Waxed cloth preparers ...	19	5	6	8	19	5
			Total, Sub-order 27 ...	666	91	149	426	356	48

TOTAL.

n.		Female.			
5 — 14.	15 and over.	Total.	0 — 4.	5 — 14.	15 and over.
5,255	12,030	*18,827*	2,884	4,534	11,409
297	738	*1,128*	170	280	678
55	113	*192*	31	56	105
......	2	*3*	......	1	2
15	42	*75*	12	16	47
6	18	*32*	4	7	21
......	2	*2*	......	......	2
21	93	*82*	14	20	48
......	......	......	......	......	......
5,649	13,038	*20,341*	3,115	4,914	12,312
8,628	17,657	*37,834*	5,565	8,141	24,128
237	398	*666*	157	158	351
......	......	......	......	......	......
14	38	*49*	8	9	32
85	200	*264*	58	62	144
392	573	*3,010*	334	588	2,088
735	1,504	*3,143*	432	726	1,985
10,091	20,570	*44,966*	6,554	9,684	28,728
15,740	33,608	*65,307*	9,669	14,598	41,040
427	1,109	*1,560*	276	528	756
388	1,006	*1,756*	283	409	1,064
231	527	*1,313*	253	303	757
30	91	*138*	12	25	101
1,076	2,733	*4,767*	824	1,265	2,678
55	111	*220*	25	47	148
811	2,180	*2,950*	494	650	1,806
4,466	11,489	*17,098*	2,680	3,979	10,439
69	184	*280*	83	56	141
74	228	*351*	48	91	212
192	392	*645*	128	134	383
......	2	......	......	......	......
122	207	*105*	20	23	62
5,789	14,883	*21,599*	3,428	4,980	13,191
6,865	17,616	*26,366*	4,252	6,245	15,869
27	65	*76*	12	20	44
39	304	*210*	43	30	137
66	369	*286*	55	50	181
101	237	*283*	40	62	181
2	6	*2*	......	......	2
......	......	......	......	......	......
103	243	*285*	40	62	183
30	74	*129*	22	33	74
5	6	*16*	1	5	10
2	6	*13*	2	3	8
......	......	......	......	......	......
......	......	......	......	......	......
37	86	*158*	25	41	92
206	698	*729*	120	153	456
24	85	*110*	11	30	69
40	109	*182*	27	36	119
11	25	*18*	5	2	11
6	8	......	......	......	......
81	227	*310*	43	68	199

Total.				Town.			
Total.				Male.			
Total.	0 — 4.	5 — 14.	15 and over.	Total.	0 — 4.	5 — 14.	15 and over.
11,511	1,624	2,952	6,935	5,794.	773	1,561	3,460
796	111	194	491	368	47	97	224
281	43	88	150	141	22	43	76
2	...	...	2	2	...	...	2
119	18	28	73	53	8	14	31
27	6	6	15	15	3	4	8
4	...	...	4	2	...	...	2
196	32	38	126	119	18	19	82
......	...	...	...	...	...	...	......
12,936	1,834	3,306	7,796	6,494	871	1,738	3,885
10.457	1,518	2,473	6,466	4,749	730	1,302	2,717
116	15	29	72	59	5	19	35
......	...	...	...	...	...	...	......
43	8	10	25	15	1	5	9
120	16	39	65	68	8	25	35
774	88	163	523	156	40	51	65
1.709	240	426	1,043	849	111	216	522
13,219	1,885	3,140	8,194	5,896	895	1,618	3,383
26.155	3,719	6,446	15,990	12,390	1,766	3,356	7,268
463	66	114	283	226	35	52	139
1,181	163	284	734	552	60	143	340
312	68	75	169	143	32	38	73
36	1	10	25	14	...	2	12
1.992	298	483	1,211	935	136	235	564
330	41	79	210	149	22	44	83
3.653	544	850	2,259	1,780	250	443	1,087
20,930	2,998	4,933	12,999	10,687	1,505	2,607	6,575
260	33	71	156	130	17	39	74
628	83	155	390	320	45	70	205
265	61	53	151	122	28	28	66
2	...	...	2	2	...	...	2
495	85	117	293	447	75	107	265
26,563	3,845	6,258	16,460	13,637	1,942	3,338	8,357
28,555	4,143	6,741	17,671	14,572	2,078	3,573	8,921
167	24	43	100	100	14	25	61
319	53	27	239	213	26	14	173
486	77	70	339	313	40	39	234
178	30	45	103	112	16	31	65
8	1	2	5	6	1	2	3
......	...	...	...	...	...	...	......
186	31	[illegible]7	108	118	17	33	68
203	37	48	118	98	19	21	58
29	3	10	16	13	2	5	6
21	2	5	14	8	...	2	6
......	...	...	...	..	...	...	......
......	...	...	...	..	...	...	......
253	42	63	143	119	21	28	70
925	150	180	595	550	78	100	372
214	28	47	139	117	17	21	79
288	36	65	187	133	13	35	85
46	6	11	29	38	5	11	21
19	5	6	8	19	5	6	8
567	75	129	363	307	40	73	194

XVII.

	Female.			Country. Total.				Male.				Female.			
Total.	0—4.	5—14.	15 and over.	Total.	0—4.	5—14.	15 and over.	Total.	0—4.	5—14.	15 and over.	Total.	0—4.	5—14	15 and over.
6,717	851	1,391	3,475	27,323	3,982	6,837	16,504	14,213	1,949	3,694	8,570	13,110	2,033	3,143	7,934
138	64	97	267	1,534	226	383	925	834	120	200	514	700	106	183	411
140	21	45	74	107	16	23	68	55	6	12	37	52	10	11	31
...	...	...	...	3	...	1	2	......	...	...	...	3	...	1	2
66	10	14	42	23	4	3	16	14	2	1	11	9	2	2	5
12	3	2	7	34	3	7	24	14	2	2	10	20	1	5	14
2	...	...	2	......	...	......	...	......	...	...	...	......	...	...	...
77	14	10	44	19	1	3	15	14	1	2	11	5	...	1	4
...	...	...	...	......	...	......	...	......	...	...	...	......	...	...	...
6,448	963	1,568	3,911	29,043	4,232	7,257	17,554	15,144	2,080	3,911	9,153	13,899	2,152	3,346	8,401
5,708	788	1,171	3,749	58,653	8,838	14,296	35,519	26,527	4,061	7,326	15,140	32,126	4,777	6,970	20,379
57	10	10	37	1,343	300	366	677	734	153	218	363	609	147	148	314
...	...	...	...	......	...	......	...	......	...	...	...	......	...	...	...
28	7	5	16	61	3	13	45	40	2	9	29	21	1	4	16
52	8	14	30	470	83	108	279	258	33	60	165	212	50	48	114
618	43	112	458	3,453	498	817	2,138	1,061	212	341	508	2,392	286	476	1,630
860	120	210	521	4,096	615	1,035	2,446	1,813	312	519	982	2,283	303	516	1,464
7,323	990	1,522	4,811	68,076	10,337	16,635	41,104	30,433	4,773	8,473	17,187	37,643	5,564	8,162	23,917
13,765	1,953	3,090	8,722	97,119	14,569	23,892	58,658	45,577	6,853	12,384	26,340	51,542	7,716	11,508	32,318
837	31	62	144	2,908	485	841	1,582	1,585	240	375	970	1,323	215	466	612
629	94	141	394	2,171	322	513	1,336	1,044	133	245	666	1,127	180	268	670
169	36	37	96	1,930	356	459	1,115	786	139	193	454	1,144	217	266	661
22	1	8	13	247	35	45	167	131	24	28	79	116	11	17	88
1,057	162	248	647	7,256	1,198	1,858	4,200	3,546	536	841	2,169	3,710	662	1,017	2,031
181	19	35	127	84	12	23	49	45	6	11	28	39	6	12	21
1,873	294	407	1,172	2,764	426	611	1,727	1,687	226	368	1,093	1,077	200	243	634
10,843	1,493	2,326	6,424	14,738	2,297	3,512	8,929	7,883	1,110	1,859	4,914	6,855	1,187	1,658	4,015
130	16	32	82	251	28	54	169	151	11	30	110	100	17	24	59
308	38	85	185	76	16	10	50	33	6	4	23	43	10	6	27
143	33	25	85	1,037	170	273	624	565	75	164	326	502	95	109	298
...	...	...	...	......	...	......	...	......	...	...	...	......	...	...	...
48	10	10	28	115	21	28	66	58	11	15	32	57	10	13	34
12,926	1,903	2,920	8,103	19,095	2,970	4,511	11,614	10,422	1,445	2,451	6,526	8,673	1,525	2,060	5,088
13,983	2,065	3,168	8,750	26,351	4,168	6,369	15,814	13,968	1,981	3,292	8,695	12,383	2,187	3,077	7,119
67	10	18	39	18	5	4	9	9	3	2	4	9	2	2	5
106	27	13	66	287	43	42	202	183	27	26	131	104	16	17	71
173	37	31	105	305	48	46	211	192	30	27	135	113	18	19	76
66	14	14	38	495	62	118	315	278	36	70	172	217	26	48	143
2	...	...	2	3	...	......	3	3	...	...	3	......	...	...	...
...	...	...	...	......	...	......	...	......	...	...	...	......	...	...	...
68	14	14	40	498	62	118	318	281	36	70	175	217	26	48	143
105	18	27	60	55	10	15	30	31	6	9	16	24	4	6	14
16	1	5	10	......	...	......	...	......	...	...	...	......	...	...	...
13	2	3	8	......	...	......	...	......	...	...	...	......	...	...	...
...	...	...	...	......	...	......	...	......	...	...	...	......	...	...	...
...	...	...	...	......	...	......	...	......	...	...	...	......	...	...	...
134	21	35	78	55	10	15	30	31	6	9	16	24	4	6	14
375	72	80	223	858	120	179	559	504	72	106	326	354	48	73	233
97	11	26	60	26	4	7	15	13	4	3	6	13	...	4	9
155	23	30	102	59	7	11	41	32	3	5	24	27	4	6	17
8	1	...	7	14	5	2	7	4	1	...	3	10	4	2	4
...	...	...	...	......	...	......	...	......	...	...	...	......	...	...	...
260	35	56	169	99	16	20	63	49	8	8	33	50	8	12	30

Occupation and Class.				Total.				Provincial … Ma…	
Class.	Order.	Sub-order and Group.	Occupation.	Total.	0 – 4.	5 – 14.	15 and over.	Total.	0 – 4.
D.—Preparation and Supply of Material Substances—*continued.*	XI. Supplementary Requirements—*contd.*	28 Books and Prints, &c. ...	157 Press proprietors, printers, &c.	725	98	141	486	410	54
			158 Book-binders	61	12	14	85	42	9
			159 Book sellers and publishers	160	14	22	124	90	10
			160 Newspaper proprietors, &c.	4	......	1	3	1	......
			161 News agents, &c.	2	......	1	1	1	......
			162 Print and picture dealers	13	1	3	8	6	1
			Total, Sub-order 28 ...	964	125	182	657	550	74
		29 Watches, clocks and scientific instruments.	163 Watch makers and sellers	280	32	70	178	169	18
			164 Opticians	6	......	2	4	4	......
			165 Surgical instrument makers	......	......	......	......	......	......
			166 Photographic apparatus dealers	2	......	......	2	......	......
			167 Other scientific instrument dealers	52	7	11	34	25	4
			168 Scale makers and sellers	11	2	2	7	11	2
			Total, Sub-order 29 ...	351	41	85	225	209	24
		30 Carving, engraving, &c.	169 Wood and ebony carvers	166	19	53	94	97	12
			170 Ivory carvers	218	30	48	140	109	15
			171 Cotton-stamp makers and sellers	60	3	14	43	58	3
			172 Turners and lacquerers	1,415	207	321	887	764	107
			173 Die-sinkers, &c.	474	62	97	315	244	24
			174 Type-founders	17	2	1	14	6	1
			175 Mica, flint, talc workers...	8	......	2	6	4	......
			176 Mosaic and Alabastor workers	35	3	13	19	19	1
			Total, Sub-order 30 ...	2,393	326	549	1,518	1,281	163
		31 Toys, curiosities, &c.	177 Toy, kite, &c., dealers, Bird-stuffers ...	1,697	260	370	1,058	1,045	101
			178 Hukka-stem makers and sellers	291	39	62	190	116	14
			179 Papier-maché workers	16	2	5	9	16	2
			180 Card makers and sellers...	65	8	15	42	31	3
			181 Tábut makers and sellers	1	......	......	1	......	......
			182 Curiosity dealers	113	15	20	77	61	6
			Total, Sub-order 31 ...	2,182	324	481	1,377	1,259	186
		32 Music and musical instruments.	183 Music dealers	48	4	13	31	25	2
			184 Conch makers, &c.	720	106	172	442	432	62
			Total, Sub-order 32 ...	768	110	185	473	457	64
		33 Necklaces, Bracelets, beads, sacred threads, &c.	185 Bangle makers, &c., in lac	347	59	83	205	100	31
			186 Bangle makers, &c., in stone	1	......	......	1	1	......
			187 Bangle makers, &c., in wood and bone ...	2,759	396	703	1,651	1,399	187
			188 Bangle makers, &c., in clay	41	6	3	32	39	6
			189 Bangle makers, &c., in glass	1,897	235	401	1,261	1,020	109
			189a Bangle (unspecified) makers, &c.	602	76	129	397	318	31
			190 Bangle fitters	404	61	83	260	197	30
			191 Imitation jewellery makers	145	23	32	90	10	......
			192 Bead makers and sellers...	137	21	38	78	55	10
			193 Rosary and necklace makers	242	31	60	151	126	12
			194 Flower garland makers	994	100	211	683	511	54
			195 Artificial flower makers	7	......	......	7	2	......
			196 Sacred thread makers and sellers ...	381	44	107	230	178	24
			Total, Sub-order 33 ...	7,948	1,052	1,850	5,046	4,017	494
		34 Furniture	197 Upholsterers	18	14	2	2	3	......
			198 Furniture makers...	236	38	67	101	141	18
			199 Frame makers	2	......	1	1	......	......
			200 Looking-glass makers and sellers	58	8	16	34	52	8
			Total, Sub-order 34 ...	344	60	86	198	196	26

Total.		Female.			
5 — 14.	15 and over.	Total.	0 — 4.	5 — 14.	15 and over.
84	272	315	44	57	214
10	23	19	3	4	12
14	66	70	4	8	58
......	1	3	......	1	2
......	1	1	......	1	......
1	4	6	......	2	4
109	367	41[illegible]	51	73	290
47	104	111	14	23	74
2	2	2	......	......	2
......	......	......	......	......	......
......	......	2	......	......	2
4	17	27	3	7	17
2	7	......	......	......	......
5[illegible]	130	14[illegible]	17	30	95
27	58	69	7	26	36
23	71	109	15	25	69
8	27	22	......	6	16
154	503	651	100	167	384
53	167	230	38	44	148
......	5	11	1	1	9
2	2	4	......	......	4
6	12	16	2	7	7
273	845	1,112	163	276	673
250	634	652	99	129	424
29	73	175	25	33	117
5	9	......	......	......	......
9	19	34	5	6	23
......	......	1	......	......	1
9	36	61	9	11	41
302	771	923	138	179	606
10	13	23	2	3	18
102	268	2[illegible]8	44	70	174
112	281	311	46	73	192
37	98	181	28	46	107
......	1	......	......	......	......
370	842	1,351	209	333	809
3	30	2	......	......	2
7	694	877	126	184	567
	210	284	45	52	187
36	131	207	31	47	129
..	10	155	23	32	60
21	24	82	11	17	54
41	73	116	19	19	78
120	397	483	46	91	346
......	2	5	......	......	5
51	98	208	20	56	132
973	2,550	3,931	558	877	2,496
2	1	15	14	......	1
38	85	125	20	29	76
......	......	2	......	1	1
18	31	6	......	3	3
53	117	148	34	33	81

Town.							
Total.				Male.			
Total.	0 — 4.	5 — 14.	15 and over.	Total.	0 — 4.	5 — 14.	15 and over
694	92	137	465	392	52	81	25
58	12	13	33	40	9	9	2
136	11	19	106	73	7	11	5
4	...	1	3	1	...	...	1
2	...	1	1	1	...	...	1
13	1	3	8	6	1	1	4
903	116	174	616	513	69	102	342
265	32	63	170	156	18	41	97
......	...	...	...	...	...	...	.....
......	...	...	...	...	...	...	.....
......	...	...	...	...	...	...	.....
30	3	6	21	20	3	2	15
11	2	2	7	11	2	2	7
306	37	71	198	187	23	45	119
147	14	48	85	87	9	24	54
176	23	42	111	91	10	21	60
49	2	11	36	31	2	6	23
1,129	165	252	712	612	89	121	402
149	17	37	95	75	4	23	49
11	...	...	11	4	...	...	4
8	...	2	6	4	...	2	2
......	...	...	...	...	...	...	.....
1,669	221	392	1,056	904	114	197	593
360	50	78	232	193	27	43	123
237	33	49	145	93	12	24	57
4	...	2	2	4	...	2	2
60	7	14	39	29	3	9	17
1	...	...	1	...	...	...	.....
73	7	14	51	38	5	6	27
7.4	97	157	470	357	47	84	226
33	4	11	18	25	2	10	13
142	28	34	80	69	11	17	41
175	32	45	98	94	13	27	54
184	32	43	109	86	15	18	53
......	...	...	...	...	...	...	.....
2,181	305	559	1,317	1,092	136	284	672
......	...	...	...	...	...	...	.....
535	74	101	360	300	36	66	198
109	17	33	60	54	7	18	29
171	26	29	116	86	14	13	59
13	...	...	13	9	...	...	9
102	16	28	58	33	6	11	16
217	20	56	141	116	12	38	68
637	59	180	448	341	35	77	229
4	...	...	4	...	......	...	.....
148	19	32	97	49	12	13	24
4,301	568	1,010	2,723	2,166	273	588	1,355
15	14	...	1	...	...	...	.....
194	24	50	120	90	10	26	54
......	...	...	...	...	...	...	.....
34	8	14	17	29	8	11	15
243	41	64	138	119	13	37	69

XVII.

Female.				Country.											
				Total.				Male.				Female.			
Total.	0 — 4.	5 — 14.	15 and over.	Total.	0 — 4.	5 — 14.	15 and over.	Total.	0 — 4.	5 — 14.	15 and over.	Total.	0 — 4.	5 — 14.	15 and over.
302	40	56	206	31	6	4	21	18	2	3	18	13	4	1	8
18	3	4	11	3	...	1	2	2	...	1	1	1	...	...	1
63	4	8	51	24	3	3	18	17	3	3	11	7	...	...	7
3	...	1	2	......	...	......	...	......	...	...	...	...	...	...	...
1	...	1	...	......	...	......	...	......	...	...	...	...	...	...	...
6	...	2	4	......	...	......	...	......	...	...	...	...	...	...	...
393	47	72	274	58	9	8	41	37	5	7	25	21	4	1	16
109	14	22	73	15	...	7	8	13	...	6	7	2	...	1	1
...	...	...	...	6	...	2	4	4	...	2	2	2	...	...	2
...	...	...	...	......	...	......	...	......	...	...	...	...	...	...	...
...	...	...	...	2	...	......	2	......	...	...	...	2	...	...	2
10	...	4	6	22	4	5	13	5	1	2	2	17	3	3	11
...	...	...	...	......	...	......	...	......	...	...	...	...	...	...	...
119	14	26	70	45	4	14	27	22	1	10	11	23	3	4	16
60	5	24	31	19	5	5	9	10	3	3	4	9	2	2	5
85	13	21	51	42	7	6	29	18	5	2	11	24	2	4	18
18	...	5	13	11	1	3	7	7	1	2	4	4	...	1	3
517	76	131	310	236	42	69	175	152	18	33	101	134	24	36	74
74	13	14	47	325	45	60	220	169	20	30	119	156	25	30	101
7	...	...	7	6	2	1	3	2	1	...	1	4	1	1	2
4	...	...	4	......	...	......	...	......	...	...	...	...	...	...	...
...	...	...	...	35	3	13	19	19	1	6	12	16	2	7	7
765	107	195	463	724	105	157	462	377	49	76	252	347	56	81	210
167	23	35	100	1,337	210	301	826	852	134	207	511	485	76	94	315
134	21	25	88	64	6	13	45	23	2	5	16	41	4	8	29
...	...	...	...	13	2	3	7	12	2	3	7	...	...	...	...
31	4	5	22	5	1	1	3	2	...	...	2	3	1	1	1
1	...	...	1	......	...	......	...	......	...	...	...	...	...	...	...
34	2	8	24	40	8	6	26	13	1	3	9	27	7	3	17
367	50	73	244	1,458	227	324	907	902	139	218	545	556	88	106	362
8	2	1	5	15	...	2	13	......	...	...	...	15	...	2	13
73	17	17	39	578	78	138	362	363	51	85	227	215	27	53	135
81	19	18	44	593	78	140	375	363	51	85	227	230	27	55	148
98	17	25	56	163	27	40	96	80	16	19	45	83	11	21	51
...	...	...	...	1	...	......	1	1	...	...	1	...	...	...	...
1,083	169	275	645	569	91	144	334	307	51	86	170	262	40	58	164
...	...	...	...	41	6	3	32	39	6	3	30	2	...	...	2
235	38	35	162	1,362	161	300	901	720	73	151	406	642	88	149	405
55	10	14	31	493	59	97	337	264	24	59	181	229	35	32	156
85	12	16	57	233	35	54	144	111	10	23	72	122	19	31	72
4	...	...	4	132	23	32	77	1	...	...	1	131	23	32	76
69	10	17	42	35	5	10	20	22	4	10	8	13	1	...	12
101	8	18	75	25	11	4	10	10	...	3	7	15	11	1	3
296	24	63	219	357	41	81	235	170	19	43	108	187	22	38	127
4	...	...	4	3	...	......	3	2	...	...	2	1	...	...	1
99	7	19	73	233	25	75	133	124	12	38	74	109	13	37	59
2,135	295	472	1,368	3,647	484	840	2,823	1,851	221	435	1,195	1,796	263	405	1,126
15	14	...	1	3	...	2	1	3	...	2	1	...	...	...	...
104	14	24	60	72	14	17	41	51	8	12	31	21	6	5	10
...	...	...	...	2	...	1	1	......	...	...	...	2	...	1	1
5	...	3	2	24	5	2	17	23	5	2	16	1	...	...	1
124	28	27	69	101	19	22	60	77	13	16	48	24	6	6	12

Occupation and Class.				Total.				Provincial Ma…	
Class.	Order.	Sub-order and Group.	Occupation.	Total.	0—4.	5—14.	15 and over.	Total.	0—4.
D.—Preparation and Supply of Material Substances—*continued*.	XI. Supplementary requirements—*continued*.	35 Harness	201 Saddlers	759	111	178	470	393	56
			202 Saddle-cloth makers	73	11	21	41	30	6
			203 Whip, goad, &c., makers	43	7	12	24	24	3
			Total, Sub-order 35 ...	875	129	211	535	456	65
		36 Tools and Machinery ...	204 Knife and tool makers	762	103	194	465	398	51
			204a Plough makers	4	1	...	3	1	...
			205 Knife and tool grinders...	1,684	219	392	1,073	835	106
			206 Loom makers and sellers	531	74	120	337	301	37
			207 Mechanic (not Railway)	135	16	25	94	68	5
			208 Machinery dealers, &c.	109	18	20	71	36	5
			Total, Sub-order 36 ...	3,225	431	751	2,043	1,637	204
		37 Arms and ammunition...	209 Gun-makers and sellers	58	8	20	30	26	4
			210 Ammunition and Cap dealers	46	4	12	30	27	1
			211 Gunpowder makers and sellers	389	53	87	249	229	30
			212 Fire-work makers and sellers	187	27	59	101	102	15
			213 Sword makers and sellers	319	37	90	192	183	15
			214 Spear-head, &c., makers	144	31	30	83	86	17
			215 Bow and arrow makers	584	90	180	314	315	45
			216 Cudgel (láthi) makers	24	2	5	17	17	2
			Total, Sub-order 37 ...	1,751	252	483	1,016	985	129
	Total, Order XI ...		....	21,467	2,941	5,012	13,514	11,403	1,477
	XII. Textile Fabrics and Dress.	38 Wool and Fur	217 Carpet weavers and sellers	32	...	4	28	...	...
			218 Shawl weavers and sellers	45	7	7	31	19	1
			219 Felt and pashm workers	315	47	99	219	172	24
			220 Blanket weavers and sellers	9,536	1,667	2,100	5,739	4,887	843
			221 Woollen cloth makers, &c.	3,413	459	821	2,133	1,673	234
			222 Woollen yarn spinners and sellers	1,706	252	370	1,084	530	88
			223 Wool carders	75	6	22	47	42	5
			224 Wool dyers...	166	18	51	97	81	8
			224a Wool dealers	1,025	157	289	579	491	71
			225 Fur dealers...	451	64	122	265	224	28
			Total, Sub-order 38 ...	16,784	2,677	3,885	10,222	8,119	1,302
		39 Silk...	226 Silk-worm rearers...	25	7	9	9	16	5
			227 Silk carders and spinners	3,453	374	592	2,487	863	148
			228 Silk weavers and dealers	3,979	527	903	2,549	2,121	261
			229 Silk printers and dyers	1,014	186	272	556	469	92
			230 Braid makers	1,070	133	264	673	582	60
			Total, Sub-order 39 ...	9,541	1,227	2,040	6,274	4,051	566
		40 Cotton	231 Cotton cleaners, pressers and ginners ...	33,233	4,617	7,557	21,059	16,357	2,188
			231a Mill mukádams	3,132	478	840	1,814	1,452	222
			232 Cotton carpet and rug makers and sellers ...	248	34	45	169	138	8
			233 Cotton spinners, sizers and yarn beaters ...	35,655	2,915	5,560	27,180	4,079	894
			234 Cotton weavers, mill owners and managers	222,113	34,497	52,421	135,195	115,346	16,805
			234a Mill clerks	...	...	...	...	...	...
			235 Cotton factory hands (undefined)	1,116	153	257	706	616	79
			236 Calenderers, fullers and printers	1,133	145	274	714	551	65
			237 Cotton dyers	25,650	3,600	6,281	15,769	12,895	1,810
			238 Tape makers and sellers...	1,938	258	421	1,259	1,057	135
			239 Tent manufacturers and sellers	2,076	296	515	1,265	898	131
			Total, Sub-order 40 ...	233,204	40,093	74,171	205,130	153,389	22,427

Total.

le,		Female.			
5 — 14.	15 and over.	Total.	0 — 4.	5 — 14.	15 and over.
92	245	366	55	86	225
14	19	34	5	7	22
6	15	19	4	6	9
112	279	419	64	99	256
101	246	364	52	93	219
	1	3	1	......	2
194	535	849	113	198	538
65	199	230	37	55	138
11	50	69	11	14	44
7	24	73	13	13	47
378	1,055	1,588	227	373	998
9	13	32	4	11	17
8	18	19	3	4	12
51	148	160	23	36	101
36	51	85	12	23	50
56	112	136	22	34	80
16	53	58	14	14	30
114	156	269	45	66	158
4	11	7	...	1	6
294	562	766	123	189	454
2,742	7,184	10,064	1,464	2,270	6,330
...	...	32	...	4	28
2	16	26	6	5	15
45	103	193	23	54	116
1,087	2,957	4,619	824	1,013	2,782
406	1,033	1,740	225	415	1,100
137	305	1,176	164	233	779
11	26	33	1	11	21
27	46	85	10	24	51
144	276	534	86	145	303
64	132	227	36	58	133
1,928	4,894	8,665	1,375	1,962	5,328
5	6	9	2	4	3
213	502	2,590	226	379	1,985
480	1,380	1,858	266	423	1,169
135	242	545	94	137	314
160	362	488	73	104	311
993	2,492	5,490	661	1,017	3,782
3,841	10,328	16,876	2,429	3,716	10,731
418	812	1,680	256	422	1,002
28	102	110	26	17	67
1,422	1,763	31,576	2,021	4,138	25,417
28,072	70,379	106,767	17,602	24,849	64,316
...	...	...	...	...	...
144	393	500	74	113	313
135	351	582	80	139	363
3,197	7,888	12,755	1,790	3,084	7,881
226	696	881	123	195	563
256	511	1,178	165	259	754
37,739	93,233	172,005	24,566	36,432	111,907

Town.							
Total.				Male.			
Total.	0 — 4.	5 — 14.	15 and over.	Total.	0 — 4.	5 — 14.	15 and over
450	72	99	289	217	35	49	133
10	3	...	7	3	1	...	2
2	...	...	2	2	...	...	2
472	75	99	298	222	36	49	137
403	56	109	241	181	26	45	110
......	...	...	...	...	...	...	...
920	112	208	602	441	52	97	292
357	50	80	227	214	29	48	137
49	9	8	32	21	2	3	16
......	...	...	...	...	...	...	...
1.732	227	403	1,102	857	109	193	555
57	8	20	29	25	4	9	12
18	3	3	12	5	...	1	4
135	17	44	75	72	7	25	40
171	26	58	87	91	15	35	41
165	18	46	101	94	8	31	55
35	3	6	26	19	1	4	14
41	4	7	30	9	...	4	5
1	...	...	1	...	...	...	...
624	79	184	361	315	35	109	171
11.719	1,568	2,728	7,423	6,041	772	1,454	3,815
......	...	...	...	...	...	...	...
26	2	3	21	16	1	2	13
140	14	40	86	62	6	15	41
2.101	367	456	1,278	1,088	177	257	654
633	73	123	437	333	41	66	226
205	32	56	117	85	15	26	44
13	2	3	8	4	2	...	2
40	5	10	25	21	3	8	10
188	30	50	108	88	14	24	50
101	10	32	59	45	...	16	29
3.447	535	773	2,139	1,742	259	414	1,069
......	...	...	...	...	...	...	...
3.055	300	524	2,231	697	110	175	412
3.576	465	802	2,309	1,953	242	431	1,280
845	157	228	460	434	85	126	223
854	108	223	523	442	46	133	263
8.330	1,030	1,777	5,523	3,526	483	865	2,178
7.902	1,099	1,708	5,095	4,032	555	922	2,555
1.902	297	524	1,081	706	121	260	415
85	6	15	64	60	1	12	47
6.739	605	1,165	4,969	1,139	223	398	518
57,158	8,276	12,786	36,096	29,841	4,126	6,751	18,964
...	...	...	...	...	...	...	...
778	112	178	488	442	55	104	283
391	53	93	245	225	23	55	147
11.875	1,624	2,084	7,167	5,756	783	1,373	3,600
593	70	116	407	336	40	64	232
586	82	131	373	263	36	69	158
87,509	12,124	19,400	55,985	42,890	5,963	10,008	26,919

Female.				Country. Total.				Male.				Female.			
Total.	0—4.	5—14.	15 and over.	Total.	0—4.	5—14.	15 and over.	Total.	0—4.	5—14.	15 and over.	Total.	0—4.	5—14.	15 and over.
843	37	50	156	299	39	79	181	176	21	43	112	123	18	36	69
7	2	...	5	63	8	21	34	36	5	14	17	27	3	7	17
...	...	...	...	41	7	12	22	22	3	6	13	19	4	6	9
250	39	50	161	403	54	112	237	234	29	63	142	169	25	49	95
225	30	64	131	353	47	85	224	217	25	56	136	139	22	29	88
...	...	...	...	4	1	...	3	1	...	...	1	3	1	...	2
479	60	109	310	764	107	186	471	394	54	97	243	370	53	89	228
145	21	32	90	174	24	40	110	87	8	17	62	87	16	23	48
28	7	5	16	86	7	17	62	45	3	8	34	41	4	9	28
...	...	...	...	109	18	20	71	36	5	7	24	73	13	13	47
875	118	210	547	1,493	204	348	941	780	95	185	500	713	109	163	441
33	4	11	17	1	...	...	1	1	...	...	1	...	...	...	...
13	3	2	8	28	1	9	18	22	1	7	14	6	...	2	4
64	10	19	35	253	36	43	174	157	23	26	108	96	13	17	66
80	11	23	46	16	1	1	14	11	...	1	10	5	1	...	4
71	10	15	46	154	19	44	91	89	7	25	57	65	12	19	34
16	2	2	12	109	28	24	57	67	16	12	39	42	12	12	18
32	4	3	25	543	86	173	284	306	45	110	151	237	41	63	133
1	...	...	1	23	2	5	16	17	2	4	11	6	...	1	5
309	44	75	190	1,127	173	299	655	670	94	185	391	457	79	114	264
5,678	796	1,274	3,608	9,748	1,373	2,284	6,091	5,362	705	1,288	3,369	4,386	668	996	2,722
...	...	...	...	32	...	4	28	...	...	...	...	32	...	4	28
10	1	1	8	19	5	4	10	3	...	...	3	16	5	4	7
78	8	25	45	225	33	59	133	110	18	30	62	115	15	29	71
1,013	190	199	624	7,405	1,300	1,644	4,461	3,799	666	830	2,303	3,606	634	814	2,158
300	32	57	211	2,730	386	698	1,696	1,340	193	340	807	1,440	193	358	889
120	17	30	73	1,501	220	314	967	445	73	111	261	1,056	147	203	706
9	...	3	6	62	4	19	39	38	3	11	24	24	1	8	15
19	2	2	15	123	13	41	72	60	5	19	36	66	8	22	36
100	16	26	58	837	127	239	471	403	57	120	226	434	70	119	245
56	10	16	30	350	54	90	206	179	28	48	103	171	20	42	103
1,705	276	359	1,070	13,357	2,142	3,112	8,083	6,377	1,043	1,509	3,825	6,960	1,099	1,603	4,258
...	...	...	...	25	7	9	9	16	5	5	6	9	2	4	3
2,358	190	349	1,819	398	74	68	256	166	38	38	90	232	36	30	166
1,623	223	371	1,029	403	62	101	240	168	19	49	100	235	43	52	140
411	72	102	237	169	29	44	96	25	7	9	19	134	22	35	77
413	63	90	260	216	25	41	150	140	14	27	99	76	11	14	51
4,804	547	912	3,345	1,211	197	263	751	525	83	128	314	686	114	135	437
3,870	544	786	2,540	25,331	3,518	5,849	15,964	12,325	1,633	2,919	7,773	13,006	1,885	2,930	8,191
1,106	176	264	666	1,230	181	316	733	656	101	158	397	574	80	158	336
25	5	3	17	163	28	30	105	78	7	16	55	85	21	14	50
5,600	382	767	4,451	27,911	2,310	4,395	22,211	2,040	671	1,024	1,245	25,976	1,639	3,371	20,966
27,317	4,150	6,035	17,132	164,955	26,221	39,635	99,099	85,505	12,769	21,321	51,415	79,450	13,452	18,314	47,684
...	...	...	...	...	...	...	...	...	...	...	...	...	...	...	...
336	57	74	205	328	41	70	218	174	24	40	110	164	17	39	108
166	30	38	98	742	92	181	469	326	42	80	204	416	50	101	265
5,619	741	1,311	3,567	14,275	2,076	3,597	8,602	7,139	1,027	1,824	4,288	7,136	1,049	1,773	4,314
257	30	52	175	1,345	188	305	852	721	95	162	464	624	93	143	388
325	46	62	215	1,490	214	384	892	635	95	187	353	855	110	107	639
44,019	6,161	9,392	29,066	233,735	34,869	54,771	140,145	110,499	16,434	27,731	66,304	123,283	18,405	27,040	82,[illegible]41

Class.	Order.	Sub-order and Group.	Occupation.	Total. Total.	Total. 0—4.	Total. 5—14.	Total. 15 and over.	Provincial Ma[les] Total.	Provincial Ma[les] 0—4.
D.—Preparation and Supply of Material Substances—*continued.*	XII. Textile Fabrics and Dress—*contd.*	41 Jute, flax, coir, &c. ...	240 Flax-spinners, weavers and sellers	469	70	117	282	240	39
			241 Hemp rope makers and sellers	11,938	2,280	2,704	6,954	6,105	1,103
			242 Jute manufacturers, and agents	1	......	......	1	1	......
			243 Sacking, &c., makers and sellers	964	103	202	659	435	61
			244 Net makers and sellers	83	6	20	56	45	2
			245 Fancy work dealers	545	75	159	311	177	34
			246 Coir preparers, manufacturers and sellers ...	1,233	176	306	751	610	87
			Total, Sub-order 41 ...	15,232	2,710	3,508	9,014	7,613	1,326
		42 Dress	247 Tailors and darners	57,048	8,064	13,897	35,087	27,820	3,892
			248 Milliners and dress-makers	154	30	42	82	82	16
			249 Outfitters and clothes dealers	4,445	521	1,070	2,854	2,030	190
			250 Hosiers and Haberdashers	490	79	108	303	206	35
			251 Hat and turban makers...	176	31	28	117	69	10
			252 Turban-binders	242	28	55	159	144	17
			253 Umbrella makers and sellers	49	8	13	28	19	1
			254 Embroiderers	1,621	160	318	1,143	415	63
			255 Button makers and sellers	31	2	9	20	9	......
			256 False-plait makers	85	16	22	47	30	7
			257 Piece-goods dealers	28,557	4,476	7,123	16,958	14,061	2,202
			Total, Sub-order 42 ...	92,898	13,415	22,685	56,793	44,945	6,432
	Total, Order XII ...		....	460,749	67,022	106,289	287,438	218,117	32,053
	XIII. Metals and Precious Stones.	43 Gold, silver and precious stones.	258 Gold and silver dealers	1,891	225	460	1,206	1,022	112
			259 " " assayers	98	10	28	60	52	8
			260 " " workers...	54,406	7,553	13,210	33,643	28,240	3,758
			261 Gold beaters	1,652	226	379	1,047	867	111
			262 Goldsmith's dust washers	1,073	151	247	675	581	80
			263 Gold miners, managers, agents	19	3	3	13	12	2
			264 Enamellers...	92	14	18	60	43	6
			265 Electro-platers	76	8	24	44	27	3
			266 Wire drawers and braid makers	1,200	150	311	739	624	79
			267 Plate and plated ware dealers	97	7	19	71	62	5
			268 Diamond polishers and dealers	35	5	10	20	23	4
			269 Diamond diggers, washers, &c.	......	......	......	......	......	......
			270 Ruby workers	26	2	4	20	17	2
			271 Ruby and emerald, &c., dealers	76	9	22	45	40	6
			272 Pearl divers	5	1	......	4	5	1
			273 Pearl & other precious stone (unspcfd.) dealers.	931	139	239	553	429	71
			274 Coral-dealers	759	90	210	459	397	53
			275 Cornelian and Agate cutters	2,135	192	377	1,566	1,082	97
			Total, Sub-order 43 ...	64,571	8,785	15,561	40,225	33,508	4,398
		44 Brass, copper and bell-metal.	276 Brass workers and sellers	1,735	202	410	1,123	930	91
			277 Brass pot makers and sellers	1,353	167	333	852	730	86
			278 Brass image casters and sellers	135	16	37	83	79	11
			279 Copper workers and sellers	935	101	219	615	517	47
			280 Brass and copper wire drawers and sellers ...	23	1	6	16	......	......
			281 Bell-metal workers and sellers...	162	22	28	112	83	7
			282 Brass, copper and bell-metal workers ...	3,351	439	790	2,122	1,806	222
			283 Brass and copper dealers	1,860	232	405	1,223	931	118
			Total, Sub-order 44 ...	9,554	1,180	2,228	6,146	5,066	583
		45 Tin, zinc, mercury and lead.	284 Tin workers and sellers	1,031	155	247	629	535	76
			285 Tinfoil makers and sellers	101	23	25	53	46	9
			286 Zinc workers and sellers	16	2	3	11	16	2
			287 Lead and quicksilver workers	4	1	......	3	......	......
			288 Tin, lead and zinc workers	254	28	77	149	154	14
			Total, Sub-order 45 ...	1,403	209	352	845	751	101

TOTAL.

E.		Female.			
5 — 14.	15 and over.	Total.	0 — 4.	5 — 14.	15 and over.
65	186	229	31	52	146
1,491	3,511	5,833	1,177	1,213	3,443
......	1	......	......	......	......
106	268	529	42	96	391
15	28	37	4	5	28
76	68	368	41	84	243
170	353	623	89	136	398
1,922	4,365	7,619	1,334	1,586	4,649
7,051	16,877	29 228	4,172	6,846	18,210
19	47	72	14	23	35
505	1,326	2,415	322	565	1,528
59	172	224	44	49	131
14	45	107	21	14	72
27	100	98	11	28	59
7	11	30	7	6	17
121	241	1,206	107	197	902
3	6	22	2	6	14
5	18	55	9	17	29
3,717	8,142	14,496	2,274	3,406	8,816
11,528	26,985	47,953	6,983	11,157	29,813
54,105	131,059	242,652	34,069	52,184	155,479
247	663	869	113	218	543
16	28	46	2	12	32
6,893	17,598	26,157	3,795	6,317	16,045
201	555	785	115	178	492
139	362	492	71	108	313
2	8	7	1	1	5
7	30	49	8	11	30
8	16	49	5	16	28
165	350	606	71	146	389
13	44	35	2	6	27
7	12	12	1	3	8
......	......	......	......	......	......
2	13	9	......	2	7
10	24	30	3	6	21
......	4	......	......	......	......
107	251	502	68	132	302
121	223	362	37	89	236
216	769	1,053	95	161	797
8,160	20,050	31,063	4,387	7,401	19,275
212	617	815	111	198	506
172	472	622	81	161	380
18	50	57	5	19	33
115	355	418	54	104	260
......	......	23	1	6	16
10	57	79	15	9	55
414	1,170	1,545	217	376	952
195	618	929	114	210	605
1,145	3,339	4,488	598	1,083	2,807
122	337	496	79	125	292
11	26	55	14	14	27
3	11	......	......	......	......
......	......	4	1	......	3
47	93	100	14	30	56
183	467	655	108	169	378

Town.							
Total.				Male.			
Total.	0 — 4.	5 — 14.	15 and over.	Total.	0 — 4.	5 — 14.	15 and over.
103	18	25	60	57	10	16	31
1,865	314	411	1130	501	91	179	231
1	...	...	1	1	...	...	1
212	24	56	132	92	13	26	53
30	3	5	22	21	1	4	16
543	75	158	310	176	34	74	68
463	58	125	280	220	27	66	127
3,207	492	780	1,935	1,068	176	315	577
16,300	2,153	3,692	10,455	7,695	1,034	1,879	4,782
2	...	...	2	......	...	...	...
2,458	325	598	1,535	1,143	152	290	701
219	33	41	145	112	13	23	76
145	25	23	97	55	8	11	36
185	24	44	117	106	16	21	69
25	3	8	15	10	1	4	5
861	90	208	563	315	38	90	187
13	...	3	10	6	...	2	4
73	14	19	39	26	6	5	15
16,042	2,559	4,162	9,321	7,359	1,225	2,116	4,018
36,323	5,226	8,798	22,299	16,827	2,493	4,441	9,893
138,816	19,407	31,528	87,881	66,053	9,374	16,043	40,636
969	118	219	637	502	51	110	341
87	9	21	57	41	7	9	25
21,345	2,843	5,009	13,493	10,818	1,394	2,577	6,847
175	18	28	129	93	9	15	69
714	104	161	449	372	56	89	227
10	2	2	6	8	2	2	4
70	10	13	47	32	4	4	24
76	8	24	44	27	3	8	16
1,107	136	281	690	566	73	153	340
54	3	9	42	42	2	7	33
27	3	8	16	15	2	5	8
......	...	...	...	......	...	...	...
16	1	1	14	13	1	1	11
74	9	22	43	44	6	16	22
1	...	...	1	1	...	...	1
698	114	191	393	307	61	80	166
756	90	209	457	397	53	121	223
2,054	178	363	1,513	1,041	91	212	738
28,233	3,641	6,561	18,031	14,319	1,815	3,409	9,095
1,014	112	248	654	768	73	186	509
871	114	223	534	462	61	117	284
126	16	33	77	74	11	16	47
560	60	133	367	293	27	64	202
11	...	4	7	......	...	...	...
110	13	20	77	58	3	14	41
2,478	343	580	1,555	1,306	176	295	835
837	112	172	553	400	57	87	256
6,007	770	1,413	3,824	3,361	408	779	2,174
754	119	167	468	391	58	69	264
55	14	13	28	22	6	4	12
3	...	...	3	3	...	...	3
......	...	...	...	......	...	...	...
178	20	52	106	101	9	29	63
990	153	232	605	517	73	122	322

Occupation.

Female.				Country. Total.				Country. Male.				Country. Female.			
Total.	0 — 4.	5 — 14.	15 and over.	Total.	0 — 4.	5 — 14.	15 and over.	Total.	0 — 4.	5 — 14.	15 and over.	Total.	0 — 4.	5 — 14.	15 and over.
46	8	9	29	366	52	92	222	183	29	49	105	183	23	43	117
1,334	223	282	849	10,083	1,966	2,293	5,824	5,604	1,012	1,362	3,230	4,479	954	931	2,594
...	...	...	...	......	...	......	...	......	...	...	...	...	...	...	...
120	11	30	79	752	79	146	527	343	48	80	215	409	31	66	312
9	2	1	6	52	3	15	34	24	1	11	12	28	2	4	22
367	41	84	242	2	...	1	1	1	...	1	...	1	...	...	1
243	31	59	153	770	118	181	471	390	60	104	226	380	58	77	245
2,139	316	465	1,358	12,025	2,218	2,728	7,079	6,545	1,150	1,607	3,788	5,480	1,068	1,121	3,291
8,605	1,119	1,813	5,673	40,748	5,911	10,205	24,632	20,125	2,858	5,172	12,095	20,623	3,053	5,033	12,537
2	...	...	2	152	30	42	80	82	16	19	47	70	14	23	33
1,315	173	308	834	1,937	196	472	1,319	887	47	215	625	1,100	149	257	694
107	20	18	69	271	46	67	158	154	22	36	96	117	24	31	62
90	17	12	61	31	6	5	20	14	2	3	9	17	4	2	11
79	8	23	48	57	4	11	42	38	1	6	31	19	3	5	11
16	2	4	10	23	5	5	13	9	...	3	6	14	5	2	7
546	52	118	376	760	70	110	580	100	15	31	54	660	55	79	526
7	...	1	6	18	2	6	10	3	...	1	2	15	2	5	8
46	8	14	24	13	2	3	8	4	1	...	3	9	1	3	5
8,683	1,334	2,046	5,303	12,515	1,017	2,961	7,637	6,702	977	1,601	4,124	5,813	940	1,360	3,513
19,436	2,733	4,357	12,406	56,575	8,1[illegible]9	13,887	34,499	28,118	3,939	7,087	17,092	28,457	4,250	6,800	17,407
77,763	10,033	15,485	47,245	321,933	47,615	74,761	199,557	152,064	22,079	38,062	91,323	169,869	24,936	36,699	108,234
467	62	109	296	923	112	241	569	520	61	137	322	403	51	104	247
46	2	12	32	11	1	7	3	11	1	7	3	...	...	...	...
10,527	1,449	2,432	6,646	33,031	4,710	8,201	20,150	17,431	2,364	4,316	10,751	15,650	2,346	3,885	9,399
83	9	13	60	1,477	208	351	918	774	102	186	486	703	106	165	432
342	48	72	222	359	47	86	226	209	24	50	135	150	23	36	91
2	...	..	2	9	1	1	7	4	...	..	4	5	1	1	3
38	6	9	23	22	4	5	13	11	2	3	6	11	2	2	7
49	5	16	28	.....	...	......	..	......	...	...	...	...	...	...	...
541	63	128	350	93	14	30	49	28	6	12	10	65	8	18	39
12	1	2	9	43	4	10	29	20	3	6	11	23	1	4	18
12	1	3	8	8	2	2	4	8	2	2	4	...	...	...	...
..	...	..	...	.....	...	......	...	.....	...	...	...	...	...	..	..
3	...	..	3	10	1	3	6	4	1	1	2	6	...	2	4
30	3	6	21	2	...	......	2	2	...	..	2	...	...	...	...
	...	...	...	4	1	......	3	4	1	..	3	...	...	...	...
391	53	111	227	233	25	48	160	122	10	27	85	111	15	21	75
359	37	88	234	3	...	1	2	......	...	...	...	3	...	1	2
1,013	87	151	775	81	14	14	53	41	6	4	31	40	8	10	22
13,014	1,826	3,152	8,036	36,333	5,144	9,000	22,194	19,189	2,583	4,751	11,855	17,149	2,561	4,249	10,339
246	39	62	145	731	90	162	469	152	18	26	108	569	72	136	361
409	53	106	250	481	53	110	318	268	25	55	188	213	28	55	130
52	5	17	30	10	...	4	6	5	...	2	3	5	...	2	3
267	33	69	165	375	41	86	248	224	20	51	153	151	21	35	95
11	..	4	7	13	1	2	9	......	...	...	...	13	1	2	9
52	10	6	36	53	9	8	35	25	4	5	16	27	5	3	19
1,178	167	285	720	873	96	210	567	500	46	119	335	373	50	91	232
437	55	85	297	1,023	120	233	670	531	61	108	362	458	59	125	308
2,646	362	634	1,650	3,517	410	815	2,292	1,705	174	366	1,165	1,843	230	449	1,157
363	61	78	224	277	36	80	161	144	18	33	93	133	18	47	68
33	8	9	16	46	9	12	25	24	3	7	14	22	6	5	11
...	...	...	...	13	2	3	8	13	2	3	8	...	...	...	...
...	...	...	...	4	1	......	3	......	...	...	...	4	1	...	3
77	11	23	43	76	8	25	43	53	5	18	30	23	8	7	13
473	80	110	283	416	56	120	240	234	28	61	145	182	28	69	95

Occupation.

Class.	Order.	Sub-order and Group.	Occupation.	Total.	0—4.	5—14.	15 and over.	Provincial … M… Total.	0—4.
D.—Preparation and Supply of Material Substances—*continued.*	XIII. Metals and Precious Stones—*continued.*	46 Iron and steel ...	289 Iron and steel founders...	4.658	701	1,271	2,686	2,371	333
			290 Blacksmiths	40.877	6,207	10,433	24,237	21,199	3,091
			291 Iron and hardware dealers	5.069	813	1,295	2,961	2,642	408
			292 Nail makers and sellers	150	20	38	92	102	12
			293 Lock makers, menders, and sellers ...	74	10	13	51	37	4
			294 Weight makers and stampers	49	8	15	26	37	4
			Total, Sub-order 46 ...	50,877	7,759	13,065	30,053	26,388	3,856
		Total, Order XIII ...	...	126,408	17,933	31,206	77,269	65,713	8,937
	XIV. Glass, Pottery and Stoneware.	47 Glass and Chinaware ...	295 Glass-blowers	...	...	...	...	...	...
			296 Bottle dealers	30	5	5	20	17	2
			297 Glass and Chinaware dealers	399	62	91	246	192	33
			Total, Sub-order 47 ...	429	67	96	266	209	35
		48 Earthen and stoneware.	298 Potters	91.070	13,724	22,795	54,551	46,033	6,763
			299 Grindstone makers	3,585	632	924	1,979	1,809	322
			300 Pestle makers	1	...	...	1	...	...
			301 Quartz and soapstone powder preparers ...	14	1	6	8	8	...
			Total, Sub-order 48 ...	94.620	14,357	23,724	56,539	47,850	7,084
		Total, Order XIV ...	......	95.049	14,424	23,820	56,805	48,059	7,119
	XV. Wood, Cane and Leaves, &c.	49 Timber and wood ...	302 Timber and Bamboo dealers	7,435	1,166	1,924	4,345	3,755	594
			303 Wood cutters and sawyers	6.776	1,020	1,649	4,107	3,593	493
			304 Carpenters...	92,819	13,732	23,425	55,662	48,551	6,797
			305 Coopers and box makers	426	56	94	276	224	21
			Total, Sub-order 49 ...	107.456	15,974	27,092	64,390	56,123	7,904
		50 Canework, matting and leaves, &c.	306 Bamboo and rattan workers	7,505	1,205	1,746	4,554	3,478	557
			307 Basket weavers	21,429	3,439	5,524	12,466	10,826	1,683
			308 Mat makers and sellers...	239	47	61	131	84	25
			309 Screen (chik) makers	46	7	13	26	31	6
			310 Leaf-plate makers and sellers	1.759	268	407	1,084	941	145
			311 Tooth stick sellers	8,751	1,605	2,369	4,777	4,417	739
			312 Leaf-fan makers and sellers	75	13	21	41	28	4
			313 Brush and comb makers and sellers ...	479	62	135	282	260	39
			314 Broom makers and sellers	1,304	223	323	758	608	99
			315 Pith and bark collectors...	331	55	111	215	185	25
			Total, Sub-order 50 ...	41.958	6,024	10,710	24,334	20,878	3,284
		Total, Order XV ...	......	149.424	22,898	37,802	88,724	77,001	11,188
	XVI. Drugs, Gums, Dyes, &c.	51 Gums, wax and similar Forest produce.	316 India-rubber collectors	60	7	4	49	45	4
			317 Camphor and gum collectors... ...	491	86	111	294	212	43
			318 Gallnut (myrobolan) collectors ...	4	...	2	2	4	...
			319 Catechu preparers and sellers	375	58	89	228	168	25
			320 Lac collectors and sellers	161	25	43	93	87	13
			321 Sealing-wax makers	6	1	1	4	3	...
			322 Tar preparers and sellers	88	16	30	42	44	6
			323 Forest produce collectors	328	53	86	189	199	28
			Total, Sub-order 51 ...	1.513	246	366	901	762	118
		52 Drugs, dyes, pigments, &c.	324 Chemists and druggists	4.375	726	1,177	2,472	1,952	318
			325 Borax workers and sellers	4	...	1	3	...	...
			326 Saltpetre workers and sellers	113	13	19	81	57	6
			327 Alum, soda, &c., workers	394	53	103	238	199	27
			328 Soap makers and sellers	480	63	101	316	172	21
			329 Sulphur workers and sellers	48	6	11	31	[illegible]	4
			330 Indigo workers and dealers	333	61	75	207	157	25

TOTAL.

le.		Female.			
5 — 14.	15 and over.	Total.	0 — 4.	5 — 14.	15 and over.
632	1,404	2,287	366	639	1,282
.5575	12,533	19,678	3,116	4,858	11,704
709	1,525	2,427	405	586	1,436
23	67	48	8	15	25
6	27	37	6	7	24
12	19	12	2	3	7
6,957	15,575	24,489	3,903	6,108	14,478
16,445	40,331	60,695	8,996	14,761	30,938
...	...	...	...	...	...
2	13	13	3	3	7
40	119	207	29	51	127
42	132	220	32	54	134
12,078	27,193	45,037	6,962	10,717	27,358
496	991	1,726	310	428	988
...	...	1	...	...	1
3	5	6	1	2	3
12,577	28,189	46,770	7,273	11,147	28,350
12,619	28,321	46,990	7,305	11,201	28,484
1,038	2,123	3,680	572	886	2,222
866	2,235	3,183	528	783	1,872
12,481	29,273	44,268	6,935	10,944	26,389
52	161	202	35	42	125
14,437	33,782	51,333	8,070	12,6	30,608
891	2,050	4,027	668	855	2,504
2,913	6,251	10,603	1,777	2,611	6,215
23	36	155	22	38	95
11	14	15	1	2	12
227	566	818	120	180	518
1,255	2,423	4,334	866	1,114	2,354
14	10	47	9	7	31
80	161	199	23	55	121
179	330	696	124	144	428
58	102	196	30	53	113
5,651	11,943	21,090	3,640	5,059	12,391
20,088	45,725	72,423	11,710	17,714	42,999
3	38	15	3	1	11
49	121	279	44	62	173
2	2	...	...	...	...
47	96	207	38	42	132
19	55	74	12	24	38
1	2	3	1	...	2
17	21	44	10	13	21
54	117	129	25	32	72
192	452	751	128	174	449
684	1,050	2,423	408	593	1,422
...	...	4	...	1	3
6	.45	56	7	13	36
54	118	195	26	49	120
42	109	308	42	59	207
6	21	17	2	5	10
45	114	149	23	33	93

Town,							
Total.				Male.			
Total.	0 — 4.	5 — 14.	15 and over.	Total.	0 — 4.	5 — 14.	15 and over.
222	31	65	126	94	13	27	54
7,238	1,109	1,763	4,366	3,684	555	958	2,171
2,218	352	582	1,284	1,082	157	310	615
58	11	12	35	54	10	12	32
26	3	7	16	18	2	5	11
11	4	...	7	5	2	...	3
9,773	1,510	2,429	5,834	4,937	739	1,212	2,886
45,003	6,074	10,635	28,294	23,134	3,085	5,612	14,477
...	...	...	...	...	...	...	...
4	1	1	2	4	1	1	2
290	45	70	175	139	26	29	84
294	46	71	177	143	27	30	86
13,083	1,892	3,082	8,109	6,494	949	1,641	3,904
266	40	70	156	139	27	35	77
...	...	...	...	...	...	...	...
10	1	4	5	4	...	2	2
13,359	1,933	3,156	8,270	6,637	976	1,678	3,983
13,653	1,979	3,227	8,447	6,780	1,003	1,708	4,069
3,130	492	765	1,873	1,587	258	413	916
2,379	362	563	1,454	1,241	170	302	769
19,041	2,593	4,446	12,002	10,046	1,313	2,432	6,301
151	14	30	107	97	8	19	70
24,701	3,461	5,804	15,436	12,971	1,749	3,166	8,056
298	50	67	181	113	18	30	65
2,871	472	670	1,729	1,338	222	347	769
57	9	16	32	13	4	3	6
6	1	...	5	4	1	...	3
238	28	37	173	91	8	17	66
1,679	277	432	970	832	132	218	482
42	9	13	20	21	4	11	6
72	9	18	45	40	4	10	26
288	35	68	185	147	20	48	79
21	5	8	8	10	3	3	4
5,572	895	1,329	3,348	2,409	416	687	1,306
30,273	4,356	7,133	18,784	15,580	2,165	3,853	9,562
11	2	3	6	11	2	3	6
32	8	1	23	14	1	...	13
4	...	2	2	4	...	2	2
67	9	15	43	13	2	6	5
12	1	1	10	5	...	...	5
6	1	1	4	3	...	1	2
78	14	27	37	40	6	16	18
99	13	20	66	78	8	18	52
309	48	70	191	168	19	46	103
2,744	479	793	1,472	1,141	203	395	543
4	...	1	3	...	...	...	...
8	...	...	8	3	...	...	3
106	14	31	61	66	10	22	34
442	57	9[illegible]	293	153	18	37	[illegible]
13	2	3	8	9	2	3	4
81	15	13	53	58	9	10	39

Female.				Country. Total.				Country. Male.				Country. Female.			
Total.	0 — 4.	5 — 14.	15 and over	Total.	0 — 4.	5 — 14.	15 and over.	Total.	0 — 4.	5 — 14.	15 and over.	Total.	0 — 4.	5 — 14.	15 and over.
123	18	38	72	4,433	670	1,206	2,560	2,277	322	605	1,350	2,159	348	601	1,210
3,554	554	805	2,195	33,639	5,098	8,670	19,871	17,515	2,536	4,617	10,362	16,124	2,562	4,053	9,509
1,136	195	272	669	2,851	461	713	1,677	1,560	251	399	910	1,291	210	314	767
4	1	...	3	93	9	26	57	48	2	11	35	44	7	15	22
8	1	2	5	43	7	6	35	19	2	1	16	29	5	5	19
6	2	...	4	38	4	15	19	32	4	12	16	6	...	3	3
4,836	771	1,117	2,918	41,104	6,249	10,636	24,219	21,451	3,117	5,645	12,689	19,653	3,132	4,991	11,530
61,869	3,039	5,013	13,817	81,405	11,859	20,571	48,975	42,579	5,902	10,823	25,854	38,826	5,957	9,748	23,121
...	...	...	...	...	...	...	...	...	...	...	...	...	...	...	...
...	...	...	...	26	4	4	18	13	1	1	11	13	3	3	7
151	19	41	91	109	17	21	71	53	7	11	35	56	10	10	36
151	19	41	91	135	21	25	89	66	8	12	46	69	13	13	43
6,589	943	1,441	4,205	77,987	11,832	19,713	46,442	39,539	5,813	10,437	23,289	38,448	6,019	9,276	23,153
127	13	35	79	3,269	592	854	1,823	1,670	295	461	914	1,599	297	393	909
...	...	...	...	1	...	...	1	...	...	...	...	1	...	...	1
6	1	2	3	4	...	1	3	4	...	1	3	...	...	...	...
6,722	957	1,478	4,287	81,261	12,424	20,568	48,269	41,213	6,108	10,899	24,206	40,048	6,316	9,669	24,063
6,873	976	1,519	4,378	81,396	12,445	20,593	48,358	41,279	6,116	10,911	24,252	40,117	6,329	9,682	24,106
1,543	234	352	957	4,305	674	1,159	2,472	2,168	336	625	1,207	2,137	338	534	1,265
1,139	192	261	685	4,397	658	1,086	2,653	2,352	322	564	1,466	2,045	336	522	1,187
8,995	1,280	2,014	5,701	73,778	11,139	18,979	43,660	38,505	5,484	10,049	22,972	35,273	5,655	8,930	20,688
54	6	11	37	275	42	64	169	127	13	33	81	148	29	31	88
11,730	1,712	2,638	7,380	82,755	12,513	21,284	48,954	43,152	6,155	11,271	25,726	39,603	6,358	10,017	23,228
185	32	37	116	7,207	1,155	1,679	4,373	3,365	519	861	1,985	3,842	636	818	2,388
1,533	250	323	960	18,558	2,967	4,854	10,737	9,488	1,440	2,566	5,482	9,070	1,527	2,288	5,255
44	5	13	26	182	38	45	99	71	21	20	30	111	17	25	69
2	...	...	2	40	6	13	21	27	5	11	11	13	1	2	10
147	20	20	107	1,521	240	370	911	850	140	210	500	671	100	160	411
847	145	214	488	7,072	1,328	1,937	3,807	3,585	607	1,037	1,941	3,487	721	900	1,866
21	5	2	14	33	4	8	21	7	...	3	4	26	4	5	17
33	5	8	19	407	53	117	237	240	35	70	135	167	18	47	102
141	15	20	106	1,015	188	255	573	461	79	131	251	555	100	124	322
11	2	5	4	350	50	103	207	175	22	55	98	185	28	48	109
2,963	479	642	1,842	36,396	6,029	9,381	20,986	18,269	2,868	4,964	10,437	18,127	3,161	4,417	10,549
14,693	2,191	3,280	9,222	119,151	18,542	30,069	69,940	61,421	9,023	16,235	36,163	57,730	9,519	14,484	33,777
...	...	...	...	49	5	1	43	34	2	...	32	15	3	1	11
18	7	1	10	459	78	110	271	198	41	49	108	261	37	61	163
...	...	...	...	...	...	...	...	...	...	...	...	...	...	...	...
54	7	9	38	308	49	74	185	155	23	41	91	153	26	33	94
7	1	1	5	149	24	42	83	82	13	19	50	67	11	23	33
3	1	...	2	...	...	...	...	...	...	...	...	...	...	...	...
38	8	11	19	10	2	3	5	4	...	1	3	6	2	2	2
21	5	2	14	229	40	66	123	121	20	36	65	108	20	30	58
141	20	24	88	1,204	198	296	710	594	99	146	349	610	99	150	361
1,603	276	398	929	1,681	247	384	1,000	811	115	189	507	820	132	195	493
4	...	1	3	...	...	...	...	...	...	...	...	...	...	...	...
...	...	...	...	110	13	19	78	54	6	6	42	56	7	13	36
40	4	9	27	288	39	72	177	133	17	32	84	155	22	40	93
289	30	55	103	38	6	9	23	19	3	5	11	19	3	4	12
4	...	...	4	35	4	8	23	22	2	3	17	13	2	5	6
23	6	3	14	155	36	65	154	129	19	35	75	126	17	30	79

Occupation and Class.				Total.				Provincial Ma[les]	
Class.	Order.	Sub-order and Group.	Occupation.	Total.	0—4.	5—14.	15 and over.	Total.	0—4.
D.—Preparation and Supply of Material Substances—*concluded.*	XVI. Drugs, Gums, Dyes, &c.—*contd.*	52 Drugs, dyes, pigments, &c.—*continued.*	331 Madder and Logwood workers	175	33	88	104	101	10
			332 Ink-makers and sellers...	214	28	47	139	95	14
			333 Antimony preparers and sellers	24	3	3	18	6	2
			334 Henna do. do.	153	10	43	94	99	13
			335 Carmine do. do.	19	4	4	11	6	1
			336 Kunku (red powder) preparers	240	44	58	138	125	23
			337 Perfume preparers and sellers	3,436	358	590	1,483	1,252	185
			Total, Sub-order 52 ...	9,014	1,401	2,273	5,840	4,282	661
	Total, Order XVI ...		......	10,527	1,647	2,639	6,241	5,044	779
	XVII. Leather, Horns, Bones and Grease.	53 Leather, &c.	338 Tanners, curriers and hide-sellers	34,377	5,806	8,917	19,054	17,631	2,733
			339 Shoe, sandal, boot makers and sellers ...	57,541	9,184	14,484	33,873	30,553	4,493
			340 Leather dyers	40,304	6,314	10,602	23,388	20,544	3,020
			341 Water-bag, &c., makers...	5,659	1,271	1,391	2,997	2,840	647
			342 Hide, horns and bone dealers	833	117	189	527	417	46
			343 Catgut preparers	75	4	11	60	47	4
			344 Glue makers and sellers	40	7	7	26	32	7
			345 Grease preparers and sellers	130	15	42	73	71	10
			Total, Sub-order 53 ...	138,959	22,718	35,643	80,598	72,135	10,965
	Total, Order XVII ...		......	138,959	22,718	35,643	80,598	72,135	10,965
	Total, Class D.			1,506,335	222,705	364,466	919,164	751,267	108,522
E.—Commerce, Transport and Storage.	XVIII. Commerce.	54 Dealers in money and securities.	346 Bankers and Bank managers...	4,126	585	1,035	2,506	1,987	253
			347 Money-lenders and pawnbrokers	46,733	6,027	11,258	29,451	22,277	2,905
			348 Bill-discounters, &c.	30	3	1	26	24	1
			349 Insurance agents and underwriters ...	193	22	40	131	91	8
			350 Money changers and testers	7,317	1,001	1,883	4,433	3,495	605
			351 Bank clerks, bill-collectors, &c.	883	125	217	541	451	54
			Total, Sub-order 54 ...	59,285	7,763	14,434	37,088	28,325	3,726
		55 General Merchandise ...	352 General merchants	14,741	1,954	3,642	9,145	7,762	945
			353 Merchants' managers, clerks, &c.	8,264	1,032	1,800	5,432	4,265	535
			Total, Sub-order 55 ...	23,005	2,986	5,442	14,577	12,027	1,480
		56 Dealing unspecified ...	354 Shopkeepers' clerks, salesmen, &c.	11,853	1,571	2,840	7,452	6,695	801
			355 Shopkeepers' and money-lenders' servants..	13,495	1,712	3,144	8,639	7,215	835
			356 Shopkeepers, otherwise unspecified	80,074	12,456	19,934	47,684	41,723	6,077
			357 Pedlars, hawkers...	4,631	780	1,296	2,555	2,229	374
			Total, Sub-order 56 ...	110,063	16,519	27,214	66,330	56,763	8,087
		57 Middlemen, &c. (a) Brokers, &c.	358 Brokers, agents, Dubásh	22,887	2,989	5,339	14,559	11,951	1,421
			359 Auctioneers, auditors, actuaries, &c.	174	23	37	114	103	15
			Total ...	23,061	3,012	5,376	14,673	12,054	1,436
		(b) Contractors and farmers.	360 Farmers of tolls and ferries	1,611	224	419	968	911	125
			361 Farmers of liquor, opium, &c.	1,094	172	260	663	587	88
			362 Superintendents of markets, &c.	65	8	16	41	37	3
			363 Contractors otherwise unspecified	2,329	340	600	1,380	1,150	162
			364 Contractors for labour, &c.	167	23	51	93	71	12
			Total ...	5,266	776	1,346	3,144	2,758	390
			Total, Sub-order 57 ...	28,327	3,788	6,722	17,817	14,810	1,826
	Total, Order XVIII, ...		......	220,680	31,056	53,812	135,812	111,924	15,119
	XIX.—Transport and Storage.	58 Railway. (a) Administration.	365 Agents, directors, &c.	19	7	3	9	13	6
			366 Traffic managers, &c.	18	2	4	12	14	2
			367 Locomotive superintendents, &c.	183	26	59	98	63	8
			368 Auditors, accountants, &c.	31	5	10	16	27	4
			369 Engineers	39	6	12	21	24	3
			370 Clerical staff	1,454	184	285	985	826	88
			Total ...	1,744	230	373	1,141	972	111
		(b) Working Staff.	371 Stationmasters, Inspectors, &c.	946	140	149	657	560	79
			372 Guards, drivers, firemen, &c.	447	62	83	302	253	31
			373 Pointsmen, porters, signallers, &c.	3,089	403	455	2,231	1,862	191
			Total ...	4,482	605	687	3,190	2,674	301
			Total, Sub-order 58 ...	6,226	835	1,060	4,331	3,646	412

Total.

le.		Female.			
5—14.	15 and over.	Total.	0—4.	5—14.	15 and over.
26	56	74	14	12	48
25	56	119	14	22	83
...	4	18	1	3	14
31	55	57	6	12	39
3	2	13	3	1	9
34	68	115	21	24	70
316	751	1,184	178	274	737
1,172	2,449	4,732	740	1,101	2,891
1,364	2,901	6,483	868	1,275	3,840
4,799	10,099	16,746	3,073	4,118	9,555
7,746	18,309	26,988	4,686	6,738	15,564
5,652	11,872	19,760	3,294	4,950	11,516
699	1,494	2,819	624	692	1,503
107	264	416	71	82	263
10	33	23	...	1	27
7	18	8	...	...	8
22	89	59	5	20	34
19,042	42,128	66,824	11,753	16,601	38,470
19,042	42,128	66,824	11,753	16,601	38,470
190,959	451,786	755,068	114,183	173,507	467,378
540	1,194	2,139	332	495	1,312
5,702	13,670	24,459	3,122	5,556	15,781
1	22	6	2	...	4
19	64	102	14	21	67
957	2,033	3,822	496	926	2,400
107	290	432	71	110	251
7,326	17,273	30,960	4,037	7,108	19,815
1,935	4,882	6,979	1,009	1,707	4,263
951	2,779	3,999	497	849	2,653
2,886	7,661	10,978	1,506	2,556	6,916
1,429	3,365	6,268	770	1,411	4,087
1,840	4,540	6,280	877	1,304	4,099
10,412	25,234	33,351	6,379	9,523	22,450
682	1,173	2,402	406	614	1,382
14,363	34,312	53,301	8,432	12,851	32,018
2,731	7,799	10,936	1,568	2,608	6,760
20	68	71	8	17	46
2,751	7,867	11,007	1,576	2,625	6,806
236	550	700	99	183	418
135	364	507	84	125	298
8	26	28	5	8	15
304	684	1,179	187	296	696
29	30	96	11	22	63
712	1,654	2,510	386	634	1,490
3,463	9,521	13,517	1,962	3,259	8,296
28,038	68,767	108,756	15,937	25,774	67,045
2	5	6	1	1	4
2	10	4	...	2	2
14	46	115	18	45	52
10	13	4	1	...	3
7	14	15	3	5	7
142	596	628	96	143	389
177	684	773	119	196	457
74	407	336	61	75	250
48	173	195	31	35	129
211	1,460	1,837	212	244	771
333	2,040	1,808	304	354	1,150
510	2,724	2,580	423	550	1,607

Town.							
Total.				Male.			
Total.	0—4.	5—14.	15 and over.	Total.	0—4.	5—14.	15 and over.
31	2	8	21	22	1	6	15
137	18	30	89	69	12	19	38
7	3	...	4	4	2	...	2
68	6	15	47	31	3	9	19
13	2	3	8	6	1	3	2
94	18	26	50	48	8	16	24
1,318	20[illegible]	353	760	603	104	182	317
5,031	821	1,368	2,872	2,213	373	702	1,138
5,370	8[illegible]9	1,438	3,063	2,381	392	748	1,241
2,488	410	617	1,461	1,294	199	3[illegible]6	759
11,704	1,876	2,829	6,999	5,982	842	1,487	3,653
4,645	681	1,209	2,755	2,381	346	645	1,390
744	110	168	466	412	65	95	252
212	9 22	53	137	100	10	28	62
33	1	...	32	9	1	...	8
24	5	5	14	22	5	5	12
24	...	6	18	3	...	...	3
19,874	3,105	4,887	11,882	10,203	1,468	2,596	6,139
19,874	3,105	4,887	11,882	10,203	1,468	2,596	6,139
416,351	68,834	93,008	259,519	204,726	28,737	51,165	124,824
2,777	378	681	1,718	1,343	162	370	811
13,553	1,596	3,122	8,838	6,200	787	1,651	3,762
30	3	1	26	24	1	1	22
191	22	38	131	89	8	17	64
3,977	528	931	2,518	1,862	273	468	1,121
168	24	39	105	81	11	21	49
20,699	2,551	4,812	13,336	9,599	1,242	2,528	5,829
5,337	661	1,265	3,411	2,790	326	684	1,780
5,264	657	1,187	3,420	2,579	346	641	1,593
10,601	1,318	2,452	6,831	5,369	672	1,325	3,372
9,117	1,188	2,162	5,767	4,277	611	1,112	2,554
9,434	1,230	2,193	6,011	4,855	612	1,258	2,985
16,747	2,538	4,208	10,001	8,350	1,272	2,170	4,908
1,944	349	563	1,032	852	172	292	388
37,242	5,305	9,126	22,811	18,334	2,667	4,832	10,835
7,610	938	1,797	4,875	3,857	458	916	2,483
41	6	9	26	18	4	3	11
7,651	944	1,806	4,901	3,875	462	919	2,494
642	88	153	401	353	52	82	219
387	59	100	228	209	31	54	124
16	...	2	14	11	...	1	10
1,202	179	295	728	598	91	151	356
143	19	46	78	57	8	26	23
2,390	345	596	1,449	1,228	182	314	732
10,041	1,289	2,403	6,350	5,103	644	1,233	3,226
78,583	10,463	18,792	49,328	38,405	5,225	9,918	23,262
...	...	...	...	...	...	...	...
18	2	4	12	14	2	2	10
46	6	6	34	12	1	3	8
11	3	3	5	7	2	3	2
24	2	6	16	20	2	5	13
989	115	213	661	552	57	103	392
1,088	128	232	728	605	64	116	425
535	60	100	369	300	33	56	220
177	20	32	125	106	9	16	81
1,784	209	232	1,343	1,214	114	131	969
2,496	295	364	1,837	1,620	156	208	1,270
3,534	423	596	2,565	2,234	220	319	1,615

Female.				Country. Total.				Country. Male.				Country. Female.			
Total.	0 — 4.	5 — 14.	15 and over.	Total.	0 — 4.	5 — 14.	15 and over.	Total.	0 — 4.	5 — 14.	15 and over.	Total.	0 — 4.	5 — 14.	15 and over.
9	1	2	6	114	31	30	83	79	18	20	41	65	13	10	42
63	6	11	51	77	10	17	50	26	2	6	18	51	8	11	32
3	1	...	2	17	...	3	14	2	...	...	2	15	...	3	12
37	3	6	28	88	13	28	47	68	10	22	36	20	3	6	11
7	1	...	6	6	2	1	3	...	...	...	...	6	2	1	3
46	10	10	26	145	26	33	88	77	15	18	44	69	11	14	44
715	101	171	443	1,118	153	237	728	649	81	134	434	469	72	103	294
2,548	418	666	1,734	3,953	580	905	2,468	2,069	288	470	1,311	1,884	292	435	1,157
2,939	477	690	1,822	5,157	778	1,201	3,178	2,663	387	616	1,660	2,494	391	585	1,518
1,194	211	281	702	31,889	5,396	8,300	18,193	16,337	2,534	4,463	9,340	15,552	2,862	3,837	8,853
4,722	1,034	1,342	3,346	45,837	7,308	11,665	26,874	24,571	3,656	6,259	14,656	21,266	3,052	5,396	12,218
2,264	585	564	1,305	35,659	5,633	9,393	20,633	18,163	2,074	5,007	10,482	17,496	2,959	4,386	10,151
332	45	73	214	4,915	1,161	1,223	2,531	2,428	582	604	1,242	2,487	579	619	1,289
112	12	25	75	631	95	136	390	317	36	79	202	304	59	57	188
24	...	...	24	42	3	11	28	38	3	10	25	4	...	1	3
2	...	...	2	16	2	2	12	10	2	2	6	6	...	...	6
21	...	6	15	106	15	36	55	68	10	22	36	38	5	14	19
9,671	1,637	2,291	5,743	119,085	19,613	30,756	68,716	61,932	9,497	16,446	35,989	57,153	10,116	14,310	32,727
9,671	1,637	2,291	5,743	119,085	19,613	30,756	68,716	61,932	9,497	16,446	35,980	57,153	10,116	14,310	32,727
211,635	30,097	46,843	134,695	1,089,974	163,871	266,458	659,645	546,541	79,785	139,794	326,962	543,433	84,086	126,664	332,683
1,434	216	311	907	1,349	207	354	788	644	91	170	383	705	116	184	405
7,356	809	1,471	5,076	33,180	4,431	8,136	20,613	16,077	2,118	4,051	9,908	17,103	2,313	4,085	10,705
6	2	...	4	...	...	...	...	...	...	...	...	...	...	...	...
102	14	21	67	2	...	2	...	2	...	2	...	...	...	...	...
2,115	255	463	1,397	3,340	473	952	1,915	1,633	232	489	912	1,707	241	463	1,003
87	13	18	56	715	101	178	436	370	43	86	241	345	58	92	195
11,100	1,309	2,284	7,507	38,586	5,212	9,622	23,752	18,726	2,484	4,798	11,444	19,860	2,728	4,824	12,308
2,547	335	581	1,631	9,404	1,293	2,377	5,734	4,972	619	1,251	3,102	4,432	674	1,126	2,632
2,685	311	546	1,828	3,000	375	613	2,012	1,686	189	310	1,187	1,314	186	303	825
5,222	616	1,127	3,450	12,401	1,668	2,990	7,746	6,658	808	1,561	4,289	5,746	860	1,429	3,457
4,840	577	1,050	3,213	2,743	383	678	1,685	1,318	190	317	811	1,433	193	361	874
4,579	618	935	3,026	4,061	482	951	2,628	2,360	233	582	1,555	1,701	259	869	1,073
8,397	1,266	2,038	5,093	63,327	9,918	15,726	37,683	33,373	4,805	8,242	20,326	29,954	5,113	7,484	17,357
1,092	177	271	644	2,687	431	733	1,523	1,377	202	390	785	1,310	229	343	738
18,908	2,638	4,294	11,976	73,821	11,214	18,088	43,519	38,428	5,420	9,531	23,477	34,393	5,794	8,557	20,042
3,753	480	881	2,392	15,277	2,051	3,542	9,684	8,091	963	1,815	5,316	7,186	1,088	1,727	4,368
23	2	6	15	133	17	28	88	85	11	17	57	48	6	11	31
3,776	482	887	2,407	15,411	2,068	3,570	9,772	8,179	974	1,832	5,373	7,231	1,094	1,738	4,399
259	36	71	182	963	136	266	567	558	73	154	331	411	63	112	236
178	28	46	104	707	113	160	434	378	57	81	240	329	56	79	194
5	...	1	4	49	8	14	27	26	3	7	16	23	5	7	11
604	88	144	372	1,127	170	305	652	552	71	153	328	575	90	162	324
86	11	20	55	24	4	5	15	14	4	3	7	10	...	2	8
1,162	163	282	717	2,876	431	750	1,695	1,528	208	398	922	1,348	228	352	773
4,938	645	1,169	3,124	18,286	2,499	4,320	11,467	9,707	1,182	2,230	6,295	8,579	1,317	2,090	5,172
40,178	5,238	8,874	26,066	142,097	20,593	85,020	86,484	73,519	9,894	18,120	45,505	68,578	10,699	16,900	40,979
...	...	...	...	19	7	3	9	13	6	2	5	6	1	1	4
4	...	2	2	...	...	...	...	...	...	...	...	...	...	...	...
34	6	3	26	137	20	53	64	56	7	11	38	81	13	42	26
4	1	...	3	20	2	7	11	20	2	7	11	...	...	...	...
4	...	1	3	15	4	6	5	4	1	2	1	11	3	4	4
437	58	110	269	465	69	72	324	274	31	39	204	191	38	33	120
483	64	116	303	656	102	141	413	387	47	61	259	269	55	60	154
226	33	44	149	411	74	49	288	251	46	18	187	160	28	31	101
71	11	16	44	270	42	51	177	146	22	32	92	124	20	19	85
570	95	101	374	1,305	194	223	888	648	77	80	491	657	117	143	397
867	139	161	567	1,986	310	323	1,353	1,046	146	130	770	941	165	193	583
1,350	203	277	870	2,642	412	464	1,766	1,412	192	191	1,029	[illegible]	220	271	739